Rethinking the Financial Crisis

Rethinking the Financial Crisis

Alan S. Blinder, Andrew W. Lo,
and Robert M. Solow, Editors

Russell Sage Foundation ♦ New York
The Century Foundation ♦ New York and Washington, D.C.

Library of Congress Cataloging-in-Publication Data

Rethinking the financial crisis / Robert M. Solow, Alan S. Blinder, and Andrew W. Lo, editors.
    pages cm
 Includes bibliographical references and index.
 ISBN 978-0-87154-810-8 (pbk. : alk. paper) 1. Global Financial Crisis, 2008–2009.
2. International finance. 3. International economic relations. 4. Economic policy.
I. Solow, Robert M. editor of compilation.
HB37172008 .R48 2012
330.9'0511—dc23

2012032496

Text design by Suzanne Nichols.

RUSSELL SAGE FOUNDATION
112 East 64th Street, New York, New York 10065
10 9 8 7 6 5 4 3 2 1

Contents

Contents

Contributors

ALAN S. BLINDER is Gordon S. Rentschler Memorial Professor of Economics and Public Affairs in the Woodrow Wilson School at Princeton University, vice chairman of Promontory Interfinancial Network, and op-ed columnist for *The Wall Street Journal.*

ANDREW W. LO is Charles E. and Susan T. Harris Professor at the MIT Sloan School of Management and director of the MIT Laboratory for Financial Engineering.

ROBERT M. SOLOW is Institute Professor Emeritus, MIT, and a Nobel laureate in economics.

BEN S. BERNANKE is chairman of the Federal Reserve.

PATRICK BOLTON is Barbara and David Zalaznick Professor of Business at the Columbia Business School.

J. BRADFORD DELONG is professor of economics at the University of California at Berkeley and research associate of the National Bureau of Economic Research.

CHRISTOPHER L. FOOTE is senior economist and policy advisor in the research department at the Bank of Boston Federal Reserve.

KRISTOPHER S. GERARDI is financial economist and associate policy adviser at the Federal Reserve Bank of Atlanta.

SIMON G. GILCHRIST is professor of economics at Boston University and research associate of the National Bureau of Economic Research.

JOHN HULL is Maple Financial Professor of Derivatives and Risk Management at the Joseph L. Rotman School of Management, University of Toronto.

ROBERT A. JARROW is Ronald P. and Susan E. Lynch Professor of Investment Management and professor of finance and economics at the Johnson Graduate School of Management, Cornell University.

Contributors

ROBERT E. LITAN is director of research at Bloomberg Government and was, at the time of writing, senior fellow in economic studies at the Brookings Institution.

BURTON G. MALKIEL is chief investment officer of AlphaShares and Chemical Bank Chairman's Professor of Economics at Princeton University.

KEVIN J. MURPHY is Kenneth L. Trefftzs Chair in Finance in the Department of Finance and Business Economics at the Marshall School, professor of business and law in the law school, and professor of economics, all at the University of Southern California.

THOMAS PHILIPPON is associate professor of finance at the Stern School of Business at New York University.

TANO SANTOS is David L. and Elsie M. Dodd Professor of Finance and codirector of the Heilbrunn Center for Graham and Dodd Investing at Columbia Business School.

JOSÉ A. SCHEINKMAN is the Theodore A. Wells '29 Professor of Economics at Princeton University.

HERSH SHEFRIN is Mario Belotti Chair in the Department of Finance at Santa Clara University's Leavey School of Business.

MEIR STATMAN is Glenn Klimek Professor of Finance at the Leavey School of Business, Santa Clara University, and visiting professor at Tilburg University in the Netherlands.

ALAN WHITE is Peter L. Mitchelson/SIT Investment Associates Foundation Chair in Investment Strategy and professor of finance at the Rotman School of Management, University of Toronto.

PAUL S. WILLEN is senior economist and policy adviser in the research department of the Federal Reserve Bank of Boston.

EGON ZAKRAJŠEK is deputy associate director in the Division of Monetary Affairs at the Board of Governors of the Federal Reserve System.

Introduction

Alan S. Blinder, Andrew W. Lo, and Robert M. Solow

S amuel Johnson once observed that "when a man knows he is to be hanged in a fortnight, it concentrates his mind wonderfully." So does the experience of a near-total financial collapse, especially when it triggers a long and deep recession and only hastily improvised and drastic actions by the Federal Reserve and the U.S. Treasury are able to ward off an even worse catastrophe. Naturally, then, more has been said and written about the financial crisis of 2008 to 2009 than anyone can hear or read. But the research and reflections described in this book are different, and perhaps more ambitious, than the usual fare. They aim to reconsider the way we think about financial activity, especially its two-way connection with the real economy of production, consumption, capital formation, and employment. Any such rethinking will, of course, have implications for financial regulation.

People sometimes forget that financial activity is a means, not an end in itself. Its function is to make the real economy work more efficiently, that is, to allow more final output to be produced from the resources at hand. When the financial system fails, the damage that matters is not so much the financial disruptions per se, but rather the damage done to the real economy. A recession is only one of several possible routes to such damage, but it is a particularly visible and painful one.

In tranquil times, the financial system makes the real economy work better in at least five overlapping ways. First, it collects the economy's savings, wherever they originate, and places them at the disposal of the most profitable investment opportunities available. For example, without this intermediation, a pension fund in Oregon could not easily invest in a timber company in Georgia. Second, the financial system transfers risks that arise inevitably in the real economy from those who find them impossible or difficult to bear to those who, for a reasonable price, are willing to take their chances. Insurance policies are perhaps the most obvious example of risk transference, but banks—which give households safe deposits and invest the proceeds in risky loans—have been in this business for centuries. Third, financial markets provide liquidity for owners of assets, making it easier for them to sell assets for cash when needed. Fourth, in the course of doing these things, the financial system reveals information about the market's evaluation of various risks and prospects for profit. If it is unbiased and reasonably accurate, this information helps guide the private and public decisions connected with the intermediation, risk transference, and liquidity provision functions already mentioned. And fifth, if the first four functions all work well, the financial markets help society allocate capital appropriately.

When these five functions are carried out smoothly and effectively, the financial sector earns its keep. And there is much evidence, especially from the experience of emerging economies, to demonstrate that failure hurts. In the years of the Great Moderation (1984 to 2007) that preceded the financial crisis, the belief became widely accepted, even in policy circles, that the modern financial system functioned well and was substantially self-regulating. It could safely be left to itself, and if left to itself, it would perform its standard functions efficiently and would not be seriously vulnerable to runaway asset bubbles or to the kind of breakdown and collapse that would inflict serious damage on the real economy.

This belief was embodied in the "strong" form of the efficient-market hypothesis (EMH). Here is a clear statement of the strong form from one of its principal advocates:

> In an efficient market, competition among the many intelligent participants leads to a situation where, at any time, actual prices of individual securities already reflect the effect of information based both on events that have already occurred and on events which, as of now, the market expects to take place in the future. In other words, in an efficient market at any point in time the actual price of a security will be a good estimate of its intrinsic value.[1]

And that "good estimate," in turn, gets capital flowing to good uses and away from bad ones.

The financial crisis and its aftermath make this view of the system, along with its implications that financial markets are self-regulating and stable, look like a caricature. If that is what people really thought, then Rethinking Finance is surely in order. It has become a commonplace to say that "a serious mispricing of risk" lay at the heart of the crisis, which would seem to be a direct contradiction of the strong EMH. Some of the chapters in this book investigate precise ways in which the EMH either works or fails; others are concerned with what a reconceived regulatory system might look like.

The chapter by Burton Malkiel concentrates, instead, on the "weak" form of the EMH. Malkiel was one of the early advocates of efficient-market theory but—and this is a very big "but"—his preferred version of the theory insists only that securities markets are efficient in the narrow sense that opportunities for arbitrage arise rarely and are eliminated quickly. This weak EMH does not claim that security prices always represent intrinsic values properly, but only that the market itself offers no hint as to whether current security prices are above or below their intrinsic values. The weak EMH is therefore compatible with the existence of bubbles, positive or negative. It just says that it's remarkably hard to "beat the market."

Yet the weak EMH is hardly vacuous. It has major implications for public policy, even if they are not quite as sharp as those of the strong version. In particular, the weak EMH says that governments have no reason to intervene directly in securities markets unless they have information (about the relation of prices to fundamental values) that is not available to the public at large. And even in that case, there is an obvious alternative: simply make the information publicly available. Malkiel points out that, under the weak EMH, it is difficult to know if a sustained price rise represents a bubble or a price movement driven by fundamentals. If it is a bubble, however, its eventual collapse will be especially dangerous if it has been financed by high levels of debt. Thus, avoiding the buildup of excessive leverage is a legitimate objective of financial regulation even under the weak EMH.

Shefrin and Statman reconsider the theory of efficient markets, in both strong and weak forms, from the perspective of behavioral finance. They argue, first, that neither version of the EMH can be held responsible for the crisis—if only because most participants in capital markets did not believe in them, or acted as if they did not. After all, it is departures from efficiency that enable (some) market participants to earn abnormal returns. But EMH may have been conflated in the minds of the public with a widespread belief in free or unregulated markets—which did stand in the way of necessary regulation.

Shefrin and Statman discuss some standard psychological mechanisms, such as tendencies toward self-confirmation and herd behavior, that are likely to lead to unstable capital markets. These possibilities were raised decades ago by John Maynard Keynes, Hyman Minsky, and others, but vanished from view under the influence of the EMH and its close macroeconomic cousin, rational expectations. There is hardly anything new in the combination of (a) the individually rational tendency to head for the lifeboats at the first sign of trouble; (b) the herd instinct that wants to head for the lifeboats when others do so; and (c) the radical uncertainty, especially about the solvency of others, that surrounds financial crises. It is all part of standard bank-run scenarios, just as it was when Walter Bagehot wrote his classic *Lombard Street* in the nineteenth century. Brad DeLong's chapter exploits this broad similarity to place current thinking about financial instability and crisis in historical perspective. This is also a useful way to draw attention to the differences created by changes in institutions and in financial technology.

What has emerged is characterized by Shefrin and Statman as a "tug-of-war" between those who favor free markets and those who favor regulation. Everyone is aware that financial regulation is bound to be imperfect and therefore to impose costs. But those costs must be weighed against the enormous real social costs of even occasional financial breakdowns. For example, the Congressional Budget Office estimates that the Great Recession and the sluggish recovery that followed it have already cost the U.S. economy over $3.5 trillion (in 2005 dollars) in lost output. By the time the economy is back to full employment, the total could easily surpass $6 trillion, which is about 40 percent of a year's real GDP. That's an enormous number compared to standard estimates of efficiency losses from taxation or regulation.

In the United States, the financial sector has recently been growing larger and becoming more costly and more exotic, as the chapter by Thomas Philippon shows. This development raises further questions. Does the increasing size of the financial services sector reflect an increasing contribution to the efficiency of the real economy? Or is at least some of the stunning growth in finance parasitic—using more resources, especially skilled labor and human capital, than its contribution can justify? Philippon points toward the latter explanation, the chapter by Robert Jarrow gives a mixed answer, and the chapter by Patrick Bolton, Tano Santos, and José Scheinkman highlights one particular area in which unregulated, opaque financial activity generates profits by building an information barrier between insiders and retail investors. Such barriers constitute a classic inefficiency.

The book begins with the keynote address delivered by Federal Reserve chairman Ben Bernanke, who has been, in his academic life, a major figure in the analysis of the relation between the financial sector and the real economy, especially via the so-called credit channel. It was great good luck for the nation that its top central banker in 2008, as one of the foremost students of the financial and economic collapse of the 1930s, had vowed not to let it happen again.[2]

In his talk, Bernanke pointed to critical sources of vulnerability in financial institutions that were already visible before the crisis hit: their heavy dependence on short-term—even overnight—funding, their use of very high leverage, and their reliance on risk management techniques that were inadequate for complex financial products and, especially, for the interconnectedness of the whole system through interlocking debtor–creditor relations. The regulatory and supervisory arrangements either ignored these danger signals or proved inadequate to the tasks of heading off the financial collapse and then of defending the real economy against its consequences. Gaps had been allowed to open up in the statutory structure of regulation. On top of that, the response of existing regulatory bodies was weak and slow.

The chapter by Simon Gilchrist and Egon Zakrajšek makes a strong case that the macroeconomic response to the financial crisis was too little too late. They first quantify the often slippery notion of financial stress and then embed it in a macroeconomic model that can, in principle, throw some light on two aggregative questions: How and how strongly does financial stress harm the real economy? And how, in turn, do events in the real economy create or diminish financial stress? Their analysis suggests that causation is strong in both directions.

Gilchrist and Zakrajšek measure financial stress by the interest rate spreads that financial institutions have to pay on their own borrowing, over and above what would be normal at the current stage of the business cycle.[3] When they include this measure in a vector autoregression, which is the standard atheoretical way of accounting for the main macroeconomic time series, they find that it plays a quantitatively significant role both as cause and as effect. An exogenous increase in the financial stress index brings about a corresponding deterioration in the real economy—lower output, higher unemployment, and some downward pressure on the price level. In turn, when the economy encounters difficulties from other sources, the measure of financial stress rises. When Gilchrist and Zakrajšek include their index of financial stress in a conventional macroeconomic model, with a financial sector added, they find that adding the stress variable clearly improves the model's ability to explain recent events.

Finally, they conduct a fascinating simulation experiment. The model includes a "Taylor rule" that instructs the Fed to ease (tighten) monetary policy when the output gap increases (decreases) or the rate of inflation falls (rises). When Gilchrist and Zakrajšek modify the rule to require the Fed also to ease (tighten) when the index of financial stress increases (decreases), the policy response is so much stronger and faster that it reduces the recessionary fall in output and employment by about two-thirds. This eye-catching result is, of course, model-dependent; it will have to be checked for robustness. At a minimum, however, it points to great potential gains in macroeconomic performance from taking account of financial instability.

The chapter by Christopher Foote, Kristopher Gerardi, and Paul Willen takes a close look at one particular piece of financial technology that malfunctioned badly: the mortgage mess. Dodgy mortgages were, of course, at the epicenter of the crisis. It was a story of bad decisions and aftereffects that were devastating to the real economy. Many families found themselves overburdened by mortgages that they could not afford and that often exceeded the value of their house. The result has been waves of foreclosures, and the overhang of foreclosures has kept home building deeply depressed. All this is well known. Rather than review it, the chapter asks an important analytical question: were predatory lending practices and the practice of securitizing and offloading mortgage loans at the heart of the crisis? Their surprising and controversial answer: no.

This conclusion is not a whitewash of NINJA loans, teaser rates, and all that. The question is not about personal losses or improprieties, of which there were many, but about responsibility for the meltdown. The chapter provides evidence, for instance, that default rates on adjustable rate mortgages were not that much higher than those on fixed rate loans. One major reason is that, as interest rates fell across the economy, many of the resets were downward. Instead, Foote, Gerardi, and Willen lay the blame on the bubble itself, in particular on the epic underestimation of the probability that house prices would ever fall. They cite internal documentary evidence that buyers and sellers of mortgage-backed securities (MBSs) understood rather well that disaster would follow if house prices were to drop sharply. They simply did not believe that could happen. So we are back to general instability and the economics of bubbles.

The evolution of the pre-crash financial system is in part a story of financial innovation, the invention and diffusion of novel instruments and techniques for financing investment and managing wealth and risks. Some of this innovation was motivated by the desire to escape regulation; it was part of the aforementioned regulatory tug-of-war. The four chapters of part III concentrate on interesting aspects of financial innovation, their value to the real economy, and the pitfalls they create.

As already mentioned, Philippon documents not only the sheer increases in the size of the financial services industry relative to real GDP but also the increasing cost per unit of intermediation. Despite the large-scale introduction of information technology hardware and software, there does not appear to have been any corresponding improvement in the real productivity of financial activity. To paraphrase something one of us wrote many years ago, computers seem to have been everywhere except in the industry's productivity statistics.[4]

Philippon makes an unfavorable comparison with retail and wholesale trade, where the introduction of IT has indeed improved productivity dramatically. His suggestion is that the financial sector's growing use of skilled labor and information technology has mainly supported a huge increase in the volume of trading. More trading activity may enhance liquidity and perhaps even improve the information content of prices, but he sees little evidence that it has measurably improved the efficiency of the real economy.

Robert Jarrow's chapter looks in detail at some of the major types of exotic securities developed by financial engineers and describes how they work. Asset-backed securities (ABSs) are securities that provide claims to a collection of non-traded assets; collateralized debt obligations (CDOs) are backed by collections of traded assets and usually have a more complicated structure than ABSs; credit default swaps (CDSs) are essentially a way for one party to pay another to accept the risk of default on a particular debt obligation—or to make bets on or against default.

Jarrow asks—and attempts to answer—the most important question about the social utility of these securities: do these classes of credit derivatives make it possible to conduct real economic activity more efficiently? He concludes that ABSs are or can be reasonably transparent and that they serve a useful purpose: enlarging the potential supply of capital for mortgages, student loans, and so on. CDSs provide the risk-sharing properties of insurance generally, and their availability presumably enlarges and perfects bond markets. Jarrow even justifies the controversial "naked CDS," in which neither party has an insurable interest in the event that is being insured against, on the grounds that CDS prices have useful information content.

On the other hand, he concludes that CDOs, because they are excessively complex and because their underlying assets are already traded, probably add little or nothing to the efficient functioning of either the capital market or the real economy. He also suggests that credit derivatives should be traded and cleared on public exchanges, where market participants could be required to post adequate capital and transaction prices, volumes, and counterparty exposures would be public knowledge. The absence of such knowledge certainly added to the rampant uncertainty that led to market meltdowns during the financial crisis.

In financial markets, as in others, absence of information and the existence of information asymmetries among participants tend to destroy efficiency—both in good times and in bad. Since financial innovation often generates novel and highly complex securities, it is socially desirable that there be an easily available and unbiased source of information about their risk-return characteristics. This is the role of the rating agencies, of which there are currently three major ones: Moody's, Standard & Poor's, and Fitch. The chapter by John Hull and Alan White considers the institutional role of these agencies and the techniques they use to rate securities.

The purpose of a rating is to provide prospective investors with a grade (AAA, B+, etc.) that enables them to place the security in the same risk class as other, more familiar, securities. Such information is particularly vital when it comes to novel and complicated securities. Hull and White point out that the indicator of underlying risk used by Moody's was substantively different from (though related to) the indicators used by the other two agencies. This fact, along with the uncertainty that inheres in any rating system, opened the door to ratings shopping, whereby issuers searched for the most favorable ratings.

This worry, in turn, opens up the question of how rating agencies are compensated for their work. When, as now, the agencies are paid by the issuers, an immediate conflict of interest arises that can undermine the whole system. Compensation from the consumers of ratings would seem to be more appropriate, but it is not feasible because of the free-rider problem. Why should anyone buy a rating when, once it's out there, he can probably get it for free? And in that case, who pays the rating agency for its work? Hull and White look for ways to improve the current system. One alternative has recently been proposed in the United Kingdom: encourage the entry of more agencies and require issuers to rotate among them. Another alternative would be to force complex derivatives to be traded on exchanges and have the exchanges hire and assign rating agencies. In fact, once credit derivatives become standardized and exchange-traded, this may eliminate the need for ratings altogether.

Part IV turns explicitly to regulatory matters. The chapter by Robert Litan reviews briefly the logic of industrial regulation in general and then looks at what the Dodd-Frank Wall Street Reform and Consumer Protection Act of 2010 accomplishes, what it partly accomplishes, and what it leaves unaddressed. His accent is on the political economy of financial regulation, that is, the interplay between powerful private interests and the needs of public policy. Like many other observers, Litan argues that several regulatory failures contributed to the onset of the crisis, or at least allowed it to become worse than it might otherwise have been. Some of these weaknesses came in response to pressures from the industry, while others were results of regulatory fragmentation and other failings. But those are all bygones.

Litan goes on to consider a number of remedies that have been proposed, ranging from more, and more competent, oversight to higher capital standards. Many of these ideas have found a place in Dodd-Frank, though their exact shape and likely effectiveness will have to wait for details to be determined by the relevant regulators. He points out that interest-group pressure is intense. Two salient examples are the campaigns by the industry to expand the class of exemptions from clearing rules for derivatives and to weaken the so-called Volcker Rule against proprietary trading by commercial banks. These struggles may never end. Just one month after the conference, huge trading losses at JPMorgan Chase brought these issues into sharp relief once again. Was it proprietary trading or hedging that went wrong?

The bottom line, according to Litan, is that Dodd-Frank will turn out to be an imperfect patchwork, which is more or less inevitable given the harsh political economy of financial regulation. Dodd-Frank will not prevent the next financial crisis. But it may well delay the onset and diminish its amplitude. That in itself would be welcome. Be thankful for small favors.

The chapter by Kevin Murphy serves two purposes. It evaluates the widespread belief that the "bonus culture" on Wall Street created incentives for excessive risk-taking at the top—which many believe helped mightily in setting the table for the crisis. (His verdict is negative.) It also considers possibilities for the regulation of executive compensation in the financial services.

Murphy documents the enormous bulge in the compensation of the CEOs of the large broker-dealer firms that occurred from about 1995 until the crisis struck. But Murphy argues that this observation does not imply that CEO bonuses induced excessive risk-taking. In fact, those famous—or is it infamous?—CEOs had huge equity stakes in their firms. So they were by no means protected from the downside of excessive risk-taking. Instead, the more likely place to look for perverse incentives is lower down the scale, particularly among traders in the large firms. That danger is traceable not to bonuses per se, but rather to tying compensation to short-run trading profits rather than to longer-run measures of profitability. The obvious remedy is for traders' compensation agreements to contain clawback provisions if trades that are profitable at first go sour later on.

As Murphy points out, that is easier said than done: taxes will have been paid in the meanwhile, and some traders will have changed jobs. Although he describes some ways in which this sort of short-termism can be mitigated, in the end he regards most attacks on high Wall Street compensation as motivated by jealousy, primarily punitive in intent, and unlikely to improve matters.

A book like this, the work of many minds, cannot follow a single line of argument to a single, unified set of conclusions. Our reading of the various chapters does lead, however, to a handful of tentative implications that we list here for others to mull over.

1. Left to itself, the financial sector is likely to grow to a size and complexity that serves its own interests, using up resources and creating instabilities that may outweigh its contributions to real economic efficiency.

2. Such prospects may be particularly prevalent in financial innovation. While many of the products of financial engineering are indeed useful in managing real economic risks, others serve mainly as opportunities to exploit superior information and analytical capacity at the expense of less informed or less competent players.

3. Those same opportunities can lead to extraordinarily generous compensation packages, often based on making short-term killings, that may skew decisions in favor of short-horizon gains rather than long-horizon growth.

4. Such a complex, interconnected, and highly leveraged financial system evinces tendencies toward instability that may occasionally inflict serious damage on

the real economy. So the need for regulation is real. So is the need for central banks to take financial innovation and instability into account when formulating monetary policy.

5. Regulators should not be paralyzed by the realization that it is hard to tell a bubble from a well-justified rise in some relative prices. Here, as everywhere, there are two kinds of error—acting when one shouldn't, and failing to act when one should. The costs and benefits of the two sorts of error have to be appraised and balanced.

6. Society should be exploring new ways to rate complex securities, to compensate rating agencies, and to compensate traders. Even allowing for some learning from past errors, current arrangements leave much to be desired.

7. More broadly, we now realize that the global economy is indeed a system, meaning that its individual components are connected and interact in dynamic ways. When those interactions either fail or are interrupted, the consequences can be disastrous. In particular, the macroeconomy and the financial system are inextricably linked, and the importance of the so-called shadow banking system for providing individuals and institutions with liquidity and leverage also creates vulnerabilities when panic sets in and fire sales are triggered.

These observations highlight the benefits of sifting through the wreckage and systematically piecing together the causal factors that created one of the worst economic disasters of the last century. As George Santayana put it, "Those who cannot learn from history are condemned to repeat it." We are grateful to the talented authors of the insightful contributions in this volume for helping us rethink finance, and we hope their fresh perspectives will motivate current and future generations of scholars to continue with this critical research agenda.

NOTES

1. Eugene Fama, "Random Walks in Stock Market Prices," *Financial Analysts Journal*, 21(5, 1965): 56.

2. Ben S. Bernanke, "On Milton Friedman's Ninetieth Birthday," remarks at the conference to honor Milton Friedman, University of Chicago, November 8, 2002.

3. Spreads rise in cyclical downturns and fall in booms.

4. Robert Solow, "We'd Better Watch Out," *New York Times Book Review*, July 12, 1987, 36.

Part I

Rethinking Macroeconomics and Finance

Chapter 1

Some Reflections on the Crisis and the Policy Response

Ben S. Bernanke

I would like to thank the conference organizers for the opportunity to offer a few remarks on the causes of the 2007 to 2009 financial crisis, as well as on the Federal Reserve's policy response. The topic is a large one, and today I will be able only to lay out some basic themes. In doing so, I will draw from talks and testimonies that I gave during the crisis and its aftermath, particularly my testimony to the Financial Crisis Inquiry Commission in September 2010 (Bernanke 2010). Given the time available, I will focus narrowly on the financial crisis and the Federal Reserve's response in its capacity as liquidity provider of last resort, leaving discussions of monetary policy and the aftermath of the crisis to another occasion.

TRIGGERS AND VULNERABILITIES

In its analysis of the crisis, my testimony before the Financial Crisis Inquiry Commission drew the distinction between triggers and vulnerabilities. The *triggers* of the crisis were the particular events or factors that touched off the events of 2007 to 2009—the proximate causes, if you will. Developments in the market for subprime mortgages were a prominent example of a trigger of the crisis. In contrast, the *vulnerabilities* were the structural, and more fundamental, weaknesses in the financial system and in regulation and supervision that served to propagate and amplify the initial shocks. In the private sector, some key vulnerabilities included high levels of leverage; excessive dependence on unstable short-term funding; deficiencies in risk management in major financial firms; and the use of exotic and nontransparent financial instruments that obscured concentrations of risk. In the public sector, my list of vulnerabilities would include gaps in the regulatory structure that allowed systemically important firms and markets to escape comprehensive supervision; failures of supervisors to effectively apply some existing authorities; and insufficient attention to threats to the stability of the system as a whole (that is, the lack of a macroprudential focus in regulation and supervision).

The distinction between triggers and vulnerabilities is helpful in that it allows us to better understand why the factors that are often cited as touching off the crisis seem disproportionate to the magnitude of the financial and economic reaction. Consider subprime mortgages, on which many popular accounts of the crisis focus. Contemporaneous data indicated that the total quantity of subprime mortgages outstanding in 2007 was well less than $1 trillion; some more recent accounts place the figure somewhat higher. In absolute terms, of course, the potential for losses on these loans was large—on the order of hundreds of billions of dollars. However, judged in relation to the size of global financial markets, aggregate exposures to subprime mortgages were quite modest. By way of comparison, it is not especially uncommon for one day's paper losses in global stock markets to exceed the losses on subprime mortgages suffered during the entire crisis, without obvious ill effect on market functioning or on the economy. Thus, losses on subprime mortgages can plausibly account for the massive reaction seen during the crisis only insofar as they interacted with other factors—more fundamental vulnerabilities—that served to amplify their effects.

On the surface, the puzzle of disproportionate cause and effect seems somewhat less stark if one takes the boom and bust in the U.S. housing market as the trigger of the crisis, as the paper gains and losses associated with the swing in house prices were many times the losses associated directly with subprime loans. Indeed, the 30 percent or so aggregate decline in house prices since their peak has by now eliminated nearly $7 trillion in paper wealth. However, on closer examination, it is not clear that even the large movements in house prices, in the absence of the underlying weaknesses in our financial system, can account for the magnitude of the crisis. First, much of the decline in house prices has occurred since the most intense phase of the crisis; the decline in prices since September 2008 is probably better viewed as largely the result of, rather than a cause of, the crisis and ensuing recession. More fundamentally, however, any theory of the crisis that ties its magnitude to the size of the housing bust must also explain why the fall of dot-com stock prices just a few years earlier, which destroyed as much or more paper wealth—more than $8 trillion—resulted in a relatively short and mild recession and no major financial instability.[1] Once again, the explanation of the differences between the two episodes must be that the problems in housing and mortgage markets interacted with deeper vulnerabilities in the financial system in ways that the dot-com bust did not. Let me turn, then, to a discussion of those vulnerabilities and how they amplified the effects of triggers like the collapse of the subprime mortgage market.

A number of the vulnerabilities I listed earlier were associated with the increased importance of the so-called shadow banking system. Shadow banking, as usually defined, comprises a diverse set of institutions and markets that, collectively, carry out traditional banking functions, but do so outside, or in ways only loosely linked to, the traditional system of regulated depository institutions. Examples of important components of the shadow banking system include securitization vehicles, asset-backed commercial paper (ABCP) conduits, money market mutual funds, markets for repurchase agreements ("repos"), investment banks, and mortgage companies. Before the crisis, the shadow banking system had come to play a major role in global finance.

Economically speaking, as I noted, shadow banking bears strong functional similarities to the traditional banking sector. Like traditional banking, the shadow banking sector facilitates maturity transformation (that is, it is used to fund longer-term, less-liquid assets with short-term, more-liquid liabilities), and it channels savings into specific investments, mostly debtlike instruments. In part, the rapid growth of shadow banking reflected various types of regulatory arbitrage—for example, the minimization of capital requirements. However, instruments that fund the shadow banking system, such as money market mutual funds and repos, also met a rapidly growing demand among investors, generally large institutions and corporations, seeking cashlike assets for use in managing their liquidity. Commercial banks were limited in their ability to meet this growing demand by prohibitions on the payment of interest on business checking accounts and by relatively low limits on the size of deposit accounts that can be insured by the Federal Deposit Insurance Corporation (FDIC).

As became apparent during the crisis, a key vulnerability of the system was the heavy reliance of the shadow banking sector, as well as some of the largest global banks, on various forms of short-term wholesale funding, including commercial paper, repos, securities lending transactions, and interbank loans. The ease, flexibility, and low perceived cost of short-term funding also supported a broader trend toward higher leverage and greater maturity mismatch in individual shadow banking institutions and in the sector as a whole.

While banks also rely on short-term funding and leverage, they benefit from a government-provided safety net, including deposit insurance and backstop liquidity provision by the central bank. Shadow banking activities do not have these safeguards, so they employ alternative mechanisms to gain investor confidence. Among these mechanisms are the collateralization of many shadow banking liabilities; regulatory or contractual restrictions placed on portfolio holdings, such as the liquidity and credit quality requirements applicable to money market mutual funds; and the imprimaturs of credit rating agencies. Indeed, the very foundation of shadow banking and its rapid growth before the crisis was the widely held view (among both investors and regulators) that these safeguards would protect shadow banking activities against runs and panics, similar to the protection given to commercial banking by the government safety net. Unfortunately, this view turned out to be wrong. When it became clear to investors that these alternative protections might not be adequate to protect against losses, widespread flight from the shadow banking system occurred, with pernicious dynamics reminiscent of the banking panics of an earlier era.

Although the vulnerabilities associated with short-term wholesale funding and excessive leverage can be seen as structural weaknesses of the global financial system, they can also be viewed as a consequence of poor risk management by financial institutions and investors, which I would count as another major vulnerability of the system before the crisis. Unfortunately, the crisis revealed a number of significant defects in private-sector risk management and risk controls, importantly including insufficient capacity by many large firms to track firmwide risk exposures, such as off-balance-sheet exposures.

This lack of capacity by major financial institutions to track firmwide risk exposures led in turn to inadequate risk diversification, so that losses, rather than being dispersed broadly, proved in some cases to be heavily concentrated among relatively few, highly leveraged companies. Here, I think, is the principal explanation of why the busts in dot-com stock prices and in the housing and mortgage markets had such markedly different effects. In the case of dot-com stocks, losses were spread relatively widely across many types of investors. In contrast, following the housing and mortgage bust, losses were felt disproportionately at key nodes of the financial system, notably highly leveraged banks, broker-dealers, and securitization vehicles. Some of these entities were forced to engage in rapid asset sales at fire-sale prices, which undermined confidence in the counterparties exposed to these assets, led to sharp withdrawals of funding, and disrupted financial intermediation, with severe consequences for the economy.

Private-sector risk management also failed to keep up with financial innovation in many cases. An important example is the extension of the traditional originate-to-distribute (OTD) business model to encompass increasingly complex securitized credit products, with wholesale market funding playing a key role. In general, the originate-to-distribute model breaks down the process of credit extension into components or stages—from origination to financing and to the postfinancing monitoring of the borrower's ability to repay—in a manner reminiscent of how manufacturers distribute the stages of production across firms and locations. This general approach has been used in various forms for many years and can produce significant benefits, including lower credit costs and increased access of consumers and small and medium-sized businesses to capital markets. However, the expanded use of this model to finance subprime mortgages through securitization was mismanaged at several points, including the initial underwriting, which deteriorated markedly, in part because of incentive schemes that effectively rewarded originators for the quantity rather than the quality of the mortgages extended. Loans were then packaged into securities that proved complex, opaque, and unwieldy; for example, when defaults became widespread, the legal agreements underlying the securitizations made reasonable modifications of troubled mortgages difficult. Rating agencies' ratings of asset-backed securities were revealed to be subject to conflicts of interest and faulty models. At the end of the chain were investors who often relied mainly on ratings and did not make distinctions among AAA-rated securities. Even if the ultimate investors wanted to do their own credit analysis, the information needed to do so was often difficult or impossible to obtain.

Dependence on short-term funding, high leverage, and inadequate risk management were critical vulnerabilities of the private sector prior to the crisis. Derivative transactions further increased risk concentrations and the vulnerability of the system, notably by shifting the location and apparent nature of exposures in ways that were not transparent to many market participants. But even as private-sector activities increased systemic risk, the public sector also failed to appreciate or sufficiently respond to the building vulnerabilities in the financial system—both because the statutory framework of financial regulation was not well suited to addressing some key vulnerabilities and because some of the authorities that did exist were not used effectively.

In retrospect, it is clear that the statutory framework of financial regulation in place before the crisis contained serious gaps. Critically, shadow banking activities were, for the most part, not subject to consistent and effective regulatory oversight. Much shadow banking lacked meaningful prudential regulation, including various special-purpose vehicles, ABCP conduits, and many nonbank mortgage-origination companies. No regulatory body restricted the leverage and liquidity policies of these entities, and few if any regulatory standards were imposed on the quality of their risk management or the prudence of their risk-taking. Market discipline, imposed by creditors and counterparties, helped on some dimensions but did not effectively limit the systemic risks these entities posed.

Other shadow banking activities were potentially subject to some prudential oversight, but weaknesses in the statutory and regulatory framework meant that in practice they were inadequately regulated and supervised. For example, the Securities and Exchange Commission (SEC) supervised the largest broker-dealer holding companies, but only through an opt-in arrangement that lacked the force of a statutory regulatory regime. Large broker-dealer holding companies faced serious losses and funding problems during the crisis, and the instability of such firms as Bear Stearns and Lehman Brothers severely damaged the financial system. Similarly, the insurance operations of American International Group, Inc. (AIG) were supervised and regulated by various state and international insurance regulators, and the Office of Thrift Supervision (OTS) had authority to supervise AIG as a thrift holding company. However, oversight of AIG Financial Products, which housed the derivatives activities that imposed major losses on the firm, was extremely limited in practice.

The gaps in statutory authority had the additional effect of limiting the information available to regulators and consequently may have made it more difficult to recognize the underlying vulnerabilities and complex linkages in the overall financial system. Shadow banking institutions that were unregulated or lightly regulated were typically not required to report data that would have adequately revealed their risk positions or practices. Moreover, the lack of preexisting reporting and supervisory relationships hindered any systematic gathering of information that might have helped policymakers in the early days of the crisis.

A broader failing was that regulatory agencies and supervisory practices were focused on the safety and soundness of individual financial institutions or markets—what we now refer to as microprudential supervision. In the United States and most other advanced economies, no governmental entity had either a mandate or sufficient authority—now often called macroprudential authority—to take actions to limit the systemic risks that could result from the collective behavior of financial institutions and markets.

Gaps in the statutory framework were an important reason for the buildup of risk in certain parts of the system and for the inadequate response of the public sector to that buildup. But even when the relevant statutory authorities did exist, they were not always used forcefully or effectively enough by regulators and supervisors, including the Federal Reserve. Notably, bank regulators did not do enough to force large financial institutions to strengthen their internal risk-management systems or to curtail risky practices. The Federal Reserve's Supervisory Capital Assessment Program, undertaken in the spring of 2009 and popularly known as the "stress tests," played a critical role in restoring confidence in the U.S. banking system, but it also demonstrated that many institutions' information systems could not provide timely, accurate information about bank exposures to counterparties or complete information about the aggregate risks posed by different positions and portfolios. Regulators had recognized these problems in some cases but did not press firms vigorously enough to fix them.

Even without a macroprudential mandate, regulators could also have done more to try to mitigate risks to the broader financial system. In retrospect, stronger bank capital standards—notably those relating to the quality of capital and the amount of capital required for banks' trading book assets—and more attention to the liquidity risks faced by the largest, most interconnected firms would have made the financial system as a whole more resilient.

THE CRISIS AS A CLASSIC FINANCIAL PANIC

Having laid out some of the triggers and vulnerabilities that set the stage for the crisis, I can briefly sketch the evolution of the crisis itself. As I have noted, developments in housing and mortgage markets played an important role as triggers. Beginning in 2007, declining house prices and rising rates of foreclosure raised serious concerns about the values of mortgage-related assets and considerable uncertainty about where those losses would fall. The economy officially fell into recession in December 2007, following several months of financial stress. However, the most severe economic consequences followed the extreme market movements in the fall of 2008.

To a significant extent, the crisis is best understood as a classic financial panic— differing in details but fundamentally similar to the panics described by Bagehot (1873/1897) and many others.[2] The most familiar type of panic that has occurred historically, involving runs on banks by retail depositors, has been made largely obsolete by deposit insurance, central bank backstop liquidity facilities, and the associated government supervision of banks. But a panic is possible in any situation in which longer-term, illiquid assets are financed by short-term, liquid liabilities and in which providers of short-term funding either lose confidence in the borrower or become worried that other short-term lenders may lose confidence. The combination of dependence on wholesale, short-term financing, excessive leverage, generally poor risk management, and the gaps and weaknesses in regulatory oversight created an environment in which a powerful, self-reinforcing panic could begin (for further discussion, see Bernanke 2009).

Indeed, paniclike phenomena arose in multiple contexts and in multiple ways during the crisis. The repo market, a major source of short-term credit for many financial institutions, notably including the independent investment banks, was an important example. In repo agreements, loans are collateralized by financial assets, and the maximum amount of the loan is the current assessed value of the collateral less a safety margin, or "haircut." The secured nature of repo agreements gave firms and regulators confidence that runs were unlikely. But this confidence was misplaced. Once the crisis began, repo lenders became increasingly concerned about the possibility that they would be forced to receive collateral instead of cash, collateral that would then have to be disposed of in falling and illiquid markets. In some contexts, lenders responded by imposing increasingly higher haircuts, cutting the effective amount of funding available to borrowers. In other contexts, lenders simply pulled away, as in a deposit run; in these cases, some borrowers lost access to repo entirely, and some securities became unfundable in the repo market. In either case, absent sufficient funding, borrowers were frequently left with no option but to sell assets into illiquid markets. These forced sales drove down asset prices, increased volatility, and weakened the financial positions of all holders of similar assets. Volatile asset prices and weaker borrower balance sheets in turn heightened the risks borne by repo lenders, further boosting the incentives to demand higher haircuts or withdraw funding entirely. This unstable dynamic was operating in full force around the time of the near-failure of Bear Stearns in March 2008, and again during the worsening of the crisis in mid-September of that year.[3]

Classic panic-type phenomena occurred in other contexts as well. Early in the crisis, structured investment vehicles and many other asset-backed programs were unable to roll over their commercial paper as investors pulled back, and the programs were forced to draw on liquidity lines from banks or to sell assets.[4] The resulting pressure on the bank liquidity providers, evident especially in the market for dollar-denominated loans in short-term funding markets, impeded the functioning of the financial system throughout the crisis. Following the Lehman collapse and the "breaking of the buck" by a money market mutual fund that held commercial paper issued by Lehman, both money market mutual funds and the commercial paper market were also subject to runs.[5] More generally, during the crisis, runs of short-term uninsured creditors created severe funding problems for a number of financial firms, including several large broker-dealers and also some bank holding companies. In some cases, withdrawals of funds by creditors were augmented by "runs" in other guises—for example, by prime brokerage customers of investment banks concerned about the safety of the cash and securities held at those firms or by derivatives counterparties demanding additional margin.[6] Overall, the emergence of runlike phenomena in a variety of contexts helps explain the remarkably sharp and sudden intensification of the financial crisis, its rapid global spread, and the fact that standard market indicators largely failed to forecast the abrupt deterioration in financial conditions.

The multiple instances of runlike behavior during the crisis, together with the associated sharp increases in liquidity premiums and dysfunction in many markets, motivated much of the Federal Reserve's policy response (see Madigan 2009). Bagehot advised central banks—the only institutions that have the power to increase the aggregate liquidity in the system—to respond to panics by lending freely against sound collateral. Following that advice, from the beginning of the crisis the Fed, like other major central banks, provided large amounts of short-term liquidity to financial institutions, including primary dealers as well as banks, on a broad range of collateral.[7] Reflecting the contemporary institutional environment, it also provided backstop liquidity support for components of the shadow banking system, including money market mutual funds, the commercial paper market, and the asset-backed securities markets. To be sure, the provision of liquidity alone can by no means solve the problems of credit risk and credit losses, but it can reduce liquidity premiums, help restore the confidence of investors, and thus promote stability. It can also reduce panic-driven credit problems in cases in which such problems result from price declines during liquidity-driven fire sales of assets.

The pricing of the liquidity facilities was an important part of the Federal Reserve's strategy. Rates could not be too high; to have a positive effect, and to minimize the stigma of borrowing, the facilities had to be attractive relative to the rates available (or nominally available) in illiquid, dysfunctional markets. At the same time, pricing had to be sufficiently unattractive that borrowers would voluntarily withdraw from these facilities as market conditions normalized. This desired outcome in fact occurred: by early 2010, emergency lending had been drastically reduced, along with the demand for such lending.

The Federal Reserve's responses to the failure or near-failure of a number of systemically critical firms reflected the best of bad options, given the absence of a legal framework for winding down such firms in an orderly way in the midst of a crisis—a framework that we now have. However, those actions were, again, consistent with the Bagehot approach of lending against collateral to illiquid but solvent firms. The acquisition of Bear Stearns by JPMorgan Chase was facilitated by a Federal Reserve loan against a designated set of assets, and the provision of liquidity to AIG was collateralized by the assets of the largest insurance company in the United States. In both cases the Federal Reserve determined that the loans were adequately secured, and in both cases the Federal Reserve has either been repaid with interest or holds assets whose assessed values comfortably cover remaining loans.

To say that the crisis was purely a liquidity-based panic would be to overstate the case. Certainly, an important part of the resolution of the crisis involved assuring markets and counterparties of the solvency of key financial institutions, and that assurance was provided in significant part by the injection of capital, including public capital, and the issuance of guarantees—measures not available to the Federal Reserve. In these respects, the Treasury-managed Troubled Asset Relief Program (TARP) and the FDIC's Temporary Liquidity Guarantee Program (TLGP) played critical roles. As I have noted, the Federal Reserve did help restore confidence in the solvency of the banking system by leading the stress tests of the nineteen largest U.S. bank holding companies in the spring of 2009. These stress tests, which were both rigorous and transparent, helped make it possible for the tested banks to raise $120 billion in private capital in the ensuing months.

The response to the panic also involved an extraordinary amount of international consultation and coordination. Following a key meeting of the Group of Seven finance ministers and central bank governors in Washington on October 10, 2008, the governments of other industrial countries took strong measures to stabilize key financial institutions and markets. Central banks collaborated closely throughout the crisis; in particular, the Federal Reserve undertook swap agreements with fourteen other central banks to help ensure adequate dollar liquidity in global markets and thus keep credit flowing to U.S. households and businesses.

CONCLUSION

The financial crisis of 2007 to 2009 was difficult to anticipate for two reasons: First, financial panics, being to a significant extent self-fulfilling crises of confidence, are inherently difficult to foresee. Second, although the crisis bore some resemblance at a conceptual level to the panics known to Bagehot, it occurred in a rather different institutional context and was propagated and amplified by a number of vulnerabilities that had developed outside the traditional banking sector. Once identified, however, the panic could be addressed to a significant extent using classic tools, including backstop liquidity provision by central banks, both here and abroad.

To avoid or at least mitigate future panics, the vulnerabilities that underlay the recent crisis must be fully addressed. This process is well underway at both the national and international levels. I will have to leave to another time a discussion of the extensive changes in regulatory frameworks, as well as the changes in the Federal Reserve's own organization and practices, that have been or are being put in place. Instead, I will close by noting that the events of the past few years have forcibly reminded us of the damage that severe financial crises can cause. Going forward, for the Federal Reserve as well as other central banks, the promotion of financial stability must be on an equal footing with the management of monetary policy as the most critical policy priorities.

NOTES

1. According to the Federal Reserve's statistical release "Flow of Funds Accounts of the United States," the value of real estate held by households fell from $22.7 trillion in the first quarter of 2006 to $20.9 trillion in the fourth quarter of 2007 (down 8.1 percent from the first quarter of 2006). It then declined to $18.5 trillion in the third quarter of 2008 (down 18.6 percent from the first quarter of 2006) and to $16.0 trillion in the fourth quarter of 2011 (down 29.7 percent from the first quarter of 2006). The stock market wealth of U.S. households peaked at $18.1 trillion in the first quarter of 2000 and fell $6.2 trillion to $11.9 trillion through the third quarter of 2001. After a short-lived recovery, stock market wealth bottomed at $9.9 trillion in the third quarter of 2002. Overall, stock market wealth fell $8.3 trillion (or 46 percent) between its peak in the first quarter of 2000 and its trough in the third quarter of 2002. The "Flow of Funds Accounts" are published quarterly and are available at www.federalreserve.gov/releases/z1.

2. The classic theoretical analysis of "pure" banking panics is Diamond and Dybvig (1983). Note that the term "panic" does not necessarily imply irrational behavior on the part of depositors or investors; it is perfectly rational to participate in a run if one fears that the bank will be forced to close. However, the collective action of many depositors or investors can lead to outcomes that are undesirable from the point of view of the economy as a whole.

3. For a theoretical discussion of "margin spirals" and related phenomena, see Brunnermeier and Pedersen (2009). Institutional details on the triparty repo market and a description of developments in that market during the crisis are provided in Copeland, Martin, and Walker (2010). The role of the "run on repo" in the crisis is discussed in Gorton and Metrick (2009).

4. An empirical analysis of the run on ABCP is provided in Covitz, Liang, and Suarez (forthcoming).

5. For an analysis of the determinants of runs on money market mutual funds during the crisis, see McCabe (2010).

6. Prime brokers provide a variety of services for hedge funds and other sophisticated institutional investors. Their services include clearing of trades, financing of long securities positions, and borrowing of securities to facilitate the establishment of short positions.

7. Primary dealers are broker-dealers that are designated as counterparties by the Federal Reserve Bank of New York for its conduct of open market operations in the implementation of monetary policy.

REFERENCES

Bagehot, Walter. 1897. *Lombard Street: A Description of the Money Market.* New York: Charles Scribner's Sons. (Originally published in 1873.)

Bernanke, Ben S. 2009. "Reflections on a Year of Crisis." Speech delivered at "Financial Stability and Macroeconomic Policy," a symposium sponsored by the Federal Reserve Bank of Kansas City, Jackson Hole, Wyo. (August 20–22).

———. 2010. "Causes of the Recent Financial and Economic Crisis." Statement before the Financial Crisis Inquiry Commission, Washington, September 2.

Brunnermeier, Markus K., and Lasse Heje Pedersen. 2009. "Market Liquidity and Funding Liquidity." *Review of Financial Studies* 22(6): 2201–38.

Copeland, Adam, Antoine Martin, and Michael Walker. 2010. "The Tri-Party Repo Market Before the 2010 Reforms." Staff Report 477. New York: Federal Reserve Bank of New York (November). Available at: http://www.copeland.marginalq.com/res_doc/sr477.pdf.

Covitz, Daniel, Nellie Liang, and Gustavo Suarez. Forthcoming. "The Evolution of a Financial Crisis: Collapse of the Asset-Backed Commercial Paper Market." *Journal of Finance.*

Diamond, Douglas W., and Philip H. Dybvig. 1983. "Bank Runs, Deposit Insurance, and Liquidity." *Journal of Political Economy* 91(3): 401–19.

Gorton, Gary B., and Andrew Metrick. 2009. "Securitized Banking and the Run on Repo." Working Paper 15223. Cambridge, Mass.: National Bureau of Economic Research (August).

Madigan, Brian F. 2009. "Bagehot's Dictum in Practice: Formulating and Implementing Policies to Combat the Financial Crisis." Speech delivered at "Financial Stability and Macroeconomic Policy," a symposium sponsored by the Federal Reserve Bank of Kansas City. Jackson Hole, Wyo. (August 20–22).

McCabe, Patrick. 2010. "The Cross-section of Money Market Fund Risks and Financial Crises." Finance and Economics Discussion Series 2010-51. Washington, D.C.: Board of Governors of the Federal Reserve System (September).

Chapter 2

This Time, It Is *Not* Different: The Persistent Concerns of Financial Macroeconomics

J. Bradford DeLong

When the *Financial Times*'s Martin Wolf asked former U.S. Treasury secretary Lawrence Summers what in economics had proved useful in understanding the 2007 to 2009 financial crisis and recession, Summers answered: "There is a lot about the recent financial crisis in Bagehot." "Bagehot" here is Walter Bagehot's 1873 book, *Lombard Street.* How is it that a book written 150 years ago is still state-of-the-art in economists' analysis of episodes like the recent one that we hope is just about to end? There are three reasons. The first is that modern academic economics has long possessed drives toward analyzing empirical issues that can be successfully treated statistically and theoretical issues that can be successfully modeled on the foundation of individual rationality. But those drives are disabilities in analyzing episodes like major financial crises that come too rarely for statistical tools to have much bite, and for which a major ex post question asked of wealth-holders and their portfolios is: just what were they thinking? The second is that even though the causes of financial collapses like the one we saw in 2007 to 2009 are diverse, the transmission mechanism—in the form of the flight to liquidity and/or safety in asset holdings—and the consequences for the real economy in the freezing-up of the spending flow and its implications have always been very similar since at least the first proper industrial business cycle in 1825. Thus, a nineteenth-century author like Walter Bagehot is in no wise at a disadvantage in analyzing the downward financial spiral. The third reason is that the proposed cures for the current financial crises still bear a remarkable family resemblance to those proposed by Walter Bagehot. And so he is remarkably close to the best we can do, even today.

At the Institute for New Economic Thinking (INET) conference in Bretton Woods, New Hampshire, in the spring of 2011, *Financial Times* correspondent and columnist Martin Wolf asked: "[Doesn't] what has happened in the past few years simply suggest that [academic] economists did not understand what was going on?" Former U.S. Treasury secretary Lawrence Summers, in the course of his long answer, said: "There is a lot in [Walter] Bagehot that is about the crisis we just went through. There is more in [Hyman] Minsky, and perhaps more still in [Charles] Kindleberger."[1]

Summers is referring here to Walter Bagehot (1826–1877), who published his *Lombard Street: A Study of the Money Market* in 1873. Hyman Minsky (1919–1996) was a twentieth-century observer and theorist of financial crises who is best approached not through his books or his collected essay volume—*Can "It" Happen Again?* (Minsky 1982, 1986; see also Yellen 2009)—but rather through the use that economic historian Charles Kindleberger (1910–2003) made of his work in *Manias, Panics, and Crashes: A History of Financial Crises* (1978). Asked to name where to turn in the works of economists to understand what was going on from 2005 to 2011, Summers cited three dead economists—one of them long dead. Summers did then enlarge his answer to include living economists, starting with the economic historian Barry Eichengreen and then moving on to mention "[George] Akerlof, [Robert] Shiller, many, many others." Summers stressed the success of empirical work in aiding understanding, in contrast to the failure of modern macroeconomic theory to "keep up with [the] revolution" in finance "as it was realized that asset prices show large volatility that does not reflect anything about fundamentals" (see Shiller 1980).[2]

How is it that Walter Bagehot's *Lombard Street,* a book written 150 years ago, is still state-of-the-art in economists' analysis of episodes like the one that we hope will be dated as ending in 2014? And what exactly did Bagehot say that is still useful?

There are three reasons why Bagehot (1873) still has authority. The first is that modern academic macroeconomics has long possessed two drives. It has possessed a drive toward analyzing empirical issues that can be successfully treated statistically, and it has possessed a drive toward analyzing theoretical issues that can be successfully modeled on the foundation of a representative agent possessing individual rationality. These drives are often very useful: most of the successes of modern macroeconomics as a policy science are built on them. These drives, however, become positive disabilities in analyzing episodes like major financial crises, which arise too rarely for statistical tools to have much bite. Given that a major ex post question we can ask of wealth-holders and their portfolios after a crisis is "Just what were you thinking?" a baseline assumption of individual rationality forecloses too many issues—as does any assumption of a representative agent.

The second reason is that, while the causes of financial collapses are diverse, the effects are pretty much constant across time. Ever since the first proper industrial business cycle occurred in 1825, we have seen a single mechanism, in the form of the flight to liquidity and/or safety in asset holdings, transmit financial distress to the real economy of production and employment, and the consequences for the real economy, in the freezing-up of the spending flow and its implications for employment and production, have looked much the same in episode after episode. Thus, a nineteenth-century author like Walter Bagehot is in no wise at a disadvantage in analyzing the causes and spread of a downward financial spiral or its consequences for the real economy.

The basic story is simple. Through the arrival of new information, through sheer panic, or through the effects of government policies, wealth-holders lose their confidence that a good chunk of the financial assets that they had thought were safe, liquid stores of value and potential means of payment are in fact safe and liquid. Such assets thus lose their attractiveness as safe stores of value and liquid potential means of payment. This causes wealth-holders to attempt to dump their holdings of such now-impaired assets to try to rebalance their portfolios with respect to safety and liquidity. But the dumping of those assets makes them even less safe and less liquid. The recognition of reality (or the simple panic) triggers an attempted shift of portfolios in the direction of holding more safe, liquid stores of value just at the moment when the value of assets that count as such declines. This was the story from 2007 to now. And this was also the story of the period from 1825 to 1826. Thus, it is not surprising that an analysis as good as Bagehot's (1873) of 1825 to 1826 and similar downturns driven by financial crisis is still a (nearly) state-of-the-art analysis of 2007 to the present.

Bagehot's (1873) key relevant insight was that expansionary policies affect both the demand for and the supply of safe, liquid stores of value. When households and businesses are convinced that they need to hold more safe, liquid stores of value, they try to push their spending on currently produced goods and services below their incomes. But since economy-wide incomes are nothing but spending on currently produced goods and services, the net effect is only to push incomes, production, and spending down until households and businesses feel so poor that they forget about building up their stocks of safe, liquid stores of value.

This brings us to the third reason—the additional feature of the situation that Bagehot saw back in 1873. The natural cure for the financial system and for the real economy is for something to lead households and businesses to lower their demand or something to expand the supply of safe, liquid savings vehicles. If the desired safe and liquid asset holdings at full employment once again become equal to asset supplies, the economy will recover. Bagehot saw aggressive expansionary policies as desirable, both to increase the supplies of the safe, liquid stores of value that households and businesses wished to hold and to dampen demand for such assets by demonstrating that risks would be managed and reduced. And those are still the policies—admittedly, in many different flavors—that are advocated today.

Thus, Walter Bagehot is remarkably close to the best we can do, even today.

AGGREGATE SUPPLY AND AGGREGATE DEMAND

Say's Law

At the beginning of economics, back at the very start of the nineteenth century, Jean-Baptiste Say (1803/1855) wrote that the idea of a "general glut"—of economy-wide "overproduction" and consequent mass unemployment—was incoherent. Nobody, Say argued, would ever produce anything beyond what they expected to use themselves unless they planned to sell it, and nobody would sell anything unless they expected to use the money they earned to buy something else.

Thus, "by a metaphysical necessity," as John Stuart Mill (1844) put it back in 1829, there can be no imbalance between the aggregate value of planned production-for-sale, the aggregate value of planned sales, and the aggregate value of planned purchases. This is what would become "Say's Law." Say pointed out that producers could certainly guess wrong about what consumers wanted—and thus produce an excess of washing machines when what consumers really wanted was more yoga lessons. But, Say argued, that would produce a clear market signal in the form of an excess demand for and high profits in making commodities short supply, and an excess supply of and losses in making commodities in surplus. The market system would have the incentive and the power to quickly iron out such imbalances. The fact remained that planned spending had to equal planned production. And in reply to those who claimed that general depression could be produced if the economy's money supply was too low, Say said that producers could and would always give credit:

> To say that sales are dull, owing to the scarcity of money, is to mistake the means for the cause. . . . Should the increase of traffic require more money to facilitate it, the want is easily supplied. . . . Merchants know well enough how to find substitutes for the product serving as the medium of exchange or money. (Say 1803/1855, 137)

Thomas Robert Malthus thought at the start of the 1820s that there was something wrong with Say's argument. Malthus believed that he could see the excess supply, but not the corresponding excess demand:

> We hear of glutted markets, falling prices, and cotton goods selling at Kamschatka lower than the costs of production. It may be said, perhaps, that the cotton trade happens to be glutted; and it is a tenet of [Say's] new doctrine on profits and demand that if one trade be overstocked with capital it is a certain sign that some other trade is understocked. But where, I would ask, is there any considerable trade that is confessedly understocked, and where high profits have been long pleading in vain for additional capital? The [Napoleonic] war has now been at an end above four years; and though the removal of capital generally occasions some partial loss, yet it is seldom long in taking place, if it be tempted to remove by great demand and high profits. (Malthus 1820/1836, 59)

But Malthus did not have a coherent view of what was wrong with Say's basic argument. Malthus tended to see what we would call cyclical unemployment as, rather, an aspect of his other Malthusian concerns about the causes of poverty—and thus as something, like the rest of poverty, best addressed through long-run reform measures to strengthen monarchy, patriarchy, and religion (see Malthus 1798).[3]

The proper answer to Say was given by John Stuart Mill in a piece he wrote in 1829 but did not publish until 1844:

> There cannot be an excess of all other commodities, and an excess of money. . . . But those who have . . . affirmed that there was an excess of all commodities,

never pretended that money was one of these commodities. . . . Persons in general, at that particular time, from a general expectation of being called upon to meet sudden demands, liked better to possess money than any other commodity. Money, consequently, was in request, and all other commodities were in comparative disrepute. . . . When this happens to one single commodity, there is said to be a superabundance of that commodity; and if that be a proper expression, there would seem to be in the nature of the case no particular impropriety in saying that there is a superabundance of all or most commodities, when all or most of them are in this same predicament. (Mill 1829/1844, 37)

What has the potential, according to Mill, to break Say's Law (the equality of expected production and incomes, on the one hand, and planned spending "by metaphysical necessity," on the other) is that people do not just buy currently produced goods and services with their incomes—they also buy money, or, more generally, financial assets. The easiest way for wealth-holders to build up their holdings of financial assets is not to spend the financial assets they already own—that is, to attempt to cut planned spending below expected income. But while each individual can cut planned spending below expected income, an economy as a whole cannot cut its actual spending below its actual income, because what is one economic agent's income can come from nowhere but some other economic agent's spending.

The British Downturn of 1825 to 1826

It is unfair to expect Jean-Baptiste Say to have seen this back in 1803. He did not live in an industrial economy. He had not seen a deflationary financial panic or elevated cyclical unemployment. John Stuart Mill had the advantage of having seen the first industrial business cycle in Britain in the form of the 1825 to 1826 downturn, a downturn generated by the 1825 financial crisis, which was produced in turn by the collapse of the early-1820s canal boom.

Figure 2.1 plots the percentage change in British apparent cotton consumption across most of the nineteenth century. In the forty-five years of peace between the end of the Napoleonic Wars in 1815 and the disruption of the global cotton industry by the U.S. Civil War that started in 1861, apparent cotton consumption by the textile factories of Great Britain declined in only seven episodes. Cotton textile production was the high-tech, high-profit, rapidly expanding leading sector of Britain's first industrial revolution, growing at a pace of more than 8 percent per year on average. The year 1826 saw the second-worst decline in this leading sector, and in British industrial production in general.

It was this episode that John Stuart Mill was looking back on in 1829 when he developed his view of the relationship between aggregate supply and aggregate demand as mediated by the potential for an excess demand for money and other financial assets.

FIGURE 2.1 / Annual Percentage Change in Apparent British Cotton
Consumption, 1810 to 1875

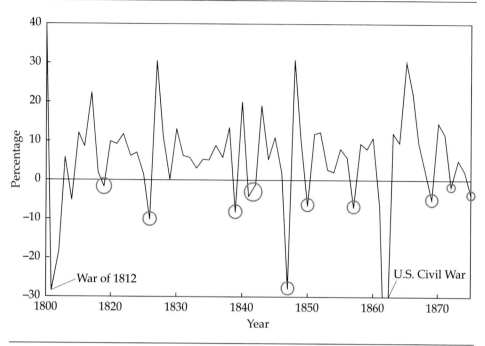

Source: Author's calculations based on Woytinsky and Woytinsky (1952).

Also in 1829, it was looking back on this episode that led Jean-Baptiste Say to revise his doctrine. In his *Complete Course of Applied Political Economy,* Say began his analysis of 1825 to 1826 with the Bank of England's recognition in late 1825 that many of its potential counterparties had overleveraged and overinvested in speculative canals and were now of questionable solvency, either on their own account or because many of their debtors had overleveraged and overinvested in speculative canals. The Bank of England therefore decided in 1825 to reduce its own risk by applying stricter standards:

> [It] cease[d] to discount commercial bills. Provincial banks were in consequence obliged to follow the same course, and commerce found itself deprived at a stroke of the advances on which it had counted, be it to create new businesses, or to give a lease of life to the old.

And the consequence, Say wrote, was financial collapse:

> As the bills that businessmen had discounted came to maturity, they were obliged to meet them, and finding no more advances from the bankers, each

was forced to use up all the resources at his disposal. They sold goods for half what they had cost. Business assets could not be sold at any price. As every type of merchandise had sunk below its costs of production, a multitude of workers were without work. Many bankruptcies were declared among merchants and among bankers, who having placed more bills in circulation than their personal wealth could cover, could no longer find guarantees to cover their issues beyond the undertakings of individuals, many of whom had themselves become bankrupt. (Say 1829, 474–75, author's translation)

What of Say's 1803 declaration that when there is a shortage of *money* in an economy, merchants "know well enough how to find substitutes for the product serving as the medium of exchange"?

What Say had missed in 1803 was that such "inside money" can be quite difficult to create. Only those economic agents whose solvency is common knowledge can create money. Only they can create the safe savings vehicles and stores of value that serve as means of payment and mediums of exchange that everybody will accept, and that everybody will accept because everybody will accept them.

But what economic agency enjoys unquestioned solvency in a time of over-leverage, overinvestment, and significant but unrealized losses whose location is unknown?

That was the problem created in 1825 and 1826 by the collapse of the canal boom and by the Bank of England's first reaction to the potential insolvency of its counterparties.

THE ORIGINS OF CENTRAL BANKING

The Market Failure

Thus, by late 1825 in Britain the revaluation of assets in response to the collapse of the canal boom had created a situation in which "money" was "in request": safe, liquid stores of value were scarce relative to demand, both because the financial crisis had led banks and businesses to seek to hold a greater share of their wealth in safe, liquid form and because the financial crisis had made a substantial proportion of safe and liquid "inside" assets—the debts of bankers, merchants, and industrialists presumed to be well capitalized—not so safe and liquid.

Note that the assets that households and businesses scramble for during a financial crisis and in its aftermath do not have to be, exclusively, means of payment themselves; assets that are still trusted will do as well, or almost as well. In the fall and winter of 1825 to 1826, economic agents throughout Britain were attempting to build up their stocks of safe, liquid financial assets out of a fear that they might need them because their creditors, who were also trying to build up their stocks of safe, liquid financial assets, might not roll over their loans. All across the British economy, economic agents were trying to cut their flow of spending below their expected flow of income—and finding themselves unable to do so, since one agent's income came from another agent's spending. The consequence was that currently produced goods and services became "in comparative disrepute": as spending fell, production and employment fell.

What, then, was it appropriate for the government to do?

Neither Say (1803/1855, 1829) nor Mill (1844) connected the dots and drew out the implications. But they are clear. In normal times, banks exist to make their profits by undertaking liquidity and safety transformations: turning illiquid and risky claims on the capital stock of the economy and on its income into the safe, liquid claims that businesses and households demand and that are used for transaction purposes. They thus create "inside money" by bearing risks, by figuring out which risks to bear, and by convincing their creditors that their liabilities are safe assets—and thus liquid means of payment—because they know their business.

But what if the private financial sector is at the moment unable to perform these safety and liquidity transformations at the scale needed to satisfy demand? What if merchants and bankers are not able to create inside-money substitutes for the product serving as the medium of exchange? What if the private market fails?

"Inside Money" and "Outside Money"

The natural way to repair such a market failure is for the government to temporarily supplement the "inside money" that the financial system can no longer create with its own "outside money." It is then the task of the government to create the safe and liquid financial assets that the private market desires. The central bank should then act as the financial system's "lender of last resort" (Humphrey and Keleher 1984). It can do so through any of a number of policies:

- *Expansionary monetary policy:* Buying relatively risky and illiquid bonds in exchange for its own safe and liquid liabilities.

- *Expansionary banking policy:* Taking risk onto its balance sheet by guaranteeing the liabilities of private banks.

- *Expansionary fiscal policy:* Making investments in bridges, in the human capital of twelve-year-olds, and in social welfare and paying for them by issuing its own relatively safe and liquid debt.

All of these policy channels were attempts to resolve the problem noted by John Stuart Mill and Jean-Baptiste Say in 1829: an excess demand for safe and liquid financial assets, an excess demand that by Walras's Law—which states that planned spending on all commodities must equal expected income—is matched by an excess supply of currently produced goods and services.

Economic theory would not get to this destination in a clear and coherent fashion until Bagehot (1873). But economic practice and policy ran ahead of theory, getting there at the end of 1825. Such an attempt to compensate for the failure of the market to create sufficient "outside money" to cure a financial crisis and the resulting downturn in real activity—to create the safe, liquid financial assets to match market demand—was undertaken by the Bank of England at the end of 1825. And this first such attempt is the origin of what we today would see as modern central banking.

"Outside Money," Financial Crisis Policy, and E. M. Forster's Great-Aunt Marianne

Our single best window onto the origin of central banking in 1825 comes from English novelist E. M. Forster, whose great-aunt Marianne Thornton had helped raise him after his father's death and left him a legacy of £8,000; as a consequence, Forster wrote *Marianne Thornton: A Domestic Biography, 1797–1887,* a book that strings her letters together with scene-setting prose.

In the middle of 1825, Marianne Thornton's younger brother, the twenty-five-year-old Henry Thornton, was invited to join what had in earlier generations been the Thornton family bank as the most junior of its six partners. Marianne's letters mentioned profits of £40,000 a year to be split among six partners.[4] In a letter of December 1825 to her friend Hannah More, she wrote that "there is just now a great pressure in the mercantile world, in the consequence of the breaking of so many of these scheming stock company bubbles." And she criticized the management of the bank that young Henry had just joined. The bank's managing partner "had been inexcusably imprudent in not keeping more cash in the House, but relying on [the bank's] credit . . . which would enable them to borrow whenever they pleased" (Forster 1956, 49).

Today we would say that the bank was overleveraged and had made the mistake of including in its core capital reserves assets that had been misclassified as "AAA." Marianne Thornton wrote of an "inexcusably imprudent" reliance on the bank's credit. But the essence of the mistake is the same. The story that Marianne Thornton tells in her letter to Hannah More has a modern ring.

Then there came a "dreadful Saturday" that Marianne proclaimed she would "never forget": on that day, a run—a wave of depositors liquidating their accounts and depleting the bank's reserves—left the bank vault "literally empty." According to Marianne, all the other partners of the company Pole, Thornton panicked: the managing partner "insisted on proclaiming themselves bankrupts at once, and raved and self-accused himself . . . [and senior partner Scott] cried like a child of 5 years old." Partner Pole was away at his country estate. Another partner was on a business trip. It fell to twenty-five-year-old Henry to deal with the fact that in the last business hour of that Saturday, Pole, Thornton was expected "to pay 33,000 [pounds], and they should receive only 12,000 [pounds]. This was certain destruction" (Forster 1956, 51).

Henry Thornton quickly found another banker, John Smith. Smith asked if the bank was solvent. Henry lied and said that it was. Well then, Smith said, Pole, Thornton would have all he could spare:

Never, [Henry] says, shall he forget watching the clock to see when 5 would strike, and end their immediate terror. . . . The clock did strike . . . as Henry heard the door locked, and the shutters put up, he felt [Pole, Thornton] would not open again but would be forcibly liquidated Monday morning. (Forster 1956, 52)

Other wheels, however, had already been set in motion.

The First Lord of the Treasury, Robert Banks Jenkinson, Lord Liverpool, had been having conversations with Bank of England governor Cornelius Buller about the need for the Bank of England to do something to calm the crisis by acting as a "lender of last resort."[5] John Smith had gotten wind of these conversations between Liverpool and Buller. That Saturday evening, after the banks had closed, John Smith told Henry Thornton that if Henry truly believed that Pole, Thornton was solvent, he, John Smith, would undertake to get it cash from the Bank of England. This was a shock. As Marianne Thornton wrote: "The Bank [of England] had never been known to do such a thing in the annals of banking" (Forster 1956, 53).

On Sunday at 8:00 A.M., the members of the Court of the Bank of England who were in London were assembled to meet John Smith and Henry Thornton: "John Smith began by saying that the failure of [Pole, Thornton] would occasion so much ruin that he should really regard it as a national misfortune . . . then turned to Henry and said, 'I think you give your word the House is solvent?' Henry said he could . . . [and] had brought the books." "'Well then,' said the governor and the deputy governor of the Bank, 'you shall have 400,000 pounds by 8 tomorrow morning, which will I think float you.' Henry said he could scarcely believe what he had heard" (Forster 1956, 55).

On Monday morning, in the predawn dark, Henry Thornton was at the Bank of England as Governor Buller and Deputy Governor Richards personally counted out £400,000 in bank notes. Marianne Thornton claimed that one of the two said: "I hope this won't overset you, my young man, to see the governor and deputy governor of the Bank [of England] acting as your two clerks." She added: "Rumors that the Bank of England had taken [Pole, Thornton] under its wing soon spread, and people brought back money [on Monday] as fast as they had taken it out on Saturday" (Forster 1956, 55).

Henry Thornton had been irrationally exuberant and in error when he swore that the bank was solvent. The bank was eventually closed, and the partners lost their capital shares. The Bank of England had to wait years before getting its emergency loan back in nominal terms, and it never recovered accrued interest. (But it did not care much.)[6]

The particular intervention to support Pole, Thornton was only a small part of what the Bank of England did in the Panic of 1825. To quote from Bank of England director Jeremiah Harman:

We lent [cash] by every possible means and in modes we had never adopted before; we took in stock on security, we purchased Exchequer bills, we made advances on Exchequer bills, we not only discounted outright, but we made advances on the deposit of bills of exchange to an immense amount, in short, by every possible means consistent with the safety of the Bank, and we were not on some occasions over-nice. Seeing the dreadful state in which the public were, we rendered every assistance in our power. (Bagehot 1873, electronic file)

Did it work? Relative to the 8 percent annual trend rate of increase in cotton consumption in Britain, it appears that cotton consumption in 1826 was some 24 percent below trend before rebounding with a 30 percent growth rate in 1827. Relative to trend, it looks like a deep, albeit short downturn. There is good reason to fear that the downturn would have been considerably worse had the Bank of England behaved like the U.S. Treasury and the Federal Reserve in the early 1930s and washed its hands of the situation.

From the standpoint of Mill's theory that the flip side of deficient general demand for currently produced commodities is an excess demand for safe and liquid financial assets, it is straightforward to understand how the Bank of England's interventions in the Panic of 1825 would have boosted the economy. That the Bank of England was willing to guarantee the liabilities of Pole, Thornton turned them from shaky, risky assets back into "inside money"—safe, liquid assets that would satisfy the unusual demand at that moment for near-riskless stores of value and sources of liquidity. That the Bank of England was itself printing up extra banknotes—expanding its balance sheet—raised the supply of "outside money" that the government was providing to the banking system. That the Bank of England was taking action to deal with the crisis may have restored that elusive "confidence" that diminishes the desired portfolio demand for an unusually high amount of safe, liquid assets. And when banks, businesses, and households no longer wish to cut their planned expenditure below their expected income, the economic downturn is over. As A. C. Pigou (1923, electronic version) quotes Alfred Marshall, the industrial depression "could be removed almost in an instant if confidence could return, touch all industries with her magic wand, and make them continue their production and their demand for the wares of others."

THE DEVELOPMENT OF CENTRAL-BANKING PRACTICE IN THE MIDNINETEENTH CENTURY

Robert Peel and "Moral Hazard"

In 1844 the British Parliament took a look at the system of central-bank support for the economy in a financial crisis that resulted from the Bank of England's intervention in 1825. It held a debate on the terms on which the charter of the Bank of England should be renewed. The conclusion of the 1844 bank recharter debate was twofold:[7]

1. The Bank of England should not have the power to print unlimited amounts of money to support the banking system in a financial crisis—in fact, it should be illegal for the Bank of England to print extra banknotes in a crisis. The important

principle was that bankers should be on notice that they should not expect a bailout—for that would create too great a risk of substantial losses from moral hazard.

2. In the event of a real emergency—which, Prime Minister Robert Peel claimed, should not happen—the government could and would request that the Bank of England print as many banknotes as needed to fix the financial crisis.

The reason for (1) was very clear to the parliamentary debaters back in 1844. Any confident expectation on the part of the financial community that the Bank of England stood behind it and would intervene to prevent large-scale bankruptcy in a financial crisis would greatly amplify the chances of such a crisis by removing fear and caution. Bankers confident that in the last analysis they were gambling with the public's money would do what bankers tend to do in such situations. Hence, Robert Peel and his majority in the Parliament thought, it was very important to establish the principle that the Bank of England could not be relied upon to bail out the banking system. And, Peel thought, the best way to establish that principle would be to make it illegal for the Bank of England to do so. As of 1844, the worry was that a government backstop for financial markets would enable moral hazard, lead financiers confident of rescue in an emergency to gamble with the government's and the taxpayers' money, and in the end, because of the expectation of rescue, bring on the financial crises that lender-of-last-resort activities were supposed to cure.

This chain of logic leads to the conclusion that, as Charles Kindleberger put it, "if the market is sure that a lender of last resort exists, its self-reliance is weakened." Therefore, according to Kindleberger,

the lender of last resort . . . should exist . . . but his presence should be doubted. . . . This is a neat trick: always come to the rescue in order to prevent needless deflation, but always leave it uncertain whether rescue will arrive in time or at all, so as to instill caution in other speculators, banks, cities, or countries . . . some sleight of hand, some trick with mirrors . . . [because] fundamentalism has such unhappy consequences for the economic system. (Kindleberger 1978, 12)

Hence the legal prohibition of unlimited expansions of the note issue: Parliament made it illegal for the Bank of England to expand its balance sheet by buying up other assets and issuing additional Bank of England notes, unless the extra note issues were matched by additional gold reserves. The difficulty with this prohibition is that the supply of "outside money" is thereby rendered inelastic, and as Charles Kindleberger (1978, 92) noted, "the difficulty in making the note issue inelastic . . . is that it became inelastic at all times, when the requirement in an internal financial crisis is that money be freely available."

Much earlier, in 1848, Karl Marx had complained that the Bank Recharter Act of 1844 was by its nature destructive, for it

put into practice a self-acting principle for the circulation of paper money. . . . The issuing department is by law empowered to issue notes to the amount of fourteen millions sterling. . . . Beyond these fourteen millions, no note can be issued which is not represented in the vaults of the issuing department by bullion to the same amount. . . . Suppose now that a drain of bullion sets in, and successively abstracts various quantities of bullion from the issuing department. . . . This is not a mere supposition. On October 30, 1847, the reserve of the banking department had sunk to £1,600,000 while the deposits amounted to £13,000,000. With a few more days of the prevailing alarm, which was only allayed by a financial coup d'état on the part of the Government, the Bank reserve would have been exhausted and the banking department would have been compelled to stop payments. . . . Sir Robert Peel's much vaunted Bank law does not act at all in common times; [and] adds in difficult times a monetary panic created by law to the monetary panic resulting from the commercial crisis. (Marx and Engels 1980, 379–84)

Marx's scorn for Peel stemmed in large part from Peel's role in passing the Bank Recharter Act:

Peel himself has been apotheosized in the most exaggerated fashion. . . . One thing at least distinguished him from the European "statesmen"—he was no mere careerist. . . . The statesmanship of this son of the bourgeoisie . . . consisted in the view that there is today only one real aristocracy: the bourgeoisie. . . . He continually used his leadership of the landed aristocracy to wring concessions from it for the bourgeoisie. . . . Catholic emancipation . . . the reform of the police . . . the Bank Acts of 1818 and 1844, which strengthened the financial aristocracy . . . tariff reform . . . free trade . . . with which the aristocracy was nothing short of sacrificed to the industrial bourgeoisie. . . . His power over the House of Commons was based upon the extraordinary plausibility of his eloquence. If one reads his most famous speeches, one finds that they consist of a massive accumulation of commonplaces, skillfully interspersed with a large amount of statistical data. (Marx and Engels 1850/1980, 5)

And indeed, Marx's complaints about the 1844 Bank Recharter Act would have been well taken—if the act had been applied.

Robert Peel's Successors and "Suspension Letters"

As Robert Peel wrote in 1844, looking back on the Bank Recharter Act, the mere fact that the act had made lender-of-last-resort operations illegal did not mean that they should not or would not be undertaken:

My confidence is unshaken that we have taken all the Precautions which legislation can prudently take up against the Recurrence of a pecuniary Crisis. It may occur in spite of our Precautions, and if it does, and if it be necessary to assume a grave responsibility for the purpose of meeting it, I dare say men will be found willing to assume such a responsibility. I would rather trust to this than impair the efficiency and probable success of those measures by which one hopes to control evil tendencies in their beginning, and to diminish the risk that extraordinary measures may be necessary. (*British Parliamentary Papers* [1847], 1969, xxix)

Peel saw a choice: either (1) give the Bank of England explicit powers—and so run the risk that financiers, expecting that those powers would be used, would exploit moral hazard and so produce irrational exuberance, extravagant overleverage, and repeated frequent financial crises—or (2) forbid the Bank of England from acting and rely on financial statesmen in the future to take actions "ultra vires" under the principle that in the end "salus populi suprema lex." Peel chose (1). To him and his peers, the risk of enabling moral hazard by granting explicit powers appeared greater than the risk that the makers of monetary policy would not understand in a crisis that their proper role was to create enough "outside money" to satisfy the panic demand for safe, liquid assets and so eliminate the gap between planned economy-wide spending and expected income that would otherwise generate a deep economic downturn.

And indeed, Peel's expectations of how his successors would act in a crisis were rational. Men were indeed found willing to assume a grave responsibility and go ultra vires and undertake actions that they had no legal power to perform—indeed, actions that they were expressly forbidden by the terms of the Bank of England's new charter from undertaking. The governors of the Bank of England, however, would not expand their balance sheet beyond its legal limit purely on their own initiative. They required first a blessing from the government of the day.

The blessing took the form of a "suspension letter" written by the chancellor of the Exchequer—the British Treasury secretary. First in 1847 and then in 1857, and then again in 1866, the chancellor wrote a letter to the governor of the Bank of England stating that he was suspending for the duration of the financial crisis those provisions of the Bank Recharter Act of 1844 that restricted the Bank of England's ability to expand its balance sheet. Nothing in the black-letter law or in previous custom gave the chancellor any such power to at his will suspend provisions of a corporation charter and grant the corporation extra privileges and powers above those Parliament had granted it. Successive chancellors did so anyway. They judged it, as Peel had foretold, "necessary to assume a grave responsibility for the purpose of meeting" the crisis. They did so. And few people complained.

One who did complain was the irate Karl Marx. He asked whether

it [will] be believed that the Committee has contrived to simultaneously vindicate the perpetuity of the law and the periodical recurrence of its infraction? Laws have usually been designed to circumscribe the discretionary power of Government. Here, on the contrary, the law seems only continued in order to continue to the Executive the discretionary power of overruling it. (Marx 1868, 1)

The reason few people complained was that the system seemed to work less badly than other systems that could be envisioned. The system was inconsistent—and that annoyed Marx. But the granting by the act's originator of ultra vires lender-of-last-resort powers coupled with the forbidding of those powers in the act's text accomplished Charles Kindleberger's "neat trick . . . sleight of hand . . . trick with mirrors . . ." and made it possible for the "lender of last resort . . . [to] exist . . . but [for] his presence [ex ante] to be doubted," and for the Bank of England to "come to the rescue in order to prevent needless deflation, but always leave it uncertain whether rescue will arrive in time or at all, so as to instill caution."

And more often than not, in the third quarter of the nineteenth century at least, it was unnecessary to take risks onto the Bank of England's books and issue additional banknotes above the legal limit; the simple declaration that the chancellor of the Exchequer had sent a suspension letter to the governor of the Bank of England—or even just that he was planning to send a suspension letter—was enough to eliminate the high demand for additional safe, liquid savings vehicles.

FROM PRACTICE BACK TO THEORY: WALTER BAGEHOT'S *LOMBARD STREET*

Bagehot's Rules

When Walter Bagehot settled down to write *Lombard Street,* he had at his back not only the analytical apparatus of British classical political economy but also half a century's worth of policymakers' experience in dealing with financial crises, as well as policymakers' memoirs in which they reflected upon their experience. He thus had several rich veins of material to draw upon as he attempted to systematize what was known about how central banking worked in a financial crisis. The midnineteenth-century practice of central banking he took it upon himself to rationalize and explain can be summed up simply: when, in a financial crisis, private savers want desperately to hold more safe, liquid savings vehicles, *give them what they want.*

Bagehot explained how a central bank should go about doing this with four rules. His first rule was that the central bank exists to keep the fall in the supply of safe, liquid savings vehicles in a financial crisis as small as possible, and that it does so by lending freely to all—or at least to all who have collateral to indicate that they would be solvent if times were normal and if the financial crisis had passed:

> They must lend to merchants, to minor bankers, to "this man and that man," whenever the security is good. In wild periods of alarm, one failure makes many, and the best way to prevent the derivative failures is to arrest the primary failure which causes them. . . . On the surface there seems a great inconsistency . . . like saying—first, that the reserve should be kept, and then that it should not be kept. But there is no puzzle. . . . The ultimate banking reserve of

a country (by whomsoever kept) is not kept out of show, but for . . . meeting a demand for cash caused by an alarm within the country. . . . We keep that treasure for the very reason that in particular cases it should be lent.

Bagehot's second rule was that it is very dangerous to place an ex ante limit on how much the monetary authority will commit to operation as a lender of last resort: the central bank needs to stand ready to expand the supply of safe, liquid assets by as much as turns out to be necessary, which may be more (or less) than anybody thinks possible (or necessary):

An opinion that most people, or very many people, will not pay their credi- tors; and this too can only be met by enabling all those persons to pay what they owe, which takes a great deal of money. . . . Just so before 1844, an issue of notes, as in 1825, to quell a panic entirely internal did not diminish the bul- lion reserve. The notes went out, but they did not return. They were issued as loans to the public, but the public . . . never presented them for payment. . . . We must keep a great store of ready money always available, and advance out of it very freely in periods of panic, and in times of incipient alarm.

Bagehot's third rule was that the central bank must not play favorites:

Advances should be made on all good banking securities, and as largely as the public ask for them. . . . The object is to stay alarm. . . . But the way to cause alarm is to refuse some one who has good security to offer. . . . If it is known that the Bank of England is freely advancing on what in ordinary times is reckoned a good security—on what is then commonly pledged and easily convertible—the alarm of the solvent merchants and bankers will be stayed.

The purpose is to destroy risk. And the risk that a particular firm's assets will not receive symmetrical treatment with the assets of other, more favored firms is an extra source of risk that does not need to be introduced.

Bagehot is often glossed as if he had declared that a central bank in a financial crisis should lend to *illiquid* but not *insolvent* institutions.[8] But it is difficult to see how any institution whose solvency is common knowledge could possibly be illiq- uid. Indeed, it is only because the central bank's solvency is common knowledge that it can create the safe, liquid "outside money" needed to reflate the financial system in a financial crisis.[9] Bagehot did not say "illiquid but not insolvent." He said something more clever: that the central bank should be seen to be "freely advancing on what in ordinary times is reckoned a good security—on what is then commonly pledged and easily convertible"; then "the alarm of the solvent merchants and bankers will be stayed."[10]

Bagehot's fourth rule is that central-bank lending in a financial crisis should be undertaken at a "penalty rate": nobody—no organization, no manager, no trader, no investor—should end the crisis in any sense happy about having been forced to rely on the government. This would appear to mean, particularly, that equity should be extinguished before the central bank begins providing support at inter-est rates that are at all concessionary. To the extent that equity rights are preserved as less than a proper penalty rate is charged, the criticism that the central bank has unnecessarily provided incentives for moral hazard is unanswerable (Castiglionesi and Wagner 2012).

The Great Depression

How effective are these rules? How necessary are these rules? They are a system-atization of nineteenth-century British central-banking practice. They do have a theoretical basis in John Stuart Mill's observation that deficient aggregate demand—planned, total, economy-wide spending that is less than expected income—is the flip side of excess demand for financial assets or for some subset thereof. These rules do also, at least in Peel's formulation, attempt the sleight of hand and tricks with mirrors (the "ambiguity, verging on duplicity . . . promis[ing] not to rescue banks and merchant houses . . . to force them to take responsibility for their behavior, and then rescu[ing] them . . . for otherwise trouble might spread") that Kindleberger calls for in the hope of minimizing ex ante moral hazard. But are there alternative public policy strategies that would do as well?

We do not really know. We do know, however, that the one major time when Bagehot's rules were *not* followed in a deep financial crisis turned into the Great Depression (see Eichengreen 1992, 2008).

In part this was because of the sovereign debt aspect of the crisis. In Europe there was no actor large enough to be a lender of last resort. The United States did not want to step in and serve as a lender of last resort for Europe. In part this was because there was no visible shortage of "liquidity." Money remained very cheap, in the sense that short-term interest rates remained very low and safe. So how could there have been a role for the central bank? What point was there in swapping cash for short-term government bonds when both were indistinguish-able, zero-yielding government assets? Today we would presumably distinguish between a shortage of liquidity pure and simple—investors dumping interest-earning assets at almost any price in order to build up their stocks of means of payment—and a shortage of safe assets—investors dumping risky assets in order to build up their stocks of safe assets. We would say that there is a strong case for the central bank to rebalance the economy by increasing the *money supply* in the first case and by increasing the *safe asset supply* in the second.[11] But interwar poli-cymakers did not make that leap—in part because of the rising Austrian tide. The 1920s and 1930s saw the heyday of the doctrine that business-cycle depressions are the necessary breathing of the economic mechanism (see Hayek 1931/1999; Schumpeter 1934; Robbins 1934).

Interwar policymakers also feared that large deficits and rising government debt would shake business confidence, add to the uncertainty, and raise fears of destructive inflation.[12] Monetary experts like R. G. Hawtrey (1938) could denounce those who called for fiscal austerity to fight the danger of inflation as "crying 'Fire!

Fire!' in Noah's Flood."[13] But they had little effect on policy at the end of the 1920s, and less effect on policy in the post-trough 1930s than they wished.

Kindleberger's judgment was that Bagehot's rules could be applied because more often than not they had worked reasonably well:

> Whether there is a theoretical rationale for letting the market find its way out of a panic or not, the historical fact is that panics that have been met most successfully almost invariably found some source of cash to ease the liquidation of assets before prices fell to ruinous levels. (Kindleberger 1984, 91)

The fact remains that when policymakers and commentators confronted the financial crisis of 2007 to 2009, they almost invariably reached for the rules of Walter Bagehot. It is in that sense that Lawrence Summers was correct when he said, "There is a lot in Bagehot that is about the crisis we just went through."

CONCLUSION: FROM 1873 TO 2009

It is traditional for economic historians and historians of economic thought to lament productive research programs of the past that were subsequently developed only a little further, with many threads left dangling for decades if not longer. And it is indeed a fact that the number of economists who build on Bagehot and whose work makes it into the graduate curriculum is relatively small. Minsky (1982, 1986) is present to a small degree. Kindleberger (1978, 1984) is present to a somewhat larger one. Eichengreen (1992, 2008) is present in economic history courses. Otherwise, Bagehot (1873) remains remarkably good preparation for reading modern works that attempt to pick up the same or similar threads, like Richard Koo (2003, 2009) and Carmen Reinhart and Kenneth Rogoff (2008).

One reason why Bagehot still has considerable authority is that the tools of modern academic macroeconomics are not a great deal of help in weaving together the threads trailing off from Bagehot. Rare and complex events that produce deep and lengthy downturns, like large financial crises, do not occur frequently enough for statistical methods to have much purchase. Financial crises are generated when leveraged agents make large bets and get them wrong, but modern economics has a hard time sustaining models in which agents make bets at all: it is difficult to construct economic actors who not only are believable but who fail to realize that they know less than their potential counterparty and that any deal their potential counterparty is willing to offer is not one they should accept. Academic macroeconomics can and has made progress on lots of issues, but working in the tradition of Bagehot goes against the grain.

Alongside the lack of comparative advantage to be found in the analytical tools of modern economics in making progress on Bagehot-type issues is the fact that, qualitatively, our knowledge base is little better than Bagehot's was. Bagehot or his predecessors had seen the industrial-economy financial crises of 1825–1826, 1847–1848, 1857, and 1866. Since then, we have seen global-scale crises in 1873,

1884, 1893, 1907, 1929 to 1933, and 2007 to 2009, alongside a host of local-scale crises. However, the qualitative mechanism has remained the same. Since 1825, we have seen a single mechanism transmit financial distress to the real economy of production and employment. It takes several forms: a recognition that previous confidence in the liquidity or safety of assets was built on sand; an attempted flight to liquidity and/or quality in asset holdings; and a consequent excess demand for financial assets that generates, via Walras's Law, deficient demand for currently produced goods and services. The freezing-up of the spending flow and its implications for employment and production look much the same in episode after episode. Thus, a nineteenth-century author like Walter Bagehot is at little disadvantage in analyzing the causes and spread of a downward financial spiral or in analyzing its consequences for the real economy.

Although it would certainly have been helpful and productive had the threads left dangling by *Lombard Street* been woven further than they have been over the past 140 years, that failure to make more rapid progress was not a great disability for economics. What was, however, a great disability for economics was a failure to pick up the tool kit of *Lombard Street* and use it to its full effect over the past five years. And here I do not have answers: I have only questions. Specifically:

1. Why were economists so confident that highly leveraged money-center banks—banks that had just switched from a partnership to a corporate structure—had effective control over their risks?

2. Why were economists so confident that the Federal Reserve had both the power and the will to easily stabilize the growth path of nominal GDP?

3. And what happened to economists' effective consensus on the technocratic goals of macroeconomic policy?

The presumption since at least 1936 had been that it is the business of government to intervene strategically in asset markets to stabilize the growth path of nominal GDP and thus to attempt to attain both effective price stability and maximum feasible employment and purchasing power. Yet when the crunch came in late 2008, the technocratic policy consensus on even the goal of maintaining the flow of spending proved to be fragile and ephemeral.

By contrast, Bagehot was very clear and vocal on the root cause of the problem:

Any sudden event which creates a great demand for actual cash may cause, and will tend to cause, a panic in a country where cash is much economised, and where debts payable on demand are large. . . . Some writers have endeavoured to classify panics according to the nature of the particular accidents producing them. But little, however, is, I believe, to be gained by such classifications. There is little difference in the effect of one accident and another upon our credit system. We must be prepared for all of them, and we must prepare for all of them in the same way. . . . Owners of savings not finding, in adequate quantities, their usual kind of investments, rush into anything that promises speciously. . . . The first taste is for high interest, but that taste soon becomes secondary. There is a second appetite for large gains to be made by selling the principal which is to yield the interest. So long as such sales can be effected the mania continues; when it ceases to be possible to effect them, ruin begins.

He was equally clear on what needed to be done in response:

Ordinarily discredit does not at first settle on any particular bank. . . . [It] amounts to a kind of vague conversation: Is A.B. as good as he used to be? Has not C.D. lost money? . . . A panic, in a word, is a species of neuralgia, and according to the rules of science you must not starve it. The holders of the cash reserve must be ready not only to keep it for their own liabilities, but to advance it most freely for the liabilities of others. They must lend to merchants, to minor bankers, to "this man and that man." . . . The problem of managing a panic must not be thought of as mainly a "banking" problem. It is primarily a mercantile one. . . . At the slightest symptom of panic many merchants want to borrow more than usual; they think they will supply themselves with the means of meeting their bills while those means are still forthcoming. If the bankers gratify the merchants, they must lend largely just when they like it least; if they do not gratify them, there is a panic. On the surface there seems a great inconsistency. . . . First, you establish in some bank or banks a certain reserve. . . . And then you go on to say that this final treasury is also to be the last lending-house; that out of it unbounded, or at any rate immense, advances are to be made when no one else lends. This seems like saying—first, that the reserve should be kept, and then that it should not be kept. But . . . the ultimate banking reserve of a country (by whomsoever kept) is not kept out of show, but for certain essential purposes, and one of those purposes is the meeting a demand for cash caused by an alarm within the country.

NOTES

1. See "Larry Summers and Martin Wolf on New Economic Thinking," Institute for New Economic Thinking conference, Bretton Woods, N.H., April 8, 2011 (video), available at: http://tinyurl.com/dl201108a (accessed July 17, 2012).

2. The conclusion of a very long subsequent literature was that Shiller was right: assuming that standard tools for constructing estimates of rational expectations can be applied, only a small part of aggregate equity price variation comes from revisions of rational expectations of future dividends and earnings flows.

3. John Maynard Keynes (1936) took Malthus to be in some sense a predecessor, but it is not clear in what sense.

4. Jane Austen's hero in *Pride and Prejudice* (1813), Fitzwilliam Darcy, receives £10,000 a year from his Pemberley estate and is thus richer than any other non-noble character we meet in the novel.

5. "Critical debate over who should act as lender of last resort . . . took place behind closed doors in December 1825. . . . Lord Liverpool, having warned the market . . . that the speculators were going too far and that the government would not save them . . . threatened to resign if Exchequer bills were provided. . . . The emergency required action by someone. . . . Lord Liverpool . . . applied enormous pressure on the Bank to force it to issue special advances" (Kindleberger 1984, 91).

6. Henry Thornton's career prospered thereafter: even though the bank he had seized command of as a junior partner foundered, the consensus was that he had displayed great energy, good judgment, a cool head, and a facility with figures that made him worth backing. Thereafter, Nathan Meyer Rothschild was willing to back him.

7. The Bank Charter Act of 1844 is available at: http://www.ledr.com/bank_act/1844032.htm (accessed June 25, 2012). See also Whale (1944) and Horsefield (1944).

8. A November 17, 2011, Google search for the string "lend to illiquid but not insolvent institutions" brought up "about 431,000" results.

9. And if the central bank's own solvency is doubted—if it has or accepts sufficient harder-currency liabilities, for example—then its lender-of-last-resort operations directed at supporting the private financial system may well trigger a sovereign debt crisis in which it too needs rescue and support (see Schubert 1991).

10. Thus, Kindleberger's worry that "the central bank presumably seeks to follow rules of helping only sound houses with good paper" and that "the dilemma is that if it holds off too long, what had been good paper becomes bad," is not an argument that Bagehot would recognize for not intervening if the crisis is already bad enough that no financial institution would be solvent if it were immediately marked-to-market. Indeed, since the risk of bankruptcy makes the value of assets to creditors less than the cost of liabilities to debtors, it is hard to see how there could be any institutions that started out with any leverage at all that could be solvent in a mark-to-market sense in a deep financial crisis.

11. Bailouts and loan guarantees, purchases of long-duration and risky assets for cash and safe near-cash, and sales of cash and near-cash for other things—equities, roads, bridges, investments in the human capital of twelve-year-olds, investments in health—retain what power they have to boost the stock of safe assets even when the economy is awash in liquidity, when cash and short-term Treasury bonds are perfect substitutes, and when conventional open-market operations lose their traction. The question of whether such interventions are classified as monetary policy, banking policy, or fiscal policy is in large part a matter of definitions and labels.

12. See, for example, Herbert Hoover's budget message for 1933 (1932): "1933 should ask for only the minimum amounts which are absolutely essential for the operation of the Government. . . . The appropriation estimates for 1933 reflect a drastic curtailment of the expenses of Federal activities in all directions where a consideration of the public welfare would permit. . . . The welfare of the country demands that the financial integrity of the Federal Government be maintained. . . . We are now in a period where Federal finances will not permit of the assumption of any obligations which will enlarge . . . expenditures. . . . To those individuals or groups who normally would importune the Congress to enact measures in which they are interested, I wish to say that the most patriotic duty which they can perform at this time is to themselves refrain and to discourage others from seeking any increase in the drain upon public finances."

13. Hawtrey noted that "the [United Kingdom's] National Government . . . made strenuous efforts to balance the budget, but it was too late to stem the flight from the pound. On the 21st September the convertibility of the currency into gold was suspended. On that day Bank Rate was raised to 6 per cent [per year]. Once the gold standard was suspended, there could be no doubt of the purpose of that step. In the face of the exchange risk [created by abandoning the peg to gold] the high rate could not possibly attract foreign money. It could only be intended as a safeguard against inflation. Fantastic fears of inflation were expressed. That was to cry 'Fire! Fire!' in Noah's Flood. It is after depression and unemployment have subsided that inflation becomes dangerous" (Hawtrey 1938, 145).

REFERENCES

Austen, Jane. 1813. *Pride and Prejudice.* Available at: http://www.pemberley.com/janeinfo/pridprej.html (accessed July 17, 2012).

Bagehot, Walter. 1873. *Lombard Street: A Study of the Money Market.* London: Henry S. King. Available at: http://www.econlib.org/library/Bagehot/bagLomCover.html (accessed July 17, 2012).

British Parliamentary Papers [*1847*]. 1969. Vol. 2. London: Her Majesty's Stationary Office.

Castiglionesi, Fabio, and Wolf Wagner. 2012. "Turning Bagehot on His Head: Lending at Penalty Rates When Banks Can Become Insolvent," *Journal of Money, Credit, and Banking* 44(1, February): 201–19.

Eichengreen, Barry J. 1992. *Golden Fetters: The Gold Standard and the Great Depression.* Oxford: Oxford University Press.

———. 2008. *Globalizing Capital.* Princeton, N.J.: Princeton University Press.

Forster, E. M. 1956. *Marianne Thornton: A Domestic Biography, 1797–1887.* New York: Harcourt Brace.

Hawtrey, R. G. 1938. *A Century of Bank Rate.* London: Longmans, Green and Co.

Hayek, Friedrich von. 1999. "The Fate of the Gold Standard" (1931). In *The Collected Works of F. A. Hayek: Good Money.* Chicago: University of Chicago Press.

Hoover, Herbert. 1932. "Budget Message for Fiscal 1933." Washington: U.S. Government Printing Office.

Horsefield, J. K. 1944. "The Origins of the Bank Charter Act, 1844." *Economica* NS 11(43, November): 180ff.

Humphrey, Thomas M., and Robert E. Keleher. 1984. "The Lender of Last Resort: A Historical Perspective." *Cato Journal* 4(Spring-Summer 1984): 275–318.

Keynes, John Maynard. 1936. *The General Theory of Employment, Interest, and Money.* London: Macmillan. Available at: http://www.marxists.org/reference/subject/economics/keynes/general-theory (accessed July 17, 2012).

Kindleberger, Charles. 1978. *Manias, Panics, and Crashes: A History of Financial Crises.* New York: John Wiley.

———. 1984. *A Financial History of Western Europe.* London: Routledge.

Koo, Richard. 2003. *Balance-Sheet Recession.* New York: John Wiley.

———. 2009. *The Holy Grail of Macroeconomics.* New York: John Wiley.

Malthus, Thomas Robert. 1798. *An Essay on the Principle of Population.* London: J. Johnson. Available at: http://goo.gl/OqHVA (accessed July 17, 2012).

———. 1836. *Principles of Political Economy Considered with a View Toward Their Practical Application.* 2nd ed. London: W. Pickering. Available at: http://goo.gl/IYvxI (accessed July 17, 2012). (First edition published in 1820.)

Marx, Karl. 1868. "The English Bank Act of 1844." *New York Tribune,* August 23. Available at: http://marxengels.public-archive.net/en/ME1077en.html (accessed July 17, 2012).

Marx, Karl, and Friedrich Engels. 1850/1980. *Collected Works,* vol. 16. London: Lawrence and Wishart.

Mill, John Stuart. 1844. *Essays on Some Unsettled Questions in Political Economy.* London: John W. Parker. Available at: http://tinyurl.com/dl201108e (accessed July 17, 2012).

Minsky, Hyman. 1982. *Can "It" Happen Again? Essays on Instability and Finance.* New York: M. E. Sharpe.

———. 1986. *Stabilizing an Unstable Economy.* New York: Twentieth Century Fund.

Pigou, A. C. 1923. *Essays in Applied Economics.* London: P. S. King and Son.

Reinhart, Carmen, and Kenneth Rogoff. 2008. *This Time It's Different.* Princeton, N.J.: Princeton University Press.

Robbins, Lionel. 1934. *The Great Depression.* London: Macmillan.

Say, Jean-Baptiste. 1829. *Cours complet d'économie politique pratique (Complete Course of Applied Political Economy).* Available in the original French at: http://tinyurl.com/dl201108c (accessed July 17, 2012).

———. 1855. *Treatise d'économie politique (A Treatise on Political Economy).* Translated from the French by C. R. Prinsep, edited by Clement C. Biddle. Philadelphia: Lippincott, Grambo and Co. Available at: http://tinyurl.com/dl201108b (accessed July 17, 2012). (Originally published in 1803 in French as *Treatise d'économie politique.*)

Schubert, Aurel. 1991. *The Credit-Anstalt Crisis of 1931.* Cambridge: Cambridge University Press.

Schumpeter, Joseph A. 1934. "Depressions." In *Economics of the Recovery Program,* edited by Douglass Brown. New York: McGraw-Hill.

Shiller, Robert. 1980. "Do Stock Prices Move Too Much to Be Justified by Subsequent Movements in Dividends?" Working Paper 456. Cambridge, Mass.: National Bureau of Economic Research (February). Available at: http://www.nber.org/papers/w0456.pdf (accessed July 17, 2012).

Whale, P. Barrett. 1944. "A Retrospective View of the Bank Charter Act of 1844." *Economica* NS 11(43, August): 109ff.

Woytinsky, Wladimir, and Emma Woytinsky. 1952. *World Population and Production.* New York: Twentieth Century Fund.

Yellen, Janet. 2009. "A Minsky Meltdown: Lessons for Central Bankers." San Francisco: Federal Reserve Bank of San Francisco). Paper presented to the Eighteenth Annual Hyman P. Minsky Conference on the State of the U.S. and World Economies, "Meeting the Challenges of the Financial Crisis." New York (April 16). Available at: http://www.frbsf.org/news/speeches/2009/0416.html (accessed July 17, 2012).

Chapter 3

Credit Supply Shocks and Economic Activity in a Financial Accelerator Model

Simon G. Gilchrist and Egon Zakrajšek

This chapter uses the canonical "New Keynesian" macroeconomic model—augmented with the standard financial accelerator mechanism—to study the extent to which disruptions in financial markets can account for U.S. economic fluctuations during the 1985 to 2009 period. The key feature of the model is that financial shocks drive a wedge between the required return on capital and the safe rate of return on household savings. A widening of this wedge causes a decline in investment spending and a worsening in the quality of borrowers' balance sheets, factors that lead to a mutually reinforcing deterioration in financial conditions. We employ the methodology we have developed (Gilchrist and Zakrajšek 2012) to construct a measure of distress in the financial sector, which is used to simulate the model. Our simulations indicate that an intensification of financial stresses implies a sharp widening of credit spreads, a significant slowdown in economic activity, a decline in short-term interest rates, and a persistent disinflation. Moreover, such financial market disruptions account for the bulk of the contraction in U.S. economic activity that occurred during the last three recessions; these disturbances also generated the investment booms that characterized the 1995 to 2000 and 2003 to 2006 periods. We also consider the potential benefits of a monetary policy rule that allows the short-term nominal rate to respond to changes in financial conditions as measured by movements in credit spreads. We show that such a spread-augmented policy rule can effectively dampen the negative consequences of financial disruptions on real economic activity.

The acute financial turmoil that raged in global financial markets following the collapse of Lehman Brothers in the early autumn of 2008 plunged the United States into the most severe recession since the Great Depression. The roots of this economic calamity can be found in the meltdown of the subprime mortgage market in the wake of an unexpected and prolonged decline in house prices that materialized in late 2006. The ensuing financial stresses caused enormous liquidity problems in interbank funding markets and ultimately led to the sudden collapse of several major financial institutions and a sharp reduction in credit intermediation (for a detailed account of the 2007 to 2009 financial crisis, see Brunnermeier 2009; Gorton 2009). Responding to the cascade of massive shocks that roiled financial markets in the latter part of 2008, the U.S. government—in the hope of preventing the financial meltdown from engulfing the real economy—intervened in financial markets on an unprecedented scale and took actions that continue to divide economists, policymakers, and the public at large.

In this chapter, we assess the implications of such financial disruptions for the real economy. We first discuss the various linkages between the financial sector and the real economy and then outline three main channels by which disruptions in financial markets influence macroeconomic outcomes:

1. A pullback in spending due to reductions in wealth

2. Balance sheet mechanisms that lead to a widening of credit spreads, which curtails the ability of households and businesses to obtain credit

3. The direct effect of impairments in the ability of financial institutions to intermediate credit

Although these channels are relatively well understood from a theoretical perspective, assessing their quantitative implications remains a considerable challenge for macroeconomists. For example, a fall in output that follows a drop in lending associated with a major financial disruption reflects both supply and demand considerations. In addition, in a world characterized by a rapidly evolving financial landscape, it is difficult to gauge the extent to which various financial asset-market indicators provide consistent and credible information about the relationship between the health of the financial system and economic activity.

We then describe what is in our view a particularly informative indicator of financial market distress. Building on our recent work (see Gilchrist and Zakrajšek 2012), we construct this indicator of financial market distress using secondary market prices of bonds issued by U.S. financial institutions. Specifically, using a flexible, empirical credit-spread pricing framework, we decompose financial intermediary credit spreads into two components: (1) a component capturing the usual countercyclical movements in expected defaults; and (2) a component representing the cyclical changes in the relationship between default risk and credit spreads—the "financial bond premium," which, we argue, represents the shifts in the risk attitudes of financial intermediaries, that is, the marginal investors pricing corporate debt claims.

To study the relationship between the financial bond premium and the macro-economy, we use an identified vector autoregression (VAR) framework that, under reasonable assumptions, allows us to trace out the dynamic effect of an unexpected increase in the financial bond premium on the key macroeconomic and financial variables. In our terminology, such a "financial shock" is associated with a period of temporary, but significant, distress in financial markets. We also show that in response to such an unexpected increase in the financial bond premium—which, by construction, is contemporaneously uncorrelated with the current state of the economy—the net worth position of the nonfinancial sector deteriorates significantly, real economic activity slows appreciably, and both the short- and longer-term risk-free rates decline noticeably.

To provide further insight into the linkages between the financial sector and economic activity, we then study the effect of financial market disruptions in a macroeconomic framework that incorporates financial market frictions into an otherwise standard model of the macroeconomy (along the lines of Christiano, Eichenbaum, and Evans [2005] and Smets and Wouters [2007]). The main purpose of this analysis is to disentangle movements in the supply and demand for credit by imposing a structural framework on macroeconomic data. In particular, using quarterly U.S. macroeconomic data, we study simulations of the U.S. economy over the 1985 to 2009 period based on the canonical "New Keynesian" model augmented with the financial accelerator framework developed by Bernanke, Gertler, and Gilchrist (1999).[1]

In our simulation exercises, we use fluctuations in the estimated financial bond premium as a proxy for exogenous disturbances to the efficiency of private financial intermediation within the model of Christiano et al. (2005) and Smets and Wouters (2007) augmented with the financial accelerator of Bernanke et al. (1999). We calibrate the key parameters of the model, so that the responses of macroeconomic aggregates to our measure of financial shocks match the corresponding responses that are estimated using the actual data. Using this realistic calibration of the U.S. economy, we explore the extent to which observable fluctuations in the financial bond premium—an indicator of financial market distress—can account for macroeconomic dynamics during the 1985 to 2009 period. The results indicate that the model can account well for the overall movements in consumption, investment, output, and hours worked that were observed during this period. The model also does well at matching both the observed decline in inflation and nominal interest rates and the sharp widening of nonfinancial credit spreads that typically occurs during recessionary periods.

Finally, we use this framework to analyze the potential benefits of an alternative monetary policy rule that allows for nominal interest rates to respond to changes in financial conditions, as measured by movements in credit spreads. The results indicate that by allowing the nominal interest rate to respond to credit spreads, as suggested recently by John Taylor (2008), Paul McCulley and Ramin Toloui (2008), and Laurence Meyer and Brian Sack (2008), monetary policy can effectively dampen the negative consequences of financial disruptions on real economic activity. This result is consistent with the recent empirical evidence suggesting that increases in credit spreads may be one of the earliest and clearest aggregators of accumulating evidence of incipient recession (see, for example, Gertler and Lown 1999; King, Levin, and Perli 2007; Mueller 2009; Gilchrist, Yankov, and Zakrajšek 2009; Faust et al. 2011; Gilchrist and Zakrajšek 2012).

In the next section, we discuss the various channels by which financial factors may influence economic outcomes. That discussion is followed by a review of the empirical methodology we use to estimate the financial bond premium and a presentation of evidence that financial shocks—identified vis-à-vis unexpected disturbances to the financial bond premium in a standard monetary VAR framework—have significant adverse consequences for the real economy. We then outline the macroeconomic framework we use to study the impact of financial disturbances on the macroeconomy and present the corresponding results before offering a brief conclusion.

FINANCE AND THE REAL ECONOMY

The benchmark macroeconomic model used to study the behavior of firms and households is predicated on the assumption that the composition of agents' balance sheets has no effect on their optimal decisions. Within this Modigliani-Miller paradigm, households make consumption decisions based solely on permanent income—the sum of their financial wealth and the per-period income obtained from the present discounted value of future wages; movements in financial asset prices shape agents' spending decisions to the extent that they influence households' financial wealth, whereas changes in interest rates affect spending decisions because they alter the present discounted values and hence reflect appropriately calculated user-costs for financing real consumption expenditures. On the business side, firms make investment decisions by comparing the expected marginal profitability of new investment projects with the appropriately calculated after-tax user-cost of capital. The relevant interest rate used in such calculations reflects the maturity-adjusted, risk-free rate of return appropriate to discount the future cash flows.

Financial market imperfections—stemming from asymmetric information or moral hazard on the part of borrowers vis-à-vis lenders—provide a theoretical link between the financial health of households and firms and the amount of borrowing and hence economic activity in which they are able to engage. Although models differ on details, contracts between borrowers and lenders generally require that borrowers post collateral or maintain some stake in the project in order to mitigate the contracting problems associated with such financial market imperfections. For example, when the borrower's net worth is low relative to the amount borrowed, the borrower has a greater incentive to default on the loan. Lenders recognize these incentive problems and consequently demand a premium to provide the necessary external funds.

In general, the external finance premium is increasing in the amount borrowed relative to the borrower's net worth. Because net worth is determined by the value of assets in place, declines in asset values during economic downturns result in a deterioration of borrowers' balance sheets and a rise in the premiums charged on the various forms of external finance. The increases in external finance premiums, in turn, lead to further cuts in spending and production. The resulting reduction in economic activity causes asset values to fall further and amplifies the economic downturn—the so-called financial accelerator mechanism.

Although the theoretical impact of changes in financial conditions on household and business spending decisions through the financial accelerator mechanism is well understood, quantifying the overall strength of this mechanism remains a challenge for macroeconomists. This task is complicated by the fact that it is very difficult to distinguish the effect of a slowdown in economic activity on household and firm spending due to the usual demand channels absent financial market frictions from the effect that such a slowdown may have through the financial accelerator itself. Nonetheless, a careful assessment of the empirical implications of models that allow for financial frictions—relative to those that assume perfect capital markets—has allowed researchers to make substantial progress in assessing the empirical relevance of changes in financial conditions for real activity.

On the household side, the permanent income model of consumption has stark implications for the responsiveness of consumption to both income and asset values. Transitory changes in income should have very little effect on permanent income and hence consumption. Reasonably calibrated versions of such models imply that households are relatively insensitive to changes in asset values, suggesting that households should increase consumption by three to four cents for every dollar increase in their financial wealth. More important, to a first approximation, the value of housing does not represent net wealth for the household sector because an increase in home values is also an increase in the implicit rental cost of housing. As a result, the household sector is no better or worse off when home values rise (for a thorough discussion, see Buiter 2010).

Empirical research provides compelling evidence against the permanent income model of consumption in favor of models in which the quality of household balance sheets plays an important role in determining their consumption decisions. A variety of studies have shown that household consumption is excessively sensitive to movements in transitory income. Whereas the exact cause of this excess sensitivity is subject to considerable debate, the excess sensitivity is generally attributed to the fact that at least a subset of households face significant borrowing constraints or engage in precautionary savings behavior because of imperfect insurance.

In contrast to the predictions of the permanent income model, both microeconomic and macroeconomic studies also suggest an important link between house prices and household consumption (see, for example, Case, Quigley, and Shiller 2005; Campbell and Cocco 2008; Carroll, Otsuka, and Slacalek 2011). Estimates of the housing wealth effect vary, but generally they imply that household consumption increases by an amount ranging from three to ten cents for every dollar increase in housing wealth. This response is generally attributed to the fact that at higher equity levels households can obtain larger home mortgage loans and thus maintain high consumption levels while financing a home. Similarly, existing homeowners may engage in mortgage equity withdrawals to finance high levels of consumption relative to their income.

Empirical research also provides evidence that supports the notion that corporate balance sheets influence investment spending, though this evidence is more contentious. It is well known that business investment spending is strongly correlated with corporate cash flow. Earlier research, initiated by Fazzari, Hubbard, and Petersen (1988), has argued that cash flows stimulate investment because internal funds are a cheaper source of finance than external funds. Critics point out, however, that current cash flows may also provide signals about future profits, which in turn determine the firm's net worth and hence the strength of its balance sheet. That said, the available evidence suggests that the cash flow mechanism is quite strong for smaller firms, firms with limited access to corporate credit and equity markets, and firms with weak balance sheets (see, for example, Gilchrist and Himmelberg 1995).

More recent research has questioned the macroeconomic relevance of this effect by arguing that for the large firms that account for the bulk of investment spending, current cash flows serve mainly as signals about future profit opportunities rather than as indicators of the strength of their balance sheets (see, for example, Cummins, Hassett, and Oliner 2006; Rebelo, Eberly, and Vincent 2008). Nonetheless, studies that have analyzed investment spending during financial crises show that large negative shocks to firms' balance sheets can have important adverse consequences for the investment decisions of large firms, at least during periods of acute financial distress (see, for example, Aguiar 2005; Gilchrist and Sim 2007). At the same time, credit spreads on a wide variety of corporate debt instruments typically widen significantly in recessionary periods, a development that is consistent with a deterioration in the overall financial condition of the corporate sector or a worsening of conditions within the financial sector that serves as an originator and guarantor of corporate debt instruments. Although macroeconomic evidence offers mixed guidance on the importance of interest rates for investment spending, our recent work (Gilchrist and Zakrajšek 2007), using firm-level data, shows that capital formation is highly responsive to changes in corporate credit spreads.

The financial mechanism linking the balance sheet conditions of borrowers to real activity is often described as the "broad credit channel." Financial institutions are also likely to suffer from asymmetric information and moral hazard problems when raising funds to finance their lending activities. The focus of this "narrow credit channel" is the health of financial intermediaries and its impact on the ability of financial institutions to extend credit. In a fractional reserve banking system, deposits provide a source of funds for lending with only a small fraction of total deposits held as reserves. Because a tightening of monetary policy drains reserves from the banking system, poorly capitalized banks that are unable to raise external funds cut back on their lending. As a result, bank-dependent borrowers, in particular small firms and households that have few alternative sources of credit, reduce spending (see, for example, Bernanke and Blinder 1988; Bernanke and Lown 1991; Kashyap and Stein 1994, 2000; Peek and Rosengren 1995a, 1995b, 2000; Ashcraft 2005; Gilchrist and Zakrajšek 2011a).

In an important paper, Anil Kashyap and Jeremy Stein (2000) document the empirical validity of this mechanism by showing that small U.S. commercial banks that are poorly capitalized are especially sensitive to changes in the stance of monetary policy. Although this bank lending channel appears to have important effects on the lending behavior of smaller banks, such banks account for only a small fraction of total bank lending in the United States, which suggests that the bank lending channel may not be a quantitatively important channel through which monetary policy affects the real economy. In a recent paper, however, Nicola Cetorelli and Linda Goldberg (forthcoming) argue that this lending channel may also be at work at large commercial banks operating primarily in domestic markets. In contrast, commercial banks with global operations are able to offset declines in domestic deposits through internal funds obtained from their global subsidiaries. In times of a worldwide financial distress, however, the ability of global subsidiaries to provide internal funds to U.S. financial institutions is also likely to be limited in scope, a development that would further strengthen the bank lending channel in the United States.

Although monetary policy may not have a large direct impact through the bank lending channel, reductions in bank capital during economic downturns can also reduce lending activity. As economic growth slows and defaults and delinquencies rise, the quality of bank loan portfolios deteriorates. Banks seeking to shore up their capital or to meet regulatory capital requirements tighten their credit standards and cut back on lending, an inward shift in loan supply that curtails the spending of bank-dependent borrowers (see, for example, Van den Heuvel 2007, forthcoming; Bassett et al. 2012).

The strength of this mechanism, of course, depends on the overall health of the banking sector and on the extent to which firms and households are bank-dependent. In the United States, the bulk of investment spending is financed by relatively large firms that rely primarily on corporate bond and equity markets to finance their capital expenditures. Nonetheless, certain corporate debt instruments—most notably commercial paper—are typically backed by lines of credit at commercial banks. In addition, a substantial portion of business financing through commercial and industrial loans relies on such credit lines. In times of financial turmoil, even large nonfinancial firms may have a difficult time raising capital in arm's-length markets. As these firms tap their backup lines of credit to finance inventories or operating expenditures in the face of falling revenues, banks may be forced to make further cuts in lending to bank-dependent borrowers (see, for example, Ivashina and Scharfstein 2010).

The direct effect of falling values of assets held by the financial sector is more difficult to assess. Although there is clear evidence that reductions in bank capital have important implications for the lending behavior of small banks, there is less direct evidence to support the claim that a capital channel has important implications for the lending behavior of large banks and nonbank financial intermediaries. Nonetheless, a sharp pullback in lending by large commercial banks and nonbank financial institutions during the recent financial crisis—owing to lack of liquidity in the interbank funding markets or a retrenchment in lending as these institutions sought to replenish depleted capital—very likely caused a severe slowdown in economic activity by constricting the supply of credit.

More generally, spurred by the extraordinary events of the 2007 to 2009 financial crisis, an emergent theoretical literature emphasizes the implications of the capital position of financial intermediaries for asset prices. For example, Zhiguo He and Arvind Krishnamurthy (2009, 2010) show that adverse macroeconomic conditions, by depressing the capital base of financial intermediaries, can reduce the risk-bearing capacity of the marginal investor, causing a sharp increase in the conditional volatility and correlation of asset prices and a drop in risk-free interest rates. Relatedly, Viral Acharya and S. "Vish" Viswanathan (2010) have developed a theoretical framework in which financial intermediaries—in response to a sufficiently severe aggregate shock—are forced to de-lever by selling their risky assets to better-capitalized firms, causing asset markets to clear only at "cash-in-the-market" prices (but see Allen and Gale 1994, 1998). Markus Brunnermeier and Lasse Pedersen (2009) and Nicolae Gârleanu and Pedersen (2009), in contrast, explore how margins, or "haircuts"—the difference between the security's price and the collateral value that must be financed with the trader's own capital—interact with liquidity shocks in determining asset price dynamics.

Empirical support for this type of mechanism is provided by our recent work (Gilchrist and Zakrajšek 2012), in which we employ a large panel of unsecured corporate bonds issued by U.S. nonfinancial firms to decompose the associated credit spreads into two components: a default-risk component capturing the usual countercyclical movements in expected defaults, and a non-default-risk component that captures the cyclical fluctuations in the relationship between default risk and credit spreads. According to our results, the majority of the information content of credit spreads for future economic activity is attributable to movements in this excess bond premium—that is, to deviations in the pricing of corporate debt claims relative to the expected default risk of the issuer. Moreover, we show that shocks to this premium that are orthogonal to the current macroeconomic conditions cause economically and statistically significant declines in economic activity and inflation, as well as in risk-free rates and broad measures of equity valuations.

Importantly, this recent work also shows that fluctuations in their excess bond premium are closely related to the financial condition of broker-dealers, the highly leveraged financial intermediaries that play a key role in most financial markets, according to Tobias Adrian and Hyun Song Shin (2010).[2] Taken together, the evidence we present supports the notion that deviations in the pricing of long-term corporate bonds relative to the expected default risk of the underlying issuer reflect shifts in the effective risk aversion of the financial sector. Increases in risk aversion, in turn, lead to a contraction in the supply of credit, through both the corporate bond market and the broader commercial banking sector.

FINANCIAL BOND PREMIUM AS AN INDICATOR OF FINANCIAL STRESS

The origins of the 2007 to 2009 crisis undoubtedly lie within the U.S. financial sector, which, after a massive buildup in leverage and a prolonged period of loose underwriting standards and mispricing of risk, underwent an abrupt deleveraging process that sharply curtailed the availability of credit to businesses and households. To measure the cyclical fluctuations in the risk-bearing capacity of the financial sector, we apply our methodology (Gilchrist and Zakrajšek 2012) to credit spreads on bonds issued by a broad set of U.S. financial institutions. We then use the excess bond premium based on financial intermediary spreads—which we term the "financial bond premium"—as a summary statistic for distress in the financial system.

The key information underlying our analysis comes from a sample of fixed income securities issued by U.S. financial corporations.[3] Specifically, for the period from January 1985 to June 2010, we extracted from the Lehman/Warga (LW) and Merrill Lynch (ML) databases month-end prices of outstanding financial corporate bonds that are actively traded in the secondary market.[4] To guarantee that the borrowing costs of different firms are measured at the same point in their capital structure, we restricted our sample to include only senior unsecured issues with a fixed coupon schedule. After eliminating a small number of extreme observations, our sample contains 886 individual securities, issued by 193 distinct financial firms (for a complete description of the data and the construction of financial intermediary credit spreads, see Gilchrist and Zakrajšek 2011b).

We focus the analysis on the period from the mid-1980s onward, a period marked by a stable monetary policy regime and by significant deregulation of financial markets—for example, the Riegle-Neal Act (1994), the Gramm-Leach-Bliley Act (1999), and the repeal of Regulation Q (1986). In addition, rapid advances in information technology over the past quarter-century have significantly lowered the information and monitoring costs of investments in public securities, thereby increasing the tendency for corporate borrowing to take the form of negotiable securities issued directly in capital markets. By improving liquidity in both the primary and secondary markets, these changes in the financial landscape have facilitated more efficient price discovery and are likely to have improved the information content of credit spreads, both for future economic outcomes and as indicators of financial market distress.

The time-series evolution of credit spreads for our sample of bonds is depicted in figure 3.1. With the exception of the recent financial crisis, the median credit spread on bonds issued by financial institutions—although countercyclical—fluctuated in a relatively narrow range. In spite of focusing on a relatively narrow segment of the U.S. financial system—namely, the publicly traded financial corporations with senior unsecured debt trading in the secondary market—the interquartile range of spreads indicates a fair amount of dispersion in the price of debt across different institutions, information that is potentially useful for identifying shocks to the financial system.

The Financial Bond Premium

Before presenting our indicator of financial stress, we briefly outline the empirical methodology underlying the construction of the financial bond premium. Our decomposition of credit spreads (Gilchrist and Zakrajšek 2012) is based on the credit-spread regression of the following type:

$$\ln S_{it}[k] = -\beta DD_{it} + \boldsymbol{\lambda}' \mathbf{Z}_{it}[k] + \varepsilon_{it}[k] \tag{3.1}$$

FIGURE 3.1 / U.S. Financial Intermediary Credit Spread, 1985 to 2010 (Monthly)

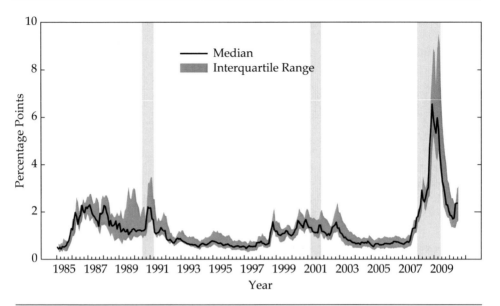

Source: Authors' calculations based on data from Lehman/Warga (Warga 1991) and Merrill-lynch (2012).

Note: Sample period is January 1985 to June 2010. The solid line depicts the median spread on senior unsecured bonds issued by 193 financial firms in our sample, and the shaded band depicts the corresponding interquartile range. The shaded vertical bars denote the recessions as dated by the National Bureau of Economic Research.

where $S_{it}[k]$ denotes the credit spread on bond k (issued by firm i); DD is the distance-to-default (DD) for firm i; $\mathbf{Z}_{it}[k]$ is a vector of bond-specific characteristics that controls for the optionality features embedded in most corporate securities as well as for potential term and liquidity premiums; and $\varepsilon_{it}[k]$ is a credit-spread "pricing error." The key feature of our approach is that the firm-specific credit risk is captured by the distance-to-default, a market-based indicator of default risk based on the option-theoretic framework developed in the seminal work of Robert Merton (1974).

Using the estimated parameters of the credit-spread regression model, the financial bond premium in month t is defined by the following linear decomposition:

$$FBP_t = \bar{S}_t - \widehat{\bar{S}}_t \qquad (3.2)$$

where $\bar{S}_t$ denotes the average credit spread in month t and $\widehat{\bar{S}}_t$ is its predicted counterpart. As shown in figure 3.2, our empirical credit-spread pricing model (Gilchrist and Zakrajšek 2011b, 2012) explains a substantial portion of the cyclical fluctuations in financial intermediary credit spreads, a result indicating that the distance-to-default provides an accurate measure of default risk. Note also that the financial bond premium is, by construction, uncorrelated with the observed measures of default risk, so that movements in the financial bond premium are

FIGURE 3.2 / Actual and Predicted Financial Intermediary Credit Spreads, 1985 to 2010 (Monthly)

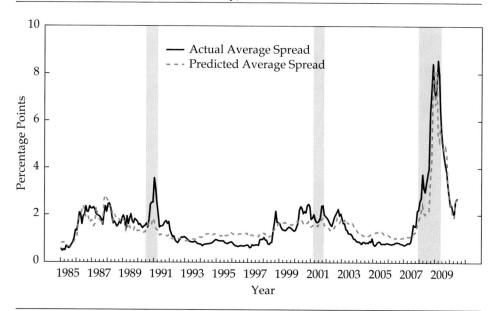

Source: Authors' calculations based on Gilchrist and Zakrajšek (2012) and text.

Note: Sample period is January 1985 to June 2010. The solid line depicts the average credit spread on senior unsecured bonds issued by 193 financial firms in our sample. The dashed line depicts the predicted average credit spread using the methodology in Gilchrist and Zakrajšek (2011b). The shaded vertical bars denote the recessions as dated by the National Bureau of Economic Research.

likely to reflect variation in the price of default risk rather than changes in the risk of default in the U.S. financial sector.

The solid line in figure 3.3 shows the estimated monthly financial bond premium —the difference between the solid and dotted lines in figure 3.2—while the overlaid solid dots denote the quarterly (annualized) return on assets (ROA) in the U.S. financial corporate sector. The high degree of negative comovement between this broad measure of profitability of the financial sector and the financial bond premium is consistent with the view that risk premiums in asset markets fluctuate closely in response to movements in the capital and balance sheet conditions of financial intermediaries, a fact also emphasized by Adrian and Shin (2010) and Adrian, Moench, and Shin (2010a, 2010b).

Note that the financial bond premium appears to be a particularly timely indicator of strains in the financial system. The sharp run-up in the premium during the early 1990s, for example, is consistent with the view that capital pressures on commercial banks in the wake of the Basel I capital requirements significantly exacerbated the 1990 to 1991 economic downturn by reducing the supply of bank-intermediated credit (Bernanke and Lown 1991). In contrast, the robust health of the financial system at the start of the 2001 recession has been cited as an important

FIGURE 3.3 / Financial Bond Premium and Financial-Sector Profitability, 1985 to 2010 (Monthly)

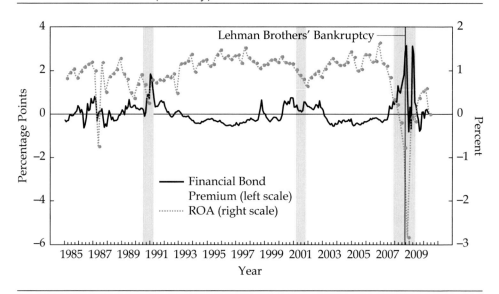

Source: Authors' calculations based on Standard & Poor's Compustat database (2011).

Note: Sample period is January 1985 to June 2010. The solid line depicts the estimated financial bond premium based on financial intermediary credit spreads. The solid dots depict the quarterly (annualized) return on assets (ROA) for the U.S. financial corporate sector, calculated using quarterly firm-level Compustat data. The shaded vertical bars denote the recessions as dated by the National Bureau of Economics.

factor in the absence of a "credit crunch," which, in turn, probably contributed to the fact that the downturn remained localized in certain troubled industries, particularly the high-tech sector (Stiroh and Metli 2003).

With regard to the recent financial crisis, the intensifying downturn in the housing market and the emergence of significant strains in term funding markets in the United States and Europe during the summer of 2007 precipitated a sharp increase in the financial bond premium. At that time, banking institutions, in addition to their mounting concerns about actual and potential credit losses, recognized that they might need to take a large volume of assets onto their balance sheets, given their existing commitments to customers and the heightened reluctance of investors to purchase an increasing number of securitized products. The recognition that the ongoing turmoil in financial markets could lead to substantially larger-than-anticipated calls on their funding capacity and investors' concerns about valuation practices for opaque assets were the primary factors behind the steady climb of the financial bond premium during the remainder of 2007 and over the subsequent year. Once these funding pressures receded and conditions in financial markets—following the unprecedented government interventions in the financial system—stabilized, the financial bond premium returned to its pre-crisis level.

The Financial Bond Premium and the Macroeconomy

To examine systematically the macroeconomic consequences of financial distur-bances, we incorporate the financial bond premium into an otherwise standard VAR. The specification includes the following endogenous variables: (1) consumption growth as measured by the log-difference of real personal consumption expendi-tures on nondurable goods and services; (2) investment growth as measured by the log-difference of real private investment (residential and business) in fixed assets; (3) the log-difference of hours worked in the nonfarm business sector; (4) output growth as measured by the log-difference of real GDP; (5) inflation as measured by the log-difference of the GDP price deflator; (6) the growth of the market value of net worth in the nonfinancial (nonfarm) corporate sector; (7) the ten-year (nominal) Treasury yield; (8) the effective (nominal) federal funds rate; and (9) the financial bond premium.[5]

The choice of endogenous variables is motivated in part by the macroeconomic framework considered in the next section—a New Keynesian model augmented with the financial accelerator mechanism formulated by Bernanke, Gertler, and Gilchrist (1999)—which emphasizes credit constraints for nonfinancial borrow-ers and treats financial intermediaries largely as a veil. Although recent work by Mark Gertler and Nobuhiro Kiyotaki (2010), Vasco Cúrdia and Michael Woodford (2010), and Gertler and Peter Karadi (2011) has made important strides in incorpo-rating a financial intermediary sector into a canonical macroeconomic framework, the highly stylized nature of the credit intermediation process in these models poses significant challenges for the quantitative evaluation of financial shocks. Our approach, by contrast, sidesteps these difficult calibration issues by assuming that fluctuations in the estimated financial bond premium provide an adequate description of the disruptions in the financial intermediation process.

The cost of this simplifying assumption is that it ignores the intricacies surround-ing the significant dislocations—and their implications for asset prices, monetary and fiscal policy, financial stability, and the real economy—experienced by many asset markets during the 2007 to 2009 crisis. Also, by including only the net worth of the nonfinancial corporate sector, it abstracts from the massive deleveraging in the household sector that occurred in the wake of the bursting of the housing bubble.[6] With these caveats in mind, we use the multivariate framework specified earlier to trace out the effect of an unexpected increase in the financial bond pre-mium that is contemporaneously uncorrelated with measures of economic activity and inflation, the balance sheet position of the nonfinancial sector, and the level of short- and long-term interest rates. The responses of key macroeconomic aggre-gates to the impact of such a financial shock will then provide a benchmark for the calibration of the macroeconomic model considered in the next section.

Figure 3.4 depicts the responses of the nine endogenous variables to such an unanticipated increase in the financial bond premium. These responses are based on a VAR(2) model that is estimated over the January 1985 to June 2010 period and in which the financial bond premium is ordered last. An unanticipated increase

FIGURE 3.4 / Macroeconomic Implications of a Financial Shock, 1985 to 2010

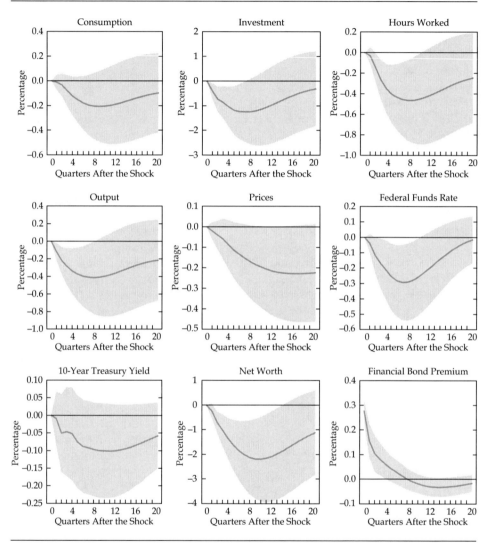

Source: Authors' calculations based on data from the National Income and Product Accounts (BEA 2012), and Federal Reserve Board (2012a, 2012b).

Note: The figure depicts the impulse response functions from a nine-variable VAR(2) model to a one-standard-deviation orthogonalized shock to the excess financial bond premium (see text for details). Shaded bands denote 95 percent confidence intervals based on 1,000 bootstrap replications.

of one standard deviation in the financial bond premium—almost thirty basis points—is associated with a significant slowdown in economic activity. In economic terms, the implications of this financial disruption are substantial: although the decline in consumption is relatively mild, total private fixed investment drops significantly, bottoming out a full percentage point below trend about five quarters after the shock; hours worked also decelerate markedly, and the output of the economy as a whole does not begin to recover until about a year and a half after the initial impact.

The downturn in economic activity is amplified in part by the substantial drop in the net worth of nonfinancial firms. Moreover, the repair of corporate balance sheets is slow and protracted, as evidenced by the fact that net worth remains significantly below its trend four years after the shock. The combination of the economic slack and appreciable disinflation in the wake of the financial shock elicits a significant easing of monetary policy, as evidenced by the decline in the federal funds rate.

A MACROECONOMIC FRAMEWORK

The impulse response functions shown in figure 3.4 are consistent with important linkages between changes in financial conditions and macroeconomic outcomes. Quantifying these links, however, requires structural models of the macroeconomy that can distinguish between movements in credit supply and demand and that can account for the feedback effects between developments in the financial and real sectors of the economy. Recent work by Virginia Queijo von Heideken (2009), Ferre De Graeve (2008), Ian Christensen and Ali Dib (2008), and Lawrence Christiano, Roberto Motto, and Massimo Rostagno (2009) seeks to quantify these mechanisms by estimating medium-scale macroeconomic models that incorporate credit market imperfections through the financial accelerator mechanism described in Carlstrom and Fuerst (1997) and Bernanke et al. (1999).[7]

Although details differ in terms of model specification, all of these papers document an important role for financial factors in business cycle fluctuations. Queijo von Heideken (2009), for example, shows that the ability of a model with a rich array of real and nominal rigidities to fit both the U.S. and the Euro-area data improves significantly if one allows for the presence of a financial accelerator mechanism; Christiano and his colleagues (2009) demonstrate that shocks to the financial sector have played an important role in economic fluctuations over the past two decades, both in the United States and in Europe.

For tractability, the model used in our analysis is kept purposefully simple. As in Bernanke et al. (1999), it allows for a household sector that consumes, saves, and supplies labor; an investment goods sector that produces new capital goods from current output; and a retail sector that faces nominal price rigidities that result in a standard New Keynesian Phillips curve. The model also allows for gradual adjustment of consumption by assuming that households find it costly to change their consumption levels relative to past consumption (habit formation); gradual adjustment of business investment is achieved by assuming that capital goods–producing firms face increasing marginal costs when the investment goods–producing sector expands rapidly (higher-order investment adjustment costs). These adjustment costs imply that asset prices—the value of capital in place—increase during economic expansions. Monetary policy in the model is conducted according to a modified Taylor-like rule that assumes that the monetary authority, given interest-rate smoothing, adjusts nominal short-term interest rates in response to changes in current inflation and output growth.

As in Bernanke et al. (1999), the model also allows for an entrepreneurial sector that faces significant credit market frictions in the process of owning and operating the existing capital stock. These frictions give rise to an external finance premium that creates a wedge between the required return on capital—the rate at which entrepreneurs can borrow to finance capital accumulation—and the risk-free rate of return received by the household sector for its savings. In this environment, an expansion in output causes an increase in the value of assets in place and, as a result, an increase in the entrepreneurial net worth. As entrepreneurs' net worth expands relative to their borrowing, the external finance premium falls, causing a further increase in both asset values and investment demand. These feedback effects, in turn, further amplify the financial accelerator mechanism.

The key parameters of the model are chosen so that the responses of macroeconomic aggregates to a financial disruption roughly match the corresponding responses shown in figure 3.4. Using this procedure, we explore the extent to which observable fluctuations in the financial bond premium can account for the business cycle dynamics of the U.S. economy during the 1985 to 2009 period. We then use this framework to analyze the potential benefits of an alternative monetary policy rule, a rule that allows for nominal interest rates to respond to changes in financial conditions as measured by movements in credit spreads.

This analysis is prompted by the observation that the behavior of key private interest rates during the recent crisis diverged markedly from their usual comovement with the federal funds rate. In response, a number of prominent observers have suggested that credit spreads should be given independent weight in monetary policy decisions. Most notably, John Taylor (2008) has argued that the intercept term of his famous rule should be adjusted downward in proportion to observed movements in the spread of term Libor over rates on comparable-maturity overnight index swaps (OIS).[8] Others have suggested that monetary policy should pay close attention to the balance sheets of financial intermediaries. Christiano and his colleagues (2008), for example, have developed a model in which financial disruptions are an important source of economic fluctuations and a Taylor rule modified to include a response to aggregate credit delivers superior macroeconomic outcomes.

In our framework, disturbances in the financial intermediation sector are the sole source of cyclical fluctuations. To assess the degree to which this type of modification of our baseline policy rule would improve macroeconomic stability, we consider a policy rule in which monetary authorities also respond to movements in observed credit spreads. Specifically, the monetary authority allows the nominal interest rate r_{t+1}^n to respond to inflation (π_t), output growth (y_t), and the credit spread (s_t), according to

$$r_{t+1}^n = r^n + \phi_r r_t^n + \phi_\pi \pi_t + \phi_y y_t + \phi_s s_t \qquad (3.3)$$

where $0 < \phi_r < 1$ is the parameter governing the degree of interest rate smoothing, while $\phi_\pi > 0$, $\phi_y > 0$, and $\phi_s \leq 0$ determine the response of the policy interest rate to inflation, output growth, and changes in financial conditions, respectively, where the latter is summarized by the movements in credit spreads.[9] Note that this adjustment implies that the policy rate be reduced—relative to what our baseline policy rule would prescribe—when credit spreads are higher than normal; conversely, the policy rate should be raised in response to an unusual easing of financial conditions.[10] Of course, in the case where $\phi_s = 0$—the baseline case—the monetary authority does not respond directly to changes in financial conditions.

Baseline Results

Figure 3.5 shows the impulse responses of the selected macroeconomic variables implied by the model in response to a financial shock, assuming the baseline specification of the monetary policy rule ($\phi_s = 0$). We show impulse responses for two hypothetical economies that differ only in the extent to which the credit intermediation process is subject to frictions arising from the agency problem in financial markets. In our framework, the severity of financial frictions is governed by the value of parameter $0 \leq \chi < 1$, with $\chi = 0.05$, implying a relatively modest degree of financial market imperfections, while $\chi = 0.10$ implies a somewhat greater inefficiency in the process of credit intermediation.[11]

According to these results, the model with a relatively high degree of financial market frictions captures remarkably well the shape of the corresponding responses based on the actual data shown in figure 3.4. Consumption, investment, hours, and output all exhibit significant declines in response to an adverse financial shock, with the peak decline in the response of each variable closely matching its empirical counterpart. Although the model delivers the qualitative dynamics for each of the variables that are consistent with those observed in the data, the model does produce a peak response that is somewhat earlier than the peak response observed in figure 3.4.

The decline in the price level implied by the model with a relatively high degree of financial market frictions also roughly matches the deceleration in prices seen in the data. Furthermore, given the estimated baseline policy rule—in which the coefficient on the credit spread $\phi_s = 0$—the model-implied dynamics for inflation and output generate a path for the nominal short-term interest rate that is broadly in line with the estimated response of the federal funds rate to an unanticipated increase in the financial bond premium.

We now consider the ability of the model with a relatively high degree of financial market frictions ($\chi = 0.10$) to explain economic activity over the 1985 to 2009

FIGURE 3.5 / Model-Based Impulse Responses to a Financial Shock

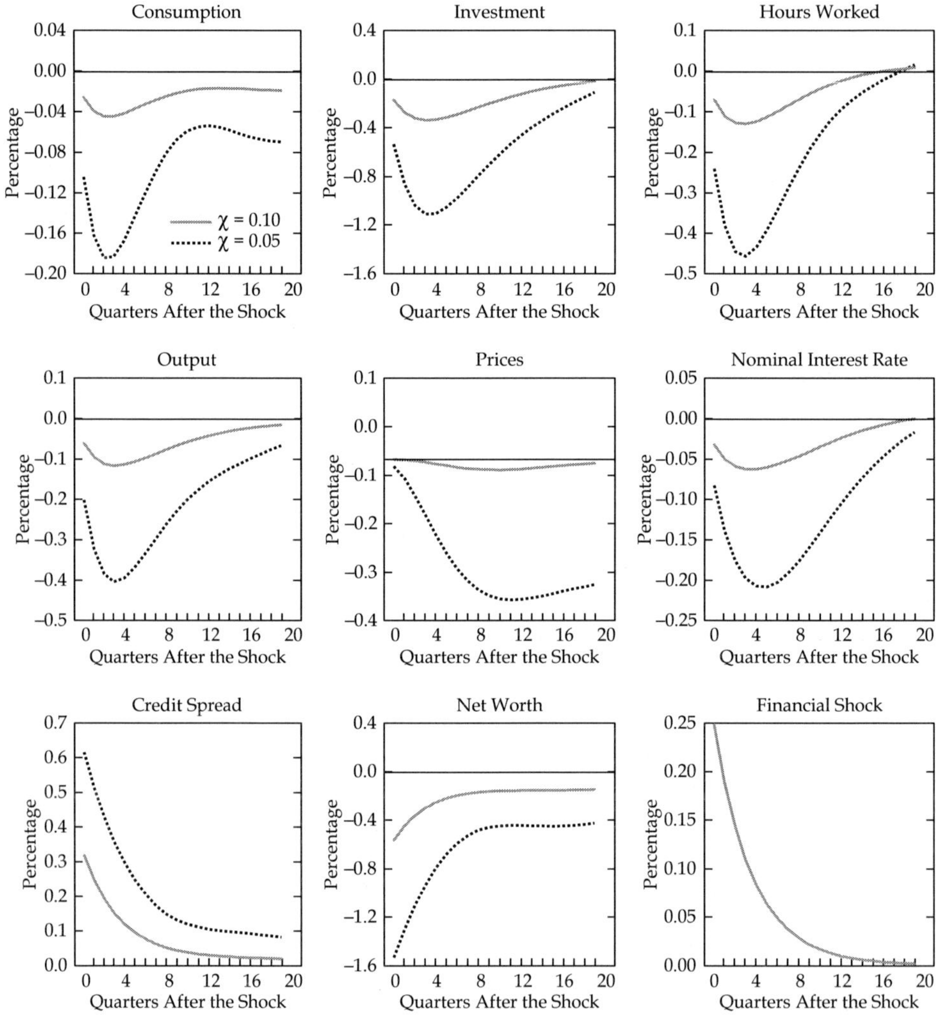

Source: Authors' calculations.

Note: The figure depicts the model-based impulse response functions—for a different degree of financial market frictions—of selected variables to a one-standard-deviation financial shock for the baseline specification of the monetary policy rule, a case in which the monetary authority does not respond to credit spreads—that is, $\varphi_s = 0$ (see text for details). All variables are in deviations from their respective steady-state values.

period. To do so, we first initialize the model to be in steady state as of the end of 1984. We then feed into the model—as disturbances to the efficiency of the credit interme-diation process—the actual innovations to the financial bond premium (based on the AR[1] model) over the January 1985 to December 2009 period. Figure 3.6 shows the evolution of the key macroeconomic variables of the U.S. economy over this period, while figure 3.7 shows the corresponding path for the model-implied variables.

According to the model, the economy experienced contractions in economic activity during all three of the recessions, as dated by the National Bureau of Economic Research, during our sample. In these episodes, a contraction in invest-ment spending drives the business cycle: relative to its trend, business investment fell about five percentage points during the 1990 recession, a bit more than three percentage points during the 2001 downturn, and more than ten percentage points during the most recent crisis. Consumption declined slightly during the 1990 recession, held up well during the dot-com bust, and declined modestly during the 2007 to 2009 recession.

Roughly speaking, model-implied fluctuations in output are also in line with historical experience: a mild contraction in output on the order of two percent-age points during the 1990 recession; a one-percentage-point decline during the bursting of the tech bubble in 2001; and a decline of about four percentage points during the most recent recession. Interestingly, financial shocks imply a strong investment boom in the mid and late 1990s and during the 2003 to 2006 period.

On the whole, financial disruptions appear to account for a substantial frac-tion of fluctuations in real economic activity during these last three recessions. The depth and timing of the contraction in the early 1990s coincides well with the historical experience, as is the case with the 2007 to 2009 downturn. In con-trast, the investment spending implied by the model clearly contracted earlier than that seen in the data during the 1999 to 2001 period, which was the tail end of the dot-com boom. On the other hand, investment also exhibited a substan-tial drag on the economy during the subsequent recovery, implying sluggish employment—a result consistent with the jobless recovery that characterized that time period.

The model also succeeds in capturing observed movements in nominal interest rates, inflation, and credit spreads over this time period. Short-term nominal inter-est rates declined substantially in each recession, and inflation declined during these contractionary phases. Credit spreads exhibited substantially more variation than the underlying financial shock and spike-up during the 1990 and 2007 to 2009 recessions. Credit spreads also widened notably in the late 1990s and early 2000s, but were driven to their all-time lows during the investment booms of the mid-1990s and mid-2000s.

An important aspect of the recent crisis that is omitted from our analysis is the fact that since December 2008 the Federal Open Market Committee (FOMC) has maintained a target range for the federal funds rate of 0 to 0.25 percent—that is, monetary policy has been effectively constrained by the presence of a zero lower bound (ZLB) on nominal interest rates. Although our empirical results are quali-tatively and quantitatively robust to the exclusion of that period from our sample,

FIGURE 3.6   /   U.S. Macroeconomic Performance, 2006 to 2009 (Quarterly)

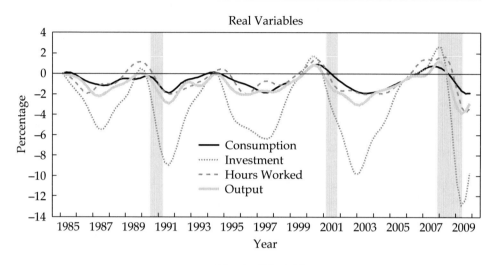

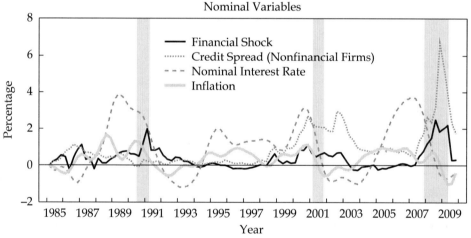

Source: Authors' calculations based on data from National Income and Product Accounts (BEA 2012) and Federal Reserve Board (2012a, 2012b).

Note: The figure depicts the path of actual U.S. macroeconomic and financial variables. Cyclical fluctuations have been eliminated from all real variables, as well as from inflation and the nominal funds rate, using the Corbae and Ouliaris (2006) frequency-domain filter. All variables are set to equal zero in January 1985. The shaded vertical bars denote the recessions as dated by the National Bureau of Economics Research.

FIGURE 3.7 / Model-Based Simulation of a Financial Shock (Baseline Monetary Policy Rule), 2006 to 2009 (Quarterly)

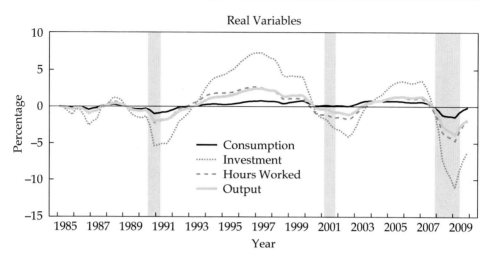

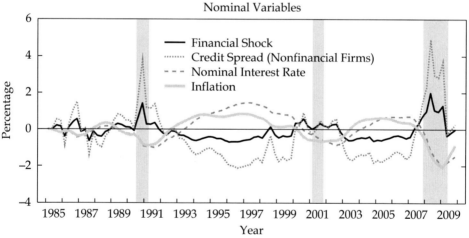

Source: Authors' calculations.

Note: The figure depicts the model-implied path of selected macroeconomic variables in response to the estimated financial shocks for the baseline specification of the monetary policy rule, a case in which the monetary authority does not respond to credit spreads ($\varphi_s = 0$). The degree of financial market frictions $\chi = 0.10$ (see text for details). All variables are in deviations from their respective steady-state values and are set to equal zero in January 1985. The shaded vertical bars denote the recessions as dated by the National Bureau of Economic Research.

the binding ZLB constraint raises important questions for the conduct of monetary policy in any model used to analyze the macroeconomic and financial developments over this period.

As emphasized by Gauti Eggertsson and Michael Woodford (2003) and by Anton Nakov (2008), forward guidance regarding the anticipated future path of short-term nominal interest rates provides a very effective way to stabilize the output gap and inflation within the New Keynesian framework. By announcing that the policy rate will be kept low during the initial phase of economic recovery, such a commitment provides stimulus to the economy by lowering expected future real interest rates, thereby avoiding deflation in the near term, while producing only mildly elevated rates of inflation once the economy has fully recovered.

However, as shown by Levin and his colleagues (2010), when the economy is hit by a large and persistent natural rate shock—the kind experienced during the recent crisis—forward guidance alone delivers relatively poor macroeconomic outcomes. According to their simulations, a combination of forward guidance and other policy measures—such as large-scale asset purchases—is needed to deliver a sufficient macroeconomic stimulus in situations where the economy experiences a "Great Recession"–style shock and the near-term path of the policy rate is constrained by the zero lower bound. While incorporating the ZLB and unconventional monetary policy actions into the analysis lies beyond the scope of our chapter, our next set of simulation results would suggest that an aggressive and timely response of monetary policy to changes in financial conditions—in our context measured by movements in credit spreads—would reduce the likelihood of interest rate policy being subsequently constrained by the zero lower bound.

The Spread-Augmented Monetary Policy Rule

To recap briefly, our baseline simulations imply that shocks to the efficiency of the intermediation process, as measured by innovations to the financial bond premium, can account quite well for the broad movements in hours worked, consumption, investment, and output during the 1985 to 2009 period. In our view, the model dynamics are sufficiently close to the actual economic outcomes to provide a useful guide for alternative policy rules that might be used to stabilize the economy in the wake of disruptions in financial markets.

In this section, we consider one such rule proposed in the literature—namely, the adjustment to the first-difference rule so that monetary policy responds to changes in financial developments as measured by the movements in credit spreads (see, for example, Cúrdia and Woodford 2010). Specifically, we augment the baseline first-difference rule by allowing for a direct response of the policy rate to the measured credit spread. The response coefficient on the spread ϕ_s is set equal to –0.5, so that the nominal rate offsets the increase (or decrease) in financial market stress by declining ten basis points for every increase of twenty basis points in credit spreads. It is important to note that this rule is not derived formally from a welfare-maximization problem.[12] Rather, our aim is to evaluate whether adding a response to credit spreads, as proposed by Taylor (2008) and McCulley and Toloui (2008), can improve the equilibrium responses of the macroeconomy to shocks emanating from the financial sector.

The solid lines in figure 3.8 depict the model-based impulse responses to a financial shock under the spread-augmented monetary policy rule, while the dotted lines denote the corresponding responses under the baseline first-difference rule ($\phi_s = 0$), replicated, for comparison purposes, from figure 3.5. The comparison of responses reveals that including the credit spread in the policy rule provides substantial stabilization of the real side of the economy. Importantly, the price level, in response to a financial shock, increases about one-half of a percentage point, rather than falling 0.3 percentage points, as in the baseline case.

In effect, this stabilization policy achieves a substantial reduction in output volatility and almost no variation in inflation. As a result, the implied movements in both nominal and real rates are also quite modest—on the order of only five basis points. In contrast, under the baseline policy rule, the monetary authority, by not reacting directly to credit market conditions, has to ease significantly more in response to an adverse financial shock, as evidenced by the decline in the short-term rate of about twenty basis points.

The spread-augmented policy rule works through agents' expectations. In response to an adverse financial shock, agents anticipate that the monetary authority will ease policy. These expectations lead to a modest reduction in real interest rates but, at the same time, to a relatively large offsetting increase in asset values and thus to a much smaller decline in net worth than one sees under the baseline monetary policy rule. As a result, the response of the credit spread under the alternative policy rule basically mimics the response of the financial shock, resulting in very little additional amplification through the financial accelerator mechanism.

Although asset prices are forward-looking, they influence the condition of firms' balance sheets—and hence the strength of the financial accelerator—immediately. Consequently, a reduction in expected future real interest rates can be very effective in offsetting an emerging disruption in credit markets. This point is made explicit in figure 3.9, which shows the model-implied path of the key macroeconomic aggregates during the 1985 to 2009 period under the spread-augmented policy rule. Consistent with the results presented in figure 3.8, such a rule leads to a substantial reduction in the variability of output, hours worked, and investment. Furthermore, the model does quite well at stabilizing inflation over this time period.

To be sure, actual disruptions in financial markets, as evidenced by the recent financial crisis, are far more complex than simple shocks to the credit spread modeled in our framework. Nevertheless, these results suggest that a monetary policy regime that is committed, in advance, to fully offsetting shocks to the financial system through active interest rate policy can be quite beneficial in mitigating the deleterious consequences of financial market disruptions.

In the simulations reported earlier, financial shocks are surprise events that result in an immediate increase in credit spreads, a jump that exceeds the size of the underlying financial shock because of the endogenous response of asset prices in the financial accelerator model. This raises the question of whether it would

FIGURE 3.8 / Model-Based Impulse Responses to a Financial Shock (Baseline Versus Spread-Augmented Monetary Policy Rule)

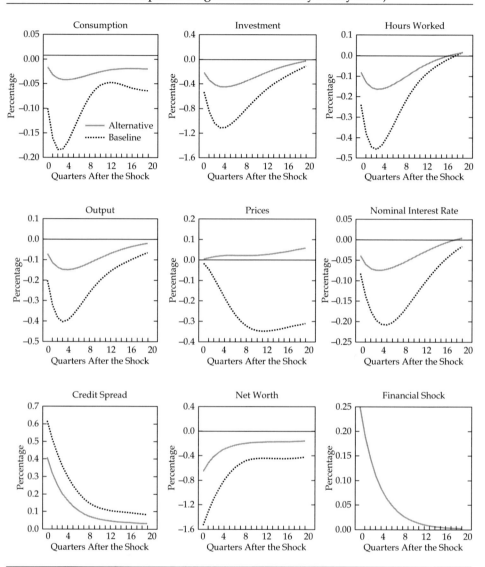

Source: Authors' calculations.

Note: The solid lines depict the model-based impulse response functions of selected variables to a one-standard-deviation financial shock for the alternative specification of the monetary policy rule, a case in which the monetary authority responds to credit spreads, with the reaction coeffcient $\varphi_s = -0.5$; the dotted lines correspond to impulse responses under the baseline specification of the monetary policy rule ($\varphi_s = 0$). The degree of financial market frictions $\chi = 0.1$ (see text for details). All variables are in deviations from their respective steady-state values.

FIGURE 3.9 / Model-Based Simulation of a Financial Shock (Spread-Augmented Monetary Rule), 2006 to 2009 (Quarterly)

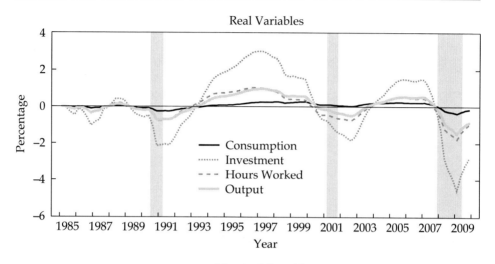

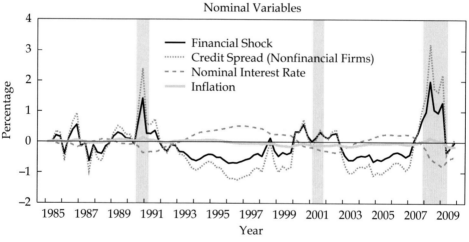

Source: Authors' calculations.

Note: The figure depicts the model-implied path of selected macroeconomic variables in response to the estimated financial shocks for the alternative specification of the monetary policy rule, a case in which the monetary authority responds to credit spreads, with the reaction coefficient $\varphi_s = -0.5$. The degree of financial market frictions $\chi = 0.1$ (see text for details). All variables are in deviations from their respective steady-state values and are set to equal zero in January 1985. The shaded vertical bars denote the recessions as dated by the National Bureau of Economic Research.

be more beneficial if the monetary authority responded directly to the exogenous component of the credit spread—that is, to the underlying disruption in the credit intermediation process. To address this question, we replace the observed credit spread in the first-difference rule with the actual financial shock. For comparison purposes, we maintain the same elasticity of interest-rate response—the coefficient ϕ_s—of −0.5 as before.

The impulse responses produced by this exercise are displayed in figure 3.10. Comparing these results to those in figure 3.8 shows that the same policy response applied to the exogenous component of financial shocks results in an appreciably less stable macroeconomic environment. This is also true in the model simulation, which is shown in figure 3.11. Although economic fluctuations are dampened relative to the baseline model in which the monetary authority is assumed to follow the standard first-difference rule, swings in real economic activity are substantially more pronounced than those implied by the spread-augmented policy rule. This result reflects the fact that by responding to the underlying financial disturbance—as opposed to the observed credit spread—the monetary authority does not take into account the endogenous decline in asset values, which depresses entrepreneurs' current net worth and thereby exacerbates the effect of financial frictions on real economic activity.

As a final exercise, we consider explicitly the role that expectations play in how the economy responds to the spread-augmented monetary policy rule. We do so by considering the benefits of such a policy in an environment where there is "news" regarding a probable deterioration in financial conditions. Agents in the economy—firms, households, and the monetary authority—interpret this news as a signal of a gradual deterioration in financial conditions that will occur sometime in the future. In this context, we again consider the macroeconomic implications of a spread-augmented policy rule with the response coefficient $\phi_s = -0.5$. Figure 3.12 depicts the results of this exercise, with the trajectory of the financial "news shock" shown in the lower right panel. For comparison, the dotted lines depict impulse responses of the key macroeconomic variables to such news in the baseline case, in which the monetary authority does not commit itself to responding directly to movements in credit spreads.

According to these results, the deterioration in financial conditions is gradual, with the financial shock building steadily and peaking at about fifteen basis points a year after the initial news. Under the baseline policy rule, this news causes a significant reduction in output, investment, consumption, and hours worked, with the responses of these variables matching closely—in terms of both their timing and magnitude—the responses in the case when the economy is hit by an unanticipated financial shock. Again, the main driving force of these macroeconomic dynamics is the effect of bad news about future financial conditions on asset prices, which works through expectations. Upon release of the news, asset prices fall immediately, causing an immediate and significant decline in net worth. As net worth falls, borrower balance sheets become impaired and economic activity slows. In contrast to the previous exercises that did not involve such news, the gradual deterioration in financial conditions engenders a slow

FIGURE 3.10   /   Model-Based Impulse Responses to a Financial Shock (Baseline Versus Shock-Augmented Monetary Policy Rule)

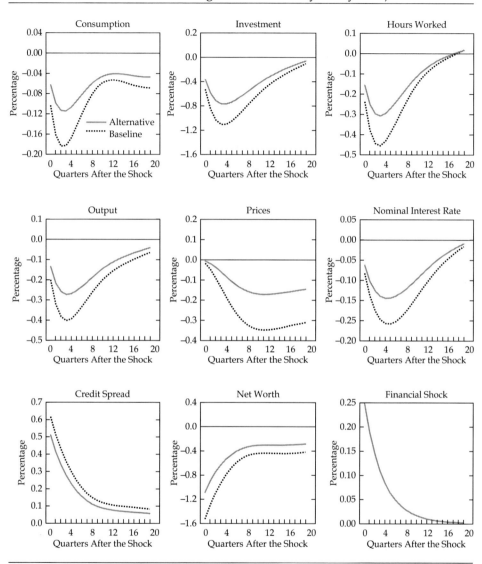

Source: Authors' calculations.

Note: The solid lines depict the model-based impulse response functions of selected variables to a one-standard-deviation financial shock for the alternative specification of the monetary policy rule, a case in which the monetary authority responds to the financial bond premium, with the reaction coeffcient $\varphi_s = -0.5$; the dotted lines correspond to impulse responses under the baseline specification of the monetary policy rule ($\varphi_s = 0$). The degree of financial market frictions $\chi = 0.1$ (see text for details). All variables are in deviations from their respective steady-state values.

FIGURE 3.11 / Model-Based Simulation of a Financial Shock (Shock-Augmented Monetary Policy Rule), 1985 to 2009 (Quarterly)

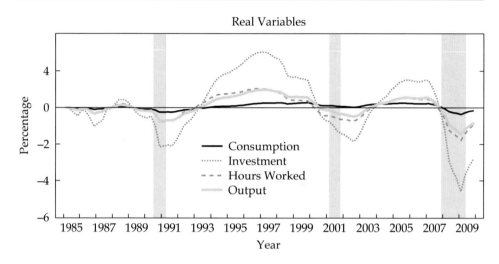

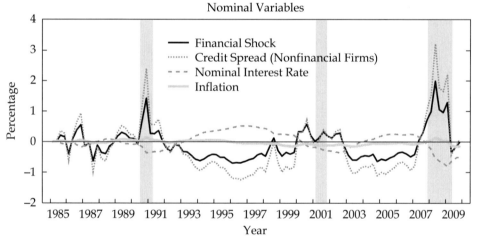

Source: Authors' calculations.

Note: The figure depicts the model-implied path of selected macroeconomic variables in response to the estimated financial shocks for the alternative specification of the monetary policy rule, a case in which the monetary authority responds to the financial bond premium, with the reaction coefficient $\varphi_s = -0.5$. The degree of financial market frictions $\chi = 0.1$ (see text for details). All variables are in deviations from their respective steady-state values and are set to equal zero in January 1985. The shaded vertical bars denote the recessions, as dated by the National Bureau of Economic Research.

FIGURE 3.12 / Model-Based Impulse Responses to Adverse Financial News
(Baseline Versus Spread-Augmented Monetary Policy Rule)

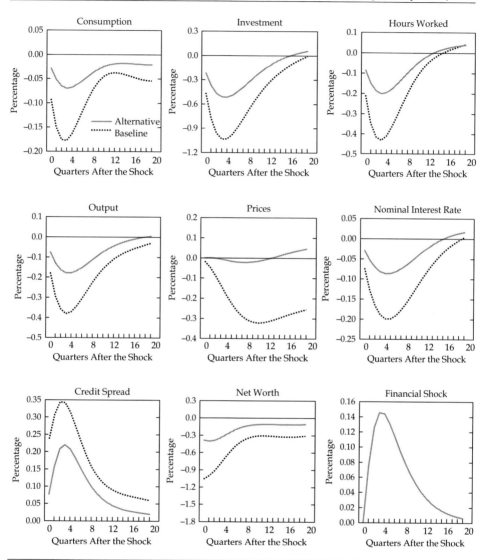

Source: Authors' calculations.

Note: The figure depicts the model-based impulse response functions of selected variables to adverse financial news. The solid lines correspond to the alternative specification of the monetary policy rule, a case in which the monetary authority responds to credit spreads, with the reaction coeffcient $\varphi_s = -0.5$; the dotted lines correspond to the baseline specification of the monetary policy rule ($\varphi_s = 0$). The degree of financial market frictions $\chi = 0.1$ (see text for details). All variables are in deviations from their respective steady-state values.

and progressive widening of credit spreads, which indicates that credit spreads by themselves do not provide an immediate signal regarding the severity of the unfolding news event.

Nonetheless, as can be seen by the solid lines in figure 3.12, a policy that commits the monetary authority in advance to responding to changes in financial conditions has significant stabilization benefits—the decline in output is roughly one-third of the decline that occurs under the baseline policy rule. Note that the fall in asset prices is also reduced by about one-third, so that there is very little immediate effect on credit spreads. Although the gradual deterioration in financial conditions does ultimately cause credit spreads to widen appreciably, the widening is significantly less pronounced than under the baseline policy rule.

Perhaps the most striking result is that by committing to adjusting the short-term nominal interest rates in response to a deterioration in financial conditions, the monetary authority needs to lower the policy rate only about ten basis points, compared with the easing of twenty basis points implied by the baseline first-difference rule. In other experiments (not shown), when we allow the monetary authority to respond even more aggressively to movements in credit spreads, we obtain virtually no change in the nominal short-term rate in response to adverse news about future financial conditions. In effect, by committing to an aggressive stabilization policy, the monetary authority can achieve its goals without resorting to large adjustments in the policy rate. The anticipation by households and firms that the monetary authority will respond aggressively to adverse financial developments leads to an understanding that the recession will not be as severe, and as a result asset prices decline only modestly. In turn, this development improves the overall economic conditions, leading to a mutually reinforcing beneficial feedback loop.

CONCLUSION

This chapter has examined the extent to which the canonical New Keynesian macroeconomic model with financial frictions is able to account for U.S. macroeconomic dynamics during the 1985 to 2009 period. We showed that by carefully constructing a sequence of financial shocks using financial intermediary credit spreads, a reasonably calibrated version of the framework of Christiano and his colleagues (2005) and Smets and Wouters (2007), augmented with the financial accelerator of Bernanke and his colleagues (1999), can account for the broad movements in consumption, investment, hours worked, and output observed during this period. The model also does well at matching the observed countercyclical movements in inflation and short-term nominal interest rates, as well as the strong procyclicality of credit spreads on bonds issued by nonfinancial firms.

Although the model is relatively simple compared with the recent work in this area, our findings nonetheless provide considerable insight into the importance of financial factors in business cycle fluctuations. In particular, our simulations suggest that by allowing the nominal interest rate to respond to credit spreads—a primary measure of financial stress in our framework—monetary policy can effectively ameliorate the negative consequences of financial market shocks on real economic activity, while experiencing very little offsetting inflationary pressures.

We thank Ben Rump and Michael Levere for outstanding research assistance. The views expressed in this chapter are solely the responsibility of the authors and should not be interpreted as reflecting the views of the board of governors of the Federal Reserve System or of anyone else associated with the Federal Reserve System.

NOTES

1. Other formulations of financial market frictions in macroeconomic models include, for example, Fuerst (1995), Carlstrom and Fuerst (1997), Kiyotaki and Moore (1997), and Cooley, Marimon, and Quadrini (2004).

2. Broker-dealers are financial institutions that buy and sell securities for a fee, hold an inventory of securities for resale, and differ from other types of institutional investors in their active procyclical management of leverage. As documented by Adrian and Shin (2010), expansions in broker-dealer assets are associated with increases in leverage as broker-dealers take advantage of greater balance sheet capacity; conversely, contractions in their assets are associated with deleveraging of their balance sheets.

3. The definition of the financial sector encompasses publicly traded financial firms in the following three-digit North American industrial classification system (NAICS) codes: 522 (credit intermediation and related activities); 523 (securities, commodity contracts, and other financial investments and related activities); 524 (insurance carriers and related activities); and 525 (funds, trusts, and other financial vehicles). Government-sponsored entities, such as Fannie Mae and Freddie Mac, are excluded from the sample.

4. These two data sources are used to construct the benchmark corporate bond indexes used by market participants. Specifically, they contain secondary market prices for a vast majority of dollar-denominated bonds publicly issued in the U.S. corporate cash market. The ML database is a proprietary data source of daily bond prices that starts in 1997. By contrast, the LW database of month-end bond prices has a somewhat broader coverage and is available from 1973 through mid-1998 (for details, see Warga 1991).

5. Consumption and investment series are constructed from the underlying National Income and Product Accounts (NIPA) data using the chain-aggregation methods outlined in Whelan (2002). The market value of net worth is taken from the U.S. Flow of Funds Accounts.

6. In a small nod to the importance of the housing market during the recent downturn, our measure of aggregate investment includes both residential and business fixed investment.

7. In an alternative approach, Andrew Levin, Fabio Natalucci, and Egon Zakrajšek (2004) employ firm-level data on credit spreads, expected default frequencies (EDFs), and leverage to estimate directly the structural parameters of the debt-contracting problem underlying the financial accelerator model of Bernanke et al. (1999).

8. The Libor-OIS spread is a conventional measure of counterparty credit risk in interbank funding markets (see, for example, Taylor and Williams 2009).

9. By specifying the rule in which the short-term interest rate responds to output *growth*—as opposed to the output *gap*—the monetary authority is assumed to follow a robust first-difference rule of the type proposed by Athanasios Orphanides (2003). As shown by Orphanides and John Williams (2006), such first-difference rules are highly success-ful in stabilizing economic activity in the presence of imperfect information regard-ing the structure of the economy; moreover, according to the simulations reported by Orphanides and Williams, such a robust monetary policy rule yields outcomes for the federal funds rate that are very close to those seen in the actual data, especially for the period since the mid-1980s.

10. The view that the central bank should raise short-term interest rates to "prick" asset bubbles is widely rejected by today's profession because monetary policy is too blunt of a tool to allow the type of surgical intervention required to deflate a bubble without plunging the economy into a recession. Nevertheless, modifications of simple policy rules to include measures of economy-wide financial conditions have been proposed by the advocates of the "leaning against the wind" principle, which argues that the central banks should cautiously raise interest rates beyond the level necessary to maintain price stability over the short to medium run when a potentially detrimental asset price boom has been identified (but see Borio and Lowe 2002, 2006). Importantly, the proponents of this view stress the nonlinear nature of the policy response, as posi-tive and negative asset-price shocks have asymmetric macroeconomic effects, as well as the strong informational requirements concerning the properties of the emerging bubble.

11. A model with frictionless financial markets corresponds to $\chi = 0$ (for a detailed discussion, see Gilchrist and Zakrajšek 2011b).

12. In the case in which credit spreads are endogenous, both financial and nonfinancial shocks will cause credit spreads to fluctuate, and the magnitude of spread adjust-ment to the policy rate will have important implications for the economy's response to various types of disturbances (for detailed analysis and discussion, see Cúrdia and Woodford 2010).

REFERENCES

Acharya, Viral V., and S. "Vish" Viswanathan. 2010. "Leverage, Moral Hazard, and Liquidity." *Journal of Finance* 66(1): 99–138.

Adrian, Tobias, Emanuel Moench, and Hyun Song Shin. 2010a. "Financial Intermediation, Asset Prices, and Macroeconomic Dynamics." Staff Report 422. New York: Federal Reserve Bank of New York.

———. 2010b. "Macro Risk Premium and Intermediary Balance Sheet Quantities." *International Monetary Fund Economic Review* 58(1): 179–207.

Adrian, Tobias, and Hyun Song Shin. 2010. "Liquidity and Leverage." *Journal of Financial Intermediation* 19(3): 418–37.

Aguiar, Mark. 2005. "Investment, Devaluation, and Foreign Currency Exposure: A Case of Mexico." *Journal of Development Economics* 78(1): 95–113.

Allen, Franklin, and Douglas Gale. 1994. "Limited Market Participation and Volatility of Asset Prices." *American Economic Review* 84(4): 933–55.

———. 1998. "Optimal Financial Crises." *Journal of Finance* 53(4): 1245–84.

Ashcraft, Adam B. 2005. "Are Banks Really Special? New Evidence from the FDIC-Induced Failure of Healthy Banks." *American Economic Review* 95(5): 1712–30.

Bassett, William F., Mary Beth Chosak, John C. Driscoll, and Egon Zakrajšek. 2012. "Changes in Bank Lending Standards and the Macroeconomy." Finance and Economics Discussion Series Paper No. 2012-24. Washington: Federal Reserve Board.

Bernanke, Ben S., and Alan S. Blinder. 1988. "Credit, Money, and Aggregate Demand." *American Economic Review* 78(2): 435–39.

Bernanke, Ben S., Mark Gertler, and Simon Gilchrist. 1999. "The Financial Accelerator in a Quantitative Business Cycle Framework." In *The Handbook of Macroeconomics*, edited by John B. Taylor and Michael Woodford. Amsterdam: Elsevier Science B.V.

Bernanke, Ben S., and Cara S. Lown. 1991. "The Credit Crunch." *Brookings Papers on Economic Activity* 2(2): 205–39.

Bureau of Economic Analysis. 2012. National Income and Product Accounts. Available at: http://www.bea.gov/national/index.htm (accessed November 1, 2011).

Borio, Claudio E., and Philip W. Lowe. 2002. "Asset Prices, Financial and Monetary Stability: Exploring the Nexus." Working Paper 114. Basel: Bank for International Settlements.

———. 2006. "Monetary and Financial Stability: Here to Stay?" *Journal of Banking and Finance* 30(12): 3407–14.

Brunnermeier, Markus K. 2009. "Deciphering the Liquidity and Credit Crunch of 2007–2008." *Journal of Economic Perspectives* 23(1): 77–100.

Brunnermeier, Markus K., and Lasse Heje Pedersen. 2009. "Market Liquidity and Funding Liquidity." *Review of Financial Studies* 22(6): 265–92.

Buiter, Willem H. 2010. "Housing Wealth Isn't Wealth." *Economics: The Open-Access, Open-Assessment E-Journal* 4(2010-22). Available at: http://dx.doi.org/10.5018/economics-ejournal.ja.2010-22 (accessed July 6, 2012).

Campbell, John Y., and Joao F. Cocco. 2008. "How Do House Prices Affect Consumption? Evidence from Micro Data." *Journal of Monetary Economics* 54(3): 591–621.

Carlstrom, Charles T., and Timothy S. Fuerst. 1997. "Agency Costs, Net Worth, and Business Cycle Fluctuations: A Computable General Equilibrium Analysis." *American Economic Review* 87(5): 893–910.

Carroll, Christopher D., Misuzu Otsuka, and Jirka Slacalek. 2011. "How Large Are Housing and Financial Wealth Effects? A New Approach." *Journal of Money, Credit, and Banking* 43(1): 55–79.

Case, Karl E., John M. Quigley, and Robert J. Shiller. 2005. "Comparing Wealth Effects: The Stock Market Versus the Housing Market." *B.E. Journal of Macroeconomics* 5(article 1).

Cetorelli, Nicola, and Linda S. Goldberg. Forthcoming. "Banking Globalization and Monetary Transmission." *Journal of Finance*.

Christensen, Ian, and Ali Dib. 2008. "The Financial Accelerator in an Estimated New Keynesian Model." *Review of Economic Dynamics* 11(1): 155–78.

Christiano, Lawrence J., Martin Eichenbaum, and Charles L. Evans. 2005. "Nominal Rigidities and the Dynamic Effects of a Shock to Monetary Policy." *Journal of Political Economy* 113(1): 1–45.

Christiano, Lawrence J., Cosmin Ilut, Roberto Motto, and Massimo Rostagno. 2008. "Monetary Policy and Stock Market Boom-Bust Cycles." Working Paper 955. Frankfurt am Main: European Central Bank (October).

Christiano, Lawrence J., Roberto Motto, and Massimo Rostagno. 2009. "Financial Factors in Economic Fluctuations." Working paper. Evanston, Ill.: Northwestern University, Department of Economics.

Cooley, Thomas F., Ramon Marimon, and Vincenzo Quadrini. 2004. "Aggregate Consequences of Limited Contract Enforceability." *Journal of Political Economy* 112(4): 817–47.

Corbae, Dean, and Sam Ouliaris. 2006. "Extracting Cycles from Nonstationary Data." In *Econometric Theory and Practice: Frontiers of Analysis and Applied Research*, edited by Dean Corbae, Steven N. Durlauf, and Bruce E. Hansen. Cambridge: Cambridge University Press.

Cummins, Jason G., Kevin A. Hassett, and Stephen D. Oliner. 2006. "Investment Behavior, Observable Expectations, and Internal Funds." *American Economic Review* 96(3): 796–810.

Cúrdia, Vasco, and Michael Woodford. 2010. "Credit Spreads and Monetary Policy." *Journal of Money, Credit, and Banking* 42(s1): 3–35.

De Graeve, Ferre. 2008. "The External Finance Premium and the Macroeconomy: U.S. Post–World War II Evidence." *Journal of Economic Dynamics and Control* 32(11): 3415–40.

Eggertsson, Gauti B., and Michael Woodford. 2003. "The Zero Bound on Interest Rates and Optimal Monetary Policy." *Brookings Papers on Economic Activity* 34(1): 139–211.

Faust, Jon, Simon Gilchrist, Jonathan H. Wright, and Egon Zakrajšek. 2011. "Credit Spreads as Predictors of Real-Time Economic Activity: A Bayesian Model-Averaging Approach." Working Paper 16725. Cambridge, Mass.: National Bureau of Economic Research.

Fazzari, Steven M., R. Glenn Hubbard, and Bruce C. Petersen. 1988. "Financing Constraints and Corporate Investment." *Brookings Papers on Economic Activity* 1(1): 141–95.

Federal Reserve Board. 2012a. *Selected Interest Rates–H.15 Statistical Release.* Available at: http://www.federalreserve.gov/releases/h15/ (accessed November 1, 2011).

———. 2012b. *Flow of Funds Accounts of the United States–Z1. Statistical Release.* Available at: http://www.federalreserve.gov/releases/z1/ (accessed November 1, 2011).

Fuerst, Timothy S. 1995. "Money and Financial Interactions in the Business Cycle." *Journal of Money, Credit, and Banking* 27(4): 1321–38.

Gârleanu, Nicolae, and Lasse Heje Pedersen. 2009. "Margin-Based Asset Pricing and Deviations from the Law of One Price." Working paper. New York: New York University, Stern School of Business (September).

Gertler, Mark, and Peter Karadi. 2011. "A Model of Unconventional Monetary Policy." *Journal of Monetary Economics* 58(1): 17–34.

Gertler, Mark, and Nobuhiro Kiyotaki. 2010. "Financial Intermediation and Credit Policy in Business Cycle Analysis." In *Handbook of Macroeconomics,* vol. 3, edited by Benjamin M. Friedman and Michael Woodford. Amsterdam: North-Holland/Elsevier.

Gertler, Mark, and Cara S. Lown. 1999. "The Information in the High-Yield Bond Spread for the Business Cycle: Evidence and Some Implications." *Oxford Review of Economic Policy* 15(3): 132–50.

Gilchrist, Simon, and Charles P. Himmelberg. 1995. "The Role of Cash Flow in Reduced-Form Investment Equations." *Journal of Monetary Economics* 36(3): 541–72.

Gilchrist, Simon, and Jae W. Sim. 2007. "Investment During the Korean Financial Crisis: A Structural Econometric Analysis." Working Paper 13315. Cambridge, Mass.: National Bureau of Economic Research.

Gilchrist, Simon, Vladimir Yankov, and Egon Zakrajšek. 2009. "Credit Market Shocks and Economic Fluctuations: Evidence from Corporate Bond and Stock Markets." *Journal of Monetary Economics* 56(4): 471–93.

Gilchrist, Simon, and Egon Zakrajšek. 2007. "Investment and the Cost of Capital: New Evidence from the Corporate Bond Market." Working Paper 13174. Cambridge, Mass.: National Bureau of Economic Research.

———. 2011a. "Bank Lending and Credit Supply Shocks." Working paper. Boston: Boston University, Department of Economics.

———. 2011b. "Monetary Policy and Credit Supply Shocks." *International Monetary Fund Economic Review* 59(2): 194–232.

———. 2012. "Credit Spreads and Business Cycle Fluctuations." *American Economic Review* 102(4): 1692–1720.

Gorton, Gary. 2009. "Information, Liquidity, and the (Ongoing) Panic of 2007." *American Economic Review* 99(2): 567–72.

He, Zhiguo, and Arvind Krishnamurthy. 2009. "A Model of Capital and Crisis." Working paper. Evanston, Ill.: Northwestern University, Kellogg School of Management.

———. 2010. "Intermediary Asset Pricing." Working paper. Evanston, Ill.: Northwestern University, Kellogg School of Management.

Ivashina, Victoria, and David Scharfstein. 2010. "Bank Lending During the Financial Crisis of 2008." *Journal of Financial Economics* 97(3): 319–38.

Kashyap, Anil K., and Jeremy C. Stein. 1994. "Monetary Policy and Bank Lending." In *Monetary Policy,* edited by N. Gregory Mankiw. Chicago: University of Chicago Press.

———. 2000. "What Do a Million Observations on Banks Say About the Transmission of Monetary Policy?" *American Economic Review* 90(3): 407–28.

King, Thomas B., Andrew T. Levin, and Roberto Perli. 2007. "Financial Market Perceptions of Recession Risk." Finance and Economics Discussion Series Paper 2007-57. Washington, D.C.: Federal Reserve Board.

Kiyotaki, Nobuhiro, and John H. Moore. 1997. "Credit Cycles." *Journal of Political Economy* 105(2): 211–48.

Levin, Andrew T., David López-Salido, Edward M. Nelson, and Tack Yun. 2010. "Limitations on the Effectiveness of Forward Guidance at the Zero Lower Bound." *International Journal of Central Banking* 6(1): 143–89.

Levin, Andrew T., Fabio M. Natalucci, and Egon Zakrajšek. 2004. "The Magnitude and Cyclical Behavior of Financial Market Frictions." Finance and Economics Discussion Series Paper 2004-70. New York: Federal Reserve Board.

McCulley, Paul A., and Ramin Toloui. 2008. "Chasing the Neutral Rate Down: Financial Conditions, Monetary Policy, and the Taylor Rule." *Global Central Bank Focus* (February 20).

Merrill Lynch. 2012. Corporate Master and High-Yield Databases. Proprietary data. (accessed November 1, 2011).

Merton, Robert C. 1974. "On the Pricing of Corporate Debt: The Risk Structure of Interest Rates." *Journal of Finance* 29(2): 449–70.

Meyer, Laurence H., and Brian P. Sack. 2008. "Updated Monetary Policy Rules: Why Don't They Explain Recent Monetary Policy." *Monetary Policy Insights,* Macroeconomic Advisors (March 7).

Mueller, Philippe. 2009. "Credit Spreads and Real Activity." Working paper. London: London School of Economics.

Nakov, Anton. 2008. "Optimal and Simple Monetary Policy Rules with Zero Floor on the Nominal Interest Rates." *International Journal of Central Banking* 4(2): 73–128.

Orphanides, Athanasios. 2003. "Historical Monetary Policy Analysis and the Taylor Rule." *Journal of Monetary Economics* 50(5): 983–1022.

Orphanides, Athanasios, and John C. Williams. 2006. "Monetary Policy with Imperfect Knowledge." *Journal of the European Economic Association* 4(4): 366–75.

Peek, Joe, and Eric S. Rosengren. 1995a. "Bank Regulation and the Credit Crunch." *Journal of Banking and Finance* 19(3–4): 679–92.

———. 1995b. "The Capital Crunch: Neither a Borrower nor a Lender Be." *Journal of Money, Credit, and Banking* 27(3): 625–38.

———. 2000. "Collateral Damage: Effects of the Japanese Bank Crisis on Real Activity in the United States." *American Economic Review* 90(1): 30–45.

Queijo von Heideken, Virginia. 2009. "How Important Are Financial Frictions in the U.S. and the Euro Area?" *Scandinavian Journal of Economics* 111(3): 567–86.

Rebelo, Sergio, Janice C. Eberly, and Nicolas Vincent. 2008. "Investment and Value: A Neo-classical Benchmark." Working paper. Evanston, Ill.: Northwestern University, Kellogg School of Management.

Smets, Frank, and Rafael Wouters. 2007. "Shocks and Frictions in U.S. Business Cycle: A Bayesian DSGE Approach." *American Economic Review* 97(3): 586–606.

Standard & Poor's. 2011. Compustat North American Database. Proprietary database (accessed November 1, 2011).

Stiroh, Kevin J., and Christopher Metli. 2003. "Now and Then: The Evolution of Loan Quality for U.S. Banks." *Current Issues in Economics and Finance* (Federal Reserve Bank of New York) 9(4): 1–7.

Taylor, John B. 2008. "Monetary Policy and the State of the Economy." Testimony before the House Committee on Financial Services (February 26).

Taylor, John B., and J. C. Williams. 2009. "A Black Swan in the Money Market." *American Economic Journal: Macroeconomics* 1(1): 58–83.

Van den Heuvel, Skander J. 2007. "The Bank Capital Channel of Monetary Policy." Working paper. Philadelphia: University of Pennsylvania, Wharton School.

———. Forthcoming. "Banking Conditions and the Effects of Monetary Policy: Evidence from U.S. States." B.E. Journal of Macroeconomics: Advances.

Warga, Arthur D. 1991. "A Fixed Income Database." Working paper. Houston: University of Houston.

Whelan, Karl. 2002. "A Guide to the Use of Chain-Aggregated NIPA Data." *Review of Income and Wealth* 48(2): 217–33.

Part II

Rethinking Market Efficiency

Chapter 4

The Efficient-Market Hypothesis and the Financial Crisis

Burton G. Malkiel

The worldwide financial crisis of 2008 to 2009 left in its wake severely damaged economies in the United States and Europe. The crisis also shook the foundations of modern-day financial theory, which rests on the proposition that our financial markets are basically efficient. Critics have even suggested that the efficient-market hypothesis (EMH) was in large part responsible for the crisis.

This chapter argues that the critics of EMH are using a far too restrictive interpretation of what EMH means. EMH does not imply that asset prices are always "correct." Prices are always wrong, but no one knows for sure if they are too high or too low. EMH does not imply that bubbles in asset prices are impossible, nor does it deny that environmental and behavioral factors cannot have profound influences on required rates of return and risk premiums. At its core, EMH implies that arbitrage opportunities for riskless gains do not exist in an efficiently functioning market and that, if they do appear from time to time, they do not persist. The evidence is clear that this version of EMH is strongly supported by the data. EMH can comfortably coexist with behavior finance, and the insights of Hyman Minsky are particularly relevant in eliminating the recent financial crisis.

Bubbles, when they do exist, are particularly dangerous when they are financed with debt. The housing bubble and the derivative securities associated with it left both the consumer and financial sectors dangerously leveraged. Policymakers are unlikely to be able to identify bubbles in advance, but they must be better focused on asset-price increases that are financed with debt.

The worldwide financial crisis of 2008 to 2009 left in its wake severely damaged economies in the United States and Europe. Unemployment rates soared up to and in some cases above the double-digit level, and economies in Europe and the United States were still operating in 2012 well below economic capacity. Moreover, the high indebtedness of consumers, financial institutions, and governments made the severe recession unusually persistent and limited the fiscal policy responses of governments throughout the world.

The crisis also shook the very foundations of modern-day financial theory, which rests on the hypothesis that our financial markets are basically efficient. Financial writers and economists alike were ready to write obituaries for the efficient-market hypothesis, or EMH, as it is widely known. The financial writer Justin Fox published a best-selling book in 2009 entitled *The Myth of the Rational Market*. The economist Robert Shiller (1984, 459) described EMH as "one of the most remarkable errors in the history of economic thought." Some professional investment managers went even further. Jeremy Grantham opined that EMH was "more or less directly responsible" for the financial crisis.[1] Paul Krugman (2009) agreed, writing that "the belief in efficient financial markets blinded many if not most economists to the emergence of the biggest financial bubble in history. And efficient-market theory also played a role in inflating that bubble in the first place."

In this essay, I describe what the efficient-market hypothesis implies for the functioning of our financial markets. I suggest that a number of common misconceptions about EMH have led some analysts to reject the hypothesis prematurely. I then examine the abundant evidence that leads me to believe that our financial markets are remarkably efficient and that reports of the death of EMH are greatly exaggerated. Finally, I indicate what I believe are the important lessons that policymakers should learn from the financial crisis.

WHAT THE EFFICIENT-MARKET HYPOTHESIS MEANS AND WHAT IT DOES NOT MEAN

Two fundamental tenets make up the efficient-market hypothesis. EMH first asserts that public information is reflected in asset prices without delay. Information that should beneficially (adversely) affect the future price of any financial instrument is reflected in the asset's price today. If a pharmaceutical company now selling at $20 per share receives approval for a new drug that will give the company a value of $40 tomorrow, the price will move to $40 right away, not slowly over time. Because any purchase of the stock at a price below $40 will yield an immediate profit, we can expect market participants to bid the price up to $40 without delay.

It is, of course, possible that the full effect of the new information is not immediately obvious to market participants. It is also likely that the estimated sales and profits cannot be predicted with any precision and that the value of the discovery is amenable to a wide variety of estimates. Some market participants may vastly underestimate the significance of the newly approved drug, but others may greatly overestimate its value. In some cases, therefore, the market may underreact to a favorable piece of news. But in other cases, the market may overreact, and it is far from clear that systematic underreaction or overreaction to news presents an arbitrage opportunity promising traders easy, risk-adjusted, extraordinary gains. It is this aspect of EMH that implies its second, and more fundamental, tenet: in an efficient market, no arbitrage opportunities exist.

This lack of opportunities for extraordinary profits is often explained by a joke popular with professors of finance. A professor who espouses EMH is walking along the street with a graduate student. The student spots a $100 bill lying on the ground and stoops to pick it up. "Don't bother to try to pick it up," says the professor. "If it was really a $100 bill, it wouldn't be there." Perhaps a less extreme telling of the story would have the professor advising the student to pick the bill up right away because it will not be lying around very long. In an efficient market, competition ensures that opportunities for extraordinary risk-adjusted gain do not persist.

EMH does not imply that prices are always "correct" or that all market participants are always rational. There is abundant evidence that many (perhaps even most) market participants are far from rational and suffer from systematic biases in their processing of information and their trading proclivities. But even if price-setting were always determined by rational, profit-maximizing investors, prices could never be "correct." Suppose that stock prices are rationally determined as the discounted present value of all future cash flows. Future cash flows can only be estimated and are never known with certainty. There will always be errors in the forecasts of future sales and earnings. Moreover, equity risk premiums are unlikely to be stable over time. Prices are therefore likely to be "wrong" all the time. What EMH implies is that we never can be sure whether they are too high or too low at any given time. Some portfolio managers may correctly determine when some prices are too high and others too low. But other times such judgments are in error. And in any event, the profits that are attributable to correct judgments do not represent unexploited arbitrage possibilities.

Complex financial investments are particularly susceptible to mispricing, especially when the loans that underlie the derivative are misrepresented. A full discussion of the causes of the financial crisis is beyond the scope of this essay, but there is no doubt that the mispricing of mortgage-backed securities played an important role in widening the crisis. Although the mispricing of the real estate securing the mortgages may correctly be described as a classic bubble, there was far from a lack of rationality throughout the market. Perverse incentives influenced both mortgage originators and investment bankers. And the financial institutions that held excessive amounts of the toxic instruments in highly leveraged portfolios were encouraged to do so by asymmetric compensation policies and by a breakdown of regulation that led to a failure to constrain excessive debt and inadequate liquidity. In any event, while some hedge funds profited from selling some of these instruments short, there were certainly no arbitrage opportunities that were obvious ex ante.

EMH AND THE ADJUSTMENT OF MARKET PRICES TO DIFFERENT TYPES OF NEW INFORMATION

Since Eugene Fama's (1970) influential survey article, it has been customary to distinguish between three versions of EMH depending on the type of information that is believed to be reflected in the current prices of financial assets (see also Fama 1991). In the "narrow" or "weak" form of the hypothesis, it is asserted that any information that might be contained in historical price series or trading volume is already reflected in current prices. Since past trading data are widely available, any historical patterns that might have reliably predicted future price movements will already have been exploited. If, for example, there has been a reliable "Santa Claus Rally" (suggesting that stock prices will rise between Christmas and New Year's Day), investors will act to anticipate the signal, and when they do, the historical pattern will self-destruct. According to this version of EMH, "technical analysis"—the interpretation of historical price charts—will be nugatory.

Broader forms of the hypothesis have expanded on the types of information that are reflected in current prices. According to the "semi-strong" form of the hypothesis, any "fundamental" information about individual companies or about the stock market as a whole will be reflected in stock prices without delay. Thus, investors cannot profit from acting on some favorable piece of news concerning a company's sales, earnings, dividends, and so on, because all of the available publicity on the subject will already be reflected in the company's stock price. Profit-seeking traders and investors can be expected to exploit even the smallest informational advantage, and by so doing, they incorporate all information into market prices, thereby eliminating any profit opportunities. According to this version of the hypothesis, even "fundamental analysis"—in-depth analysis of the financial situation and the prospects for individual companies—will prove fruitless because all favorable information will already have been reflected in market prices.

A third form of EMH suggests that not only anything that is known but also anything that is knowable has already been assimilated into market prices. This extreme version postulates that one cannot even benefit from "inside information." It is unlikely that this "strong" form of the hypothesis is ever completely satisfied. But trading on inside information is illegal, and in the United States the Securities and Exchange Commission (SEC) has been increasingly diligent in going after company executives and hedge fund managers who are believed to have profited from trading on inside information.

EMH AND THE RANDOM WALK HYPOTHESIS

All forms of EMH imply that market prices cannot be forecast. Much of the empirical literature has focused on the "random walk" hypothesis, a statistical description of unforecastable price changes. The term was apparently first used in an exchange of correspondence that appeared in *Nature* in the early 1900s (Pearson 1905). The subject of the correspondence was the optimal search procedure for finding a drunk who had been left in the middle of a field. The answer was quite complex, but the place to start was simply the place where the drunkard had been left. Paul Samuelson (1965) made a seminal contribution to the EMH literature in his article entitled "Proof That Properly Anticipated Prices Fluctuate Randomly." If market prices fully incorporate the information and expectations of all market participants, then price changes must be random. Prices will, of course, change as new information is revealed to the market, but true news is random—it cannot be forecast from past events. Thus, in an informationally efficient market, price changes are unforecastable. Samuelson's contribution has been extended to allow for risk-averse investors by Stephen LeRoy (1973) and Robert Lucas (1978) and in many other directions by other researchers, including directions that allow for heterogeneous expectations. Random price movements do not imply that the stock market is capricious. Randomness indicates a well-functioning and efficient market rather than an irrational one.

The earliest empirical work on the random walk hypothesis was performed by Louis Bachelier (1900). He concluded that commodity prices follow a random walk, although he did not use that term. Corroborating evidence from other time series was provided by Holbrook Working (1960) and from U.S. stock prices by Alfred Cowles and Herbert Jones (1937) and Maurice Kendall (1953). These studies generally found that the serial correlations between successive changes are essentially zero. Harry Roberts (1959) found that a time series generated from a sequence of random numbers has the same appearance as a time series of U.S. stock prices. M. F. M. Osborne (1977) concluded that stock-price movements are similar to the random Brownian motion of physical particles and that the logarithms of price changes are independent of each other.

Other empirical work, using alternative techniques and data sets, has searched for more complicated patterns in the sequence of prices in speculative markets. Clive Granger and Oskar Morgenstern (1963) used the technique of spectral analysis but were unable to find any dependably repeatable patterns in stock-price movements. Eugene Fama (1965a, 1965b) not only looked at serial correlation coefficients (which were close to zero) but also corroborated his investigation by examining a series of lagged prices and performing a number of nonparametric "runs" tests. He also examined a variety of filter techniques—trading techniques where buy (sell) signals are generated by some upward (downward) price movements from recent troughs (peaks)—and found that they could not produce abnormal profits. Other investigations have done computer simulations of more complicated technical analysis of supposedly predictive stock chart patterns (such as "double tops," "inverted head and shoulders," and so on) and found that profitable trading strategies cannot be undertaken on the basis of these patterns. Bruno Solnik (1973) measured serial correlation coefficients for daily, weekly, and monthly price changes in nine countries and concluded that profitable investment strategies cannot be formulated on the basis of the extremely small dependencies found.

Although most of the earliest studies of the stock market supported a general finding of randomness, more recent work has indicated that the random walk model does not strictly hold. Some patterns appear to exist in the development of stock prices. Over short holding periods, there is some evidence of momentum in the stock market, while mean reversion appears to be present over longer holding periods. Nevertheless, it is less clear that there are violations of the weak form of EMH, which states only that unexploited trading opportunities should not persist in any efficient market.

Andrew Lo and Craig MacKinlay (1999), in a book entitled *A Non-random Walk Down Wall Street*, have found evidence inconsistent with the random walk model. Calculating weekly and monthly holding period returns for various stock indexes, they find evidence of positive serial correlation, which implies some momentum in stock prices. Moreover, exploiting the fact that return variances scale linearly in a random walk market, they construct a variance ratio test that rejects the random walk hypothesis. This rejection of the random walk hypothesis for stock indexes may result, however, from the behavior of small company stocks that are infrequently traded. New information about the market as a whole is likely to be factored into the prices of large capitalization stocks first and into the prices of smaller stocks later. Interestingly, Lo and MacKinlay are unable to reject the random walk hypothesis when they perform tests on individual stocks. Narasimhan Jegadeesh and Sheridan Titman (1993) have also found some evidence of momentum in stock prices.

Two possible explanations for the existence of momentum have been offered: the first is based on behavioral considerations, the second on sluggish responses to new information. Shiller (2000) emphasizes a psychological feedback mechanism that imparts a degree of momentum into stock prices, especially during periods of extreme enthusiasm. Individuals see stock prices rising and are drawn into the market in a kind of "bandwagon effect." The second explanation is based on the argument that investors do not adjust their expectations immediately when news arises—especially news of company earnings that have exceeded (or fallen short of) expectations. Ray Ball and Phillip Brown (1968) and Richard Rendleman, Charles Jones, and Henry Latané (1982) have found that abnormally high returns follow positive earnings surprises as market prices appear to respond to earnings information only gradually.

There is enough evidence in support of short-term momentum that research-ers such as Mark Carhart (1997) have considered momentum to be a priced factor in explaining the cross-section of security and mutual fund returns. And Clifford Asness, Tobias Moskowitz, and Lasse Pederson (2010) have offered actual invest-ment funds where stocks showing positive momentum are overweighted in the portfolio. In these two analyses, positive momentum is considered to be strong relative performance over the preceding twelve months (not including the most recent month to allow for any short-term return reversals). As is the case with many of the so-called predictable patterns in stock-price returns, investment strategies based on these are predictive during some periods but not in others.

Although there is some evidence supporting the existence of short-term momen-tum in the stock market, many studies have shown evidence of negative serial correlation—that is, return reversals—over longer holding periods. For example, Eugene Fama and Kenneth French (1988) have found that 25 to 40 percent of the variation in long holding period returns can be predicted in terms of a negative cor-relation with past returns. Similarly, James Poterba and Lawrence Summers (1988) have found substantial mean reversion in stock market returns at longer horizons.

Some studies have attributed this forecastability to the tendency of stock mar-ket prices to "overreact." Werner De Bondt and Richard Thaler (1985), for example, argue that investors are subject to waves of optimism and pessimism that cause prices to deviate systematically from their fundamental values and later to exhibit mean reversion. They suggest that such overreaction to past events is consistent with the implication of the behavioral decision theory of Daniel Kahneman and

Amos Tversky (1974, 1979) that investors are systematically overconfident of their ability to forecast either future stock prices or future corporate earnings (see also Kahneman and Riepe 1998). These findings give some support to investment techniques that rest on a "contrarian" strategy—that is, buying the stocks, or groups of stocks, that have been out of favor for long periods of time.

However, the finding of mean reversion is not uniform across studies and is quite a bit weaker in some periods than it is for others. Indeed, the strongest empirical results come from periods including the Great Depression, which may have been a time with patterns that do not generalize well. Moreover, such return reversals for the market as a whole may be quite consistent with the efficient functioning of the market, since they could result, in part, from the volatility of interest rates and the tendency of interest rates to be mean-reverting. Since stock returns must rise or fall to be competitive with bond returns, there is a tendency when interest rates go up for prices of both bonds and stocks to go down, and for prices of bonds and stocks to go up as interest rates go down. If interest rates revert to the mean over time, this pattern tends to generate return reversals, or mean reversion, in a way that is quite consistent with the efficient functioning of markets.

Moreover, it may not be possible to profit from the tendency for individual stocks to exhibit return reversals. Zsuzsanna Fluck, Burton Malkiel, and Richard Quandt (1997) simulated a strategy of buying stocks over a thirteen-year period during the 1980s and early 1990s, and returns over smaller periods of three to five years within that time span were particularly poor. They found that stocks with very low returns over the past three to five years had higher returns in the next period, and that stocks with very high returns over the past three to five years had lower returns in the next period. Thus, they confirmed the very strong *statistical* evidence of return reversals. However, they also found that returns in the next period were similar for both groups, so they could not confirm that a contrarian approach would yield higher-than-average returns. There was a statistically strong pattern of return reversal, but not one that implied an inefficiency in the market that would enable investors to make excess returns. Moreover, many of the predictable patterns mentioned in the finance literature seemed to disappear after they were published. William Schwert (2003) suggests two possible explanations. First, researchers have a normal tendency to focus on results that challenge conventional wisdom. It is likely that in some particular sample a statistically significant result will emerge that appears to challenge EMH. Alternatively, practitioners may learn quickly about any "dependable" profit-making opportunities and exploit them until they are no longer profitable. In other words, if there are $100 bills available, they will be picked up as soon as they are discovered. My own view of the matter has been succinctly expressed by Richard Roll (1992, 28), an academic economist who also was a portfolio manager, investing billions of dollars of investment funds:

> I have personally tried to invest money, my client's money and my own, in every single anomaly and predictive device that academics have dreamed up. . . . I have attempted to exploit a whole variety of strategies supposedly

documented by academic research. And I have yet to make a nickel on any of these supposed market inefficiencies. . . . But, I have to keep coming back to my point . . . that a true market inefficiency ought to be an exploitable opportunity. If there's nothing investors can exploit in a systematic way, time in and time out, then it's very hard to say that information is not being properly incorporated into stock prices. . . . Real money investment strategies don't produce the results that academic papers say they should.

THE SEMISTRONG FORM OF EMH

The narrow or weak form of EMH suggests that any information contained in the history of stock prices will have already been reflected in current prices. Hence, "technical analysis," the analysis of past price movements, cannot be employed to produce above-average returns. But most professional investment managers are "fundamental analysts" rather than technicians. Fundamental analysts study a wide range of information, including company sales, earnings, and asset values, in forming portfolios that they hope will earn excess returns. Studies attempting to determine whether publicly available information can be used to improve portfolio performances are tests of the semistrong form of EMH. Usually a finding that abnormal returns can be earned is referred to as an EMH anomaly.

At the outset, it is important to note that any empirical test purporting to show that abnormal returns can be earned is based on some model of risk adjustment. For example, the capital asset pricing model (CAPM) is often used to adjust for risk. Thus, an anomalous finding that excess returns can be earned by exploiting publicly available "fundamental" information is actually a joint test of EMH and the risk adjustment procedures employed. If the CAPM beta is an inadequate measure of risk (or if beta is measured with error), it will be inappropriate to consider beta-adjusted excess returns to be inconsistent with EMH. Similarly, if market capitalization (size) and market-to-book factors are added to beta to account for risk, abnormal returns will be identified only if this three-factor model fully describes the cross-section of expected returns.

Tests of the semistrong form of EMH have looked at how rapidly new information is reflected in market prices and whether the use of certain valuation metrics favored by security analysts can generate abnormal returns. Studies seeking to examine the rapidity of price responses to news announcements are called "event studies." The "events" used in such studies have included dividend changes, earnings reports that have differed from estimates, and merger announcements.

Various tests have been performed to ascertain the speed of adjustment of market prices to new information. Fama and his colleagues (1969) looked at the effect of stock splits on equity prices. Although splits themselves provide no economic benefit, splits are usually accompanied or followed by dividend increases that do convey information to the market concerning management's confidence about the future progress of the enterprise. Although splits usually result in higher market valuations, the market appears to adjust to such announcements fully and immediately. Substantial returns can be earned before the split announcement, but there is no evidence of abnormal returns after the public announcement.

Similarly, merger announcements can raise market prices substantially, especially when premiums are being paid to the shareholders of the acquired firm, but it appears that the market adjusts fully to the public announcements. Arthur Keown and John Pinkerton (1981) found no evidence of abnormal price changes after the public release of merger information. James Patell and Mark Wolfson (1984) examined the intraday speed of adjustment to earnings and dividend announcements. They noted that the stock market assimilates publicly available information "very quickly." The largest portion of the price response occurs in the first five to fifteen minutes after disclosure.

Although most event studies have supported EMH, some have not. Ball and Brown (1968) found that stock-price reactions to earnings announcements are not complete. He found that abnormal returns can be earned in the period after the announcement date. Rendleman, Jones, and Latané (1982) also found that unexpected earnings announcements are not immediately reflected in stock prices and that abnormal returns can be earned by purchasing shares of companies with positive earnings surprises. These studies of sluggish adjustment (or underreaction) support the momentum arguments referred to earlier. However, the pattern of underreaction to announcements is not consistent over time. Fama (1998) has argued that overreaction to news announcements appears about as often as underreaction (see also Bernard and Thomas 1990). In any event, such anomalies tend to be so small that only professional traders could have earned economic profits.

There has been considerable work on the use of a variety of valuation metrics to isolate stocks that are expected to generate "excess" returns. An influential book by Benjamin Graham and David Dodd (1934) entitled *Security Analysis* spawned the development of a whole profession of security analysts who were trained to examine "fundamental" financial data for firms, such as earnings and asset values, and find stocks that represented "good value." The approach remains popular today, especially with the growing appeal of behavioral finance. Behaviorists such as Daniel Kahneman and Amos Tversky (1974, 1979) have argued that investors tend to be overoptimistic and far more certain of their forecasts than is warranted. Thus, they tend to overestimate future growth and to pay more than they should for "growth" stocks—those stocks promising above-average future growth. Conversely, "value" stocks—those stocks that are less exciting and therefore sell at more modest valuation metrics, such as low multiples of earnings and of book value—are likely to generate excess returns.

Of all the predictable patterns that have been discovered, this so-called value effect is among those most supported by the evidence. Basu (1977) found that portfolios of stocks with low price-to-earnings (P/E) multiples have tended to provide higher returns than portfolios of stocks with high P/E ratios. Using a somewhat different value criterion, Fama and French (1992, 1998) found that portfolios made up of stocks with low ratios of price-to-book-value (P/BV) provide relatively higher returns than the portfolios of high-P/BV firms. When the CAPM measure of risk was used to adjust for risk, the higher return from value stocks appeared to represent an inefficiency.

Another pattern that has found empirical support is the size or small-firm effect. Between 1926 and the present, an investor could have realized higher portfolio returns by concentrating on stocks with relatively small market capitalizations (see Banz 1981; Reinganum 1983; Ibbotson Associates). Fama and French (1998) have demonstrated that this effect can be documented in international as well as U.S. stock markets. In the United States, the excess returns from small-capitalization stocks appear almost entirely in January—hence this size effect is often called "the January Effect."

Findings such as these have often been considered "anomalies" or "inefficiencies." But again, we are driven back to the joint hypothesis problem. If CAPM is an insufficient model for the measurement of risk, then the result does not represent an inefficiency. Indeed, Fama and French (1993) have proposed that small company stocks and low-P/BV stocks are riskier. Small companies can be more vulnerable to economic shocks than larger firms, and low P/BV may be a reflection of some form of economic distress. For example, during the recent financial crisis, distressed bank stocks sold at unusually low prices relative to their book values. Hence, any excess returns that were earned were simply some compensation for risk. This interpretation has been vigorously disputed by Josef Lakonishok, Andrei Schleifer, and Robert Vishny (1994), who argue that these patterns are evidence of inefficiencies. Nevertheless, it has become standard to employ risk measurement techniques that augment the beta risk measure of CAPM with the addition of size and P/BV factors. In some models, a fourth factor, momentum, is added to the Fama-French three-factor risk model (see, for example, Carhart 1997).

PREDICTABLE TIME-SERIES MARKET RETURNS BASED ON VALUATION PARAMETERS

Considerable empirical research has been conducted to determine whether future returns for the overall market can be predicted on the basis of initial valuation parameters. It is claimed that valuation ratios, such as the price-to-earnings multiple or the dividend yield of the stock market as a whole, have considerable time-series predictive power.

Formal statistical tests of the ability of dividend yields (that is, the ratio of dividends to stock prices) to forecast future returns have been conducted by Eugene Fama and Kenneth French (1988) and by John Campbell and Robert Shiller (1998). Depending on the forecast horizon involved, as much as 40 percent of the variance of future returns for the stock market as a whole can be predicted on the basis of the initial dividend yield of the market index.

This finding is not necessarily inconsistent with efficiency. Dividend yields of stocks tend to be high when interest rates are high, and they tend to be low when interest rates are low. Consequently, the ability of initial yields to predict returns may simply reflect the adjustment of the stock market to general economic conditions. Moreover, the use of dividend yields to predict future returns has been much less effective since the mid-1980s. One possible explanation is that the dividend behavior of U.S. corporations has changed over time, as suggested by Laurie Bagwell and John Shoven (1989) and by Fama and French (2001). During more recent years, companies may have been more likely to institute a share repurchase program than to increase their dividends. Changing compensation practices—company executives are now more likely to be rewarded with stock options than with cash bonuses—have encouraged such a change in behavior. Buybacks tend to increase the value of executive stock options. The option holder does not receive any dividends that are paid. Finally, it is worth noting that this phenomenon does *not* work consistently with individual stocks. Investors who simply purchase a portfolio of individual stocks with the highest dividend yields in the market will *not* earn a particularly high rate of return (see, for example, Fluck et al. 1997).

Time-series empirical studies have also found that price-to-earnings multiples for the market as a whole have considerable predictive power. Investors have tended to earn larger long-horizon returns when purchasing the market basket of stocks at relatively low price-to-earnings multiples. Campbell and Shiller (1998) have shown that initial P/E ratios explain as much as 40 percent of the variance of future returns. They conclude that equity returns have been predictable in the past to a considerable extent.

Consider, however, the experience during the past fifteen years of investors who have attempted to undertake investment strategies based either on the level of the price-to-earnings multiple or on the size of the dividend yield to predict future long-horizon stock returns. Price-to-earnings multiples for the Standard & Poor's 500 stock index were unusually high in mid-1987 (suggesting very low long-horizon returns). Dividend yields fell below 3 percent. The average annual total return from the index over the next ten years was an extraordinarily generous 16.7 percent. Earnings multiples were also extremely high in the early 1990s, but returns remained extremely high until the end of the decade. We need to be very cautious in assessing the extent to which stock market returns are predictable on the basis of valuation metrics. Studies by Amit Goyal and Ivo Welch (2003) and by Kenneth Fisher and Meir Statman (2006) have found that neither dividend yields nor price-to-earnings multiples are useful in generating timing strategies to shift between stocks and bonds that would generate returns exceeding a simple buy-and-hold strategy.

VARIANCE BOUND TESTS

One kind of empirical test whose results have questioned market efficiency is called a "variance bound test." In an efficient market, all assets should be priced at the discounted present value of all of their cash flows. In one well-known model of stock valuation popularized by Myron Gordon (1959), the price of a share was taken to be the discounted present value of the future stream of dividends. Stephen

LeRoy and Richard Porter (1981), as well as Robert Shiller (1981), then compared the realized variance of the dividend stream (the components of the ex post present value) with the variance of stock prices. They found that the variance of stock prices dramatically exceeds the variance of ex post present values. Stock prices are far too volatile to be explained by the variance of future dividends. Of course, it is far from clear how much deviation from "true value" is necessary to declare that stock prices are "too volatile." In his influential article entitled "Noise," Fischer Black (1986) argued that a market should still be considered efficient even if prices deviate in a range of plus-200 percent and minus-50 percent of fundamental value. Nevertheless, Shiller concluded that the excess volatility of stock prices implies that EMH must be false.

Shiller's conclusion has been extremely controversial. Allan Kleidon (1986) and Terry Marsh and Robert Merton (1986) showed that with the kinds of sample sizes used in the tests, sampling variation alone could have generated the Shiller results. But even if the LeRoy-Porter and Shiller findings survive the statistical critiques, there are several reasons to be cautious about interpreting the results as inconsistent with EMH. For one thing, it is well established that managers tend to smooth dividends; therefore, the ex post variance of dividends may understate the true variance in the fortunes of individual companies. In addition, it is highly unlikely that either real interest rates or required risk premiums are stable over time. Stock prices should adjust with changes in required rates of return, and such price volatility may be entirely consistent with EMH.

There is no reason to believe that individual preferences and behavior are stable over time. Required risk premiums are likely to be influenced by environmental conditions, and when these conditions change, the behavior of investors can be expected to change as well. This perspective suggests a more nuanced view of the world of rational expectations. The approach has been championed by Andrew Lo and is called the "adaptive markets hypothesis." This view suggests a quite complicated process to explain the determination of equilibrium risk premiums (see Farmer and Lo 1999; Lo 2004, 2005; Brennan and Lo 2009).

BUBBLES IN ASSET PRICES

Perhaps the most persuasive argument against market efficiency is that securities markets have often experienced spectacular bubbles. During the so-called Internet bubble that inflated in the late 1990s, any security associated with the "New Economy" soared in price. Companies that changed their names to include "dot.net" or a similar suffix would often double in price. When the bubble popped, Internet-related stocks lost 90 percent or more of their value. During the housing bubble in the first decade of the 2000s, the inflation-adjusted price of the median single family house doubled after being flat for the entire past century. The associated mispricing of mortgage-backed securities had far-reaching consequences for world financial institutions and for the entire world economy. Critics have considered these episodes to be obvious cases of market inefficiency.

Bubbles often start with some exogenous factor that can be interpreted rationally as presenting large future prospects for profit. In England in the early 1700s, it was the formation of the promising new corporation, the South Sea Company, and the rise of its stock price. The wave of new companies that followed was expected to provide profitable investment outlets for the savings of individuals. In the United States during the late 1990s, it was the promise of the Internet, which was expected to revolutionize the way consumers obtained information and purchased goods and services. The generation of sharply rising asset prices that followed, however, seemed to have more to do with the behavioral biases emphasized by scholars such as Kahneman and Shiller.[2]

Kahneman and Tversky (1974, 1979) argued that people forming subjective judgments tend to disregard base probabilities and to make judgments solely in terms of observed similarities to familiar patterns. Thus, investors may expect past price increases to continue even if they know from past experience that all skyrocketing stock markets eventually succumb to the laws of gravity. This phenomenon was certainly present during the great housing bubble of 2007 to 2008. Investors also tend to enjoy the self-esteem that comes from having invested early in some "new era" phenomenon, and they are overconfident of their ability to predict the future.

Shiller (2000) emphasizes the role of "feedback loops" in the propagation of bubbles. Price increases for an asset lead to greater investor enthusiasm, which then leads to increased demand for the asset and therefore to further price increases. The very observation that prices have been rising alters the subjective judgment of investors and reinforces their belief that the price increases will continue. The news media play a prominent role in increasing the optimism of investors. The media are, in Shiller's view, "generators of attention cascades" (60). One news story begets another, and the price increases themselves (whether of common stocks or single-family houses) appear to justify the superficially plausible story that started the rise in the price of the asset(s). According to Shiller, bubbles are inherently a social phenomenon. A feedback mechanism generates continuing rises in prices and an interaction back to the conventional wisdom that started the process. The bubble itself becomes the main topic of social conversation, and stories abound about certain individuals who have become wealthy from the price increases. As the economic historian Charles Kindleberger (1989) has stated, "There is nothing so disturbing to one's well-being and judgment as to see a friend get rich."

The question naturally arises why the arbitrage mechanism of EMH does not prick the bubble as it continues to inflate. Enormous profit opportunities were certainly achievable during the Internet bubble for speculators who correctly judged that the prices of many technology stocks were "too high." But the kind of arbitrage that would have been necessary was sometimes difficult to effect and in any event, it was very risky. There appear to be considerable "limits to arbitrage" (see, for example, Shleifer, Lakonishok, and Vishny 1992; DeLong et al. 1990). For example, in one celebrated case during the Internet bubble, the market price of Palm Pilot stock (which was 95 percent–owned by the company 3Com) implied a total capitalization considerably greater than that of its parent, suggesting that the rest of 3Com's business had a negative value. But the arbitrage (sell Palm Pilot stock short and buy 3Com stock) could not be achieved because it was impossible to borrow Palm Pilot stock to accomplish the short sale.

Arbitrage is also risky; one never can be sure when the bubble will burst. The mantra of hedge fund managers (the natural arbitragers) in the United States was "markets can remain irrational much longer than we can remain solvent." Moreover, some arbitragers may recognize that a bubble exists but are unable to synchronize their strategies to take advantage of it (see Abreu and Brunnermeier 2003). They might prefer to ride the bubble for as long as possible. Indeed, one empirical study by Markus Brunnermeier and Stefan Nagel (2004) has found that rather than shorting Internet stocks, hedge funds were actually buying them during the late 1990s. Hedge funds were embarking on a strategy of anticipating that the momentum of the price increases would continue and thus were contributing to the mispricing rather than trading against it.

Critics consider the existence of spectacular bubbles in asset prices "damning" evidence against the EMH. But even when we know ex post that major errors were made, there were certainly no clear ex ante arbitrage opportunities available to rational investors.

Equity valuations rest on uncertain future forecasts. Even if all market participants rationally price common stocks as the present value of all expected future cash flows, it is still possible for excesses to develop. We know, with the benefit of hindsight, that the outlandish claims regarding the growth of the Internet (and the related telecommunications structure needed to support it) were unsupportable. We know now that projections for the rates of growth and the stability and duration of those growth rates for "New Economy" companies were unsustainable. But neither sharp-penciled professional investors nor quantitative academics were able to accurately measure the dimensions of the bubble or the timing of its eventual collapse.

As indicated earlier, there is evidence that initial dividend yields for the market as a whole have considerable predictive power to explain future long-horizon rates of return. But during the early 1990s, dividend yields in the United States fell well below 3 percent, implying very low rates of return for the next five to ten years. In fact, the U.S. stock market generated unusually large double-digit rates of return during the entire decade of the 1990s. In 1996, Campbell and Shiller presented a paper (later published as Campbell and Shiller 1998) to the board of governors of the U.S. Federal Reserve System showing that price-to-earnings multiples for the overall market possessed substantial ability to predict future rates of return. Since P/E multiples were extraordinarily high at that time, the work implied a likelihood of very low or even negative rates of return. This work influenced Alan Greenspan (1996), then chairman of the board of governors, to question whether the stock market was at bubble levels and to suggest that investors were exhibiting "irrational exuberance." The stock market rallied strongly for more than four years thereafter. We know now (ex post) that market prices were at bubble levels in late 1999 and early 2000. No one was able accurately to identify the timing of the bubble in advance. And certainly no riskless arbitrage opportunities existed, even at the height of the bubble.

HYMAN MINSKY AND THE 2007 TO 2008 FINANCIAL CRISIS

The financial crisis of 2007 to 2008 reinforces two important lessons that may sometimes be overlooked by policymakers. First, it is critical to distinguish between asset-price bubbles that are financed by debt and those that inflate without a major increase in indebtedness. The former are far more dangerous than the latter. The bursting of the Internet bubble in early 2000 did usher in a period of poor macroeconomic performance in the United States and in other world economies. But the recession that followed was moderate and relatively short-lived. The bursting of the real estate bubble in 2007 had far more serious consequences. Because individual balance sheets as well as those of financial institutions had become overextended in debt, there were serious adverse effects on consumer spending and on the ability and willingness of financial institutions to lend.

The debt-to-income ratios of individuals, which have historically measured about one-third, rose to a level well above 100 percent during the boom as people bought houses with lower and lower down payments and tapped the equity in their houses by assuming second mortgages. The leverage ratios of financial institutions also increased dramatically. The debt-to-equity ratios of investment banks such as Bear Stearns and Lehman Brothers reportedly exceeded thirty-to-one. Moreover, the debt was short-term rather than long-term. As investors in the short-term paper of those institutions began to worry about the quality of the mortgage-backed securities on the asset side of the investment banks' balance sheets, they refused to roll over their loans and we experienced a classic run on the banks. Commercial banks also became dangerously overleveraged, and a collapse of the financial system was avoided only by extraordinary measures undertaken by government authorities.

These events give us a renewed appreciation of the work of Hyman Minsky (1982, 2008), who stressed that stability itself breeds the seeds of instability in a capitalist system. Periods of economic expansion and relative stability lead individuals and institutions to reduce the premiums they demand to hold risky assets and to tolerate greater amounts of debt than they had previously accepted. The increased willingness of borrowers to borrow and lenders to lend leads to a growth in the availability and flow of credit, which in turn drives up asset prices to levels that may be inconsistent with their "fundamental valuations." Precautionary lending practices are replaced with what Minsky has called "Ponzi finance." Ponzi loans are characterized as loans to borrowers whose operating cash flow is insufficient to pay down principal so that the loans must continually be refinanced. The process ends with what has been called a "Minsky Moment."

Market participants begin to believe that asset prices are "unsustainably high," and they attempt to cash in their profits before prices collapse. Lenders are reluctant to make new loans and refuse to renew the loans already outstanding. Investors demand higher-risk premiums and attempt to alter the composition of their portfolios to increase the liquidity of the instruments they hold. As a result of a rush to exit risky holdings, there are "fire sales" of all risk assets. Prices decline dramatically, and markets become less liquid. In the extreme case, a full-fledged financial crisis ensues.

There is little doubt that the Minsky model seems an especially good description of the recent financial crisis. Minsky's "financial instability" hypothesis is also consistent with the insights of behavioral finance and with the tendency of market systems to experience periodic bubbles. But even when we know ex post that asset prices were "wrong," the fundamental characteristic of efficient markets remains valid. Markets can make "mistakes," sometimes egregious ones, and those mistakes can have extremely unfortunate macroeconomic consequences. But there were no obvious ex ante arbitrage opportunities. While some hedge funds did profit from selling short mortgage-backed securities, other investment funds and financial institutions went bankrupt because they held long positions in these same instruments and financed those positions exclusively with short-term debt.[3] What Minsky's work does make clear, however, is that policymakers need to be very alert to increases in asset prices that are financed with debt. Both the amount and the maturity of the debt on individual and institutional balance sheets are crucial variables. It is debt-financed asset-price bubbles that have the most serious macroeconomic effects.

The "mistakes" that markets sometimes make can also have undesirable microeconomic effects. We count on financial markets to allocate the economy's scarce capital resources to the most productive uses. We know that the overpricing of Internet stocks in 1999 and early 2000 led to the financing of many fanciful business ventures and to an overinvestment in long-distance fiber-optic cable that was sufficient to span the globe multiple times. We know that during the housing bubble of the first decade of the 2000s far too many houses were built and, again, investment capital was badly allocated. The more difficult question is evaluating the costs and benefits of a market-based allocation system and determining what it should be compared with. Certainly few would agree that a Soviet-type central planning system is likely to make better allocation decisions.

THE PERFORMANCE OF PROFESSIONAL INVESTORS

Perhaps the most convincing tests of market efficiency are direct tests of the ability of professional investment managers to outperform the market as a whole. If market prices are generally determined by irrational investors and it is easy to identify predictable patterns in security returns or exploitable anomalies in security prices, then professional investment managers should be able to beat the market. Direct tests of the actual returns earned by professionals, who are often compensated with strong incentives to outperform the market, should represent the most compelling evidence of market efficiency.

A large body of evidence suggests that professional investment managers are not able to outperform index funds that buy and hold the broad stock market portfolio. One of the earliest studies of mutual fund performance was undertaken by Michael Jensen (1968). He found that active fund managers are unable

FIGURE 4.1 / Returns for Surviving Funds Compared with Returns for All Funds

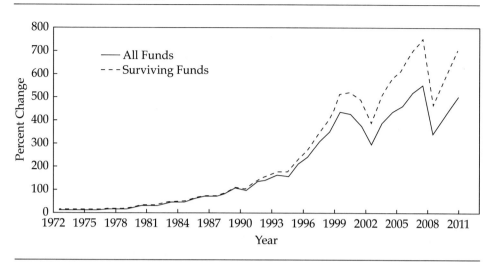

Source: Author's compilation of data from Lipper Analytic Services (various years).

to add value. Using a risk-adjustment model motivated by the capital asset pricing model, he found that actively managed mutual funds tend to underperform the market by approximately the amount of their added expenses. I repeated Jensen's study with data from a subsequent period and confirmed the earlier results (Malkiel 1995).

Carhart (1997) used a different method of risk adjustment in appraising the performance of actively managed mutual funds. He measured risk in terms of a four-factor model. In addition to the CAPM beta, he used the two Fama-French risk factors of "value" (low price to book value) and "size" as well as a "momentum" factor. Carhart found that most mutual funds underperform the market on a risk-adjusted basis. Although the best funds are able to earn back their expenses with higher gross returns, net returns are no better than could be earned by a low-cost, broad-based index fund. Carhart's study is consistent with previous work suggesting that professional investors are unable to beat the market.

Studies of mutual fund returns must take account of certain biases in many data sets. The degree of "survivorship bias" in the data is often substantial. Poorly performing funds tend to be merged into other funds in the mutual fund's family complex, thus burying the records of many of the underperformers. Figure 4.1 updates the study I performed during the mid-1990s through the first decade of the 2000s. The analysis shows that the returns for surviving funds are considerably better than the actual return for all funds, including funds liquidated or merged out of existence. Data available for mutual fund returns generally show only the returns for currently available funds—that is, for those funds that survived.

TABLE 4.1 / Percentage of U.S. Equity Funds Outperformed by Benchmarks, 2006 to 2010

Fund Category	Benchmark Index	Percentage Outperformed
All domestic equity	S&P 1500	57
All large-cap funds	S&P 500	62
All mid-cap funds	S&P Mid-Cap 400	78
All small-cap funds	S&P Small-Cap 600	63
All multi-cap funds	S&P Small-Cap 1500	66
Global funds	S&P Global 1200	59
International funds	S&P 700	85
Emerging market funds	S&P/IFCI Composite	86

Source: Author's compilation based on data from Standard & Poor's (various years).

Survivorship bias makes the interpretation of long-run mutual fund data sets very difficult. But even using data sets with some degree of survivorship bias, one cannot sustain the argument that professional investors can beat the market.

Table 4.1 shows the percentage of actively managed mutual funds that have been outperformed by their relevant passive benchmarks. In general, two-thirds of actively managed funds are outperformed by their benchmark indexes. Similar results can be shown for earlier five-year periods, as well as for ten- and twenty-year periods. Moreover, the funds that do have superior records in one base period are not the same in the next. There is little persistence in mutual fund returns—with the possible exception of very high-expense, poorly performing funds in one period, which tend to do poorly in the next. Managed funds are regularly outperformed by broad index funds with equivalent risk. The median actively managed mutual fund underperforms its benchmark by about eighty to ninety basis points (eight- to nine-tenths of 1 percent), which is approximately the additional expenses charged by the fund's management.

Of course, for any period one can find a number of fund managers who have produced well-above-average returns. But there is no dependable persistence in performance. During the 1970s, the top twenty mutual funds enjoyed almost double the performance of the index. During the 1980s, those same funds underperformed the index. The best-performing funds of the 1980s failed to outperform in the 1990s. And the funds with the best records during the 1990s, which tended to be those with concentrations of "New Economy" stocks, had disastrous returns during the first decade of the 2000s.

Figure 4.2 presents a forty-year record of actively managed mutual funds and the Standard & Poor 500 (S&P 500) stock index, a benchmark frequently used to measure overall market returns. It plots the performance of all mutual funds that have been available over the entire period. In 1970 there were 358 equity mutual funds in the United States. (Today there are thousands of funds.) Only 108 of those original funds survived through the end of 2010. All we can do is measure the relative performance versus the market for these surviving funds. We can be sure,

FIGURE 4.2 / Returns of Surviving Mutual Funds Compared with S&P 500
Returns, 1970 to 2010

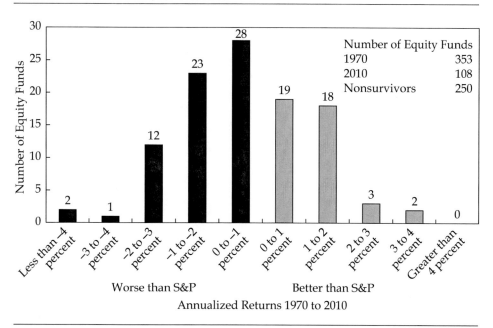

Source: Author's calculations based on data from Lipper Analytic Services (various years) and the
Vanguard Group (various years).

however, that the 250 funds that did not survive had even worse records. Yet even
though these data are tainted by survivorship bias, we find that the vast majority of
the mutual funds that have been in existence for forty years have underperformed
an index that has served as the basis for the most popular indexed mutual funds
and exchange-traded funds (ETFs). And one can count on the fingers of one hand
the number of professionally managed mutual funds that have outperformed the
S&P 500 index by two percentage points or more per year.

Similar kinds of results have been observed for other professional investors,
such as pension funds and insurance company portfolios (see, for example,
Swensen 2005, 2009). A variety of biases—such as inclusion bias, backfill bias, and
survivorship bias—make the interpretation of hedge fund returns problematic
(see, for example, Malkiel and Saha 2005). But it does not appear that hedge funds,
as a group, are able to produce abnormal returns for their clients.[4] If markets were
dominated by irrational investors who make systematic errors in valuing equities,
we should expect that professional investors, who are well incentivized to beat the
market, would realize relatively generous returns. If persistent anomalies were
obvious and bubbles were easy to spot, a simple passively managed equity fund
that buys and holds all the stocks in the market would not display the degree of
superiority that it does.

Large arbitrage opportunities do not persist. And while markets can and do make mistakes—some of them horrendous—it is extraordinarily difficult to recognize such situations ex ante. Certainly such examples of mispricing that are recognized ex post do not provide opportunities for risk-adjusted extraordinary returns.

The wisdom of the market appears to produce a tableau of prices that is certainly not always correct but is hard to second-guess. It is therefore difficult for me to resist the conclusion that our financial markets are remarkably efficient, and that EMH remains a most useful hypothesis approximating how our financial markets actually work.

CONCLUSION

In the final analysis, it is probably useful to think of the stock market in terms of "reasonable market efficiency" or "relative market efficiency" rather than absolute efficiency. Andrew Lo (2008) has suggested that few engineers would even contemplate performing a statistical test to determine whether a given engine is perfectly efficient. But they would attempt to measure the efficiency of that engine relative to a frictionless ideal. Similarly, it is unrealistic to require our financial markets to be perfectly efficient in order to accept the basic tenets of EMH. Indeed, as Sanford Grossman and Joseph Stiglitz (1980) argued, the perfect efficiency of our financial markets is an unrealizable ideal. Those traders who ensure that information is quickly reflected in market prices must be able at least to cover their costs. But it is reasonable to ask if our financial markets are relatively efficient, and I believe that the evidence is very powerful that our markets come very close to the EMH ideal.

Information does get reflected rapidly in security prices. Thus, to return to our analogy of the $100 bill lying on the ground, it is highly unlikely that it will stay there—that is, that we will find those prices persisting for any length of time. There may well be some loose pennies around. They will be picked up only if justified by the cost involved in exploiting the opportunities available. Thus, some professional managers may even earn the fees they charge. Their profits, in effect, reflect economic rents. But what seems abundantly clear is that investors in actively managed funds do not reap any benefits over and above those they would earn from a low-cost, broad-based, passively managed index fund.

I would draw one more conclusion from this discussion of the efficient-market hypothesis. EMH and behavioral finance should not be considered as competitive models. Behavioral finance provides important insights into the formation of expectations and the process by which valuations are determined. And as Hersh Shefrin and Meir Statman (this volume) make clear, behavioral finance does not argue that the behavioral biases of investors make the market "beatable." Moreover, the insights of Minsky help explain how required risk premiums are influenced by environmental conditions. Policymakers will be well served by internalizing Minsky's central theses that financial markets—even if efficient in the sense I have used the term—are able to inflict substantial damage on the real economy.

NOTES

1. As quoted by Joe Nocera, "Poking Holes in a Theory of Markets," *New York Times,* June 5, 2009, p. 81.

2. For excellent surveys of the behavioral finance literature, see Statman (2010).

3. Highly complex derivatives invite asymmetries of information and therefore present opportunities for large profits. Such opportunities are inconsistent with the strong form of EMH, which I have suggested is unlikely to hold in practice. Moreover, Robert Jarrow (this volume) has suggested that some arbitrage opportunities arose from improper ratings published by the rating agencies.

4. Not even the upwardly biased Hedge Fund Research, Inc. (HFRI) hedge fund index has outperformed the S&P 500 stock index, as shown by Jakub Jurek and Erik Stafford (2011).

REFERENCES

Abreu, Dilip, and Markus K. Brunnermeier. 2003. "Bubbles and Crashes." *Econometrica* 71(1): 173–204.

Asness, Clifford S., Tobias J. Moskowitz, and Lasse H. Pederson. 2010. "Value and Momentum Everywhere." Working paper. University of Chicago and AQR Capital Management.

Bachelier, Louis. 1900. "Théorie de la speculation." *Annales Scientifiques de l'École Normale Supérieure* 3: 17, 21–86.

Bagwell, Laurie Simon, and John B. Shoven. 1989. "Cash Distributions to Shareholders." *Journal of Economic Perspectives* 3(3): 129–40.

Ball, Ray. 1978. "Anomalies in Relationships Between Securities' Yields and Yield-Surrogates." *Journal of Financial Economics* 6(2–3): 103–26.

Ball, Ray, and Phillip Brown. 1968. "An Empirical Evaluation of Accounting Income Numbers." *Journal of Accounting Research* 6(2): 159–78.

Banz, Rolf W. 1981. "The Relationship Between Return and Market Value of Common Stock." *Journal of Financial Economics* 9(1): 3–18.

Basu, S. 1977. "The Investment Performance of Common Stocks in Relation to Their Price Earnings Ratios: A Test of the Efficient-Market Hypothesis." *Journal of Finance* 32(3): 663–82.

Bernard, Victor L., and Jacob K. Thomas. 1990. "Evidence That Stock Prices Do Not Fully Reflect the Implications of Current Earnings for Future Earnings." *Journal of Accounting and Economics* 13(4): 305–40.

Black, Fischer. 1986. "Noise." *The Journal of Finance* 41(3): 529–43.

Brennan, Thomas J., and Andrew W. Lo. 2009. "The Origin of Behavior." Available at: http://ssrn.com/abstract=1506264 (accessed June 24, 2012).

Brunnermeier, Markus, and Stefan Nagel. 2004. "Hedge Funds and the Technology Bubble." *The Journal of Finance* 59(5): 2013–40.

Campbell, John Y., and Robert J. Shiller. 1998. "Valuation Ratios and the Long-Run Market Outlook." *Journal of Portfolio Management* 24(winter): 11–26.

Carhart, Mark M. 1997. "On Persistence in Mutual Fund Performance." *Journal of Finance* 52(1): 57–82.

Cowles, Alfred, and Herbert Jones. 1937. "Some A Posteriori Probabilities in Stock Market Action." *Econometrica* 5(3): 280–94.

De Bondt, Werner F. M., and Richard Thaler. 1985. "Does the Stock Market Overreact?" *Journal of Finance* 40(3): 793–807.

DeLong, J. Bradford, Andrei Shleifer, Lawrence H. Summers, and Robert J. Waldmann. 1990. "Noise Trader Risk in Financial Markets." *Journal of Political Economy* 98(4): 703–38.

Fama, Eugene. 1965a. "The Behavior of Stock Market Prices." *Journal of Business* 38(1): 34–105.

———. 1965b. "Random Walks in Stock Market Prices." *Financial Analysts Journal* 21(Sept.–Oct.): 55–59.

———. 1970. "Efficient Capital Markets: A Review of Theory and Empirical Work." *Journal of Finance* 25(2): 383–417.

———. 1991. "Efficient Capital Markets: II." *Journal of Finance* 46(December): 1575–1617.

Fama, Eugene F., and Kenneth R. French. 1988. "Permanent and Temporary Components of Stock Prices." *Journal of Political Economy* 96(2): 246–73.

———. 1992. "The Cross-section of Expected Stock Returns." *Journal of Finance* 47(2): 427–65.

———. 1993. "Common Risk Factors in the Returns on Stocks and Bonds." *Journal of Financial Economics* 33(February): 3–56.

———. 1998. "Value Versus Growth: The International Evidence." *Journal of Finance* 53(6): 1975–99.

———. 2001. "Disappearing Dividends: Changing Firm Characteristics or Lower Propensity to Pay" *Journal of Financial Economics* 60(April): 3–43.

Fama, Eugene, Lawrence Fischer, Michael Jensen, and Richard Roll. 1969. "The Adjustment of Stock Prices to New Information." *International Economic Review* 10(1): 1–21.

Farmer, J. Doyne, and Andrew W. Lo. 1999. "Frontiers of Finance: Evolution and Efficient Markets." *Proceedings of the National Academy of Sciences* 96(August): 9991–92.

Fisher, L. Kenneth, and Meir Statman. 2006. "Market Timing in Regressions and Reality." *Journal of Financial Research* 29(3): 293–304.

Fluck, Zsuzsanna, Burton G. Malkiel, and Richard E. Quandt. 1997. "The Predictability of Stock Returns: A Cross-sectional Simulation." *Review of Economics and Statistics* 79(2): 176–83.

Fox, Justin. 2009. *The Myth of the Rational Market.* New York: HarperBusiness.

Gordon, Myron J. 1959. "Dividends, Earnings, and Stock Prices." *Review of Economics and Statistics* 41(2): 89–105.

Goyal, Amit, and Ivo Welch. 2003. "Predicting the Equity Premium with Dividend Ratios." *Management Science* 49(5): 639–54.

Graham, Benjamin, and David Dodd. 1934. *Security Analysis.* New York: McGraw-Hill.

Granger, Clive W. J., and Oskar Morgenstern. 1963. "Spectral Analysis of New York Stock Exchange Prices." *Kyklos* 16(1): 1–27.

Greenspan, Alan. 1996. Remarks at the annual dinner and Francis Boyer Lecture of the American Enterprise Institute for Public Policy Research. Washington, D.C. (December 5).

Grossman, Sanford J., and Joseph E. Stiglitz. 1980. "On the Impossibility of Informationally Efficient Markets." *American Economic Review* 70(3): 393–408.

Ibbotson Associates. Various years. *Stocks, Bonds, Bills, and Inflation* (annual yearbooks). Chicago: Ibbotson Associates.

Jegadeesh, Narasimhan, and Sheridan Titman. 1993. "Returns to Buying Winners and Selling Losers: Implications for Stock Market Efficiency." *Journal of Finance* 48(1): 65–91.

Jensen, Michael. 1968. "The Performance of Mutual Funds in the Period 1945–1964." *Journal of Finance* 23(2): 389–416.

Jurek, Jakub W., and Erik Stafford. 2011. "The Cost of Capital for Alternative Investments." Working paper. Cambridge, Mass.: Harvard Business School.

Kahneman, Daniel, and Mark W. Riepe. 1998. "Aspects of Investor Psychology." *Journal of Portfolio Management* 24(4): 52–65.

Kahneman, Daniel., and Amos Tversky. 1974. "Judgment Under Uncertainty: Heuristics and Biases." *Science* 185(27 Sept.): 1124–31.

———. 1979. "Prospect Theory: An Analysis of Decision Under Risk." *Econometrica* 47(2): 263–91.

Kendall, Maurice. 1953. "The Analysis of Economic Time Series, Part I: Prices." *Journal of the Royal Statistical Society* 96(1): 11–34.

Keown, Arthur J., and John M. Pinkerton. 1981. "Merger Announcements and Insider Trading Activity: An Empirical Investigation." *Journal of Finance* 36(4): 855–69.

Kindleberger, Charles. 1989. *Manias, Panics, and Crashes: A History of Financial Crises* (revised and enlarged). New York: Basic Books.

Kleidon, Allan W. 1986. "Variance Bounds Tests and Stock Price Valuation Models." *Journal of Political Economy* 94(5): 953–1001.

Krugman, Paul. 2009. "How Did Economists Get It So Wrong?" *New York Times Magazine*, September 2.

Lakonishok, Josef, Andrei Schleifer, and Robert W. Vishny. 1994. "Contrarian Investment, Extrapolation, and Risk." *Journal of Finance* 49(5): 1541–78.

Leroy, Stephen F. 1973. "Risk Aversion and the Martingale Property of Stock Returns." *International Economic Review* 14(2): 436–46.

Leroy, Stephen F., and Richard D. Porter. 1981. "The Present Value Relation: Tests Based on Variance Bounds." *Econometrica* 49(3): 555–74.

Lipper Analytic Services. Various years. Proprietary data. New York: Lipper Analytic Services.

Lo, Andrew. 2004. "The Adaptive Market Hypothesis: Market Efficiency from an Evolutionary Perspective." *Journal of Portfolio Management* 30: 15–29.

———. 2005. "Reconciling Efficient Markets with Behavioral Finance: The Adaptive Markets Hypothesis." *Journal of Investment Consulting* 7(2): 21–44.

———. 2008. "Efficient Markets Hypothesis." In *The New Palgrave: A Dictionary of Economics*, 2nd ed., edited by Steven N. Durlauf and Lawrence E. Blume. New York: Palgrave Macmillan.

Lo, Andrew W., and A. Craig MacKinlay. 1999. *A Non-Random Walk Down Wall Street.* Princeton, N.J.: Princeton University Press.

Lucas, Robert E., Jr. 1978. "Asset Prices in an Exchange Economy." *Econometrica* 46(6): 1429–46.

Malkiel, Burton G. 1995. "Returns from Investing in Equity Mutual Funds, 1971 to 1991." *Journal of Finance* 50(2): 549–72.

Malkiel, Burton G., and Atanu Saha. 2005. "Hedge Funds: Risk and Return." *Financial Analysts Journal* 61(6): 80–88.

Marsh, Terry A., and Robert C. Merton. 1986. "Dividend Variability and Variance Bounds Tests for the Rationality of Stock Market Prices." *American Economic Review* 76(3): 483–98.

Minsky, Hyman P. 1982. *Can "It" Happen Again? Essays on Instability and Finance.* Armonk, N.Y.: M. E. Sharpe.

———. 2008. *Stabilizing an Unstable Economy.* New York: McGraw-Hill.

Osborne, M. F. M. 1977. *The Stock Market and Finance from a Physicist's Viewpoint.* Washington, D.C.: Self-published by author.

Patell, James, and Mark Wolfson. 1984. "The Intraday Speed of Adjustment of Stock Prices to Earnings and Divident Announcements." *Journal of Financial Economics* 13(2): 223–52.

Pearson, Karl. 1905. "The Problem of the Random Walk." *Nature* 72(294): 294–94.

Poterba, James M., and Lawrence H. Summers. 1988. "Mean Reversion in Stock Prices." *Journal of Financial Economics* 22(1): 27–59.

Reinganum, Marc R. 1983. "The Anomalous Stock Market Behavior of Small Firms in January: Empirical Tests for Tax-Loss Selling Effects." *Journal of Financial Economics* 12(June): 89–104.

Rendleman, Richard J., Charles Jones, and Henry Latané. 1982. "Empirical Anomalies Based on Unexpected Earnings and the Importance of Risk Adjustments." *Journal of Financial Economics* 10(3): 269–87.

Roberts, Harry V. 1959. "Stock Market 'Patterns' and Financial Analysis: Methodological Suggestions." *Journal of Finance* 14(1): 1–10.

Roll, Richard. 1992. "Volatility in U.S. and Japanese Stock Markets: A Symposium." *Journal of Applied Corporate Finance* 5(1): 25–29.

Samuelson, Paul. 1965. "Proof That Properly Anticipated Prices Fluctuate Randomly." *Industrial Management Review* 6(2): 41–49.

Schwert, G. William. 2003. "Anomalies and Market Efficiency." In *Handbook of the Economics of Finance*, edited by George M. Constantinides, Milton Harris, and René M. Stulz. Amsterdam: North Holland.

Shiller, Robert. 1981. "Do Stock Prices Move Too Much to Be Justified by Subsequent Changes in Dividends?" *American Economic Review* 71(June): 421–36.

———. 1984. Comment in *Brookings Papers on Economic Activity*: 459.

———. 2000. *Irrational Exuberance*. Princeton, N.J.: Princeton University Press.

Shleifer, Andrei, Josef Lakonisok, and Robert Vishny. 1992. "The Structure and Performance of the Money Management Industry." *Brookings Papers on Economic Activity: Microeconomics* 1992: 339–91.

Solnik, Bruno H. 1973. "Note on the Validity of the Random Walk for European Stock Prices." *Journal of Finance* 28(5): 1151–59.

Standard & Poor's. Various years. Proprietary data. New York: Standard & Poor's.

Statman, Meir. 2010. *What Investors Really Want*. New York: McGraw-Hill.

Swensen, David F. 2005. *Unconventional Success: A Fundamental Approach to Personal Investment*. New York: Free Press.

———. 2009. *Pioneering Portfolio Management*. New York: Free Press.

Vanguard Group of Investment Companies. Various years. Proprietary data. Malvern, Penn.: Vanguard Group.

Working, Holbrook. 1960. "Note on the Correlation of First Differences of Averages in a Random Chain." *Econometrica* 28(4): 916–18.

Chapter 5

Behavioral Finance in the Financial Crisis: Market Efficiency, Minsky, and Keynes

Hersh Shefrin and Meir Statman

We explore lessons from behavioral finance about the origins of the financial crisis of 2007 to 2009 and the likelihood of averting the next one. We argue that the crisis highlights the need to incorporate behavioral finance into our economic and financial theories. Psychology, including aspirations, cognition, emotions, and culture, is at the center of behavioral finance. We discuss this psychology and its reflection in our behavior and the institutions that bring us together, including corporations, governments, and markets. Our discussion encompasses Keynes's view that psychology drives economic booms and busts as well as Minsky's view that crises are inevitable in capitalistic systems. It also encompasses efficient markets and free markets, bubbles, links between financial markets and the real economy, debt financing and innovation, tugs of war over government regulations and rules of fairness, and a culture where homeownership is prized beyond its economic benefits.

The financial crisis that peaked in 2008 is still roiling us in the Great Recession, in which the economy is barely growing and the unemployment rate is frighteningly high. What inflicted this crisis? And what, if anything, can we do to prevent the next one? We argue that behavioral finance offers some answers to these questions. The answers are rooted in the psychology underlying the sometimes baffling uncertainty in which we live, including our aspirations, cognition, emotions, culture, and perceptions of fairness. We discuss this psychology and its reflection in the institutions that bring us together, including corporations, markets, and governments. Our discussion encompasses Keynes's view that psychology drives economic booms and busts as well as Minsky's view that crises are inevitable in capitalistic systems. It also encompasses efficient markets and free markets, bubbles, links between financial markets and the real economy, debt financing and innovation, tugs of war over government regulations and rules of fairness, and a culture where homeownership is prized beyond its economic benefits.

John Maynard Keynes (1936/1967) highlighted the role of psychology in economics long before the study of behavioral economics and finance was developed. Arguing that sentiment, reflecting unrealistic optimism or pessimism, leads to booms and busts, he noted that securities' prices often diverge substantially from their intrinsic values over an extended period, and he explored the implications of such divergence for employment, income, and money. Keynes's framework is as relevant to our financial crisis and Great Recession as it was to the Great Depression he was studying.

Hyman Minsky (1986/2008) argued that economists, misreading Keynes, downplay the role of financial institutions. In particular, he argued that financial innovation can create economic euphoria for a while before destabilizing the economy and hurling it into crises rivaling the Great Depression. Minsky's insights are evident in the effects of innovations in mortgages and mortgage securities. His recommendation that the Federal Reserve Board elevate regulation of the financial sector to the same status as monetary policy has effectively been adopted by the Fed (see Chapter 1, this volume).

Houses have been at the heart of our current crisis, and their psychological appeal extended beyond their utilitarian benefits. Their aspirations propelled many homeowners into houses they could not afford. Moreover, those aspirations evoked certain emotions and cognitive errors, blinding homeowners to the risk involved. A mortgage banker has written that home buyers during this period were willing to sign anything placed in front of them. "After witnessing literally thousands of signings," he writes, "I will tell you that most people are so focused on getting into their new home that they have no idea what it was they just signed" (Statman 2009).

Aspirations for wealth and status blinded bankers to the risks they were taking when issuing or holding mortgages and mortgage securities. Bethany McLean and Joe Nocera (2010, 163) write that Stan O'Neal, Merrill Lynch's CEO from 2002 to 2007, in his aspiration to surpass Goldman Sachs, was constantly prodding his people to take on more risk: "You didn't want to be in Stan's office on the day Goldman reported earnings," said one of his lieutenants. Hersh Shefrin (2009, 2010) has described some of the biases that affected managers of companies associated with mortgage securities as they sped along the road that ended in the financial crisis. Overconfident Merrill Lynch executives sidelined their company's most experienced risk managers and proceeded to boost their company's exposure to subprime mortgages. Investment bankers at UBS were beset by confirmation errors as they searched for evidence that would confirm their rosy assessments of the subprime markets and ignored disconfirming evidence gathered by their own analysts. Analysts at the financial products division of AIG were misled by categorizing errors: they effectively relegated to a single category the credit default swaps they were selling and ignored differences in the subprime composition of mortgage pools. And executives at Standard & Poor's, aspiring to enhance their wealth and position, chose to lower their standards for rating mortgage securities rather than lose business to competitors.

A culture of homeownership, encouraged by government, deepened the crisis and extended it. President Bill Clinton declared in 1994: "More Americans should own their own homes, for reasons that are economic and tangible, and reasons that are emotional and intangible, but go to the heart of what it means to harbor, to nourish, to expand the American Dream" (Morgenson and Rosner 2011, 1). A culture that accepts, even applauds, mortgage debt contributed to the crisis as well. Louis, a fifty-seven-year-old man, said that a mortgage is "huge, it's a big credit, because if you had to save money to buy a house, 90 percent of people would never do it. . . . It feels like someone gave you credit so that you can live in a house" (Peñaloza and Barnhart 2011, 749).

Corporations were eager to cater to the culture of homeownership, financed by mortgages. Countrywide Financial was the largest mortgage lender in the country before it nearly collapsed into bankruptcy in 2008 and was acquired by Bank of America. In 2003, Angelo Mozilo, its chief executive, said: "Expanding the American dream of homeownership must continue to be our mission, not solely for the purpose of benefitting corporate America, but more importantly, to make our country a better place" (Morgenson and Rosner 2011, 181).

Corporations regularly engage in a tug-of-war with other corporations, consumers, and governments, whether over penalty fees for late payments of credit card bills, regulation of derivatives, or pollution of air and water. Corporations, including banks and other financial institutions, often capture regulators, turning public servants into corporate servants. "Our goal is to allow thrifts to operate with a wide breadth of freedom from regulatory intrusion," said James E. Gilleran in 2004, while serving as the director of the Office of Thrift Supervision (OTS). John M. Reich, who directed the office in 2007, canceled a scheduled lunch to have lunch instead with Kerry K. Killinger, the chief executive of Washington Mutual. "He's my largest constituent," Mr. Reich wrote (Appelbaum 2010).

Tugs-of-war are fought in a world where people subscribe to different ideologies and notions of fairness, as we observe in the debate over the "Occupy Wall Street" movement. Eugene Robinson (2011), a *Washington Post* columnist, empathizes with the movement: "Three decades of trickle-down economic theory, see-no-evil deregulation and tax-cutting fervor have led to massive redistribution. Another word for what's been happening might be theft." But Jeff Jacoby (2011), a *Boston Globe* columnist, bristles at Robinson's condemnation of "income growth among the highest-earning Americans as theft." Jacoby writes: "Economic envy may cloak itself in rhetoric about 'inequality' or 'egalitarianism' or 'redistribution of wealth,' but its oldest name is *covetousness.* That is the sin enjoined by the last of the Ten Commandments: 'Thou shalt not covet thy neighbor's house; thou shalt not covet thy neighbor's wife, or his manservant, or his maidservant, or his ox, or his ass, or anything that is thy neighbor's.'"

Moreover, tugs-of-war are fought in fields fogged not only by uncertainty about the future but also by uncertainty about the present and the effects of present actions on future outcomes. In 2004 Alan Greenspan dismissed the possibility that we were in a housing bubble, declaring that "a national severe price distortion" would be "most unlikely." Ben Bernanke said in 2005 that home-price increases "largely reflect strong economic fundamentals" (Andrews 2008). Four years later, testifying before Congress in 2008, Greenspan said: "Those of us who have looked to the self-interest of lending institutions to protect shareholders' equity, myself included, are in a state of shocked disbelief" (Andrews 2008). And in a recent speech, Bernanke (2010) placed blame for the housing bubble on financial innovation of the kind that alarmed Hyman Minsky: "The availability of these alternative mortgage products . . . is likely a key explanation of the housing bubble."

FIGURE 5.1 / Historical Series for Housing Prices, Population, Building Costs, and Interest Rates, 1890 to 2011

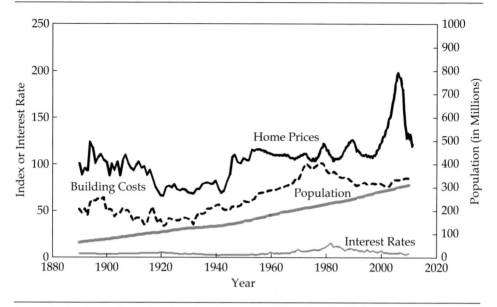

Source: Authors' compilation based on data from Shiller (2012).

The interaction between the components we noted amplified them into our crisis. Aspirations for homeownership and a culture fostering homeownership interacted with mortgage securities innovated by banks, insured by credit default swaps, and rated erroneously by rating agencies. Power in the regulatory tug-of-war shifted to banks, which used it to increase their financial leverage. The unrealistic optimism that Keynes associated with booms was paramount, as were the market dynamics emphasized by Minsky.

U.S. home prices increased from 1997 to 2006 by approximately 85 percent, adjusted for inflation, fostering the largest national housing boom in the nation's history. The cost of owning houses relative to renting them increased dramatically from 2003 to 2006, suggesting the existence of a bubble (home prices greatly exceeding their intrinsic values over an extended period). Home prices have subsequently fallen by more than 30 percent (see figure 5.1).

Bubbles pose a challenge to the efficient-market hypothesis. This hypothesis is on trial now, accused of facilitating the crisis by misleading its adherents into docility. "How did economists get it so wrong?" asked Paul Krugman (2009). Some of the blame, he asserts, belongs to the belief that markets are efficient. "In short, the belief in efficient financial markets blinded many, if not most, economists to the emergence of the biggest financial bubble in history. And efficient-market theory also played a significant role in inflating that bubble in the first place."

Our chapter consists of three parts. The first part is devoted to market efficiency and its behavioral aspects. In the second part, we discuss the insights into the crisis and human behavior that can be found in the work of Keynes and Minsky. The third part describes additional behavioral issues associated with the crisis, with a focus on financial innovation, aspirations, and tugs-of-war.

EFFICIENT MARKETS, RATIONAL MARKETS, AND BUBBLES

There are two main definitions of efficient markets, one ambitious and the other modest. The ambitious definition is better called "rational markets," which are markets where the "the price is always right." Specifically, these are markets where securities' prices always equal their intrinsic values. The modest definition of efficient markets is "unbeatable markets," which are markets where investors are unable to generate consistent excess returns (Statman 2011a).

Rational markets are unbeatable because excess returns come from exploiting gaps between prices and intrinsic values, gaps absent in rational markets. But unbeatable markets are not necessarily rational. It might be that prices deviate from intrinsic values but such deviations are hard to identify in time or difficult to exploit for generating consistent excess returns.

All citizens care about whether markets are rational since the rational allocation of capital enhances overall economic welfare. But investors, especially traders, also care about whether markets are unbeatable, since beatable markets provide opportunities to generate excess returns whereas unbeatable markets do not.

Krugman's (2009) definition of efficient markets corresponds to rational markets. He describes the efficient-market hypothesis as the claim that "financial markets price assets precisely at their intrinsic worth given all publicly available information." Krugman goes on to fault financial economists for rarely attempting to discern whether indeed "markets always get asset prices right" by investigating "whether asset prices make sense given real world fundamentals like earnings."

Bubbles cannot exist in rational markets because bubbles imply substantial deviations of prices from intrinsic values during extended periods. A positive bubble in a security exists when its price is higher than its intrinsic value, whereas a negative bubble exists when its price is lower than its intrinsic value. Bubbles can persist in unbeatable markets if investors are unable to exploit them for excess returns because, for example, digging for information about intrinsic values is difficult, trading on such information is costly, and the risk embedded in necessarily imprecise estimations of intrinsic values can bring losses. Investors who know their estimates of intrinsic values are imprecise are deterred from investing much in attempts to exploit bubbles because they risk losses if their estimates are wrong. Moreover, investors risk losses even if they are right to conclude that a bubble exists. Gaps between prices and intrinsic values can widen for months, even years, before they narrow. Investors might not have sufficient funds or fortitude to sustain their investments during extended periods when their estimates of intrinsic values are right yet prices continue to be wrong. Witness the debacle of Long-Term Capital Management.

No single investor has all the information necessary for accurate estimates of the intrinsic values of securities. The genius of the market, presumed by the rational-market hypothesis, is in its ability to aggregate our individual bits of information into securities' prices such that, in the end, prices of securities provide accurate estimates of intrinsic values. But are markets rational?

Markets aggregate information as investors exploit information for excess returns. We can think of a series of intrinsic values of a security over time as a series of mosaics. Investors gather information that uncovers portions of the mosaics, infer that the overall mosaic shows intrinsic values higher or lower than prices, and then buy or sell securities so as to gain excess returns. Although each investor might uncover only one portion of one of the series of mosaics, and perhaps a blurred one, the collective trading action of all investors on prices serves to uncover the full series of mosaics with a clarity corresponding to the aggregate information in the hands of all investors today.

Some evidence indicates that markets are indeed good at aggregating information. Gur Huberman and William Schwert (1985) examined whether announcements of the Israeli consumer price index (CPI) contain information that is not already aggregated in index-linked bond prices. Each of us is likely to see today some portions of the mosaic that make up the CPI number that will be announced by the Central Bureau of Statistics next week or next month—perhaps the price of milk or the price of automobiles. Each of us can form an imperfect inference from his or her bit of information as to whether the CPI number to be announced will be relatively high or low. And each of us can trade on that information, selling bonds if we conclude that inflation is high or buying them if we conclude that inflation is low. If the bond market aggregates our individual bits of information perfectly, we should find that the prices of bonds do not change at all when the CPI number is announced, because the market has already aggregated our bits of information about inflation and incorporated them into bond prices. Huberman and Schwert found that bond prices change little when the Central Bureau of Statistics announces the CPI numbers, consistent with the hypothesis that the market is indeed good at aggregating information. Similarly, Mark Weinstein (1977) finds that announcements of changes in bond ratings by rating agencies exert little effect on bond prices, implying that the bond market is good at aggregating information. Yet Ilia Dichev and Joseph Piotroski (2001) find that stock prices fail to aggregate information fully before changes in bond ratings are announced. Stocks of companies whose bond ratings were increased by rating companies had higher subsequent returns than stocks of companies whose bond ratings were decreased.

Gary Gorton (2008, 3) argues that the market for subprime mortgage securities before 2006 was opaque and far from able to ensure that securities' prices equaled their intrinsic values by aggregating information:

> The subprime residential mortgage securities (RMBS) bonds resulting from the securitization often populated the underlying portfolios of collateralized debt obligations (CDOs), which in turn were often designed for managed, amortizing portfolios of asset-backed securities (ABS), RMBS, and commercial

mortgage securities (CMBS). CDO tranches were then often sold to . . . off-balance sheet vehicles or their risk was swapped in negative basis trades. Moreover, additional subprime securitization risk was created . . . synthetically via credit default swaps as inputs into (hybrid or synthetic) CDOs. This nesting or interlinking of securities, structures, and derivatives resulted in a loss of information and ultimately in a loss of confidence since, as a practical matter, looking through to the underlying mortgages and modeling the different levels of structure was not possible.

Information aggregation was significantly enhanced by the introduction in 2006 of the ABX indices of subprime risk, traded over the counter. "For the first time," Gorton writes, "information about subprime values and risks was aggregated and revealed. While the location of the risks was unknown, market participants could, for the first time, express views about the value of subprime bonds, by buying or selling protection."

We hear the impediments to rational markets that aggregate information correctly in the voice of John Paulson, whose hedge fund, Paulson and Company, gained $15 billion in a bet against subprime mortgage securities. Speaking to the Financial Crisis Inquiry Commission (FCIC), Paulson described the bits of information he had. First was the bit of information, gleaned from his personal experience during years of living in New York, that real estate prices do not always go up. Instead, they often bubble up, only to deflate later. "New York periodically goes through a real estate crisis," he said, as it did in the 1970s, early 1980s, and early 1990s. "I didn't subscribe to the school that real estate only goes up."

Paulson found additional bits of information when he researched the subprime market and was astounded by the low standards set for borrowers. He compared these low standards to the high standards he had to satisfy when he bought his own home. "When I purchased my home, it was very strict underwriting standards. I had to provide two pay stubs, two years' tax returns, three months of bank statements, all sorts of credit card information. All of a sudden I saw these lowest-quality mortgages with basically no underwriting standards at all." Paulson added: "When you get to a private guy who doesn't care, he may just fill it in, state an income, appraisal and say 'Yes we checked' when they didn't. That's when you got the really bad-quality stuff" (Ahmed 2011).

Paulson inferred from his bits of information that subprime mortgages were overpriced. But the mosaic he saw was of securities as they would be priced years later. He did not see clearly the mosaics as they would be priced in the following days and months. Indeed, his bets brought him losses during those early days and months. He told the commission that professionals and peers thought that he was a misguided "novice" who was likely to lose his bet against subprime mortgage securities. "Most of them, when we did express our viewpoints, thought we were inexperienced novices in the mortgage market. We were very, very much in the minority. If I said a thousand-to-one, we were the one. Even friends of ours thought we were so wrong, they felt sorry for us" (Ahmed 2011).

The cost of digging for information impedes the uncovering of information and its aggregation. Indeed, we know from Sanford Grossman and Joseph Stiglitz (1980) that we cannot expect securities' prices to equal intrinsic values because markets where prices always equal intrinsic values provide no compensation to investors who dig for information and aggregate it, as Paulson did when he dug into subprime mortgage securities. The aggregation of information is also hampered by limits to arbitrage. Paulson inferred that subprime mortgage securities were overpriced, but he could not have been entirely sure that his inference was correct. He surely could not have been certain that securities' prices would fully reflect his inference soon, before he ran out of funds or fortitude. This uncertainty limits the amounts that investors such as Paulson are willing to bet on their bits of information. In turn, smaller bets retard and diminish the aggregation of information into prices. Moreover, some markets lack structures or securities that allow investors to bet against the securities they consider overpriced. Indeed, Paulson wanted to bet against subprime mortgage securities earlier than he did, but was delayed by the absence of structures and securities that would allow such bets. Last, some investors who infer that current prices exceed intrinsic values might choose to ride the bubble by buying overpriced securities rather than selling them; in the expectation that the bubble will inflate further, they are hoping to sell later on before the bubble deflates. Such investors move prices further away from intrinsic values rather than closer to them.

COGNITIVE ERRORS AND BUBBLES

So far in our discussion of rational prices and bubbles, we have assumed that investors are not hampered by cognitive errors or misleading emotions, but only by a failure of securities' prices to properly aggregate the bits of information available to each investor into complete mosaics reflecting the intrinsic values of securities. In Shefrin and Statman (1994), we have developed an asset-pricing model in which investors are hampered by such errors and emotions. For example, some investors might be excessively optimistic, some might be excessively pessimistic, and others might be "smart-money" investors who are free of cognitive errors and misleading emotions.

In the model, the equilibrium price of a security is a wealth-weighted average of all investors' subjective valuations of the intrinsic value of that security. Prices are rational, equaling intrinsic values, when all investors are smart-money investors. Prices can be rational even when all investors commit cognitive errors. This is the case where the cognitive errors of some completely cancel the cognitive errors of others.

Complete cancellation occurs when the wealth-weighted average error of investors is zero, a condition involving the sum of two distinct terms. First is the average error across all investors. Investor errors are nonsystematic if the average error is zero. The second term relates to nonconcentrated errors among investors. Errors are nonconcentrated when the covariance between investors' wealth and their errors is zero.

Patient smart-money investors drive prices to their rational levels in the long run, even in the presence of investors who commit cognitive errors, because, over time, wealth shifts from investors who are misled by cognitive errors to smart-money investors who are free of errors. This drives the wealth-weighted sum of investor errors toward zero. Yet prices are not necessarily rational in the short run, even in the presence of smart-money investors, because smart-money investors might lack sufficient wealth to offset the impact on prices of investors whose errors are not self-canceling. Smart-money investors are smart enough not to take on excessive risk in attempts to exploit gaps between prices and intrinsic values. Their caution serves to limit arbitrage by limiting the extent to which their trades drive prices to equal intrinsic values (see Shleifer and Vishny 1997).

Rational prices exist when investor errors are not systematic or not concentrated. Yet there is much evidence that errors tend to be systematic. For example, investors are commonly misled by availability bias: overweighting bits of information readily available to memory, while underweighting equally important bits of information not readily available to memory. To understand the role of concentration in the formation of nonrational prices, consider the evolution of a bubble.

Imagine a stock market with optimistic investors and pessimistic ones. Assume that errors at the outset are neither systematic nor concentrated, such that stock prices are rational at the outset, equal to their intrinsic values. Now imagine a long run of good news, accompanied by increases in stock prices. Optimistic investors find that their bets have paid off handsomely, while pessimistic investors find that their bets have not. As a result, wealth shifts to optimists.

If optimistic investors remain optimistic, then the shift in their relative wealth leads optimism to be concentrated among the wealthier investors. This concentration tends to inflate the prices of securities above their intrinsic values, creating bubbles. Optimists might even ride these bubbles with leveraged positions. Moreover, if bubbles last long enough, some pessimists might become persuaded that they were wrong to be pessimists and turn into optimists, probably exacerbating the bubbles in the process. Some pessimists remain true to their pessimistic beliefs, and these beliefs are indeed directionally correct. They can engage in arbitrage, making bets large enough to eliminate bubbles by pushing prices down to their rational levels. But pessimists are not likely to make large bets because large bets are very risky. This limits arbitrage and leaves bubbles inflated.

The crisis highlights the roles of optimism and pessimism. Excessive optimism leads investors to expect unwarranted increases not only in the prices of stocks and other assets, such as houses, but also in future short-term (real) interest rates. This expectation creates a steep, positively sloped yield curve in the present that provides impetus for borrowing short-term and lending long-term. Indeed, this is what financial institutions do. A bubble can make the yield curve even steeper. Yet expectations of future short-term interest rates decline as excessive optimism wanes, and prices of long-term bonds rise as long-term bonds are discounted by expectations of future short-term rates. Consequently, financial institutions earn low returns on their subsequent investments. In contrast, the expected rise in short-term rates is warranted when prices are rational, in which case the prices of long-term bonds fall over time rather than rise (see Xiong and Yan 2010).

DID OUR BELIEF THAT MARKETS ARE EFFICIENT CAUSE THE CRISIS?

Behavioral finance is perceived by some as a repudiation of the efficient-market hypothesis. And the crisis seems to provide one more piece of evidence, if one were needed, that markets are indeed not efficient. Yet discussions about market efficiency are muddled because the definition of efficient markets as rational markets is confused with their definition as unbeatable markets.

We have known that, by logic, markets cannot be efficient in the sense of rational markets since at least 1980, when Grossman and Stiglitz (1980) published their article "On the Impossibility of Informationally Efficient Markets." This is because markets in which securities' prices always equal their intrinsic values provide no compensation for the cost of digging for information that might uncover deviations of prices from intrinsic values. Moreover, there is much empirical evidence that prices regularly deviate from intrinsic values. The story of John Paulson, who dug for information about mortgage securities, is one of many examples. Paulson had incentives to uncover deviations of prices from intrinsic values and profited by exploiting them. Indeed, there is evidence that, on average, professional investors, such as hedge fund and mutual fund managers, are able to generate consistent excess returns, which compensate them for the cost of uncovering information. Yet the bulk of evidence also shows that the clients of money managers, both individual and institutional, do not share in these excess returns. This indicates that, from the perspective of clients, markets are efficient in the sense of being unbeatable.

As Statman (2011a) has noted, it is difficult to lay blame for the crisis on a belief that markets are efficient, whether rational or merely unbeatable, when more than four out of every five mutual fund dollars are in active mutual funds whose managers refuse to believe that markets are efficient, whether rational or unbeatable. And mutual fund managers are just one group among many who reject such beliefs, including hedge fund managers, security analysts, and individual investors who try to glean market-beating information from magazines and television programs. It is even more difficult to lay blame for the crisis on a belief that markets are efficient, knowing that crises occurred regularly centuries ago, long before the 1960s, when the efficient-market hypothesis was formed.

Indeed, the puzzle of beliefs in market efficiency is not that people believe that markets are efficient, whether rational or unbeatable, but that they think that markets are easily beatable. One category of attempts to beat the market takes the form of market timing or tactical asset allocation. This category is especially relevant in the context of the crisis since, in essence, it involves attempts to identify bubbles and exploit them. Price-to-earnings (P/E) ratios and dividend yields are prominent among the possible indicators of bubbles. For example, a high P/E ratio of a stock index, such as the S&P 500 index, might indicate the presence of a bubble in a market that is not rational, one in which stock prices exceed their intrinsic values. Investors who know bubbles in real time might use that knowledge to beat the market by selling stocks now or later, when bubbles are fully inflated.

Markets that are not rational are not necessarily easily beatable. High P/E ratios and low dividend yields might indicate the presence of bubbles, but not everyone agrees that investors can use P/E ratios and dividend yields to beat the market. John Campbell and Robert Shiller (1998) have found that relatively high P/E ratios and relatively low dividend yields predict relatively low subsequent long-run returns. This implies that markets are not rational and opens the door to beating the market.

The P/E ratio developed by Campbell and Shiller reached its peak of 44.2 in December 1999, and the P/E ratios of many large technology companies exceeded 100. Jeremy Siegel (2001, A20) wrote at the time: "These lofty valuations could not be justified even if these firms achieved analysts' very optimistic long-term earnings growth estimates (which ranged from 20 percent to over 55 percent annually) for periods of as long as 10 years" (see also Siegel 2000).

Yet Shefrin (2000) pointed out that large deviations of prices from intrinsic values actually reduce the ability of P/E ratios to predict future returns. In particular, the Campbell-Shiller P/E ratio stood at 27.7 in December 1996, the highest it had been since the stock market bubble and crash of 1929, when the P/E ratio reached 32.6. At the time, Campbell and Shiller predicted that in ten years, through December 2006, the real value of the market would be 40 percent lower than it was in December 1996. Shefrin (2000, 313) wrote that, "from a statistical perspective, the confidence associated with the 1996 Campbell-Shiller prediction for the 1997–2006 period is very low." We know now that real stock prices did not fall by 40 percent between December 1996 and December 2006. Instead, they rose by 49.7 percent. Moreover, several studies indicate that the relation between P/E ratios and dividend yields and subsequent returns is not tight, and that P/E ratios and dividend yields are not reliable predictors of subsequent returns (see Malkiel 2003; Fisher and Statman 2000, 2006; Goyal and Welch 2003).

Kenneth Fisher and Meir Statman (2000) have argued that cognitive errors explain why many investors believe that market timing is easy, when the evidence indicates that it is difficult. We note two of these errors here—hindsight error and confirmation error. Hindsight errors persuade us that it was clear in 2007, in foresight, that returns in 2008 would be disastrous. But the evidence indicates that few saw in 2007 foresight what we see today in hindsight. We see today that the S&P 500 index fell from 1,468 at the end of 2007 to 891 at the end of 2008, but this is not what prominent Wall Street strategists saw in foresight. *Business Week* conducted a survey among strategists at the end of 2007, asking them to forecast the level of the S&P 500 index at the end of 2008. Estimates ranged from 1,780 at the high end to 1,350 at the low end, still exceedingly higher than the actual 891 (*Business Week* 2007). Two other surveys conducted in December 2007 and January 2008— the National Association for Business Economics (NABE) "Outlook" survey and the Blue Chip Economic Indicators survey—show GDP growth forecasts much higher than actual growth and unemployment rate forecasts much lower than actual unemployment.

Confirmation errors lead some to focus on economists who were correct in forecasting the coming crisis, confirming the belief that forecasting the crisis was easy, but neglect many more economists—including those surveyed by *Business Week*, NABE, and Blue Chip—who were incorrect.

Shefrin (2000, 2008) points out that, in general, Wall Street strategists are poor forecasters, and their 2007 forecasts for 2008 are no exception. Using panel data for individual forecasters, he finds that the simple rule of the forecast of the next year's return equaling its historical mean outperforms the forecasts of every Wall Street strategist, as well as the average of all the forecasts. Yet few strategists would keep their jobs if they were to adopt a simple—even if superior—forecasting rule. Hindsight bias and confirmation errors are persistent, leading Wall Street strategists and their clients alike to believe that markets are beatable once expertise is applied.

Burton Malkiel (this volume) recognizes the distinction between rational markets and unbeatable markets. He notes that the occurrence of bubbles from time to time—prices deviating from intrinsic values—implies that markets are not always rational. Yet he argues that the crisis provides no evidence to counter the claim that markets are unbeatable. We agree. Because of limits to arbitrage, opportunities to beat the market by earning abnormally high risk-adjusted returns are typically small, even when markets are not rational. Yet the debate about the role in the crisis of the belief in efficient markets has little to do with whether markets are unbeatable and much to do with whether they are rational. Recall that Krugman's (2009) definition of efficient markets corresponds to rational markets in his description of the efficient-market hypothesis: "Financial markets price assets precisely at their intrinsic worth given all publicly available information." Moreover, Krugman blames the crisis on the belief that free markets are always better than regulated markets even more than he blames it on the belief that markets are rational.

EFFICIENT MARKETS AND FREE MARKETS

"Free markets," in their extreme form, are those in which government puts no imprint on economic activities. In their moderate form, government puts little imprint on them. Free markets are often conflated with "efficient markets" in their form as "rational markets."

Whereas Milton Friedman is most closely associated with free market advocacy, Merton Miller was foremost in advocating free financial markets. He titled a 1994 keynote address "Regulating Derivatives: Enough Already!" and wrote: "But despite what I and most other economists, at least of the Chicago variety, see as the social benefits of theses financial derivates, they have, let us face it, also been getting a very bad press recently" (Miller 1997, 67). Miller went on to "emphasize that no serious danger of a derivatives-induced financial collapse really exists," and that financial market disasters tend to be policy disasters committed by government entities, such as the Federal Reserve Bank, rather than by free financial markets. "A classic example," he wrote, "has been the turmoil in the U.S. bond market since the spring of 1994 after our Federal Reserve Bank suddenly nudged up short-term interest rates" (68).

Free markets can easily be conflated with the rational markets version of efficient markets because proponents of one are often also proponents of the other. But the two are distinct. Consider a rational market that is also free of government regulation of the pollution emitted by power plants owned by utilities. Now imagine that the government enacts regulations limiting pollution, imposing fresh costs on utilities, and reducing the intrinsic value of their shares. The market can remain rational if share prices drop instantaneously to equal the new intrinsic value, but the market is no longer as free as it has been.

A central bank takes interest in financial markets in major part because markets serve as allocators of capital. Capital is allocated productively in rational markets since prices that equal intrinsic values send correct signals as to where capital should be allocated. But capital is misallocated in bubbles, when prices deviate from intrinsic values. Free markets are best if they result in rational markets, but central bank intervention, such as popping bubbles, might be called for in markets that are not rational. A Federal Reserve Bank that identifies bubbles is likely to pop both real bubbles, doing much good, and illusory bubbles, doing much harm. A belief that bubbles cannot exist is dangerous, but so is a belief that bubbles are easy to identify. This was the quandary that Alan Greenspan posed in December 1996. Prompted by Campbell and Shiller's (1998) P/E ratios analysis, Greenspan asked how "we know when irrational exuberance has unduly escalated asset values, which then become subject to unexpected and prolonged contraction" (Greenspan 1996). Greenspan learned that the question does not have an easy answer: the dot-com bubble did not burst for another five years, and then did so only after the Fed raised interest rates six times from June 1999 to May 2000.

Consider next the housing bubble of 1997 to 2006, which came to an end after the Fed engaged in seventeen consecutive interest rate hikes between June 2004 and June 2006. There was no consensus that a bubble was underway before it burst. In 2005, TIAA-CREF published two competing views. The bubble view was expressed by Shiller (2005, 20), who based his opinion on figure 5.1 (up to 2004). Speaking about the historical record of home prices, he said: "The upswing looks quite anomalous by historical standards, suspiciously like a bubble. . . . The situation is unstable, and if expectations of further increases disappear, prices may fall sharply. . . . We should temper our expectations and recognize that there is substantial risk." The other series in figure 5.1 suggest that the increase in home prices was not driven by fundamentals such as construction costs, population growth, or interest rates.

In presenting the opposing view, Richard Peach (2005, 21), vice president of the Federal Reserve Bank of New York, acknowledged that bubbles might exist in some housing markets but argued that this is not true for all markets. Peach said: "While national average home prices are high, they do not appear to be overvalued relative to fundamentals." Moreover, Peach argued, increased home prices and the ratio of rental incomes to home prices were reflecting improvements in the quality of houses and lower interest rates. He added that the number of people who indicated that it was a good time to buy a home was historically low, even if rising; that the average loan-to-value ratio was low; and that delinquency rates on prime adjustable rate loans were somewhat lower than on prime fixed rate mortgages. None of these facts, he pointed out, indicated the presence of a national housing bubble.

Future home prices are mosaics, fully revealed only in the future. Shiller and Peach based their assessments on different portions of the mosaics. Shiller focused on the series of home prices, a series he created. Peach focused on other portions of the mosaics, such as house quality and loan-to-value ratios. Later in this chapter, we encounter a third view from 2005, that of John Dugan, who at the time, as head of the Office of the Comptroller of the Currency (OCC), was focused on weak lending practices in the market for subprime and Alternative-A (Alt-A) mortgages. Shiller's view ultimately prevailed, but note that his statements from 2005 were cautious. Moreover, Peach's view fell within the realm of plausibility. At the time, it was far from obvious to most that a national housing bubble existed. Moreover, there is not necessarily a direct line between a deflation of a housing bubble and the financial crisis that follows.

KEYNES, BUBBLES, AND RATIONAL PRICES

Our perspective on rational prices and bubbles corresponds to Keynes's ideas on economic expansions and downturns, bubbles, financial crises, rational pricing, and psychology. Indeed, Keynes wrote extensively about psychology and focused on concepts that are at the center of behavioral finance, such as optimism, confidence, and sentiment. Keynes applied these concepts in assessing conditions where securities' prices are not rational and in describing how bubbles develop and burst (see chapter 22, "Notes on the Trade Cycle," in Keynes 1936/1967). Writing about the psychology of financial booms and crises, Keynes (1936/1967, 315–17) noted:

> The later stages of the boom are characterized by optimistic expectations as to the future yield of capital goods . . . of speculators who are more concerned with forecasting the next shift of market sentiment than with a reasonable estimate of the future yield of capital assets, that when disillusion falls upon an over-optimistic and over-bought market, it should fall with sudden and even catastrophic force. Moreover, the dismay and uncertainty as to the future which accompanies a collapse in the marginal efficiency of capital naturally precipitates a sharp increase in liquidity preference. . . . It is not so easy to revive the marginal efficiency of capital, determined as it is by the uncontrollable and disobedient psychology of the business world. It is the return of confidence, to speak in ordinary language, which is so insusceptible to control in an economy of individualistic capitalism.

The portion of *The General Theory* most often mentioned in connection with rational prices and market efficiency is chapter 12, "The State of Long-Term Expectation."

It is here that Keynes introduced the concept of "animal spirits" and used a beauty contest analogy to describe the behavior of investors in stock markets and the impact of their behavior on stock prices.

In the beauty contest analogy, Keynes argued that the price of a stock does not necessarily equal its intrinsic value. Rather, it equals the average of investors' subjective valuations of that stock. Moreover, investors are not driven to find the intrinsic values of stocks. Instead, they are driven to buy the stocks that other investors will find "beautiful." Keynes (1936/1967, 151) wrote: "Thus certain classes of investments are governed by the average expectation of those who deal on the Stock Exchange as revealed in the price of shares." This property is reflected in our Shefrin-Statman model, in which security prices equal the wealth-weighted averages of investors' subjective valuations.

Keynes (1936/1967, 152, emphasis in original) was forceful in his view that an assumption that prices are rational is unwarranted:

> We are assuming, in effect, that the existing market valuation, however arrived at, is uniquely *correct* in relation to our existing knowledge of the facts which will influence the yield of the investment, and it will only change in proportion to changes in this knowledge; though philosophically speaking, it cannot be uniquely correct, since our existing knowledge does not provide a sufficient basis for a calculated mathematical expectation. In point of fact, all sorts of considerations enter into the market valuation, which are in no way relevant to the prospective yield.

MINSKY AND KEYNES

Minsky regularly criticized economists for failing to grasp Keynes's ideas. In his book *Stabilizing an Unstable Economy*, Minsky (1986/2008) argued that while economists assimilated some of Keynes's insights into standard economic theory, they failed to grasp the connection between the financial and real sectors. Specifically, he argued that finance is missing from macroeconomic theory, with its focus on capital structure, asset-liability management, agency theory, and contracts. He wrote: "Keynes's theory revolves around bankers and businessmen making deals on Wall Street. . . . One of the peculiarities of the neoclassical theory that preceded Keynes and the neoclassical synthesis that now predominates economic theory is that neither allows the activities that take place on Wall Street to have any significant impact upon the coordination or lack of coordination of the economy" (Minsky 1986/2008, 114, 132).

Minsky's work on financial crises builds on Keynes's insights, using terms such as "euphoric economy" (Minsky 1986/2008, 237) and "unrealistic euphoric expectations with respect to costs, markets, and their development over time" (233). Yet Minsky considered the issues of rational prices and market efficiency only the tip of an iceberg. His broad framework addresses issues related to the lending practices of financial institutions, central bank policy, fiscal policy, the efficacy of financial market regulation, employment policy, and income distribution.

Minsky (1986/2008, 349) argued that capitalism is inherently unstable:

> The history of capitalism is punctuated by deep depressions that are associated with financial panics and crashes in which financial relations are ruptured and institutions destroyed. Each big depression reformed the institutional structure, often through legislation. The history of money, banking, and financial legislation can be interpreted as a search for a structure that would eliminate instability. Experience shows that this search failed and the theory indicates that the search for a permanent solution is fruitless.

Minsky argued further that we seem destined to go through predictable cycles, including bubbles. These cycles involve a shift in weight across the three types of financing he called "hedge," "speculative," and "Ponzi." Hedge financing takes place when we can reasonably expect cash flows from capital assets and financial contracts to meet contractual payments today and in the future. Speculative financing takes place when we can reasonably expect cash flows to fall short of contractual payments in some periods, typically near-term ones. Nevertheless, if we separate cash receipts and payments into income and the return of principal—as we separate monthly mortgage payments—we find that expected income receipts meet interest payments. Thus, speculative financing involves the rolling over of maturing debt. Ponzi financing is similar to speculative financing except that it involves the equivalent of negative amortization. Thus, the face value of the outstanding debt increases. Borrowers engaged in speculative and Ponzi financing expect payment on debts to be met by refinancing, increasing debts, or liquidating other assets. Minsky (1986/2008, 233) wrote that "the mixture of hedge, speculative, and Ponzi finance in an economy is a major determinant of its stability. The existence of a large component of positions financed in a speculative or a Ponzi manner is necessary for financial instability."

Financial institutions, such as banks, become increasingly innovative in their use of financial products when the business cycle expands, boosting their leverage and funding projects with ever-increasing risk. Minsky's (1986/2008, 281) words on financial innovation are striking, as if foretelling the recent crisis: "Over an expansion, new financial instruments and new ways of financing activity develop. Typically, defects of the new ways and the new institutions are revealed when the crunch comes."

The horizons of the cash flows from the projects in speculative and Ponzi financing exceed the maturities of the associated debt. The prices of capital assets, interest rates, and default risk all rise during an economic expansion. The ensuing dynamic eventually leads to contractionary monetary policy, which induces economic downturn and financial crisis. The government responds by injecting economic stimulus and rescuing financial institutions that are too big to fail. These mitigate the magnitude of the downturn, but also set the stage for the next expansion and subsequent crisis.

Minsky illustrated some of his ideas with the 1974 run on commercial paper backed by real estate investment trusts (REITs). REITs offer a tax advantage, as investors avoid corporate income tax if REITs pay out at least 90 percent of their earnings in dividends. The REITs at the center of that run mainly financed the construction of multifamily housing, condominiums, and commercial properties. Construction projects do not generate cash flow until they are completed. Therefore, REITs that finance construction with commercial paper while paying dividends to shareholders must rely on their ability to roll over short-term debt. This implies speculative financing, possibly Ponzi financing, rather than hedge financing. Thus, REITs are exposed to risks stemming from rising short-term interest rates, as well as operating risks stemming from declines in the market value of their projects.

Interest rates rose during the recession of 1973 to 1975, construction projects were delayed, and the market for finished apartments weakened. REITs found it increasingly difficult to roll over their commercial paper, and the volume of REIT-issued commercial paper fell by 75 percent from 1973 to 1974. Commercial banks almost doubled lending to REITs in 1974, and they bore the brunt of the run on commercial paper. In effect, banks acquired real estate in exchange for the loans they extended. Consequently, banks headed into the subsequent expansion with weaker balance sheets.

FINANCIAL INNOVATIONS AND CRISES

Two kinds of housing-related financial innovations were central to the recent crisis. One relates to the originations of mortgages, and the other relates to their securitization.

Adjustable rate mortgages (ARMs) have been singled out as financial innovations that contributed to the crisis and are contrasted unfavorably with fixed rate mortgages. Yet ARMs come in many varieties: some are helpful and probably more stabilizing than fixed rate mortgages, and others are harmful and destabilizing. Plain ARMs can be very helpful, especially when coupled with substantial down payments. These typically include rates of interest that increase or decrease with a benchmark rate, such as that of one-year Treasury bills. But the initial interest rate in a plain ARM is usually lower than the corresponding rate in a fixed rate mortgage.

Statman (1982) showed that plain ARMs can serve homeowners as hedges superior to fixed rate mortgages. Consider the case where interest rates, salaries, and the value of houses move in tandem with inflation. A homeowner with an ARM might receive the bad news that inflation has pushed up interest rates and so her monthly mortgage payment will now be reset higher. Yet this increase in her mortgage payment might be hedged against corresponding increases, fueled by inflation, in her salary and the value of her house. Indeed, she might even choose not to increase her monthly payment, dipping into the equity of her home. Yet such a dip does not constitute negative amortization as long as the value of her home equity increases by more than her dips reduce it. Moreover, ARMs include, in effect, automatic refinancing as interest rates increase or decrease, obviating the need to refinance and saving its cost. ARMs do not prevent the loss of the home of a homeowner who encounters a calamity such as extended unemployment or crushing medical expenses, but fixed rate mortgages do no better at preventing such a loss.

The ARMs innovated in the years leading up to the crisis, however, were far from plain. Hybrid ARMs, such as 2/1 ARMs, offered an artificially low "teaser rate" for the first two years, then reset it to a substantially higher rate, which was reset further once a year thereafter. Similarly, 5/1 ARMs locked in an initial rate for five years before being reset once a year thereafter. Borrowers (and lenders) were regularly lulled into a belief that they did not need to worry about the reset rates because they would be able to refinance their original mortgages at lower rates before rates on these mortgages were reset. This belief made buying a small home possible for people who would have otherwise been disqualified from buying any home, and it made buying a large home possible for those who would have otherwise been qualified to buy only a small home.

Alternative-A loans fell in between prime and subprime loans. Financial innovations in Alt-A loans included variable monthly payments, such as interest only and payment option ARMs. Payment option ARMs allowed borrowers to choose their payment each month, subject to a prespecified minimum. Indeed, borrowers could choose, within limits, low payments that entailed negative amortization. These loans, however, converted to fixed rate loans once the limits were reached—that is, once the loan's principal became too large or the equity in the home too small.

Buying a home was made easier when down payments were reduced from the conventional 20 percent to 15 percent in 2004, and to 10 percent in 2005. Buying a home was made even easier when there was a surge of mortgage loans known as "no-documentation" or "limited-documentation" loans ("liar loans"): with these loans, buyers could state whatever income and assets they pleased, knowing that no one would check. The Financial Crisis Inquiry Committee (FCIC) was established as part of the Fraud Enforcement and Recovery Act to report on the causes of the financial crisis. Congress voted for the Act in May 2009, and the president signed it. The Commission issued its final report in January 2011. The FCIC report quoted Sheila Bair, FDIC chairman, on liar loans: "I absolutely would have been over at the Fed writing rules, prescribing mortgage lending standards across the board for everybody, bank and nonbank, that you cannot make a mortgage unless you have documented income that the borrower can repay the loan." The FCIC report stated: "In the end, companies in subprime and Alt-A mortgages had, in essence, placed all their chips on black: they were betting that home prices would never stop rising" (FCIC 2011, 111).

John Dugan, who headed the Office of the Comptroller of the Currency from 2005 to 2010, said in a 2005 speech: "It seems like only yesterday when a 5/1 ARM was considered a risky mortgage product. . . . Today's non-traditional mortgage products—interest-only, payment option ARMs, no doc and low-doc, and piggyback mortgages, to name the most prominent examples—are a different species of product, with novel and potentially risky features."

Dugan continued:

> We can readily understand why these new products have become fixtures in the marketplace in such a short time. One reason is that they have helped sustain loan volume that would otherwise almost certainly be falling, because rising interest rates have brought an end to the refinance boom. More important, lenders have scrambled to find ways to make expensive houses more affordable—although there's now a concern that the very availability of this new type of financing has done its share to help drive up house prices, which in turn stimulates demand for even more non-traditional financing. (Dugan 2005a)

Conventional fixed rate mortgages and plain ARMs with 20 percent down payments and the verification of buyers' incomes and assets correspond to Minsky's notion of hedge financing, where homeowners and bankers can reasonably expect cash flows from income and assets to meet mortgage payments now and in the future. ARMs with teaser rates—prominent among subprime mortgages—correspond to speculative financing, where homeowners must roll over mortgages, refinancing them before the teaser period ends and higher rates kick in.

Option ARMs that lead to negative amortization correspond to Ponzi financing: homeowners must count on appreciation in the prices of their homes for mortgage refinancing and to meet future mortgage payments. John Dugan said during a different speech:

> To the extent that they are planning for such contingencies, many payment-option-ARM borrowers calculate that they will be able to sell their property or refinance the mortgage by year six. But if real estate prices decline—and there already is evidence of softening in some markets—these borrowers could face the bleak prospect of loan balances that exceed the value of the underlying properties. In that case, selling the property or refinancing the loan would not be a viable escape valve for avoiding huge payment shocks. (Dugan 2005b)

Three innovations compounded the deficiencies of liar ARMs with teaser rates. The first was securitization—the pooling of mortgages into mortgage-backed securities. Securitization was innovated by Lewis Ranieri and his Salomon Brothers team in the late 1970s, and it became popular after the savings and loan crisis of the 1980s. The Resolution Trust Corporation (RTC), the government body that held nonperforming thrift assets, found it convenient to sell pools of assets instead of individual assets. The second innovation was collateralized debt obligations (CDOs), which divided cash flows from mortgage-backed securities into tranches prioritized by default risk. Mortgage-backed securities were quite opaque, combining many mortgages, and their tranches were even more opaque. Investors gained confidence about holding mortgage-backed securities and their tranches with the introduction of their ratings by rating agencies. Ratings were familiar to investors, whether AAA rating or BAA, and rating agencies, such as Standard & Poor's, were considered objective and reliable judges of securities quality. The third innovation was credit default swaps (CDSs), effectively an insurance policy against bond default. Actual credit default swaps were used to create synthetic credit default swaps.

Commercial banks sponsored conduits to finance long-term assets through special-purpose entities such as structured investment vehicles (SIVs). As off-balance-sheet entities, SIVs were subject to lower regulatory capital requirements. Special-purpose entities used commercial paper to raise funds that they then used to buy mortgages and mortgage securities. In effect, banks relied on Minsky-type speculative and Ponzi financing, borrowing short-term and using these borrowed funds to buy long-term assets. Whereas runs on commercial paper in 1974 centered on REITs, runs on commercial paper in 2007 and 2008 centered on the deteriorating conditions in the subprime market, which decimated the values of the assets of special-purpose entities. Indeed, the panic surrounding the 2007 run swept the entire commercial paper market, not just the portion related to subprime housing (see Covitz, Liang, and Suarez 2009).

Lewis Ranieri, the father of mortgage securitization, rejects the claim that mortgage securities are to blame for the housing crash. "Securitization is not the villain. Abuses in securitization are to blame," he wrote in a 2010 letter to the regulations divisions of the Department of Housing and Urban Development and the Department of the Treasury. "What went wrong?" asked Ranieri. "Over-leveraging at every level—beginning with the home buyer, the lender, the speculator, the Government Sponsored Enterprises, while rating agencies and Wall Street turned a blind eye. Home buyers began treating homes like ATM machines; lenders began offering products that preyed on unsophisticated borrowers; the GSEs loosened their standards and encouraged Alt-A lending and subprime lending; and Wall Street supported their activities and generated fees on the expanded products without any real liability" (Ranieri Partners Management LLC 2010). Indeed, mortgage securities, like most financial innovations, began as an attempt to do good—in this case, to help people buy houses. Yet the promise of good and the profits generated along the way by such innovations tend to blind us to drawbacks. Mortgage securities did not have to make it easy for homeowners to treat their houses like ATMs, but they did. Mortgage securities did not have to lead lenders to lower their lending standards, but they did.

Money market funds played a role in the crisis: they bought the commercial paper sold by the financial firms in order to purchase mortgages to package into mortgage securities. Money market funds were a major component of the speculative and Ponzi financing of which Minsky was so critical. Money market funds are also an interesting financial innovation and illustrate how the desire to provide benefits, including psychological benefits, can exacerbate crises.

Money market funds were innovated in the early 1970s to circumvent regulations that limited the rate of interest that banks could pay. They soon turned into substitutes for bank checking accounts. Money market fund investors received checkbooks similar to bank checkbooks and could write checks for use everywhere. But money market funds were not a close enough substitute for checking accounts because, as Statman (2011b) has noted, they lacked the "no-mental-loss" psychological benefit.

Investors who deposited a dollar in a checking account were assured that they would be able to withdraw a dollar the following day, week, or year. But money market fund investors had no such assurance. A dollar invested in a money market fund one day might be worth 98 cents the following day. Investors who contemplate buying a television set for $500 have to withdraw 510 shares of the money fund if its share price declines from $1 on the day of the purchase to 98 cents when their check is cashed. The extra ten shares register as a loss in the minds of money market fund investors.

Investing, whether in a stock or a money market fund, marks a hopeful beginning. We place a stock into a mental account, record its $100 purchase price, and hope to close it at a gain, perhaps selling the stock at $150. As stock fate has it, the stock's price may plummet to $40 during the following month rather than increase to $150.

Losses make us feel stupid. Hindsight error misleads us into thinking that what is clear in hindsight was equally clear in foresight. We bought the stock at $100 because, in foresight, it seemed destined to go to $150. But now, in hindsight, we remember all the warning signs displayed in plain sight on the day we bought our stock. Interest rates were about to increase. The CEO was about to resign. A competitor was ready to introduce a better product.

The cognitive error of hindsight is accompanied by the emotion of regret. We kick ourselves for being so stupid and contemplate how much happier we would have been if only we had kept our $100 in our savings account or invested it in another stock that zoomed as our stock plummeted. Pride is at the opposite end of the emotional spectrum from regret. Pride accompanies gains. We congratulate ourselves and feel proud for seeing in foresight that our $100 stock would soon zoom to $150. Mark-to-market accounting of money market funds opens the door to both regret and pride every time we write a check, but regret is more painful than pride is pleasurable. It is no wonder that money market fund investors prefer buck accounting over mark-to-market accounting, and money market fund executives hear their voices.

In 1977, following much lobbying by mutual fund companies, the Securities and Exchange Commission (SEC) approved the use of buck accounting such that the price of money market shares remains at $1 even when the market value of the shares deviates from it. Managers of money market funds promised not to "break the buck," and at last, money market funds seemed to have acquired the no-mental-loss benefits of checking accounts.

The promise of managers of money market funds not to break the buck was sincere but not guaranteed. The small print always said that the buck might be broken. Still, managers of money market funds kept their promise for many years, on occasion paying from their own pockets so as not to break the buck. But when the financial crisis arrived in 2008, the managers of the Reserve Fund, a large money market fund, announced that their fund contained securities of bankrupt Lehman Brothers and they had to break the buck, set its shares to 97 cents, and subsequently close the fund. The development was "really, really bad," said Don Phillips of Morningstar. "You talk about Lehman and Merrill having been stellar institutions, but breaking the buck is sacred territory." This breaking of the buck was prominent among the events that led Henry Paulson and Ben Bernanke—fearing the run on money market funds that would ensue if money market fund investors raced to withdraw their money at a dollar per share before the fund was forced to price its shares at less than a dollar—to recommend drastic measures, including government insurance of money market funds (see Statman 2011b).

The closing of the Reserve Fund is ironic because Bruce Bent, one of its founders, opposed buck accounting when it was considered in the 1970s. Bent feared that buck accounting would compel money market fund managers to buy risky securities in attempts to provide higher returns than their competitors. In a 1978 letter to the SEC, Bent wrote that buck accounting "presents the illusion of higher returns in times of declining interest rates" and makes money market funds "appear to have overcome the risk" of fluctuating interest rates. Bent noted further that buck accounting would encourage money market funds to buy risky securities that "pay higher interest rates than those which must achieve stability by exercising judgment" (Lyon 1984, 1015). Bent vowed not to buy such risky securities, but he broke his vow under the pressure of competition. This is why the Reserve Fund held Lehman securities when Lehman went bankrupt. What started as an attempt to turn money market funds into no-mental-loss investments ended with very real losses.

Today's money market fund agenda centers on mitigating the systemic risks associated with money market funds, risks made obvious in 2008. Yet a proposal to price money market fund shares by mark-to-market accounting has been met with fierce opposition. Paul Schott Stevens of the Investment Company Institute wrote that "investors prize the stability, simplicity, and convenience" of money market funds. David Hirschmann of the U.S. Chamber of Commerce wrote that investors would flee from money market funds burdened by "the complexity and cost of accounting" of mark-to-market funds. And Kenneth White, a Chicago investor, threatened to liquidate his money market funds if their prices were set by mark-to-market accounting (see letters to the editor of the *Wall Street Journal*, May 13, 2011).

In truth, there is nothing complex about mark-to-market money market funds and no cost of accounting. Mutual fund companies provide an annual accounting of the total gains and losses of each mutual fund their investors own, ready to be placed in their tax returns. But such real accounting is not mental accounting; it does not mitigate the cognitive error of hindsight and the sting of regret. Our normal psychology drives us to accept systemic risks to the entire economy and our own wealth so as to avoid the psychological sting of regret.

ASPIRATIONS

We know that we could have prevented the crisis. We not only know it in hindsight—we knew it in foresight. There would have been no foreclosures of homes financed by subprime mortgages if no subprime mortgages had been granted and there had been no failures of the banks holding them. Yet what we know in foresight is never this simple: we must also consider aspirations for houses, trade-offs in crisis prevention, and tugs-of-war powered by ideology and self-interest.

Minsky was well aware of these trade-offs—the trade-offs between too little innovation and its downside of stagnation, the trade-offs between too much innovation and its downside of disaster: "Ponzi finance is a usual way of debt-financing in a capitalist society. Consequently, capitalism without financial practices that lead to instability may be less innovative and expansionary; lessening the possibility of disaster might very well take part of the spark of creativity out of the capitalist system" (Minsky 1986/2008, 364). Keynes (1936/1967, 162) was equally aware of trade-offs: "Thus if the animal spirits are dimmed and the spontaneous optimism falters, leaving us to depend on but a mathematical expectation, enterprise will fade and die."

"Men will and do take great risks to distinguish themselves even when they know what the risks are," wrote Milton Friedman and L. J. Savage (1948). It is easy to characterize poor subprime borrowers as risk-seekers who lost their houses in the crisis because they were as eager to buy houses as lottery tickets. But aspirations for houses of their own drove subprime borrowers, and risk was merely payment for a chance to reach their aspirations. For instance, Sharon and Russ Gornie, a young couple with children in the 1990s, aspired to own a dream house; they were featured on the PBS program *Frontline* on January 14, 1997. "This is our dream house," said Sharon, pointing to blueprints of a house. "We look at it when we are off to work in the morning and when we come home tired. . . . Isn't it beautiful?" The rich, whether on Wall Street or Main Street, often join the poor in harboring aspirations for more. Some people who own two houses aspire to own three.

One implication of Daniel Kahneman and Amos Tversky's (1979) prospect theory, articulated in our behavioral portfolio theory (Shefrin and Statman 2000), is that people whose incomes fall short of their aspirations are inclined to take great risk as they strive to reach their aspirations. People whose wealth exceeds their aspirations are less inclined to take risk. Indeed, Kees Koedijk, Rachel Pownall, and Meir Statman (2011) have found that people whose aspirations exceed their incomes are more willing to take risk than people with equal incomes but lower aspirations. They also find that competitive people are more willing to take risk than people with equal incomes who are less competitive.

The current financial crisis is centered on houses and loans, both cultural emblems in the United States and beyond it. Central to the American dream, homes are the place of the middle class, and loans are an integral part of middle-class life, beyond the means they provide to home buyers. The central place of homes and loans made the crisis more severe than the bust that followed the technology boom of the late 1990s, or even the savings and loan crisis of the late 1980s, which centered on loans to real estate developers rather than loans to homeowners.

Aspirations for homes of our own drive us even if we should be guided by utilitarian benefits to rent rather than own. We are seduced by the expressive and emotional benefits of beautiful dream houses. We take pride in homeownership and feel powerful, knowing that no landlord can kick us out. We take comfort in our freedom to drill holes in walls for hooks to hold our favorite paintings.

The proportion of homeownership among whites in the United States remains greater than the proportions among minorities, and the proportions of families aspiring to houses out of their reach are greater among minorities than among whites. Still, the housing boom in the decade ending in 2005 narrowed the gaps in homeownership. The Pew Hispanic Center, a project of the Pew Research Center, found that homeownership rates rose more rapidly among minorities than among whites, yet blacks and Latinos remained far more likely than whites to depend on relatively expensive subprime loans. In 2007, 27.6 percent of home purchase loans to Hispanics and 33.5 percent of such loans to blacks were at relatively high rates, compared with just 10.5 percent among whites. Moreover, the ratios of loans to incomes were higher among blacks and Hispanics than among whites, making their homeownership more precarious (Kochhar, Gonzalez-Barrera, and Dockterman 2009).

The pull of homeownership remains strong even now, when the pain of the crisis is still searing. A 2011 *New York Times*/CBS News poll revealed that "owning a house remains central to Americans' sense of well-being, even as many doubt their home is a good investment after a punishing recession. Nearly nine in 10 Americans say homeownership is an important part of the American dream" (Streitfeld and Thee-Brenan 2011, B3).

Aspirations and the culture in which they are embedded explain the subsidies extended to American homeowners for many decades, channeled through Fannie Mae, Freddie Mac, and the Federal Housing Administration (FHA). As Shiller (2010, BU8) writes, American culture contains "a long-standing feeling that owning homes in healthy communities is connected to individual liberties that embody our national identity. Historically, homeownership has been associated with freedom, while renting—often in tenements or mill villages—has been linked to the oppression of a landlord." Shiller notes further that homeownership is not central in all cultures. Only 34.6 percent of Swiss families owned their homes in 2000, whereas 66.2 percent of American families owned their homes that year.

Most people need loans if they are to buy a house, and many had been precluded from buying a home by the conditions set by lending banks, including sizable down payments and documents testifying to an income sufficient to pay back a loan. Democrats wanted to help people reach their dreams for homes, and so did Republicans. Republican senator Phil Gramm was persuaded to support subprime lending by his mother's story. "Some people look at subprime lending and see evil. I look at subprime lending and I see the American dream in action. . . . My mother lived it as a result of a finance company making a mortgage loan that a bank would not make. . . . What incredible exploitation," he said sarcastically. "As a result of that loan, at a 50 percent premium, so far as I am aware, she was the first person in her family, from Adam and Eve, ever to own her own home" (Lipton and Labaton 2008, A1)

Cultural changes made loans and credit part of normal middle-class life, even when loans extended into consumption far beyond buying a house. Indeed, credit in the United States has become a necessity. Lisa Peñaloza and Michelle Barnhart (2011, 748) describe that cultural change as "the normalization of credit/debt." They quote Jill, a twenty-six-year-old woman who found it impossible to get a cell phone because she had no credit card. "I tried to get a new cell phone a couple of years ago, and I couldn't sign up for a new service because I didn't have a credit card. You know, it's like they don't care if you always have enough money to pay your bill. . . . If you don't have a credit card, you can't get the phone."

People learn to use credit by trial and error. Peñaloza and Barnhart quote Barry, a twenty-six-year-old man, who said: "I started getting credit cards, in college, you know, and would use them and say, oh, I will be fine, I'll make the minimum payments. Yeah, I never really followed through on that and I ended up getting pretty screwed. So, yeah. I learned the hard way." Many distinguish "good" credit from "bad" credit, and mortgages fall into the good category.

Banks and other financial institutions are quite willing to extend credit, and that willingness was facilitated in the late 1970s and early 1980s when federal laws permitted mainstream banks to offer home equity loans. Louise Story (2008) writes that some bank executives believed that homeowners would use these loans responsibly. She quoted a Merrill Lynch executive who predicted in 1988 that homeowners would not "pledge the house to buy a blouse." Yet many homeowners defied this prediction and used home equity loans to buy blouses, cars, vacations, and more. The ease of home equity loans and mortgage refinancing led many homeowners to extract all the equity in their homes (see Story 2008).

A major change in tax law in the early 1980s, under President Ronald Reagan, eliminated many tax deductions, including the deduction of interest paid on credit cards, auto loans, student loans, and other consumer credit. Yet it allowed tax deductions, with some limits, of interest paid on mortgages and equity lines of credit. Borrowing against home equity to buy a car, for example, now had a tax advantage over a car loan, and this change in tax law contributed to increases in the use of equity lines of credit and the normalization of the extraction of home equity for consumption.

We see the importance of constraints on borrowing against home equity in a natural experiment in Texas described by Chadi Abdallah and William Lastrapes (2010). A 1997 Texas constitutional amendment made it easier for homeowners to use home equity as collateral for loans. They found that Texas households, from the time before passage of the amendment until afterward, increased their retail spending relative to the change in spending by non-Texas households by 4 to 15 percent.

Greater household debt retards economic recovery. Atif Mian and Amir Sufi (2011, 1) conducted a microeconomic analysis of U.S. counties and found that U.S. economic weakness, especially weakness in employment growth, is closely related to the high levels of household debt incurred during the housing boom: "Counties where household debt grew moderately from 2002 to 2006," they write, "have seen a moderation of employment losses and a robust recovery in durable consumption and residential investment. By contrast, counties that experienced large increases in household debt during the boom have been mired in a severe recessionary environment even after the official end of the recession."

TUGS-OF-WAR

The search for policies that prevent crisis is complicated by varying ideologies and points of self-interest. Policies favored by libertarians are not necessarily favored by paternalists, and policies serving the interests of borrowers do not necessarily serve the interests of lenders. Interest groups regularly enlist politicians and regulators in their tugs-of-war with one another. George Stigler (1971) described this enlistment in "capture theory." He noted that each interest group, including bankers, lawyers, union members, and employers, wants regulations that maximize its wealth. Politicians have the power to direct regulators to benefit one interest group or another. At the same time, politicians need resources such as campaign contributions to maximize their chances at reelection. Similarly, regulators want to steer the regulatory process in directions that benefit them in prestige or industry jobs once they leave public service. The political process involves competition among interest groups, each of which attempts to capture politicians and regulators by some combination of votes, contributions, and favors in exchange for enacting and executing regulations that transfer wealth to them. Statman (2009) and Shefrin and Statman (2009) describe this tug-of-war in the context of the crisis. Shabnam Mousavi and Hersh Shefrin (2010) analyze how relative strength and influence among participants in the political process shape financial market regulations, such as those embodied in the Dodd-Frank Wall Street Reform and Consumer Protection Act of 2010.

Stigler emphasized that an interest group is likely to capture its regulators when the per-capita benefits to the members of the interest group are large relative to per-capita benefits to the general public. Sam Peltzman (1976) augmented capture theory, noting that interest groups will not capture their regulators when the total benefits to the general public are sufficiently large, even if the per-capita benefits are relatively small. Politicians and regulators who allow interest groups to capture them under such circumstances might lose more political support than they gain.

Politicians and regulators have limited power to tilt regulation toward interest groups, and their power varies by the environment in which they operate. Economic booms and rising financial markets placate the general public, reducing its vigilance and making it easier for politicians to tilt regulations toward interest groups. Recessions and plunging financial markets, by contrast, enrage the general public, increasing its vigilance and its clamor for regulatory protection from interest groups.

The Riegle-Neal Act illustrates this tug-of-war and its links to the crisis. The Riegle-Neal Interstate Banking and Branching Efficiency Act, implemented in June 1997, permits banks to establish branches and to buy other banks across the country. States began imposing restrictions on branching in the nineteenth century, justified in part by the argument that allowing banks to branch could give strong banks excessive financial power. Weak banks supported these restrictions because they limited competition, and state governments supported them because restriction gave them power over the supply of bank charters. Writing not long after the Riegle-Neal Act was enacted, Jith Jayaratne and Philip Strahan (1997) argued that the act would allow banks to become more efficient as they grew bigger, reducing costs, lowering loan rates, and accelerating economic growth. They cautioned, however, that "whether there is additional room for improved efficiency through the process of selection remains to be seen." We know from today's vantage point that the Riegle-Neal Act was not an unmitigated blessing and that banks that are "too big to fail" can precipitate a collapse of the entire financial system.

Public outrage against banks over their role in the crisis mobilized a drive toward stricter banking regulations. But banks were already preparing, according to Gretchen Morgenson and Don Van Natta (2009, A1), for postcrisis tugs-of-war as the crisis was unfolding: "Even in crisis, banks dig in for battle against regulation." They noted that in November 2008 the nine biggest participants in the derivatives market, including JPMorgan Chase and Goldman Sachs, created a lobbying organization, the CDS Consortium, to counter the expected attempt to rein in credit default swaps and other derivatives.

Morgenson and Van Natta (2009, A1) added that, "to oversee the consortium's push, lobbying records show, the banks hired a longtime Washington power broker who previously helped fend off derivatives regulation: Edward J. Rosen, a partner at the law firm Cleary Gottlieb Steen & Hamilton." They revealed that "Mr. Rosen's confidential memo . . . recommended that the biggest participants in the derivatives market should continue to be overseen by the Federal Reserve Board. Critics say the Fed has been an overly friendly regulator, which is why big banks favor it."

"Occupy Wall Street," the movement spurred by the crisis, reflects a tug-of-war involving two notions of fairness embedded in two fairness rights and trade-offs between fairness rights and economic efficiency. On one side is the right to freedom from coercion, which some argue accompanies economic efficiency. On the other is the right to economic justice, a form of the right to equal power.

Conflicts between fairness rights and trade-offs between fairness rights and economic efficiency are the subject of Shefrin and Statman (1992, 1993). The right to freedom from coercion implies, for example, that bank shareholders are entitled to pay bankers any compensation they choose, whether salary or bonus, free from any coercion by government. The right to economic justice implies that all people are entitled to an economic safety net, even if the construction of such a net involves coercing the relatively rich, whether bankers or not, to pay for it. The right to economic justice is reflected in Occupy Wall Street protesters' description of themselves as "the 99 percent," standing against the wealthy "1 percent."

Stark facts underlie the discontent of the 99 percent. Figure 5.2 shows that the share of income of the top 1 percent of households increased from 8 percent in 1980 to 23 percent in 2007. The average inflation-adjusted income of the top 1 percent of households increased by 275 percent, or an annualized 4.8, between 1979 and 2007, according to the Congressional Budget Office (CBO). In contrast, income

FIGURE 5.2 / Income Share of the Top 1 Percent

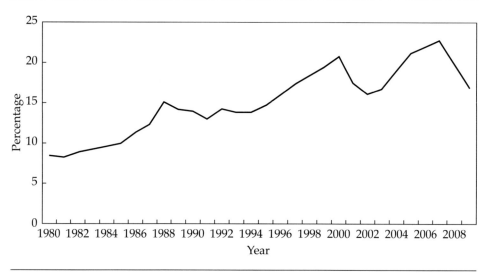

Source: Authors' compilation based on data from Tax Foundation (2012).

increased by 18 percent, an annualized 0.6 percent, for the poorest 20 percent of households. These facts are punctuated by a Census Bureau report in October 2011 that revealed that the poverty rate has now climbed to a seventeen-year high. The fate of the middle class is not much better than that of the poor. Although incomes of middle-class households increased by an annualized 1.2 percent between 1979 and 2007, Census Bureau data indicate that middle-class families suffered a 7 percent income decline between 2000 and 2010. As the incomes of the poor and middle class stagnated between 2000 and 2007, their borrowing increased dramatically according to Flow of Funds data, at approximately 10 percent per year.

As chair of the Congressional Oversight Panel, charged with overseeing implementation of the Emergency Economic Stabilization Act of 2008, Elizabeth Warren gained public attention for highlighting concerns about the fairness in consumer financial products, especially credit card debt, made complex by financial services companies. In our framework, the key fairness right associated with complexity is equal processing power: consumers are entitled to means that let them process information easily and accurately. Such means range from disclosure in plain language to prohibition of complex financial products. Warren's recommendations led to the establishment of the Bureau of Consumer Financial Protection as part of the Dodd-Frank Act of 2010. Tugs-of-war by the financial services industry blocked Warren's appointment to head the bureau, and tugs-of-war have limited the effectiveness of the bureau by restricting its budget. Warren is now recognized as a leader of those concerned about unfair practices in the financial services industry, special-interest politics, and disparities in income. She has shifted her efforts to winning a seat in the U.S. Senate.

Kevin Murphy (this volume) analyzes complaints leveled against banker bonuses. He finds, contrary to the complaints, that banker bonuses neither caused nor contributed to the financial crisis, that banker bonuses are not excessive, and that bonuses should not be regulated. So why do the Troubled Asset Relief Program (TARP) and the Dodd-Frank Act impose restrictions on pay? "I conclude," writes Murphy, "that the apparent intent of the pay restrictions in TARP and Dodd-Frank are not to reduce risk, improve pay, or protect taxpayers, but rather to attack perceived excesses in pay levels and destroy the banking-bonus culture." Murphy suggests that "the attacks on banking bonuses are driven primarily by anger, jealousy, and envy, and not by evidence that the bonuses are set in a noncompetitive market."

Murphy's argument focuses on economic efficiency and makes no explicit mention of fairness. He touches on fairness implicitly, however, when he speaks of anger, jealousy, and envy, implying that demands for social justice that reflect in anger, jealousy, and envy should be dismissed because they detract from economic efficiency and impinge on the more important fairness right of bankers and shareholders to be free from the coercion of the government and the general public. Minsky understood the trade-off between fairness rights, and between them and economic efficiency. He was particularly concerned about social frictions brought about by the high unemployment associated with economic crises resulting from the behavior of the financial sector. As we discuss later in the chapter, Minsky advocated employment programs as a remedy. He also identified the "games" played by banks against the much weaker authorities that regulate them. The authorities lose the game, but the true losers are all who are hurt by unemployment and inflation in a destabilized economy.

Minsky (1986/2008, 279) wrote:

> The standard analysis of banking has led to a game that is played by central banks, henceforth to be called the authorities, and profit-seeking banks. In this game, the authorities impose interest rates and reserve regulations and operate in money markets to get what they consider to be the right amount of money, and the banks invent and innovate in order to circumvent the authorities. The authorities may constrain the rate of growth of the reserve base, but the banking and financial structure determines the efficacy of reserves. . . . This is an unfair game. The entrepreneurs of the banking community have much more at stake than the bureaucrats of the central banks. In the postwar period, the initiative has been with the banking community, and the authorities have been "surprised" by changes in the way financial markets operate. The profit-seeking bankers almost always win their game with the authorities, but, in winning, the banking community destabilizes the economy; the true losers are those who are hurt by unemployment and inflation.

We observe the tug-of-war within the Federal Reserve Bank. The government appoints the seven members of the board of governors, and its chair regularly reports to Congress, but the Federal Reserve is not a government institution. The twelve regional Federal Reserve banks issue shares of stock to member banks, so we should not be surprised to find that the Federal Reserve Bank reflects the interests of member banks. These interests are evident in the tug-of-war between inflation hawks and doves at the Federal Reserve Bank. David Leonhardt (2011, SR8) quotes David Levey, a former managing director at Moody's: "The Fed regional banks represent, in essence, the banking community, which tends to be very conservative and hawkish." Levey continues: "Creditors don't like inflation—it's good for debtors." Thus, we should not be surprised that the Fed hawks on inflation are regional bank presidents: Richard W. Fisher of Dallas, Narayana R. Kocherlakota of Minneapolis, and Charles I. Plosser of Philadelphia.

Earlier we quoted excerpts from the public speeches of John Dugan, who headed the OCC. Dugan was a regulatory voice for prudent lending practices that would especially constrain what Minsky called Ponzi finance, such as option ARMs leading to negative amortization. Dugan worked to strengthen regulations along these lines. In a speech from December 1, 2005, he stated: "If all goes according to plan, the Federal banking agencies will propose new guidance with respect to nontraditional mortgage products by the end of this month. While the guidance will cover many other issues besides negative amortization and payment option ARMs, these will certainly be central" (Dugan 2005b, 11).

The process for developing these guidelines led to a tug-of-war. The Associated Press (2008) reported that lobbying efforts by financial institutions led to the removal of guidelines requiring banks (1) to increase efforts at verifying that mortgage applicants were employed and could afford intended home purchases; (2) to advise applicants about the risks associated with rising interest rates and consequent larger payments; and (3) to improve disclosure when bundling and selling mortgages.

Banks offered many reasons for their resistance to the proposed guidelines. Mary Jane Seebach, managing director of public affairs at Countrywide Financial Corporation, at the time the nation's largest mortgage lender, stated that the proposal "appears excessive and will inhibit future innovation in the marketplace." Ruthann Melbourne, chief risk officer of IndyMac Bank, noted: "It is not our role to be the regulator for the third-party lenders." Joseph Polizzotto, counsel to Lehman Brothers, suggested that "an open market will mean that different institutions will develop different methodologies for achieving this goal."

Dugan's side did not have the strength to win that tug-of-war. Other regulatory bodies were involved, notably the Federal Reserve, the Federal Deposit Insurance Corporation (FDIC), and the Office of Thrift Supervision (OTS). Grovetta Gardineer, the managing director for corporate and international activities at OTS, stated that the proposed guidelines "attempted to send an alarm bell that these products are bad." She told the AP that regulators were persuaded that the loans themselves were not problematic as long as banks managed the risk.

On October 17, 2006, Dugan commented that, "while the guidance applies to insured depository institutions and their affiliates, it does not apply to the many mortgage originators that have no such affiliations" (Dugan 2006, 2). Minsky

(1986/2008, 96–97) sounded cautionary notes about what he called the "fringe banking institutions" lying outside the Federal Reserve system, noting that through relationships such as lines of credit, member banks become "de facto lenders of last resort" to these institutions. He warned that these "relations can be a source of weakness for the financial system as a whole" with the "potential for a domino effect."

In June 2006, Sheila Bair became chair of the FDIC, and she criticized the OCC for being too timid. She knew that the proposed subprime guidelines were unlikely to be effective, since most subprime loans were issued by institutions outside the regulated banking system. Therefore, she advocated for applying subprime guidance to any institution financed by a regulated bank, knowing that institutions outside the regulated banking system depended on the regulated banks for their own financing. In retrospect, she noted that banks "fought us tooth and nail" and prevailed (see Nocera 2011).

Chapter 10 of the FCIC report is titled "The Madness," a term used by Lewis Ranieri to describe

> the willing suspension of prudent standards. . . . Regulators reacted weakly. As early as 2005, supervisors recognized that CDOs and credit default swaps (CDS) could actually concentrate rather than diversify risk, but they concluded that Wall Street knew what it was doing. Supervisors issued guidance in late 2006 warning banks of the risks of complex structured finance transactions—but excluded mortgage-backed securities and CDOs, because they saw the risks of those products as relatively straightforward and well understood. (Ranieri Partners Management LLC 2010, 188–89)

The Financial Crisis Inquiry Commission highlights the risks that financial institutions took in late 2006 and 2007, after housing prices peaked and defaults began to rise. Instead of winding down their CDO-CDS strategies, and consistent with the behavioral tendency to increase risk-taking when facing perceived losses relative to aspiration levels, financial institutions did the opposite. The FCIC (2011, 188) report states:

> Securities firms were starting to take on a significant share of the risks from their own deals, without AIG as the ultimate bearer of the risk of losses on super-senior CDO tranches. The machine kept humming throughout 2006 and into 2007. . . . The CDO machine had become self-fueling. Senior executives—particularly at three of the leading promoters of CDOs, Citigroup, Merrill Lynch, and UBS—apparently did not accept or perhaps even understand the risks inherent in the products they were creating.

In the end, the U.S. government had to bail out AIG and Citigroup and arrange for Bank of America to rescue Merrill Lynch by buying it. The Swiss government had to bail out UBS. These banks had become "too big to fail."

MINSKY'S PRESCRIPTIONS AND DOUBTS

Minsky noted the link between the game played by bankers against regulators and the problems of moral hazard and "too big to fail." Addressing the latter, Minsky (1986/2008, 354) wrote: "The United States has a type of contingency socialism, in which the liabilities of particular organizations are protected either by overt government intervention or by the grant of monopoly price setting powers. . . . Big or giant corporations carry an implied public guarantee (i.e., contingency liability) on their debts. This introduces a financing bias favoring giant corporations and giant banks, for the implicit public liability leads to preferred market treatment."

Addressing moral hazard, Minsky (1986/2008, 364) wrote: "Whenever the Federal Reserve steps in and refinances some positions, it is protecting organizations that engaged in a particular type of financing, and is expected to do so again. . . . The central bank virtually assures that there will be another crisis in the near future unless, of course, it outlaws the fragility inducing financial practices." Minsky made a series of recommendations about stabilizing an unstable economy, about the size of government, and employment policy, industrial policy, and financial reform. As to the size of government, Minsky advocated a government sector that comprises about 20 percent of gross domestic product, a bit larger than the 16 percent contribution of gross private domestic investment. This size of government would be large enough to run deficits whose magnitude could offset sharp declines in gross private domestic investment, as occurs during recessions.

As to employment policy, Minsky advocated that we resurrect the Roosevelt-era employment programs such as the Civilian Conservation Corps (CCC), National Youth Administration (NYA), and Works Progress Administration (WPA). He also advocated reforms to the labor participation features of transfer payment programs associated with Social Security, some of which were later changed in the direction he proposed. In particular, his recommendation to terminate the program Aid to Families with Dependent Children (AFDC) was subsequently implemented by the Clinton administration in 1996.

As to industrial policy, Minsky recommended that corporations not be allowed to grow too big to fail, be they automobile manufacturers or financial firms. Minsky advocated doing so with aggressive antitrust policy that would limit the size of corporations and the unfair advantage and moral hazard brought on by size.

As to financial reform, Minsky advocated policies to control leverage by controlling capital-asset ratios and the rate of growth of bank capital. He criticized the Fed's emphasis on open market operations relative to its operations at the discount window. In particular, he advocated that the Fed resume its practice of a century ago: engaging in rediscounting, thereby cofinancing economic activity. This activity, he suggested, would force the Fed to monitor the banking sector much more closely than it had been doing for most of the twentieth century. Fed chair Ben Bernanke belatedly came to the same general conclusion, stating: "The crisis has forcefully reminded us that the responsibility of central banks to protect financial stability is at least as important as the responsibility to use monetary policy effectively" (Appelbaum 2011). In April 2012, Bernanke reiterated his conclusion: "Going forward, for the Federal Reserve as well as other central banks, the promotion of financial stability must be on an equal footing with the management of monetary policy as the most critical policy priorities" (chapter 1, this volume).

Minsky's major objective in his recommendations about the Fed's work was to limit increases in speculative and Ponzi financing during economic expansions. Instead, he favored to-the-asset, hedge financing as being more prudent. By this he meant lending against specific project cash flows, not general corporate cash flows, with the maturity of the loan closely matched to the expected horizon of the project. Minsky also believed that the corporate income tax should be eliminated because that tax encouraged excessive investment and with it a capital structure with excessive debt.

Yet Minsky doubted that the right solutions could be implemented effectively, even if found. He wrote: "I feel much more comfortable with my diagnosis of what ails our economy and analysis of the causes or our discontents than I do with the remedies I propose. . . . Even if a program of reform is successful, the success will be transitory. Innovations, particularly in finance, assure that problems of instability will continue to crop up; the result will be the equivalent but not identical bouts of instability that are so evident in history" (Minsky 1986/2008, 319).

In the end, Minsky recommended that we expect less than we are promised: "Political leaders and the economists who advise them are to blame for promising more than they or the economy can deliver. . . . The normal functioning of our economy leads to financial trauma and crises, inflation, currency depreciations, unemployment, and poverty in the midst of what could be virtually universal affluence" (Minsky 1986/2008, 319).

CONCLUSION

Psychology is at the center of behavioral finance, and psychology underlies much of our crisis. That psychology includes aspirations, cognition, emotions, culture, and perceptions of fairness. Aspirations propelled many renters into houses they could not afford, evoking emotions and cognitive errors that blinded homeowners to risk. And the centrality of houses to the American dream in our culture deepened the crisis and extended it. Aspirations for wealth and status blinded bankers to the risk of mortgages and mortgage securities. Overconfident bankers sidelined risk managers and proceeded to boost their company's leverage. And much of the public and its political leaders were persuaded that regulations are unnecessary because free markets are not only inherently efficient but also inherently fair.

Psychology is also at the center of many of the writings of Keynes and Minsky. Long ago, Keynes identified the psychology that hurls financial markets and economies up into booms and down into busts. Minsky, building on Keynes's work, developed a framework exposing the sources of economic instability and contemplated ways to avert crises or alleviate them.

We see, in hindsight, that our crisis fits well within Minsky's framework. That framework emphasized the destabilizing effects of financial innovation, the role of euphoria, and the skill of bankers at outmaneuvering regulators. Minsky, who was pessimistic about our chances to avert financial crises, instead proposed policies for mitigating crises. These policies included a role for the Federal Reserve Bank in constraining speculative and Ponzi finance and government actions in the wake of a crisis—running budget deficits, instituting direct employment programs, and acting as a lender of last resort.

Can we hope that next time will be different? Financial crises come much too often to leave us much hope. The crisis of 1974 to 1975 was almost as long and severe as the Great Recession of 2007 to 2009. The twin Reagan-era recessions of the 1980s brought high unemployment and were followed by a sovereign debt crisis and the savings and loan crisis. The foreign currency crisis of the 1990s required action to dispose of Long-Term Capital Management without breaking the global financial system. And the recent housing bubble followed a stock market bubble.

Our world will always be uncertain, and events will often unfold in unexpected ways. Hindsight misleads us into thinking that we can see future crises as clearly as we can see past ones and that we can find policies that will prevent future crises. Moreover, we would be unable to implement policies that prevent crises even if we could identify them because those who would lose stand in the way. Limiting bank leverage might be good policy for averting crises, but bankers have the clout to resist it. We are left to remind ourselves of our psychological fallibilities so that we can avert some crises and mitigate others.

REFERENCES

Abdallah, Chadi, and William D. Lastrapes. 2010. "Home Equity Lending and Retail Spending: Evidence from a Natural Experiment in Texas." Working Paper Series (August 10, 2010; last revised April 22, 2012). Available at: http://papers.ssrn.com/sol3/papers.cfm?abstract_id=1656147# (accessed on June 29, 2012).

Ahmed, Azam. 2011. "Even Paulson's Friends Pitied His Subprime Bet." New York Times, February 14. Available at: http://dealbook.nytimes.com/2011/02/14/even-paulsons-friends-pitied-his-subprime-bet/ (accessed on June 29, 2012).

Andrews, Edmund L. 2008. "Greenspan Concedes Error on Regulation." New York Times, October 23.

Appelbaum, Binyamin. 2010. "Financial Bill to Close Regulator of Fading Industry." New York Times, July 14.

———. 2011. "Lessons from the Financial Crisis." New York Times, October 18. Available at: http://economix.blogs.nytimes.com/2011/10/18/lessons-from-the-financial-crisis/ (accessed on June 29, 2012).

Associated Press. 2008. "Bush Administration Ignored Clear Warnings: Under Pressure from Banking Industry, U.S. Government Eased Lending Rules." December 1. Available at: http://www.msnbc.msn.com/id/28001417/ns/business-stocks_and_economy/t/bush-administration-ignored-clear-warnings/#.T-35PZGDl8E (accessed on June 29, 2012).

Bernanke, Ben. 2010. "Monetary Policy and the Housing Bubble." Speech delivered at the annual meeting of the American Economic Association, Atlanta (January 3). Available at: http://www.federalreserve.gov/newsevents/speech/bernanke20100103a.htm (accessed on June 29, 2012).

Business Week. 2007. "Business Week 2008 Forecasters Expect Further Gains." *Business Week,* December 22. Available at: http://seekingalpha.com/article/58150-business-week-2008-forecasters-expect-further-gains (accessed on June 29, 2012).

Campbell, John Y., and Robert J. Shiller. 1998. "Valuation Ratios and the Long-Run Stock Market Outlook." *Journal of Portfolio Management* (Winter): 11–26.

Covitz, Daniel, Nellie Liang, and Gustavo Suarez. 2009. "The Evolution of a Financial Crisis: Runs in the Asset-Backed Commercial Paper Market." Working paper. New York: Federal Reserve Board.

Dichev, Ilia D., and Joseph D. Piotroski. 2001."The Long-Run Stock Returns Following Bond Ratings Changes." *Journal of Finance* 56(February): 173–203.

Dugan, John C. 2005a. Remarks at the American Bankers Association and American Bar Association "Money Laundering Enforcement" conference, Washington, D.C. (November 1). Available at: http://www.occ.treas.gov/news-issuances/speeches/2005/pub-speech-2005-108.pdf (accessed on June 29, 2012).

———. 2005b. Speech delivered before the Consumer Federation of America (December 1). Available at: http://www.occ.gov/news-issuances/news-releases/2005/nr-occ-2005-117.html (accessed on June 29, 2012).

———. 2006. Speech delivered before "America's Community Bankers," San Diego, Calif. (October 17). Available at: http://www.occ.gov/news-issuances/speeches/2006/pub-speech-2006-115.pdf (accessed June 29, 2012).

Financial Crisis Inquiry Commission. 2011. *Financial Crisis Inquiry Report: 2011.* Washington: U.S. Government Printing Office.

Fisher, Kenneth, and Meir Statman. 2000. "Cognitive Biases in Market Forecasts." *Journal of Portfolio Management* 26: 1–10.

———. 2006. "Market Timing in Regressions and Reality." *Journal of Financial Research* 29(3): 293–304.

Friedman, Milton, and L. J. Savage. 1948. "The Utility Analysis of Choices Involving Risk." *Journal of Political Economy* 56(4): 279–304.

Gorton, Gary B. 2008. "The Panic of 2007." Working Paper 14358. Cambridge, Mass.: National Bureau of Economic Research (September). Available at: http://www.nber.org/papers/w14358 (accessed June 29, 2012).

Goyal, Amit, and Ivo Welch. 2003. "Predicting the Equity Premium with Dividend Ratios." *Management Science* 49(5): 639–54.

Greenspan, Alan. 1996. "Remarks by Chairman Alan Greenspan." Delivered at the annual dinner and Francis Boyer Lecture of the American Enterprise Institute for Public Policy Research. Washington, D.C. (December 5). Available at: http://www.federalreserve.gov/boarddocs/speeches/1996/19961205.htm (accessed June 29, 2012).

Grossman, Sanford, and Joseph Stiglitz. 1980. "On the Impossibility of Informationally Efficient Markets." *American Economic Review* 70(3, June): 393–408.

Huberman, Gur, and William Schwert. 1985. "Information Aggregation, Inflation, and the Pricing of Indexed Bonds." *Journal of Political Economy* 93(11): 92–114.

Jacoby, Jeff. 2011. "A Sinful 'Occupation': Economic Envy Cloaks Itself in Rhetoric About 'Inequality,' but Its Oldest Name Is Covetousness." *Boston Globe,* November 2. Available at: http://articles.boston.com/2011-11-02/bostonglobe/30351341_1_zuccotti-park-protesters-tea-party-public-urination (accessed on June 29, 2012).

Jayaratne, Jith, and Philip E. Strahan. 1997. "The Benefits of Branching Deregulations." *Economic Policy Review* (Federal Reserve Bank of New York) 3(4, December): 13–29.

Kahneman, Daniel, and Amos Tversky. 1979. "An Analysis of Decision Under Risk." *Econometrica* 47(2): 263–92.

Keynes, John Maynard. 1967. *The General Theory of Employment, Interest, and Money.* London: Macmillan. (Originally published in 1936.)

Kochhar, Rakesh, Ana Gonzalez-Barrera, and Daniel Dockterman. 2009. "Through Boom and Bust: Minorities, Immigrants, and Homeownership." Washington, D.C.: Pew Hispanic Center. (May 12). Available at: http://pewhispanic.org/files/reports/109.pdf (accessed on June 29, 2012).

Koedijk, Kees, Rachel A. J. Pownall, and Meir Statman. 2011. "Aspirations, Well-being, and Risk Tolerance." Working paper. Santa Clara, Calif.: Santa Clara University.

Krugman, Paul. 2009. "How Did Economists Get It So Wrong?" *New York Times,* September 2. Available at: http://www.nytimes.com/2009/09/06/magazine/06Economic-t.html?pagewanted=print (accessed on June 29, 2012).

Leonhardt, David. 2011. "Dissecting the Mind of the Fed." *New York Times,* August 27. Available at: http://www.nytimes.com/2011/08/28/sunday-review/dissecting-why-the-fed-does-what-it-does.html (accessed on June 29, 2012).

Lipton, Eric, and Stephen Lobaton. 2008. "Deregulation Looks Back, Unswayed." *New York Times,* November 17, p. A1.

Lyon, Andrew. 1984. "Money Market Funds and Shareholder Dilution." *Journal of Finance* 39(4): 1011–20.

Malkiel, Burton G. 2003. "The Efficient Market Hypothesis and Its Critics." *Journal of Economic Perspectives* 17(1): 59–82.

McLean, Bethany, and Joe Nocera. 2010. *All the Devils Are Here: The Hidden History of the Financial Crisis.* London: Penguin.

Mian, Atif, and Amir Sufi. 2011. "Consumers and the Economy, Part II: Household Debt and the Weak U.S. Recovery." *Economic Letter* (January 18). San Francisco: Federal Reserve Bank of San Francisco. Available at: http://www.frbsf.org/publications/economics/letter/2011/el2011-02.html (accessed on June 29, 2012).

Miller, Merton. 1997. *Merton Miller on Derivatives.* New York: Wiley.

Minsky, Hyman. 2008. *Stabilizing an Unstable Economy.* New York: McGraw-Hill. (Originally published in 1986.)

Morgenson, Gretchen, and Joshua Rosner. 2011. *Reckless Endangerment: How Outsized Ambition, Greed, and Corruption Led to Economic Armageddon.* New York: Times Books/Henry Holt.

Morgenson, Gretchen, and Don Van Natta Jr. 2009. "In Crisis, Banks Dig in for Fight Against Rules." *New York Times,* June 1, p. A1.

Mousavi, Shabnam, and Hersh Shefrin. 2010. "Prediction Tools: Financial Market Regulation, Politics, and Psychology." *Journal of Risk Management in Financial Institutions* 3(4): 318–33.

Nocera, Joe. 2011. "Sheila Bair's Bank Shot." *New York Times,* July 9. Available at: http://www.nytimes.com/2011/07/10/magazine/sheila-bairs-exit-interview.html?pagewanted=all (accessed on June 29, 2012).

Peach, Richard. 2005. "Is There a Housing Bubble?" *Balance: Quarterly News and Tools from TIAA-CREF.* (Summer): 18–22.

Peltzman, Sam. 1976. "Toward a More General Theory of Regulation." *Journal of Law and Economics* 19(2): 211–40.

Peñaloza, Lisa, and Michelle Barnhart. 2011. "Living U.S. Capitalism: The Normalization of Credit/Debt." *Journal of Consumer Research* 38(4): 743–62.

Ranieri Partners Management LLC. 2010. Letter to Department of Housing and Urban Development and Department of the Treasury, July 21. Available at: http://online.wsj.com/public/resources/documents/Ranieri0723.pdf (accessed on June 29, 2012).

Robinson, Eugene. 2011. "The Study That Shows Why Occupy Wall Street Struck a Nerve." *Washington Post,* October 27. Available at: http://www.washingtonpost.com/opinions/the-study-that-shows-why-occupy-wall-street-struck-a-nerve/2011/10/27/gIQA3bsMNM_story.html (accessed on June 29, 2012).

Shefrin, Hersh. 2000. *Beyond Greed and Fear: Understanding Behavioral Finance and the Psychology of Investing.* Boston: Harvard Business School Press.

———. 2008. *A Behavioral Approach to Asset Pricing.* 2nd ed. Boston: Elsevier.

———. 2009. "Ending the Management Illusion: Preventing Another Financial Crisis." *Ivey Business Journal* (January–February). Available at: http://www.iveybusinessjournal.com/topics/innovation/ending-the-management-illusion-preventing-another-financial-crisis (accessed on June 29, 2012).

———. 2010. "How Psychological Pitfalls Generated the Global Financial Crisis." In *Voices of Wisdom: Understanding the Global Financial Crisis,* edited by Laurence B. Siegel. Charlottesville, Va.: Research Foundation of CFA Institute.

Shefrin, Hersh, and Meir Statman. 1992. *Ethics, Fairness, Efficiency, and Financial Markets.* Charlottesville, Va.: Institute of Chartered Financial Analysts Research Foundation.

———. 1993. "Ethics, Fairness, and Efficiency in Financial Markets." *Financial Analysts Journal* 49(6, November–December): 21–29.

———. 1994. "Behavioral Capital Asset Pricing Theory." *Journal of Financial and Quantitative Analysis* 29(3): 323–49.

———. 2000. "Behavioral Portfolio Theory." *Journal of Financial and Quantitative Analysis* 35(2): 127–51.

———. 2009. "Striking Regulatory Irons While Hot." *Journal of Investment Management* 7(4): 1–14.

Shiller, Robert. 2005. "Homes Are a Risky Long-Term Investment." *Balance: Quarterly News and Tools from TIAA-CREF.* (Summer): 18–22.

———. 2010. "Economic View: Mom, Apple Pie, and Mortgages." *New York Times,* March 6.

———. 2012. "Online Data, Robert Shiller: Fig2-1.xls." Available at: http://www.econ.yale.edu/~shiller/data.htm.

Shleifer, Andrei, and Robert Vishny. 1997. "The Limits of Arbitrage." *Journal of Finance* 52(1): 35–55.

Siegel, Jeremy. 2000. "Big-Cap Tech Stocks Are a Sucker Bet." *Wall Street Journal,* March 14.

———. 2001. "Manager's Journal: Not-Quite-So-Big-Cap Tech Stocks Are Still a Bad Bet." *Wall Street Journal,* March 19.

Statman, Meir. 1982. "Fixed Rate or Index Linked Mortgages from the Borrower's Point of View: A Note." *Journal of Financial and Quantitative Analysis* 17(3): 451–57.

———. 2009. "Regulating Financial Markets: Protecting Us from Ourselves and Others." *Financial Analysts Journal* 65(May/June): 22–31.

———. 2011a. "Efficient Markets in Crisis." *Journal of Investment Management* 9: 4–13.

———. 2011b. *What Investors Really Want.* New York: McGraw-Hill.

Stigler, George. 1971. "The Theory of Economic Regulation." *Bell Journal of Economics and Management Science* 2(1): 3–21.

Story, Louise. 2008. "Home Equity Frenzy Was a Bank Ad Come True." *New York Times,* August 15.

Streitfeld, David, and Megan Thee-Brenan. 2011. "Despite Fears, Owning Home Retains Allure, Poll Shows." *New York Times,* June 29, p. B1.

Tax Foundation. 2012. "Summary of 2009 Federal Individual Income Tax Data." Available at: http://taxfoundation.org/article_ns/summary-2009-federal-individual-income-tax-data (accessed June 29, 2012).

Weinstein, Mark. 1977. "The Effect of a Rating Change Announcement on Bond Price." *Journal of Financial Economics* 5(3): 329–50.

Xiong, Wei, and Hanjung Yan. 2010. "Heterogeneous Expectations and Bond Markets." *Review of Financial Studies* 23(4): 1433–66.

Chapter 6

Why Did So Many People Make So Many Ex Post Bad Decisions? The Causes of the Foreclosure Crisis

Christopher L. Foote, Kristopher S. Gerardi, and Paul S. Willen

We present twelve facts about the mortgage crisis and argue that these facts refute the popular story that the crisis resulted from finance industry insiders deceiving uninformed mortgage borrowers and investors. Instead, we argue, borrowers and investors made decisions that were rational and logical given their ex post overly optimistic beliefs about house prices. We then show that neither institutional features of the mortgage market nor financial innovations are any more likely to explain those distorted beliefs than they are to explain the Dutch tulip bubble four hundred years ago. Economists should acknowledge the limits of their understanding of asset price bubbles and design policies accordingly.

More than four years after defaults and foreclosures began to rise sharply in 2007, economists are still debating the ultimate origins of the recent U.S. mortgage crisis. Losses on residential real estate touched off the largest financial crisis in decades. Why did so many people—including home buyers and purchasers of mortgage-backed securities—make so many decisions that turned out to be disastrous ex post?

The dominant explanation is that well-informed mortgage insiders used the securitization process to take advantage of uninformed outsiders. The typical narrative follows a loan from a mortgage broker through a series of Wall Street intermediaries to an ultimate investor. According to this story, depicted graphically in the left panel of figure 6.1, deceit started with a mortgage broker, who convinced a borrower to take out a mortgage that initially appeared affordable. Unbeknownst to the borrower, the interest rate on the mortgage would reset to a higher level after a few years, and the higher monthly payment would force the borrower into default.

Brokers knew that mortgages were hardwired to explode but did not care, because the securitization process enabled them to pass these mortgages on to someone else. Specifically, investment bankers bought the loans for inclusion in mortgage-backed securities. In constructing these instruments, bankers intentionally used newfangled, excessively complex financial engineering so that investors could not figure out the problematic nature of the loans. These bankers knew

FIGURE 6.1 / Alternative Theories of the Foreclosure Crisis

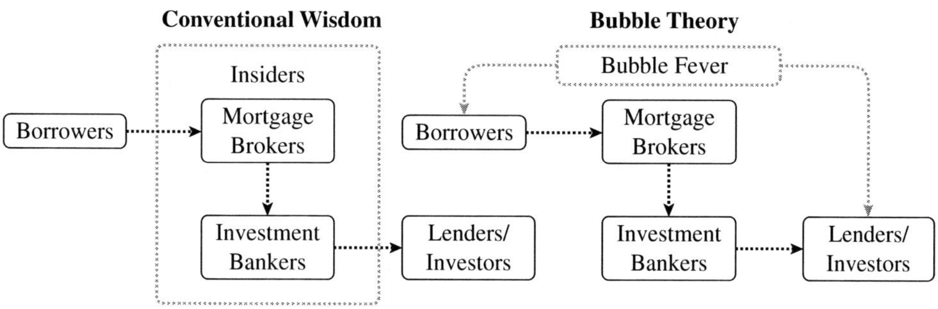

Source: Authors' figure.

that investors were likely to lose money but did not care because it was not their money. When the loans exploded, the borrowers lost their homes and the investors lost their money. But the intermediaries who collected substantial fees to set up the deals had no "skin in the game" and therefore suffered no losses.

This insider-outsider interpretation of the crisis has inspired an Academy Award–winning documentary, appropriately titled *Inside Job*. It has also motivated policies designed to prevent a future crisis, including requirements that mortgage lenders retain some skin in the game for certain mortgages in the future.

In this chapter, we lay out twelve facts about the mortgage market during the boom years and argue that they refute much of the insider-outsider explanation of the crisis. Borrowers did get adjustable rate mortgages (ARMs), but the resets of those mortgages did not cause the wave of defaults that started the crisis in 2007. Indeed, to a first approximation, "exploding" mortgages played no role in the crisis at all. Arguments that deceit by investment bankers sparked the crisis are also hard to support. Compared to most investments, mortgage-backed securities were highly transparent and their issuers willingly provided a great deal of information to potential purchasers. These purchasers could and did use this information to measure the amount of risk in mortgage investments, and their analysis was accurate, even ex post. Mortgage intermediaries retained lots of skin in the game. In fact, it was the losses of these intermediaries—who were not mortgage outsiders—that nearly brought down the financial system in late 2008. The biggest winners in the crisis, including hedge fund managers John Paulson and Michael Burry, had little or no previous experience with mortgage investments until some strikingly good bets on the future of the U.S. housing market earned them billions of dollars.

Why then did borrowers and investors make so many bad decisions? We argue that any story consistent with the twelve facts must have overly optimistic beliefs about house prices at its center. The right side of figure 6.1 summarizes this view. Rather than drawing a sharp demarcation between insiders and outsiders, it depicts a "bubble fever" that infected both borrowers and lenders. If both groups believed that house prices would continue to rise rapidly for the foreseeable future, then it is not surprising to find borrowers stretching to buy the biggest houses they could and investors lining up to give them the money. Rising house prices generate large capital gains for home purchasers. They also raise the value of the collateral backing mortgages and thus reduce or eliminate credit losses for lenders. In short, higher house price expectations rationalize the decisions of borrowers, investors, and intermediaries, including their embrace of high leverage when purchasing homes or funding mortgage investments, their failure to require rigorous documentation of income or assets before making loans, and their extension of credit to borrowers with a history of not repaying debt. If this alternative theory is true, then securitization was not a cause of the crisis. Rather, securitization merely facilitated transactions that borrowers and investors wanted to undertake anyway.

The bubble theory explains the foreclosure crisis as a consequence of distorted beliefs rather than distorted incentives. A growing literature in economics—inspired in part by the recent financial crisis—is trying to learn precisely how financial market participants form their beliefs and what can happen when these beliefs become distorted.[1] The idea that distorted beliefs are responsible for the crisis has also received some attention in the popular press. In one analysis of the crisis, *New York Times* columnist Joe Nocera referenced the famous Dutch tulip bubble of the 1630s to argue that a collective mania about house prices, rather than individual malfeasance on the part of mortgage industry insiders, may be the best explanation for why the foreclosure crisis occurred:

> Had there been a Dutch Tulip Inquiry Commission nearly four centuries ago, it would no doubt have found tulip salesmen who fraudulently persuaded people to borrow money they could never pay back to buy tulips. It would have criticized the regulators who looked the other way at the sleazy practices of tulip growers. It would have found speculators trying to corner the tulip market. But centuries later, we all understand that the roots of tulipmania were less the actions of particular Dutchmen than the fact that the entire society was suffering under the delusion that tulip prices could only go up. That's what bubbles are: they're examples of mass delusions.
>
> Was it really any different this time? In truth, it wasn't. To have so many people acting so foolishly required the same kind of delusion, only this time around, it was about housing prices. (Nocera 2011)

In both popular accounts and some academic studies, the "inside job" explanation and the bubble theory are often commingled. Analysts often write that misaligned incentives in the mortgage industry (a key part of the inside job explanation) contributed to an expansion of mortgage credit that sent house prices higher (a key part of the bubble explanation). We believe that the two explanations are conceptually distinct, and that the bubble story is a far better explanation of what actually happened. To put this another way, according to the conventional narrative, the bubble was a by-product of misaligned incentives and financial innovation. As we argue later, neither the facts nor economic theory draw an obvious causal link from underwriting and financial innovation to bubbles.

No one doubts that the availability of mortgage credit expanded during the housing boom. In particular, no one doubts that many borrowers received mortgages for which they would have never qualified before. The only question is why the credit expansion took place. Economists and policy analysts have blamed a number of potential culprits for the credit expansion, but we show that the facts exonerate the usual suspects. As noted earlier, some analysts claim that the credit expansion occurred because of improper incentives inherent in the so-called originate-to-distribute model of mortgage lending. Yet mortgage market participants had been buying and selling U.S. mortgages for more than a century without much trouble. In a similar vein, some authors blame the credit expansion on the emergence of nontraditional mortgages, like option ARMs and reduced-documentation loans, but these products had been around for many years before the housing boom occurred. Other writers blame the credit expansion on the federal government, which allegedly pushed a too-lax lending model on the mortgage industry. But government involvement in mortgage lending had been massive throughout the postwar era without significant problems. In contrast to these explanations for the credit expansion, the facts suggest that the expansion occurred simply because people believed that housing prices would keep going up—the defining characteristic of an asset bubble. Bubbles do not need securitization, government involvement, or nontraditional lending products to get started. Bubbles in many other assets have occurred without any of these things—not only tulips in seventeenth-century Holland but also shares of the South Sea Company in eighteenth-century England, U.S. equities and Florida land in the 1920s, even Beanie Babies and technology stocks in the 1990s.[2] As the housing bubble inflated, it encouraged lenders to extend credit to borrowers who had been constrained in the past, since higher house prices would ensure repayment of the loans. Much of this credit was channeled to subprime borrowers by securitized credit markets, but this does not mean that securitization "caused" the crisis. Instead, expectations of higher house prices made investors more willing to use both securitized markets and nontraditional mortgage products—because those markets and products delivered the biggest profits to investors as housing prices rose.

Another reason to keep the two explanations distinct is that they suggest very different agendas for real-world regulators and academic economists. If the inside job story is true, then the prevention of a future crisis requires regulations to ensure that intermediaries inform borrowers and investors of relevant facts and that incentives in the securitization process are properly aligned. But if the problem was some collective, self-fulfilling mania, then such regulations will not work. If house prices are widely expected to rise rapidly, then warning borrowers that their future payments will rise will have no effect on their decisions. Similarly, intermediaries will be only too willing to keep some skin in the game if they expect rising prices to eliminate credit losses.

For economists, the bubble theory implies that research should focus on a more general attempt to understand how beliefs are formed about the prices of long-lived assets. Gaining this understanding is an enormous challenge for the economics profession. From tulips to tech stocks, outbreaks of optimism have appeared repeatedly, but no robust theory has emerged to explain these episodes. As a telling example, at the peak of the housing boom economic theory could not provide academic researchers with clear predictions of where prices were going or if they were poised to fall. Scientific ignorance about what causes asset bubbles implies that policymakers should focus on making the housing finance system as robust as possible to significant price volatility rather than trying to correct potentially misaligned incentives.

The multitude of questions suggested by the financial crisis could never be answered by one single theory—or in one single paper. For example, as we discuss later, the top-rated tranches of Wall Street's mortgage-backed securities performed much better than the top-rated tranches of its collateralized debt obligations, another type of structured security. This discrepancy occurred even though both types of securities were ultimately collateralized by subprime mortgages, and even though both types of securities were constructed by the same investment banks. We do not believe that securitization alone caused the crisis, but by channeling money from investors to borrowers with ruthless efficiency, it may have allowed speculation on a scale that would have been impossible to sustain with a less sophisticated financial system. As economists, we believe that the ultimate answers to questions like these will involve information and incentives. But we also believe that an examination of the facts that we present here about the mortgage market does rule out the most common information-and-incentives story invoked to explain the crisis—that poor incentives caused mortgage industry insiders to take advantage of misinformed outsiders.

In the next section, we lay out the twelve facts about the U.S. mortgage market that are critical in rationalizing borrower and lender decisions. We follow up with a discussion that relates these facts to various economic theories about the crisis and then, in the final section, conclude with some policy recommendations.

TWELVE FACTS ABOUT THE MORTGAGE MARKET

Fact 1: Resets of adjustable rate mortgages did not cause the foreclosure crisis

One theory for why borrowers took out loans they could not repay is that their lenders misled them by granting them loans that initially appeared affordable but became unaffordable later on. Pointing to the large number of adjustable rate mortgages originated in the years immediately preceding the crisis, these analysts attribute the rise in delinquencies and foreclosures to the "payment shocks" associated with ARM-rate adjustments. Borrowers, they argue, had either not realized that their payments would rise or been assured that they could refinance to lower-rate mortgages when the resets occurred.

The "exploding ARM" theory has played a central role in narratives about the crisis since 2007, when problems with subprime mortgages first gained national attention. In April 2007, Sheila Bair, then the chair of the Federal Deposit Insurance Corporation, testified to Congress that "many subprime borrowers could avoid foreclosure if they were offered more traditional products such as 30-year fixed-rate mortgages" (Bair 2007).

Yet the data are not kind to the exploding ARM theory. Figure 6.2 shows the path of interest rates and defaults for three vintages of the most problematic type of ARM, the so-called subprime 2/28. These mortgages had fixed interest rates for the first two years, then adjusted to "fully indexed" rates every six months for the loan's twenty-eight remaining years.[3] The figure shows that, at least for subprime 2/28s, payment shocks did not lead to defaults. The top left panel depicts interest rates and cumulative defaults for subprime 2/28s originated in January 2005. For these mortgages, the initial interest rate was 7.5 percent for the first two years. Two years later, in January 2007, the interest rate rose to 11.4 percent, resulting in a payment shock of four percentage points, or more than 50 percent in relative terms. However, the lower part of the panel shows that delinquencies for the January 2005 loans did not tick up when this reset occurred. In fact, the delinquency plot shows no significant problems for the 2005 borrowers two years into

FIGURE 6.2 / Interest Rates and Cumulative Defaults for Three Vintages of Subprime 2/28 Mortgages

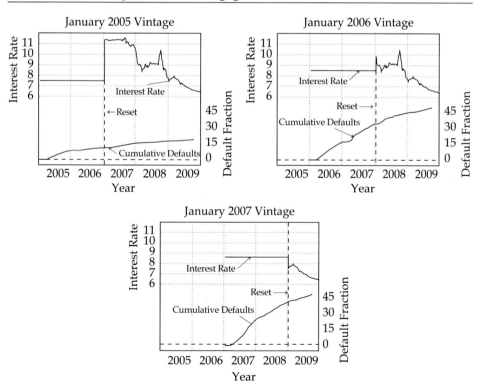

Source: Authors' calculations using data from Lender Processing Services, Inc. (various years).

their mortgages when their resets occurred. The top right panel displays data for 2/28s originated in January 2006. These loans had initial rates of 8.5 percent that reset to 9.9 percent in January 2008. This increase of 1.4 percentage points resulted in a relative increase of about 16 percent, one-third the size of the payment shock for the previous vintage. Yet even though the payment shock for the January 2006 loans was smaller than that for the 2005 loans, their delinquency rate was higher. Finally, the worst-performing loans, those originated in January 2007, are depicted in the figure's bottom panel. When these loans reset in January 2009, their fully indexed rates were actually lower than their initial rates. However, the contract on the typical 2/28 mortgage specified that the interest rate could never go below the initial rate, so for all practical purposes subprime 2/28s from January 2007 were fixed rate loans. But as the lower part of the panel indicates, these "fixed rate" loans had the highest delinquency rates of any vintage shown in the figure.

As many have pointed out, subprime 2/28s were not the only loans with payment shocks. In 2004 and 2005, lenders originated many nontraditional, or "exotic," mortgages, which often had larger payment shocks and which we discuss in more detail later. Tables 6.1 and 6.2 attempt to quantify the impact of payment shocks across the entire mortgage market by looking at all foreclosures from 2007 through 2010, regardless of the type of mortgage. The goal is to determine whether the monthly payments faced by borrowers when they first became delinquent were higher than the initial monthly payments on their loans. Table 6.1 shows that this was true for only 12 percent of borrowers who eventually lost their homes to foreclosure. The overwhelming majority of foreclosed borrowers—84 percent—were making the same payment at the time they first defaulted as when they originated their loans. A main reason for this high percentage is that fixed rate mortgages (FRMs) accounted for 59 percent of the foreclosures between 2007 and 2010. Table 6.2 shows that 52.8 percent of subprime borrowers with adjustable rate 2/28 mortgages originated from 2005 to 2007 defaulted. The comparable percentage for fixed rate mortgages is 47.6 percent—only a few percentage points lower.

Tables 6.1 and 6.2 put an upper bound on the role that deceptively low mortgage payments may have played in causing the crisis. Basically, these tables show

TABLE 6.1 / Payment Changes and Defaults, 2007 to 2010

	2007	2008	2009	2010	All
Fixed Rate Mortgage share	38%	48%	62%	74%	59%
Percentage of loans prior to delinquency spell leading to foreclosure that had . . .					
Reset	18	20	18	11	17
Payment increase	12	17	11	9	12
Payment reduction	0	0	4	8	4
No change since origination	88	82	85	83	84
Private label	68	54	37	23	41
Number of observations (in thousands)	374	641	874	756	2,646

Source: Authors' calculations using data from Lender Processing Services, Inc.

TABLE 6.2 / Relative Performance of Subprime Adjustable Rate and Fixed Rate Mortgages, 2005 to 2007

	All Subprime Mortgages		Subprime Fixed Rate Mortgages			Subprime 2/28 Mortgages		
	Number Originated (in Thousands)	Probability of Default	Number Originated (in Thousands)	Share	Probability of Default	Number Originated (in Thousands)	Share	Probability of Default
2005	529	41.9	198	37.3%	37.1	332	62.7%	44.8
2006	504	55.9	258	51.2	50.7	246	48.8	61.4
2007	246	55.9	208	84.5	53.8	38	15.5	66.8
Total	1,278	50.1	663	51.9	47.6	615	48.1	52.8

Source: Authors' calculations using data from Lender Processing Services, Inc. (various years).

us that if we had replaced all of the complex mortgage products with fixed rate mortgages, we would have prevented *at most* 12 percent of the foreclosures during this time period. But even 12 percent is a substantial overestimate, because the tables show that fixed rate borrowers also lost their homes to foreclosure.

Although FRMs accounted for most defaults, this does not mean that FRMs suffered higher default *rates*. In fact, fixed rate loans defaulted less often than adjustable rate loans; the predominance of fixed rate loans among defaulted mortgages stems from the fact that FRMs are more common than ARMs. Yet we should not overstate the better performance of fixed rate loans, particularly among subprime borrowers. Table 6.2 shows that 53 percent of subprime ARMs originated between 2005 and 2007 have experienced at least one ninety-day delinquency. The corresponding figure for FRMs is 48 percent, a difference of only five percentage points.[4] Even this small difference does not indicate that subprime ARMs were worse products than FRMs. The lack of any relationship between the timing of the initial delinquency and the timing of the reset have led most researchers to conclude that ARMs performed worse than FRMs because they attracted less creditworthy borrowers, not because of something inherent in the ARM contract itself. Even if we did believe that the ARM-versus-FRM performance difference was a causal effect and not a selection effect, almost half of borrowers with subprime FRMs became seriously delinquent. The terrible performance of subprime FRMs contradicts the claim of Martin Eakes (2007), the head of the Center for Responsible Lending, that "exploding ARMs are the single most important factor causing financial crisis for millions."

Fact 2: No mortgage was "designed to fail"

Some critics of the lending process have argued that the very existence of some types of mortgages is prima facie evidence that borrowers were misled. These critics maintain that reduced-documentation loans, loans to borrowers with poor credit histories, loans with no down payments, and option ARMs were all "designed to fail," such that no reasonable borrower would willingly have entered into such transactions.[5] In fact, the large majority of these loans succeeded for both borrower and lender alike.

In figure 6.3, we graph failure rates for four categories of securitized nonprime loans. Along the horizontal axis are years of origination; in the figure we define failure as being at least sixty days delinquent two years after the loan was originated.[6] The figure shows that the vast majority of loans originated from 2000 through 2005 were successful. For example, the lower left panel shows that in 2007, after the housing market had begun to sour, only 10 percent of the borrowers who took

FIGURE 6.3 / Failure Rates and Originations for Selected Nonprime
Mortgages, 2000 to 2007

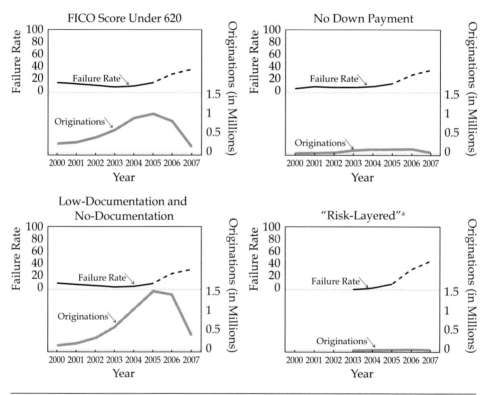

Source: Authors' calculations using data from CoreLogic, Inc. (various years; originally LoanPerformance). The sample includes all subprime and Alt-A loans in the CoreLogic database.

Notes: Failure rates are graphed by year of origination and correspond to the fraction of mortgages that were at least sixty days delinquent two years after origination. The dashed line denotes years after 2005.

[a] A risk-layered loan is low- or no-documentation, with a down payment of 10 percent or less, and negatively amortized.

out low- or no-documentation mortgages in 2005 were having serious problems. Additionally, loans requiring no down payments (top right panel) and even "risk-layered" loans (bottom right panel) originated before 2006 also displayed failure rates that are well under 10 percent. Loans in the upper left panel were made to borrowers with credit scores below 620, who typically have a history of serious debt repayment problems. Yet, after two years, more than 80 percent of low-scoring borrowers who originated loans before 2006 had either avoided serious delinquency or repaid their loans. Given their spotty credit histories, the performance of these borrowers indicates remarkable success, not failure.

Some might argue that the loans detailed in figure 6.3 succeeded only because the borrowers were able to refinance or sell. But it would be wrong to classify prepayments as failures. In many cases, simply making twelve consecutive monthly payments allowed the borrower to qualify for a lower-cost loan. In such cases, the refinance was a success for the borrower, who got a loan with better terms, as well as the lender, who was fully repaid.

In the end, the idea that subprime or Alternative-A (Alt-A) loans were designed to fail does not fit the facts. This finding should not be surprising. Marketing products that do not work is usually a bad business plan, even in the short run, whether one is producing mortgages or motorcycles. The fact that failure rates for all the loans in figure 6.3 rose at about the same time suggests that these mortgages were not designed to fail. Instead, they were not designed to withstand the stunning nationwide fall in house prices that began in 2006. We return to this theme later.

Fact 3: There was little innovation in mortgage markets in the 2000s

Another popular claim is that the housing boom saw intense innovation in mortgage markets. According to the conventional wisdom, lenders began to offer types of mortgages that they never had before, including loans with no down payments, loans with balances that increased over time,[7] and loans that lacked rigorous documentation of borrower income and assets. In more nuanced versions of the story, lenders did not innovate so much as expand the market for nontraditional mortgages. As Allen Fishbein (2006) of the Consumer Federation of America described these nontraditional mortgages in congressional testimony: "Traditionally, these types of loans were niche products that were offered to upscale borrowers with particular cash flow needs or to those expecting to remain in their homes for a short time." Figure 6.3 shows that originations of riskier loans increased dramatically from 2002 to 2006, and commentators point to such data as evidence of large-scale innovation.

The historical record paints a different picture. It is approximately true to say that prior to 1981 virtually all mortgages were either fixed rate loans or something close to it.[8] Yet the emergence of nontraditional mortgages still predates the 2000s mortgage boom by many years. Perhaps the most extreme form of nontraditional mortgage is the payment-option ARM, which allows a borrower to pay less than the interest due on the loan in a given month. The difference is made up by adding the arrears to the outstanding mortgage balance. This type of loan was invented in 1980 and approved for widespread use by the Federal Home Loan Bank (FHLB) board and the Office of the Comptroller of the Currency (OCC) in 1981 (Harrigan 1981; Gerth 1981). Large California thrifts subsequently embraced the "option ARM," which would eventually play a central role in the Golden State's housing market (Guttentag 1984). By 1996 one-third of all originations in California were option ARMs (Stahl 1996); we reproduce a 1998 advertisement for this product in the left panel of figure 6.4. The large volume of option ARMs belies the claim that this instrument was a niche product. Indeed, the lender most closely associated with option ARMs, Golden West, made a point of avoiding "upscale" borrowers. Despite originating almost two-thirds of its loans in California, the typical Golden West mortgage in 2005 was for less than $400,000 (Savastano 2005).

Some confusion about the growth of the option ARM results from the fact that it was almost exclusively held in bank portfolios until 2004. The loan was

FIGURE 6.4 / Evidence of Option ARMs and Low-Documentations Loans Before the Housing Boom

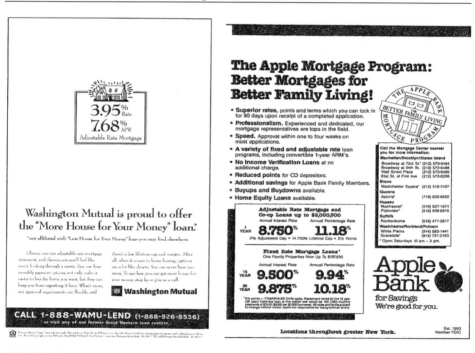

Source: New York Times (1989, 1998).

Notes: The ad on the left, from the *New York Times* on July 26, 1998, is for a payment-option ARM. The ad on the right, from the *New York Times* on June 25, 1989, is for a low-documentation loan ("no income verification"). These ads illustrate that many of the mortgages used extensively during the boom had been available many years previously.

an attractive portfolio addition because it generated floating-rate interest income and thus eliminated the lender's interest rate risk. At the same time, the option ARM's flexible treatment of amortization smoothed out payment fluctuations for the borrower. In any event, even though option ARMs were available in the 1980s and 1990s, they do not show up in data sets of *securitized* loans until 2004 (see, for example, Dokko et al. 2009, table 4). Even then, the majority of securitized option ARMs were made in the markets where they were already common as portfolio loans (Liu 2005).

Another type of nontraditional mortgage, the reduced-documentation loan, also began to spread in the 1980s; the right panel of figure 6.4 shows a 1989 ad for such a loan. By 1990, Fannie Mae was reporting that between 30 and 35 percent of the loans it insured were "low-doc" and "no-doc" loans (Sichelman 1990). Ironically, commentators raised virtually identical concerns about low-doc lending in the early 1990s as they did in 2005. For example, Lew Sichelman (1990), a veteran mortgage industry journalist, wrote in 1990 that "in recent years, lenders, spurred by competitive pressures and secure in the knowledge that they could peddle questionable loans to unsuspecting investors on the secondary market, have been approving low- and no-doc loans with as little as 10 percent down."

Fact 4: Government policy toward the mortgage market did not change much from 1990 to 2005

While the conventional wisdom blames the foreclosure crisis on too little government regulation of the mortgage market, an influential minority believes that government interventions went too far (for two leading examples of the genre, see Morgenson and Rosner 2011; Rajan 2010). According to this view, policymakers in the 1990s hoped to expand homeownership, either for its own sake or as a way to combat the effects of rising income inequality. Consequently, this narrative contends, policymakers allowed lenders to abandon traditional and prudent underwriting guidelines that had worked well for decades. In reality, government officials talked at length about lending and homeownership in the 1990s and early 2000s, but actual market interventions were modest. In fact, compared to the massive federal interventions in the U.S. mortgage market during the immediate postwar era, government interventions during the recent housing boom were virtually nonexistent.

For a concrete example, consider the size of required down payments. Gretchen Morgenson and Joshua Rosner (2011, 3) write that because of the Clinton administration's emphasis on homeownership, "in just a few short years, all of the venerable rules governing the relationship between borrower and lender went out the window, starting with the elimination of the requirements that a borrower put down a substantial amount of cash in a property."[9]

It is true that large down payments were once required to purchase homes in the United States. It is also true that the federal government was instrumental in reducing required down payments in an effort to expand homeownership. The problem for the "bad government" theory is that the timing of government involvement is almost exactly fifty years off. The key event was the Servicemen's Readjustment Act of 1944, better known as the GI Bill, in which the federal government promised to take a first-loss position equal to 50 percent of the mortgage balance, up to $2,000, on mortgages originated to returning veterans. The limits on the Veterans Administration (VA) loans were subsequently and repeatedly raised, while similar guarantees were later added to loans originated through the Federal Housing Administration (FHA). The top panel of figure 6.5 graphs average loan-to-value (LTV) ratios for various types of loans, including those with FHA and

FIGURE 6.5 / FHA and VA Loan Programs in the Immediate Postwar Era

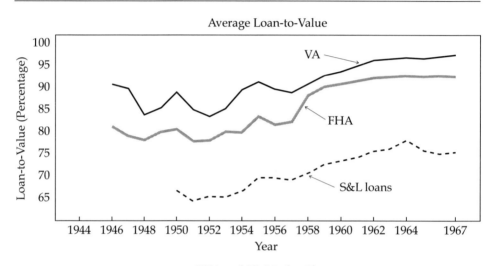

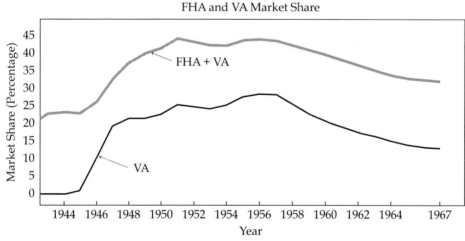

Source: Authors' compilation. LTVs from Herzog and Earley (1970), market shares from series Dc948 (FHA), Dc949 (VA), and Dc934 (total) from Carter et al. (2006).

VA insurance. It shows that borrowers took advantage of these government programs to buy houses with little or no money down. By the late 1960s, the average down payment on a VA loan was around 2 percent. A large fraction of borrowers put down nothing at all. Government involvement in the early postwar mortgage market was broad; in no sense were FHA and VA mortgages "niche products." The bottom panel of figure 6.5 shows that together the FHA and the VA accounted for almost half of originations in the 1950s before tailing off somewhat in the 1960s.

In contrast to the heavy government involvement in housing during the immediate postwar era, recent data on LTV ratios suggest no major federal mortgage market interventions in the 1990s and 2000s. Figure 6.6 shows combined LTV ratios for purchase mortgages in Massachusetts from 1990 to 2010, the period when government intervention is supposed to have caused so much trouble.[10] To be sure, the boom years of 2002 to 2006 saw an increase in zero-down financing. But the data also show that even before the boom, most borrowers got loans without needing to post a 20 percent down payment.[11] In particular, Morgenson and Rosner (2011) point to the Clinton administration's National Partners in Homeownership initiative in 1994 as the starting point for an ill-fated credit expansion that led to the crisis. But inspection of figure 6.6 does not support the assertion that underwriting behavior was significantly changed by that program. The distribution of down payments was remarkably stable after 1994. The share of zero-down loans actually fell.[12]

FIGURE 6.6 / Distribution of Combined Loan-to-Value Ratios on Home Purchases in Massachusetts, 1990 to 2011

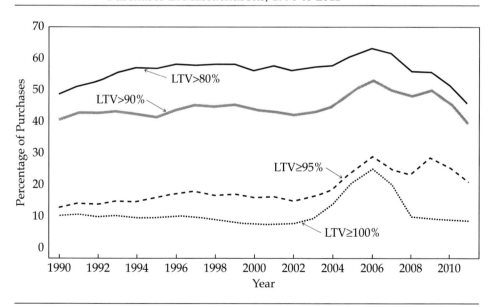

Source: Authors' calculations based on Warren Group (various years).

Note: These statistics include all mortgages taken out at the time of purchase and encompass cash buyers.

All told, it is impossible to find any government housing market initiative in recent years that is remotely comparable to the scope of the GI Bill and the FHA's subsequent expansion. It is important to stress that the FHA and the VA were widely understood to encourage high-risk lending to less-qualified borrowers. The delinquency rates on the loans they guaranteed were several times higher than delinquency rates on conventional loans. But the two government programs were also considered successful because they enabled lower-income Americans to own their own homes.[13]

Fact 5: The originate-to-distribute model was not new

One of the most important motivating principles of the Dodd-Frank Wall Street Reform and Consumer Protection Act, passed in 2010 to reduce the chance of future financial crises, was that the originate-to-distribute (OTD) model of lending shouldered much of the blame for the foreclosure crisis. Congressman Barney Frank, then the chairman of the House Financial Services Committee, put it this way: "If I can make a whole bunch of loans and sell the entire right to collect those to somebody else, at that point I don't care . . . whether or not they pay off. We have to prohibit that" (quoted in Arnold 2009). The Dodd-Frank Act requires mortgage originators to retain a slice of the credit risk of the mortgages they generate unless the credit quality of the mortgages is strong enough to earn an exemption.

Yet the OTD model was central to the U.S. mortgage market for decades before the financial crisis began. In the immediate postwar era, an important manifestation of the OTD model was the "mortgage company." These firms borrowed money from banks in order to fund mortgages for sale to outside investors, who often held the mortgages as whole loans. These lenders also "serviced" the loans on behalf of the investors and received a fixed percentage of the loan balance every month as compensation. A 1959 National Bureau of Economic Research (NBER) study of mortgage companies lists the fundamental features of the OTD model that would be familiar to modern originators as well:

> The modern mortgage company is typically a closely held, private corporation whose principal activity is originating and servicing residential mortgage loans for institutional investors. It is subject to a minimum degree of federal or state supervision, has a comparatively small capital investment relative to its volume of business, and relies largely on commercial bank credit to finance its operations and mortgage inventory. Such inventory is usually held only for a short interim between closing mortgage loans and their delivery to ultimate investors. (Klaman 1959, 239)

The importance of mortgage companies grew in the second half of the twentieth century. The top left panel of figure 6.7 shows that the market share of mortgage companies was around 20 percent in the 1970s and reached nearly 60 percent by 1995.

FIGURE 6.7 / Mortgage Statistics for Mortgage Companies and Savings and Loans, 1970 to 1997

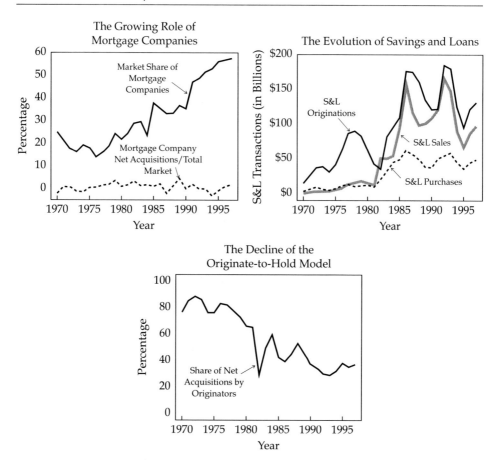

Source: Authors' compilation of data from Carter et al. (2006).

A focus on mortgage companies alone understates the role of the OTD model, however. Starting in the 1970s, the OTD model was adopted by other financial institutions, most importantly by savings and loans (S&Ls), which financed the majority of U.S. residential lending in the postwar period. S&Ls had historically followed an originate-to-hold model. By the late 1970s, however, rising interest rates had generated a catastrophic mismatch between the low interest rates that S&Ls received on their existing mortgages and their current costs of funds. This mismatch, which would eventually render more than half of S&Ls insolvent, encouraged thrifts either to turn to adjustable rate mortgages or to sell the mortgages they originated to the secondary market. The top right panel of figure 6.7 shows that by the late 1980s S&Ls were selling almost as many loans as they originated. In other words, most had adopted the OTD model and become, for all practical purposes, mortgage companies. The bottom panel of figure 6.7 shows that the decline of the originate-to-hold model was well underway thirty years before the boom of the 2000s.

Over time, the OTD model evolved. In the 1950s, mortgage companies typically sold their loans to insurance companies, which kept them on portfolio as whole loans. Starting in the 1970s, this framework gave way to mortgage-backed securities (MBSs), which were largely guaranteed by Ginnie Mae. The other government-sponsored housing agencies, Fannie Mae and Freddie Mac, became dominant players in the early 1980s. This period also saw the emergence of the private-label securities market, and in the 2000s the private-label market grew at the expense of the agency market. However, the institutional framework of the OTD model remained more or less identical to what it was in the 1950s. Lenders originated loans and sold them to other institutions. Typically the loans were then serviced by the originating lender, but other servicing arrangements were also possible.[14]

Fact 6: MBSs, CDOs, and other "complex financial products" had been widely used for decades

Another source of potential confusion lies in the distinction between the OTD model and securitization. Securitization implies originate-to-distribute, but the OTD model had existed for decades before securitization emerged. As noted earlier, early manifestations of the OTD model generally featured the sale of whole loans into investor portfolios. Only in the 1970s and 1980s did Ginnie Mae, Fannie Mae, and Freddie Mac begin to arrange or insure pass-through securities, whereby investors could buy a prorated share of a pool of mortgages. Private-label securities were also being developed at that time, but the emergence of these securities proceeded in fits and starts. In 1977, Salomon Brothers arranged the first private-label MBS deal, which was considered something of a failure (for a discussion, see Ranieri 1996). Among other problems, existing state laws prevented most of the relevant investors from buying the bonds. Issuing securities through Fannie Mae and Freddie Mac allowed issuers to address these laws, and the collateralized mortgage obligation (CMO) emerged in the early 1980s as a way to sell an array of complex securities with different repayment properties (principal only, interest only, floating rate notes, fixed rate notes, and so on) secured by a pool of mortgages. Until the 1986 Tax Reform Act, it remained difficult to construct a complex mortgage deal without the involvement of Fannie Mae or Freddie Mac. But that act created a financial structure called a real estate mortgage investment conduit (REMIC) that allowed issuers to create complex MBSs without the assistance of one of the government-sponsored enterprises (GSEs).

The emergence of collateralized debt obligations (CDOs) was the next step in the securitization of debt. The CDO was invented in the early 1990s as a way for banks to sell the risk on pools of commercial loans (Tett 2009). Over time, financial institutions realized that the CDO structure could also be used for pools of risky tranches from securities, including private-label securities backed by mortgages.

In 2000 investment banks began to combine the lower-rated tranches of mortgage securities, typically subprime asset-backed securities (ABSs), with other forms of securitized debt to create CDOs. The ABS CDO was born.[15] As Larry Cordell, Yilin Huang, and Meredith Williams (2012) show, the poor performance of ABS CDOs in the early 2000s was widely blamed on the presence of nonmortgage assets like tranches from car-loan or credit-card deals, so the ABS CDO deals became dominated by tranches from subprime ABSs. Consequently, as the housing market boomed in the mid-2000s, ABS CDOs became increasingly pure plays on the subprime mortgage market.

Looking back, we can see a remarkable feature about the boom in securitized lending in the mid-2000s: the institutional and legal framework it required had been in place since at least the early 1990s, and for some key components much earlier than that. In other words, what is significant about the evolution of the mortgage market in the 2000s is how *little* institutional change took place. As far as the mortgage and mortgage securities markets were concerned, there were few legal or institutional changes—and certainly no major ones—in the period immediately preceding the lending boom. It is true that there was dramatic growth in the *use* of subprime ABSs to fund loans, as well as in the *use* of ABS CDOs to fund the lower-rated tranches of subprime deals. But this growth did not occur because lenders and investors had been unable to use those structures earlier. In short, the idea that the boom in securitization was some exogenous event that sparked the housing boom receives no support from the institutional history of the American mortgage market.

Fact 7: Mortgage investors had lots of information

One of the pillars of the inside job theory of the mortgage crisis is that mortgage industry insiders were stingy with information about the securities they structured and sold. In fact, issuers supplied a great deal of information to potential investors. Simply put, the market for mortgage investments was awash in information.

To start with, prospectuses for pools of loans provided detailed information on the underlying loans at the time they were originated. This information included the distributions of the key credit-quality variables, such as LTV ratios, documentation status, and borrower credit scores. More importantly, they provided conditional distributions showing, for example, the share of borrowers with FICO (formerly Fair Isaac Corporation) scores between 600 and 619 or the share of borrowers with LTV ratios between 95 and 99 percent. In many cases, issuers provided loan-level details in what was known as a "free writing prospectus."

To non-experts, one of the most confusing things about the mortgage securities market is that issuers were quite careful to document the extent to which they did *not* document a borrower's income and assets. Loans were typically given a four-letter code that informed investors whether the information about income (I) and assets (A) was either verified (V), stated (S), or not collected at all (N). For example, the code SIVA means stated income/verified assets.[16] The crucial point here is that investors knowingly bought low-doc/no-doc loans. In fact, we now know that lenders provided loans to borrowers with damaged credit without documenting their incomes, not because of any after-the-fact forensic investigation, but rather because lenders were broadcasting this information to prospective investors. The origination data in figure 6.3, which shows the dramatic growth of loans to borrowers with low credit scores and less-than-full income and asset verification, come from data provided to investors—data that were known about and widely commented upon in real time.

The information flow continued after the deals were sold to investors. All issuers provided monthly loan-level information on the characteristics of every loan in the pool, including the monthly payment, the interest rate, the remaining principal balance, and the delinquency status of each loan. Issuers also disclosed the disposition of terminated loans, including the dollar amount of losses that stemmed from short sales or foreclosures. Again, these data were publicly available free of charge, but most investors used a loan-level data set from the LoanPerformance company, which was a cleaned and standardized version of raw data gathered from many different issuers and lenders.

Investors had access not only to important data but also to tools that allowed them to use these data to price securities. The MBSs and CDOs that contained the mortgages (or the mortgage risk) appeared complex on the surface, but they were in fact straightforward to model. Most investors used a program called Intex, which coded all of the rules from a prospectus for the allocation of cash flows to different tranches of a deal. To forecast the performance of a deal, an investor would input into Intex a scenario for the performance of the underlying loans. Intex would then deliver cash flows, taking into account all of the complex features of the deal, including so-called overcollateralization accounts and the treatment of interest income earned on loans that were paid off in the middle of a month. Cordell, Huang, and Williams (2012) show that using Intex, one could accurately measure the losses and value of ABS CDOs in real time throughout the crisis.

To illustrate the information available to investors on a CDO transaction, figure 6.8 shows pages from the offer documents for the notorious Abacus AC-1 CDO.[17] These documents provide amounts and CUSIPs for every security in the deal.[18] Armed with those CUSIPs, a potential investor could use LoanPerformance data to obtain the origination information and current delinquency status of every individual loan in each deal. Then, using Intex, the investor could forecast the cash flows for each reference security under different macroeconomic scenarios.

Fact 8: Investors understood the risks

Using data supplied by issuers and lenders, as well as quantitative tools designed to exploit this information efficiently, investors were able to predict with a fair degree of accuracy how mortgages and related securities would perform under various macroeconomic scenarios.[19] Table 6.3, taken from a Lehman Brothers analyst report published in August 2005, shows predicted losses for a pool of subprime loans originated in the second half of 2005 under different assumptions for

FIGURE 6.8 / The Reference Portfolio of the Abacus Deal

Reference Portfolio

Security	Type	Notional Amount	CUSIP	Fitch	Moody's	S&P	Base WAL (yrs)	Dated Date	Legal Final	Servicer
ABFC 2006-OPT1 M8	Subprime	22,222,222	00075QAM4	BBB	Baa2	BBB	3.9	8/10/2006	9/25/2036	OOMC
ABFC 2006-OPT2 M8	Subprime	22,222,222	00075XAP2	BBB	Baa2	BBB	4.1	10/12/2006	10/25/2036	OOMC
ABSHE 2006-HE3 M7	Subprime	22,222,222	04541GXK3	BBB	Baa2	BBB	3.8	4/17/2006	3/25/2036	OOMC
ABSHE 2006-HE4 M7	Subprime	22,222,222	04544GAP4	BBB	Baa2	BBB	3.8	4/28/2006	5/25/2036	SPS
ACE 2006-FM2 M8	Midprime	22,222,222	00442CAN9		Baa2	BBB	4.5	10/30/2006	8/25/2036	WFB
ACE 2006-OP2 M9	Subprime	22,222,222	00441YAP7		Baa2	BBB-	4.3	10/30/2006	8/25/2036	WFB
ARSI 2006-W1 M8	Subprime	22,222,222	040104RQ6	BBB+	Baa2	BBB+	3.8	2/7/2006	3/25/2036	AQMC
CARR 2006-FRE1 M9	Subprime	22,222,222	144538AN5	BBB+	Baa2	A	3.8	6/28/2006	7/25/2036	FREM
CARR 2006-FRE2 M8	Subprime	22,222,222	14454AAN9		Baa2	BBB+	4.2	10/18/2006	10/25/2036	FREM
CARR 2006-NC1 M8	Midprime	22,222,222	144531FF2	BBB	Baa2	BBB+	3.6	2/8/2006	1/25/2036	NCMC
CARR 2006-NC2 M8	Subprime	22,222,222	14453FAM1	BBB	Baa2	BBB	3.8	6/21/2006	6/25/2036	CARR
CARR 2006-NC3 M9	Subprime	22,222,222	144528AN6	BBB-	Baa2	BBB-	4.0	8/10/2006	8/25/2036	NCMC
CARR 2006-OPT1 M8	Subprime	22,222,222	144531FV7	BBB+	Baa2	A-	3.6	3/14/2006	2/25/2036	OOMC
CMLTI 2006-AMC1 M8	Subprime	22,222,222	17309PAL0		Baa2	BBB	4.1	9/28/2006	9/25/2036	AQMC
CMLTI 2006-NC1 M8	Subprime	22,222,222	172983AN8		Baa2	BBB	3.8	6/29/2006	8/25/2036	WFB
CMLTI 2006-WFH2 M9	Subprime	22,222,222	17309MAN3		Baa2	BBB-	4.0	8/30/2006	8/25/2036	WFB
CMLTI 2006-WMC1 M8	Midprime	22,222,222	17307G2F4	A-	Baa2	BBB+	3.7	1/31/2006	12/25/2035	WFB
CMLTI 2007-WFH1 M9	Subprime	22,222,222	17311CAM3		Baa2	BBB-	4.5	2/9/2007	1/25/2037	WFB
CWL 2006-24 M8	Subprime	22,222,222	23243HAN1		Baa2	BBB	4.9	12/29/2006	5/25/2037	CHLS
FFML 2006-FF11 M8	Midprime	22,222,222	32028PAP0	BBB	Baa2	BBB	3.9	9/6/2006	8/25/2036	WFB
FFML 2006-FF12 M8	Midprime	22,222,222	32027GAN6	BBB	Baa2	BBB	4.2	8/25/2006	9/25/2036	ALS
FFML 2006-FF14 M8	Midprime	22,222,222	32027LAP0	BBB	Baa2	BBB	4.2	9/25/2006	10/25/2036	AURA
FFML 2006-FF15 M8	Midprime	22,222,222	32028GAP0	BBB	Baa2	BBB	4.3	10/25/2006	11/25/2036	AURA
FFML 2006-FF16 M8	Midprime	22,222,222	320275AN0		Baa2	BBB+	4.3	11/30/2006	12/25/2036	NCHL
FFML 2006-FF17 M8	Midprime	22,222,222	32028KAP1	BBB	Baa2	BBB	4.4	11/25/2006	12/25/2036	ALS
FFML 2006-FF7 M8	Midprime	22,222,222	320277AP1	BBB	Baa2	BBB	3.6	5/31/2006	5/25/2036	WFB
FFML 2006-FF9 M8	Midprime	22,222,222	320276AP3	BBB+	Baa2	BBB+	3.7	7/7/2006	6/25/2036	WFB
FHLT 2006-A M7	Subprime	22,222,222	35729RAN6	BBB+	Baa2	BBB	3.9	5/10/2006	5/25/2036	WFB
FHLT 2006-B M8	Midprime	22,222,222	35729QAN8	BBB+	Baa2	BBB	4.4	8/3/2006	8/25/2036	WFB
FMIC 2006-2 M8	Midprime	22,222,222	31659EAM0		Baa2	BBB+	4.1	7/6/2006	7/25/2036	WFB
FMIC 2006-3 M8	Midprime	22,222,222	316599AN9		Baa2	BBB	4.4	10/27/2006	11/25/2036	WFB
GSAMP 2006-FM2 M8	Midprime	22,222,222	36245DAN0		Baa2	BBB+	4.0	9/29/2006	9/25/2036	WFB
HEAT 2006-3 M8	Midprime	22,222,222	437084UZ7	BBB+	Baa2	BBB+	3.5	3/30/2006	7/25/2036	SPS
HEAT 2006-5 M8	Midprime	22,222,222	437096AQ3	BBB+	Baa2	BBB+	3.8	6/25/2006	10/25/2036	WFB
HEAT 2006-6 M8	Midprime	22,222,222	437097AP3	A-	Baa2	A-	4.0	8/1/2006	11/25/2036	SPS
HEAT 2006-7 M8	Midprime	22,222,222	43709NAP8	BBB+	Baa2	BBB+	4.2	10/3/2006	1/25/2037	SPS
HEAT 2006-8 M8	Midprime	22,222,222	43709QAP1	BBB	Baa2	BBB+	4.4	12/1/2006	3/25/2037	SPS
IXIS 2006-HE3 B2	Midprime	22,222,222	46602UAM0	BBB	Baa2	BBB	4.8	9/29/2006	1/25/2037	WFB
JPMAC 2006-CW2 MV8	Midprime	22,222,222	46629BBA6	BBB	Baa2	BBB	4.3	8/8/2006	8/25/2036	CWHL
JPMAC 2006-FRE1 M8	Midprime	22,222,222	46626LFV7	BBB	Baa2	BBB	3.6	1/27/2006	5/25/2035	JPM
JPMAC 2006-WMC3 M8	Midprime	22,222,222	46629KAP4	BBB	Baa2	BBB	4.3	9/14/2006	8/25/2036	JPM
LBMLT 2006-11 M8	Midprime	22,222,222	542512AN8		Baa2	BBB	4.7	12/14/2006	12/25/2036	WMB
LBMLT 2006-4 M8	Midprime	22,222,222	54251MAN4		Baa2	A-	3.9	5/9/2006	5/25/2036	WMB
LBMLT 2006-6 M8	Midprime	22,222,222	54251RAN3	BBB+	Baa2	BBB+	4.2	7/26/2006	7/25/2036	WMB
LBMLT 2006-7 M8	Midprime	22,222,222	54251TAN9	BBB+	Baa2	A-	4.2	8/30/2006	8/25/2036	WMB

As of February 26, 2007. Goldman Sachs neither represents nor provides any assurances that the actual Reference Portfolio on the Closing Date or any future date will have the same characteristics as represented above. See the final Offering Circular for the Initial Reference Portfolio.

Reference Obligations are designated as "Midprime" herein if the weighted average FICO score of the underlying collateral that secures such Reference Obligation is greater than 625. All other Reference Obligations are designated as "Subprime" herein.

55

Reference Portfolio

Security	Type	Notional Amount	CUSIP	Fitch	Moody's	S&P	Base WAL (yrs)	Dated Date	Legal Final	Servicer
LBMLT 2006-WL1 M8	Midprime	22,222,222	542514RD8		Baa2	BBB	3.1	2/8/2006	1/25/2036	LBMC
MABS 2006-HE5 M9	Subprime	22,222,222	576455AN9		Baa2	BBB-	4.5	12/28/2006	11/25/2036	WFB
MABS 2006-NC2 M9	Subprime	22,222,222	55275BAP2	BBB	Baa2	BBB-	4.2	9/28/2006	8/25/2036	WFB
MABS 2006-WMC4 M8	Midprime	22,222,222	57645MAP7		Baa2	BBB+	4.6	11/30/2006	10/25/2036	WFB
MLMI 2006-WMC1 B2A	Midprime	22,222,222	59020U4H5		Baa2	BBB+	3.6	2/14/2006	1/25/2037	WCC
MSAC 2006-HE7 B2	Subprime	22,222,222	61750MAP0		Baa2	BBB	4.9	10/31/2006	9/25/2036	CWHL
MSAC 2006-HE8 B2	Midprime	22,222,222	61750SAP7		Baa2	BBB	5.1	11/29/2006	10/25/2036	WFB
MSAC 2006-NC4 B2	Subprime	22,222,222	61748LAN2	BBB	Baa2	BBB	4.5	6/23/2006	6/25/2036	WFB
MSAC 2006-NC5 B3	Midprime	22,222,222	61749BAQ6		Baa2	BBB-	5.3	11/28/2006	10/25/2036	CWHL
MSAC 2006-WMC1 B2	Midprime	22,222,222	61744CXV3	BBB+	Baa2	A-	4.2	1/26/2006	12/25/2035	JPM
MSAC 2006-WMC2 B2	Midprime	22,222,222	61749KAP8	BBB	Baa2	BBB	4.7	6/28/2006	7/25/2036	WFB
MSAC 2007-NC1 B2	Subprime	22,222,222	617505AN2		Baa2	BBB	5.3	1/26/2007	11/25/2036	CWHL
MSC 2006-HE2 B2	Midprime	22,222,222	617451FD6	BBB	Baa2	BBB+	4.5	4/28/2006	3/25/2036	WFB
MSIX 2006-2 B2	Midprime	22,222,222	617463AM6		Baa2	BBB	5.0	11/28/2006	11/25/2036	SAX
NHEL 2006-5 M8	Subprime	22,222,222	66988YAN2		Baa2	BBB+	4.0	9/28/2006	11/25/2036	NOVA
NHELI 2006-FM1 M8	Midprime	22,222,222	65536HCF3		Baa2	BBB+	3.3	1/30/2006	11/25/2035	WFB
NHELI 2006-FM2 M8	Midprime	22,222,222	65537FAN1	BBB+	Baa2	BBB+	4.1	10/31/2006	7/25/2036	WFB
NHELI 2006-HE3 M8	Subprime	22,222,222	65536QAN8	BBB+	Baa2	BBB+	4.0	8/31/2006	7/25/2036	WFB
OOMLT 2007-1 M8	Subprime	22,222,222	68400DAP9		Baa2	BBB	4.3	1/24/2007	1/25/2037	OOMC
SABR 2006-FR1 B2	Midprime	22,222,222	81375WJY3	BBB+	Baa2	A-	4.6	2/23/2006	11/25/2035	HSC
SABR 2006-FR3 B2	Subprime	22,222,222	813765AH7	BBB+	Baa2	BBB	5.0	8/3/2006	5/25/2036	HSC
SABR 2006-HE2 B2	Subprime	22,222,222	81377AAM4	BBB+	Baa2	BBB	4.1	9/28/2006	7/25/2036	HSC
SAIL 2006-4 M7	Subprime	22,222,222	86360WAM4	BBB	Baa2	BBB	4.1	6/25/2006	7/25/2036	ALS
SASC 2006-EQ1A M8	Subprime	22,222,222	86360RAN3		Baa2	BBB	5.2	7/17/2006	7/25/2036	AURA
SASC 2006-OPT1 M7	Subprime	22,222,222	86359UAN9	BBB	Baa2	BBB	3.7	4/25/2006	4/25/2036	AURA
SURF 2007-BC1 B2	Subprime	22,222,222	84752BAQ2		Baa2	BBB	4.9	1/24/2007	1/25/2038	WCC
SVHE 2006-EQ2 M8	Midprime	22,222,222	83611XAM6	BBB	Baa2	BBB	4.6	12/28/2006	1/25/2037	OLS
SVHE 2006-OPT1 M7	Subprime	22,222,222	83611MMF2	BBB+	Baa2	BBB	3.6	3/10/2006	3/25/2036	OOMC
SVHE 2006-OPT2 M7	Subprime	22,222,222	83611MMT2		Baa2	A-	3.6	4/7/2006	5/25/2036	OOMC
SVHE 2006-OPT3 M7	Subprime	22,222,222	83611MPR3		Baa2	BBB	3.7	5/12/2006	6/25/2036	OOMC
SVHE 2006-OPT5 M8	Subprime	22,222,222	83612CAN9		Baa2	BBB	4.2	6/19/2006	7/25/2036	OOMC
ABSHE 2006-HE7 M9	Subprime	22,222,222	04544QAP2	BBB-	Baa2	BBB-	4.4	11/30/2006	11/25/2036	SPS
BSABS 2006-HE9 M9	Subprime	22,222,222	07389MAP2		Baa2	BBB-	4.4	11/30/2006	11/25/2036	EMC
CMLTI 2007-AMC1 M8	Subprime	22,222,222	17311BAL7		Baa2	BBB	4.6	3/9/2007	12/25/2036	CWHL
FFML 2007-FF1 B2	Midprime	22,222,222	32028TAN7		Baa2	BBB	4.8	1/26/2007	1/25/2038	HLS
HASC 2006-HE2 M8	Midprime	22,222,222	44328BAP3	BBB+	Baa2	BBB+	4.3	12/5/2006	12/25/2036	CMB
HEAT 2007-1 M8	Midprime	22,222,222	43710LAN4	BBB	Baa2	BBB+	4.5	2/1/2007	5/25/2037	SPS
LBMLT 2006-8 M8	Midprime	22,222,222	54251UAN6		Baa2	A-	4.4	9/21/2006	9/25/2036	WMB
LBMLT 2006-9 M8	Midprime	22,222,222	54251WAN2		Baa2	BBB+	4.4	10/12/2006	10/25/2036	WMB
MLMI 2006-HE6 B3	Subprime	22,222,222	59023XAN6		Baa2	BBB-	4.6	12/28/2006	11/25/2037	WCC
MLMI 2006-OPT1 B2	Subprime	22,222,222	59022VAN1		Baa2	BBB	3.9	9/26/2006	8/25/2037	OOMC
MSAC 2007-HE1 B2	Subprime	22,222,222	617526AP3		Baa2	BBB	5.2	1/26/2007	11/25/2036	SM
OOMLT 2006-3 M9	Subprime	22,222,222	68389BAM5		Baa2	BBB-	4.0	10/27/2006	2/25/2037	OOMC
SASC 2006-WF3 M9	Subprime	22,222,222	86361EAP6	BBB-	Baa2	BBB-	4.3	9/25/2006	9/25/2036	ALS
SVHE 2006-OPT4 M7	Subprime	22,222,222	83611YAM4		Baa2	BBB+	3.6	5/26/2006	6/25/2036	OOMC

As of February 26, 2007. Goldman Sachs neither represents nor provides any assurances that the actual Reference Portfolio on the Closing Date or any future date will have the same characteristics as represented above. See the final Offering Circular for the Initial Reference Portfolio.

Reference Obligations are designated as "Midprime" herein if the weighted average FICO score of the underlying collateral that secures such Reference Obligation is greater than 625. All other Reference Obligations are designated as "Subprime" herein.

56

Source: Goldman Sachs, represented with permission.

TABLE 6.3 / Conditional Forecasts of Losses on Subprime Investments

Scenario	Probability	Cumulative Loss
11 percent HPA over the life of the pool (aggressive)	15%	1.4%
8 percent HPA for life	15	3.2%
HPA slows to 5 percent by end of 2005 (base)	50	5.6%
0 percent HPA for the next three years, 5 percent thereafter (pessimistic)	15	11.1%
–5 percent for the next three years, 5 percent thereafter (meltdown)	5	17.1%

Source: Lehman Brothers (Mago and Shu 2005), reprinted with permission.

U.S. house prices (Mago and Shu 2005). The top three house price scenarios, which range from "base" to "aggressive," predict losses of between 1 and 6 percent. Such losses had been typical of previous subprime deals and implied that investments even in lower-rated tranches of subprime deals would be profitable. The report also considers two adverse scenarios for house prices, one labeled "pessimistic" and the other labeled "meltdown." These two scenarios assume near-term annualized growth in house prices of 0 and –5 percent, respectively. For these scenarios, losses are dramatically worse. The pessimistic scenario generates an 11.1 percent loss, while the meltdown scenario generates a 17.1 percent loss. The report goes on to point out that while the pessimistic scenario would lead to write-offs of the lowest-rated tranches of subprime deals, the meltdown scenario would lead to massive losses on all but the highest-rated tranches.

Lehman analysts were not alone in understanding the strong relationship between house prices and losses on subprime loans. As Kristopher Gerardi and his colleagues (2008) show, analysts at other banks reached similar conclusions and were similarly accurate in their forecasts conditional on house price appreciation (HPA) outcomes. JPMorgan analysts used MSA-level variation in losses on 2003 subprime originations to produce remarkably accurate predictions about losses (Flanagan et al. 2006a). A UBS slide presentation about subprime securities given in the fall of 2005 was subtitled "It's (Almost) All About Home Prices" (Zimmerman 2005).

The Lehman analysis and others like it are crucial documents for anyone hoping to understand why investors lined up to buy securities backed by subprime loans. First, the analysis shows that investors knew about the significant risk inherent in subprime deals. Expected losses on a typical prime deal were a fraction of 1 percent—even under the worst scenarios, prime losses were expected to reach only the low single digits.[20] According to table 6.3, losses on a subprime deal could be many times higher. Given a 50 percent recovery rate in foreclosure, the 17.1 percent loss implied in Lehman's meltdown scenario assumes that lenders would foreclose on one-third of the loans in the pool. The analysis underscores investors' knowledge about the sensitivity of subprime loans to adverse movements in housing prices, and it refutes the idea that investors did not or could not determine how risky these loans were.

A second reason that table 6.3 is important is that its forecasts proved to be accurate. Despite its foreboding name, the "meltdown" scenario was actually optimistic with respect to the observed fall in housing prices that began in 2006. The current forecast for losses on deals in the ABX 2006-1 index, which largely contains loans originated in the second half of 2005, is about 22 percent (Jozoff et al. 2012). This is consistent with the relationship between losses and house prices implied by the table. The bottom line is that analysts working in real time had little trouble figuring out how much subprime investors would lose if house prices fell.

We turn to the next logical question in the next section: given how badly these loans were expected to perform if prices fell, why did investors buy them?

Fact 9: Investors were optimistic about house prices

The answer to why investors purchased subprime securities is contained in the third column of the same Lehman analysis cited in table 6.3, which lists the probabilities that were assigned to each of the various house price scenarios. It indicates that the adverse price scenarios received very little weight. In particular, the meltdown scenario—the only scenario generating losses that would threaten repayment of any AAA-rated tranche—was assigned only a 5 percent probability. The more benign pessimistic scenario received only a 15 percent probability. By contrast, the top two price scenarios, each of which assumes at least 8 percent annual growth in house prices over the next several years, received probabilities that sum to 30 percent. In other words, the authors of the Lehman report were bullish about subprime investments not because they believed that borrowers had some "moral obligation" to repay mortgages or because they did not realize that the lenders had not fully verified borrower incomes. The authors were not concerned about losses because they thought that house prices would continue to rise and that steady increases in the value of the collateral backing the loans would cover any losses generated by borrowers who would not or could not repay.

Relative to historical experience, even the baseline forecast was optimistic, and the two stronger scenarios were almost euphoric. A widely circulated calculation by Robert Shiller (2005) showed that real house price appreciation over the period from 1890 to 2004 was less than 1 percent per year. A cursory look at the Federal Housing Finance Agency (FHFA) national price index gives slightly higher real house price appreciation from 1975 to 2000—more than 1 percent—but still offers nothing to justify 5 percent nominal annual price appreciation, let alone 8 or 11 percent. Further, even sustained periods of elevated price appreciation are rare.[21]

The optimism was not unique to the Lehman report. Table 6.4, based on reports from analysts at JPMorgan, shows that optimism reigned even in 2006, after house prices had crested and begun to fall. Well into 2007, the analysts were convinced that the decline would prove transitory and that prices would soon resume their upward march.

Industry analysts were not the only ones who were optimistic about the housing market. In recent work (Gerardi, Foote, and Willen 2011), we show that there was considerable real-time debate among academic economists on whether house

TABLE 6.4 / Views on House Price Appreciation: JPMorgan Analysts

Date of Report	Date of Data	Title
December 8, 2006	October 2006	"More widespread declines with early stabilization signs"
January 10, 2007	November 2006	"Continuing declines with stronger stabilization signs"
February 6, 2007	December 2006	"Tentative stabilization in HPA"
March 12, 2007	January 2007	"Continued stabilization in HPA"
September 20, 2007	July 2007	"Near bottom on HPA"
November 2, 2007	September 2007	"UGLY! Double digit declines in August and September"

Source: Authors' compilation based on Flanagan et al. (2006b).

prices in the early 2000s were justified by fundamentals or were instead poised to fall. In any case, the contemporary evidence on what investors believed about prices suggests that their widespread optimism encouraged them to purchase subprime securities, despite the well-understood risks involved.

Fact 10: Mortgage market insiders were the biggest losers

Perhaps the most compelling evidence against the inside job theory of the crisis concerns the distribution of gains and losses among market participants. If insiders took advantage of outsiders, then those most closely associated with the origination and securitization of mortgages should have pocketed the most money or at least incurred the smallest losses. Conversely, investors with little connection to the industry should have suffered the most. In fact, the opposite pattern emerges.

First consider the losers. Table 6.5 displays losses related to the subprime crisis compiled by Bloomberg as of June 2008. Six of the top ten institutions in this unhappy group (Citigroup, Merrill Lynch, HSBC, Bank of America, Morgan Stanley, and JPMorgan) not only securitized subprime mortgages but actually owned companies that originated them. Ironically, the list omits Bear Stearns, the one firm most closely associated with the subprime market. Bear Stearns was heavily involved in every aspect of subprime lending, from origination to securitization to servicing. Yet Bear Stearns does not appear on this table because in March 2008 JPMorgan had acquired the firm in an assisted sale to prevent it from filing for bankruptcy.

In fact, a closer look at Bear Stearns's particular story provides compelling evidence against the view that mortgage industry insiders profited at the expense of outsiders. The company began experiencing problems in June 2007. Two hedge funds managed by the firm had invested heavily in subprime-related securities and reported enormous losses, requiring Bear Stearns to inject capital into the funds to protect investors. Remarkably, Bear Stearns executives were major investors in these funds (for further details, see Muolo and Padilla 2010, 244). In other words, the executives most likely to understand the subprime-lending process had made personal investment decisions that exposed them to subprime risk.[22]

TABLE 6.5 / Mortgage-Related Losses to Financial Institutions from the Subprime Crisis, June 18, 2008

	Institution	Loss (Billions of Dollars)
1	Citigroup	42.9
2	UBS	38.2
3	Merrill Lynch	37.1
4	HSBC	19.5
5	IKB Deutsche	15.9
6	Royal Bank of Scotland	15.2
7	Bank of America	15.1
8	Morgan Stanley	14.1
9	JPMorgan Chase	9.8
10	Credit Suisse	9.6
11	Washington Mutual	9.1
12	Credit Agricole	8.3
13	Lehman Brothers	8.2
14	Deutsche Bank	7.6
15	Wachovia	7.0
16	HBOS	7.0
17	Bayerische Landesbank	6.7
18	Fortis	6.6
19	Canadian Imperial (CIBC)	6.5
20	Barclays	6.3

Source: Onaran (2008). Used with permission of Bloomberg L.P. Copyright © 2012. All rights reserved.

Note: The date is chosen prior to the Lehman bankruptcy to avoid contamination from the wider financial crisis.

Indeed, the large insider losses have led many researchers to question whether lenders actually even used the OTD model. Table 6.6, based on an April 2008 Lehman Brothers report, shows that issuing institutions retained enormous amounts of both the AAA-rated private-label MBSs and the CDOs tied to their lower-rated tranches. This retention of subprime-mortgage risk occurred "even though the 'originate and distribute' model of securitization that many banks ostensibly followed was supposed to transfer risk to those institutions better able to bear it, such as unleveraged pension funds" (Kashyap 2010, 1).[23]

Fact 11: Mortgage market outsiders were the biggest winners

When we turn to the winners, the pattern is equally stark. The biggest beneficiary from the crisis was hedge fund manager John Paulson, who bought billions of dollars of credit protection on subprime deals in 2006 and 2007. When those deals defaulted en masse at the end of 2007, Paulson made $15 billion in profits (Zuckerman 2010).

Paulson and his lieutenant, Paolo Pellegrini, were complete mortgage industry outsiders. They had no investment experience in housing or mortgage markets,

TABLE 6.6 / Exposure of Financial Institutions to Housing Risk on the Eve of the Crisis, 2008

Entity	Loans	HELOC Second Liens	Agency MBSs	Non-Agency AAAs	CDOs (Residential Subordinates)	Residential Subordinates	Total Exposure
U.S. banks/ thrifts	2,020	869	852	383	90	0	4,212
GSEs/ FHLBs	444	0	741	308	0	0	1,493
Broker/ dealers	0	0	49	100	130	24	303
REITs	0	0	82	10	0	0	92
Hedge funds	0	0	50	51	0	24	126
Money managers	0	0	494	225	0	24	743
Insurance companies	0	0	856	125	65	24	1,070
Overseas	0	0	689	413	45	24	1,172
Financial guarantors	0	62	0	0	100	0	162
Others	461	185	550	21	45	0	1,262
Total	2,925	1,116	4,362	1,636	476	121	10,680

Source: Lehman Brothers U.S. Securitized Products, "Residential Credit Losses—Going into Extra Innings?" figure 4, April 11, 2008, reprinted in Acharya and Richardson (2009).

Note: Units are in billions of dollars.

and they had never traded mortgages before. Gregory Zuckerman (2010, 126) discusses investors' lukewarm response to Paulson's sales pitches, quoting one potential investor as saying: "'Paulson was a merger-arb guy and suddenly he has strong views on housing and subprime,' [the potential investor] recalls. 'The largest mortgage guys, including [Michael] Vranos at Ellington, one of the gods of the market, were far more positive on subprime.'"

Furthermore, Paulson and Pellegrini explicitly attributed their success not to insights about the underwriting process but rather to a successful bet on house prices. According to Zuckerman (2010, 107), their conclusion that house prices were going to fall was based on a simple analysis of the time series of house prices in the United States: "Housing prices had climbed a puny 1.4 percent annually between 1975 and 2000, after inflation was taken into consideration. But they had soared over 7 percent in the following five years, until 2005. The upshot: U.S. home prices would have to drop by almost 40 percent to return to their historic trend line."

It was this simple insight about prices—not any fact about credit, the origination process, or moral hazard—that led Paulson and Pellegrini to gamble on bearish bets on the subprime mortgage market. The chart showing that house prices would fall 40 percent was Paulson's "Rosetta stone, the key to making sense of the entire housing market" (Zuckerman 2010, 108). And even Zuckerman seems surprised by the failure of the insider/outsider theory of mortgage markets, posing this question at the beginning of his book: "Why was it John Paulson, a relative amateur in real estate and not a celebrated mortgage, bond, or housing specialist like Bill Gross or Mike Vranos, who pulled off the greatest trade in history?" (Zuckerman 2010, 3).

Another winner, memorably described by Michael Lewis (2010), was Michael Burry. His hedge fund Scion Capital made almost $1 billion in profits using a strategy similar to Paulson's, although on a smaller scale. Lewis writes that Burry, a medical doctor by training, was an outsider not only in the housing and mortgage industries but to society in general, as he worked largely alone. Burry attributed his success to his willingness to read complex prospectuses carefully:

> Burry had devoted himself to finding exactly the right ones to bet against. He'd read dozens of prospectuses and scoured hundreds more, looking for the dodgiest pools of mortgages, and was still pretty certain even then (and dead certain later) that he was the only human being on earth who read them, apart from the lawyers who drafted them. In doing so, he likely also became the only investor to do the sort of old-fashioned bank credit analysis on the home loans that should have been done before they were made. (Lewis 2010, 50)

In other words, Burry's bets were based on publicly available information.

Taking a broad view, the most useful demarcation to make when thinking about the mortgage market is not between insiders and outsiders—the division made in the left panel of figure 6.1—but rather between those people who thought house prices would continue to rise and those who were willing to bet that they would fall. Sadly for the economy, the overly optimistic group included not only the investors at the end of the securitization chain but the lenders and securitizers who sold them the bonds and whose losses precipitated the financial crisis.

Fact 12: It was top-rated bonds in collateralized debt obligations, not top-rated bonds backed by mortgages, that turned out to be "toxic"

No discussion of the causes of the financial crisis would be complete without some discussion of the rating agencies. To some analysts, the simple fact that rating agencies gave AAA ratings to subprime securities is patently absurd. An AAA rating is supposed to signal a near-complete absence of credit risk. Yet these bonds were often backed by reduced-documentation loans to borrowers with previous credit problems. Other critics are more specific, noting that the issuers paid the rating agencies to evaluate their deals. The implication is that these payments generated a conflict of interest for the agencies that encouraged them to bestow unjustifiably high ratings. At the very least, commentators often claim that rating agencies abetted finance industry insiders by endorsing securities backed by problem mortgages. Yet the facts paint a more nuanced picture.

To start with, the top-rated tranches of subprime securities fared better than many people realize. The left panels of figure 6.9 are generated from data on AAA-rated bonds created in 2006 and 2007 from private-label securitization deals.[24] Specifically, the panels show the fraction of these bonds on which investors suffered losses or, using industry jargon, the fraction that were "impaired." In some of these deals, 70 percent of the underlying subprime loans terminated in foreclosure (Jozoff et al. 2012). Yet despite these massive losses, the figure shows that investors lost money on fewer than 10 percent of private-label AAA-rated securities. How is that possible? As many have explained, the AAA-rated securities were protected by a series of lower-rated securities that absorbed most of the losses. If a borrower defaulted and the lender was unable to recover the principal, the resulting loss would be deducted from the principal of the deal's lower-rated tranches. For subprime deals, the degree of so-called AAA credit protection—the principal balance

FIGURE 6.9 / Impairments Among AAA-Rated Mortgage-Backed Securities and Collateralized Debt Obligations, 2006 and 2007

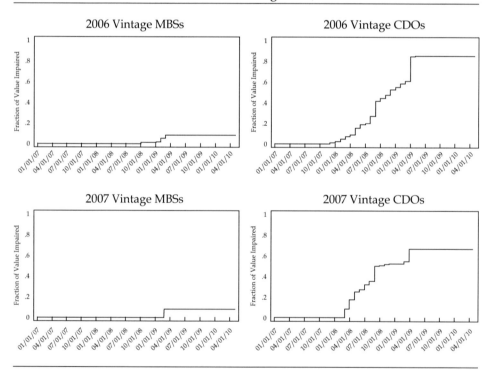

Source: Authors' compilation of data in figures 12, 13, 17, and 18 in Financial Crisis Inquiry Commission (2010).

Note: The 2007 data cover the second half of that year only. In 2006, there were 9,029 tranches of AAA-rated MBSs ($869 billion of total value) and 565 tranches of AAA-rated CDOs ($162 billion in total value). In the second half of 2007, there were 1,455 tranches of MBSs ($112 billion of total value) and 175 tranches of CDOs ($40.9 billion of total value).

of the non-AAA securities—was often more than 20 percent. Given a 50 percent recovery rate on foreclosed loans, 20 percent credit protection meant that 40 percent of the borrowers could suffer foreclosure before the AAA-rated investors suffered a single dollar of loss. For riskier deals, credit protection was higher, often substantially so. The key takeaway is that for subprime securities, credit protection largely worked, and investors in the AAA-rated securities were largely spared.

The relatively robust performance of private-label AAA-rated securities is explained clearly in the final report of the Financial Crisis Inquiry Commission (2011), among other sources. Yet it still surprises many people. If these AAA-rated securities did not suffer losses, where were the famous "toxic mortgage-related securities" that caused the financial crisis? The answer is that banks used lower-rated securities from private-label deals to construct other securities, such as the CDOs discussed earlier. Recall that because these CDOs were backed by tranches of subprime securities, which were technically labeled asset-backed securities (ABSs), the resulting CDOs were called ABS CDOs. The main difference between the original ABSs and the ABS CDOs was that the CDOs were not backed by two thousand or so subprime loans, but rather by a collection of ninety to one hundred lower-rated tranches of subprime ABS deals, with most of these tranches having BBB ratings. Yet the organizing principal of CDOs and the original ABS securities was the same: senior AAA-rated tranches were protected from losses by lower-rated tranches. For the original ABSs, losses would occur if individual homeowners defaulted. For the CDOs, losses would occur if the BBB-rated securities from the original ABS deals defaulted.

The right panels of figure 6.9 show the share of 2006 and 2007 ABS CDOs that were impaired. The results are nearly the mirror image of the previous panels. Whereas investors suffered losses on fewer than 10 percent of the AAA-rated tranches from the original subprime securities, they suffered losses on the vast majority of AAA-rated ABS CDOs.[25] To make matters worse, a large portion of the ABS CDOs were known as "super-senior" securities because they were senior even to the AAA-rated tranches of the CDO. Super-seniors were often retained by the Wall Street firm that issued the CDO. But CDO losses were commonly large enough to wipe out both the AAA tranches and super-senior ones, leaving the issuing institution with large losses. In short, it was the ABS CDOs, not the original subprime ABSs, that proved so toxic to the financial system. And the main failure of the rating agencies was not a flawed analysis of the original subprime securities, but a flawed analysis of the CDOs composed of these securities.

The disparate performance of top-rated tranches from ABSs and CDOs is one of the great puzzles of the crisis. Because issuers were paid to rate both types of securities, it is hard to blame the bad CDO ratings on the "issuer pays" model of rating-agency compensation. But if a conflict of interest did not cause the bad ratings on the CDOs, what did? Some institutional evidence provides a clue to the answer.

The key insight is that ABSs and CDOs were evaluated by using very different methods. This was true both at the investment banks that issued these two types of securities and the agencies that rated them. When forecasting subprime ABS performance, analysts modeled the default probabilities of the individual loans. Recall that the data for this type of analysis were widely available—for example, in the loan-level data sets collected and standardized by LoanPerformance. To forecast the performance of a subprime pool, analysts could first estimate an individual-level default model based on loan-level predictors like the credit score, the debt-to-income ratio, the interest rate, and the current level of the borrower's equity. The current equity level could be inferred by the original down payment on the loan, the loan's amortization schedule, and the subsequent behavior of housing prices. Armed with an individual-level model of default, the analyst could then simulate what would happen to all the mortgages in the pool if housing prices declined by, say, 5 or 10 percent.

Three comments on this ABS analysis are in order to set up the contrast with the method used to evaluate CDOs. The first is that the ABS analysis was *accurate*. Recall the Lehman Brothers analysis from table 6.3, which gives a basically accurate prediction of how bad ABS losses would be if housing prices declined. Second, in the jargon of economists, the analysis was *structural*, in that it modeled how individual decisions were likely to change as economic conditions evolved. Falling prices make it more likely that a homeowner will have negative equity, and economic theory predicts that "underwater" owners will default more often.[26] This prediction receives a great deal of support in empirical default models, so analysts knew that defaults would rise if prices declined. Moreover, they knew that the lower-rated tranches of subprime ABSs would be wiped out if the price decline was especially large. This knowledge encouraged the issuers of subprime ABSs to build a great deal of credit protection into their deals at the outset, in order to ensure that their top-rated bonds would pay off no matter what happened to the housing market.

A third point about the analysis of private-label mortgage securities is that this analysis could examine how *correlation* in individual mortgage defaults might arise.[27] The basic idea behind securitization is that individual loans might have high individual probabilities of default, but these probabilities are not likely to be correlated with one other. This assumption is violated, however, if there is some aggregate shock to all the mortgages in a pool—for example, if house prices decline on a nationwide basis. The loan-level models allowed analysts to predict how such a shock could affect mortgage pools, even though no such shock had occurred in recent history. The analysts simply noted how the individual equity positions of homeowners would change if prices declined by some assumed amount. They could then use their models to generate expected default probabilities for individual loans, then add these probabilities together. Not surprisingly, these exercises implied that a common negative price shock would induce a large correlation in expected defaults. Mortgages across the country would be much more likely to default at the same time if house prices fell everywhere.

Unfortunately, this type of structural analysis was not performed by Wall Street's CDO analysts, who were organizationally independent of the researchers analyzing mortgage pools. The CDO analysts did not devise structural models for the individual BBB-rated tranches in their CDOs. Instead, they essentially skipped ahead to the step of asking how correlated BBB defaults were likely to be.

To do this, the CDO analysts looked at past financial market data, including the prices of default insurance on individual BBB tranches.[28] As it happened, the past data implied that default correlations among the BBB tranches were low. Tranches from some deals might have paid better or worse than tranches from other deals, but there was never a time when large numbers of BBB tranches defaulted simultaneously. Crucially, the CDO analysts' backward-looking approach assumed that these low correlations would continue into the future. There was no way to model the effect of a nationwide decline in house prices because past data did not encompass such a decline. Of course, when national house prices did fall, the CDO analysts learned that defaults among BBB tranches were far more correlated than their methods had implied. As the mortgage analysts had predicted, the nationwide house price decline generated a massive correlation in defaults among individual mortgages, which wiped out the BBB tranches of the original subprime deals. Because these losses occurred on virtually all private-label securities at the same time, BBB tranches from many different securities went bust at the same time too. As a result, CDO losses extended far into the AAA-rated and super-senior tranches, with disastrous implications for the financial system.

At one level, the institutional facts resolve the puzzle over disparate ABS and CDO performance because they provide a simple explanation for why rating agencies and banks viewed the two similar types of securities so differently. The different outlooks could have stemmed from the backgrounds of the two groups of analysts. CDOs were originally constructed from various corporate bonds, for which historical correlations have been excellent guides to future performance, even during the recent crisis. CDO analysts probably assumed that the same type of historical analysis would also work well for CDOs made up of subprime mortgage bonds. By contrast, mortgage analysts were trained to model mortgages individually, and they had the data and the tools to do so.

Yet the institutional facts deepen the puzzle as well. In hindsight, it is hard to see how two groups of analysts could work in close proximity at the same financial institution and not notice the colossal dissonance implied by their respective analyses. For example, during the peak of the mortgage boom, mortgage analysts at UBS published reports showing that even a small decline in house prices would lead to losses that would wipe out the BBB-rated securities of subprime deals (Zimmerman 2005). At the same time, UBS was both an issuer of and a major investor in ABS CDOs, which would be nearly worthless if this decline occurred. Why did the mortgage analysts fail to tell their coworkers how sensitive the CDOs would be to a price decline? This question goes to the heart of why the financial crisis occurred. The answer may well involve the information and incentive structures present inside Wall Street firms. Employees who could recognize the iceberg looming in front of the ship may not have been listened to, or they may not have had the right incentives to speak up. If so, then the information and incentive problems giving rise to the crisis would not have existed between mortgage industry insiders and outsiders, as the inside job story suggests. Rather, these problems would have existed between different floors of the same Wall Street firm.

ECONOMIC THEORIES AND THE FACTS

Our twelve facts consistently point to higher price expectations as a fundamental explanation for why credit expanded during the housing boom. In this section, we ask what could have generated those higher expectations. Theories of "asymmetric information" argue that mortgage originators failed to adequately screen loans and passed them on to unsuspecting investors in mortgage-backed investments. The resulting expansion in credit then drove prices higher. Some of our facts have argued directly against this line of reasoning; in this section, we show that explanations based on asymmetric information fail on theoretical grounds as well. A second group of explanations claims that mortgage market developments related to "financial innovation" allowed credit to expand and prices to rise. We show that these explanations also have theoretical and empirical problems. Finally, we discuss the only set of theories left standing. These theories claim that the U.S. housing market was a classic "asset bubble," just like previous bubbles in tulips and tech stocks.

Explanations Based on Asymmetric Information

Economists have long studied what happens when sellers know more about the good being traded than buyers do. A key insight from this research can be conveyed with a simple example. Suppose you see an advertisement for a one-owner 1995 Oldsmobile Cutlass Ciera on Craigslist with an asking price of $1,500. You reason that a lightly driven Ciera built in 1995 should have about 100,000 miles on it, making it worth about $1,500 to you. So you call the seller and tell him you are interested, though you would like to know how many miles are on the car. The seller responds that the odometer reads about 90,000 miles, but he does not know the mileage for sure, because the odometer has stopped working. The owner is pretty sure, however, that the odometer broke only last month, so the 90,000-mile figure should be about right.

Given these facts, how much would you be willing to pay for the car? Certainly not $1,500, and most likely much less. Even though the seller reports a mileage that is less than 100,000 miles, you cannot verify this information yourself because the odometer does not work. Further, you realize that if the odometer had actually broken several years ago, the seller would have no incentive to tell you the truth. Perhaps most importantly, you realize that not all owners of 1995 Cieras are trying to sell them; many are happily driving them.[29] The willingness of this particular owner to part with his Ciera indicates that he may know something bad about it that you do not—like its true mileage. Given all this, you are likely to offer a very low price for the Ciera or refuse to buy it altogether.

In this example, you as the potential buyer are at an informational disadvantage. The seller (the informed insider) has years of experience with the car, while you (the uninformed outsider) do not even know its true mileage. Even so, you recognize the seller's incentives and understand that some information about the car is unverifiable. Then, by using common sense, you are able to form what is most likely an accurate view of the car's value, some amount less than $1,500. This simple example illustrates a bedrock result in the theory of asymmetric information: uninformed parties who trade with informed parties do not usually get exploited. Not only do the uninformed parties realize they are uninformed, but they also realize that the informed party will try to use his superior information to exploit them.[30]

How does the used-car example relate to securitization and the mortgage market? In the securitization process, lenders screen potential borrowers and originate mortgages, then package the mortgages for sale to outside investors. Yet investors cannot verify how carefully the screening is actually done. The problem is worse if the lender retains no skin in the game, so that any credit losses on the mortgages are borne solely by the investor.[31] Given these informational problems, it is reasonable to think that investors would be concerned about purchasing any mortgage-backed securities. This is the prediction of textbook theories of asymmetric information, which imply that if such asymmetries *had* been a problem for mortgage-backed securities, we would not have seen an explosion of securitized mortgage credit driving housing prices higher while investors were cheated. Rather, the opposite would have occurred. Mortgage credit would have dwindled as investors, like buyers looking over used cars with broken odometers, walked away from the deals.

Yet even though buying and selling mortgages involves some degree of asymmetric information, securitized mortgage credit *did* explode and house prices *did* move higher. The best explanation for this correlation places higher price expectations at the front of the causal chain. If investors believed that housing prices would continue rising rapidly, then it did not matter what a mortgage borrower's income or credit score was. In the event that the borrower defaulted, then the higher price of the house serving as collateral would eliminate any credit losses.[32] In the words of Gary Gorton (2010), higher housing prices cause securitized mortgages to become less "information sensitive," meaning that their profitability depends less on potentially unverifiable characteristics like borrower credit scores and incomes. So in the early 2000s, when price expectations rose, investors became eager to invest in securitized mortgages—even those that were clearly identified as "reduced-documentation" or "no-documentation," for which originators avowed that the loans had not been painstakingly underwritten.

Some authors have tried to rescue the asymmetric information theory of the crisis by arguing that investors did not know about the information problems involved, or that they were too trusting of mortgage originators. The claim is that in the future investors will not be fooled again, but in 2007 and 2008, their naïveté caused massive losses. Perhaps the most famous example of such a claim is Mian and Sufi (2009, 1482), which references an "*undetected* moral hazard on behalf of originators selling [mortgages] for the purpose of securitization as a potential cause for higher mortgage default rates" (emphasis added).

The naive investor theory can be thought of as an out-of-equilibrium behavior in a standard asymmetric information model. Equilibria in these models posit that buyers do not get cheated, but this result assumes that buyers recognize both their informational disadvantage and the willingness of sellers to exploit it. The problem with this theory is that the facts do not support it. To make an obvious point, many Wall Street investors who lost money were seasoned financial professionals, a group generally not known for being overly trusting of those on the other side of high-stakes deals. More importantly, facts 3 and 5 showed that the institutional framework behind mortgage securitization was not new. Investors had ample time to discern the relevant incentives and act accordingly. Public discussions of the potential moral hazard issues surrounding mortgage-backed securities had been common as well. Recall the quote from housing industry journalist Lew Sichelman, who noted with alarm that lenders were originating low-documentation loans for sale to investors—in 1990. Years later, when the subprime market was peaking, the front page of the "Money and Investing" section of the *Wall Street Journal* also highlighted the potential for moral hazard: "Lenders have long sold all or most of their standard mortgage loans to packagers of securities backed by these assets. But when it comes to riskier loans, some investors like to see lenders retain a large amount of exposure, so that both lenders and investors have skin in the game" (Simon and Hagerty 2005).

In short, the idea that the underwriting standards of lenders who sold loans might be different from the standards of portfolio lenders is not a sophisticated idea from a graduate seminar in information economics. Rather, it is a simple concept that was understood by virtually everyone. It does not imply that well-informed insiders were able to expand credit by taking advantage of ill-informed or neophyte outsiders. Instead, it implies that higher price expectations expanded credit by lessening the impact of any informational problems inherent in the securitization process.

The strong growth in low-doc and no-doc lending during the housing boom provides the clearest example of how informational problems were pushed to the background by higher price expectations. As the lower left panel of figure 6.3 shows, the use of such loans exploded from 2002 to 2006. The growth of reduced-documentation lending is often presented as exhibit A in narratives of how the declining standards of mortgage lenders caused the housing crisis. What this growth really shows is the declining standards of investors. These loans were clearly marked as "stated income/stated assets" loans, so investors knew what they were getting. In particular, investors knew that borrowers were likely to have inflated their incomes and assets. Yet investors purchased the loans anyway because they expected these loans to be profitable.[33] For later commentators to complain that lenders did not bother to verify income or employment is like complaining that McDonald's sometimes sells hamburgers without cheese on them. McDonald's sells hamburgers because some people prefer them to cheeseburgers. Low-doc and no-doc loans were sold because some investors preferred them to loans for which incomes and assets had been rigorously verified. Investors were willing to take their chances with the riskier loans because they thought that higher house prices would make that risk worth taking, not because of misaligned incentives in the securitization process.

It is important to reiterate that information economics implies that informed sellers generally prefer to trade with informed buyers, not uninformed buyers. The reason for this seemingly counterintuitive result is that uninformed buyers are likely to be suspicious. Returning to our used-car example, the broken odometer means that potential buyers will be uninformed about the true mileage of the car and thus suspicious about the car's true condition. Consequently, even if the Ciera is in exceptionally good condition, the seller will never get a good price for it. In other words, the broken odometer confers an informational advantage to the seller, but this is an "advantage" that the seller would very much like to avoid. The implication for mortgage markets is that originators would prefer to trade in more transparent markets. Some have suggested that Fannie Mae and Freddie Mac did a better job of aligning incentives than the issuers of private-label securities. But if that were true, then information economics would predict that sellers would have been reluctant to trade in the private-label market, where the informational asymmetries were more severe and prices were likely to be lower.

Finally, while asymmetric information may not have driven a credit expansion during the housing boom, this is not to say that asymmetric information played no role in the crisis. However, the truly damaging asymmetric information problem was not between investors and originators but between trading counterparties in the acute phase of the crisis. During this phase, market participants knew that financial institutions were facing hundreds of billions of dollars of losses, but it was unclear precisely where these losses would fall. In a sense, many financial institutions were like cars with broken odometers, and as economic theory predicts, trading ceased. Whatever role in the crisis was played by asymmetric information among potential counterparties, it obviously cannot explain the decisions made by borrowers or investors before the crisis, which is the focus of this paper. Asymmetric information probably also figured in the decisions of lenders regarding mortgage modifications. Most borrowers who default have negative equity, but most negative equity borrowers do not default. Because lenders are unsure of the borrowers who really do need modifications to stay in their homes, they are likely to deny modifications to everyone (Foote, Gerardi, and Willen 2008; Adelino, Gerardi, and Willen 2009). Even though both borrowers and lenders are better off if modifications are given to the truly needy, asymmetric information prevents those Pareto-improving trades from occurring.

Theories Based on Financial Innovation

A second group of theories argue that the source of rising house prices was some fundamental change in mortgage market institutions, though this change may not have resulted from asymmetric information. One possible example is a decline in the down payments required of potential home buyers. Researchers have constructed careful, fully optimizing models that imply that financial innovations will raise house prices, by essentially shifting out the effective demand curve for owner-occupied homes. A key goal of these researchers' papers is to explain the run-up in prices without having to resort to irrational asset price bubbles.

Four comments about financial innovation theories are in order. First, it may seem intuitive that financial innovation causes higher asset prices, but economic theory makes no such prediction. In fact, the one "folk theorem" from the literature is that a financial innovation, by improving risk-sharing, reduces the demand for precautionary saving and *lowers* asset prices.[34]

A second and more fundamental point is that a model of a financial innovation that generates an increase in asset prices typically cannot generate the subsequent fall in prices necessary to trigger a crisis. As a general rule, price movements in fully optimizing models are sustainable; to our knowledge, the phrase "unsustainable price increase" does not appear in any standard asset-pricing textbook.[35] Without an exogenous change in the innovation that caused prices to go up in the first place, optimizing models simply cannot generate asset price declines.

In a leading example of the financial innovation approach, Jack Favilukis, Sydney Ludvigson, and Stijn Van Nieuwerburgh (2010) developed an elegant general equilibrium model and attempted to replicate the path of U.S. house prices from 2002 to 2011. Specifically, they contend that the observed movement in the price-rent ratio for houses can be explained in an optimizing model by relaxed credit constraints (in the form of lower required down payments) and lower transactions costs (including lower closing costs).[36] Their analysis is correct, but in our opinion, the authors come to the wrong conclusion. Rather than illustrating how financial innovations caused the housing crisis, in our view the model perfectly illustrates how financial innovation could *not* have caused it.

To see why we think Favilukis, Ludvigson, and Van Nieuwerburgh (2010) show the impossibility of the financial innovation story as an explanation of the crisis, note that there is nothing "unsustainable" about the price increase that financial innovation is supposed to have generated. As a result, to be consistent with the 2006 to 2008 fall in housing prices, the authors must presume that the economy underwent "a surprise reversal of the financial market liberalization" in 2006. The liberalization does not end because it was unsustainable—that is, because it was not justified by fundamentals. In particular, the liberalization does not end because borrowers have trouble repaying their debts, as all borrowers repay in full by assumption. Rather, the reversal occurs exogenously because it is the only way the model has any chance to explain the data. In particular, to generate a substantial fall in house prices, the authors must impose not only a massive reversal but also the ex ante belief among market participants that such a reversal cannot happen. If home buyers had suspected that future borrowers would be unable to access the same financial innovation that they could access, then these home buyers would not have bid up house prices so much. Put simply, the more likely the financial reversal, the smaller the initial increase in prices.

If Favilukis, Ludvigson, and Van Nieuwerburgh' (2010) paper had been written before the housing market crash in 2006, housing optimists could have pointed to it as evidence that prices were on a permanently high plateau. There would have been no need to worry that the U.S. housing market was experiencing a bubble, as house prices could have been shown to be consistent with a forward-looking and fully optimizing model. Now that prices have fallen, their analysis implies that policymakers could revive the housing market easily by undoing whatever exogenous reversal caused it to contract. Of course, the inability of a rational model to explain the evolution of house prices is not unique to Favilukis, Ludvigson, and Van Nieuwerburgh (2010). The Achilles' heel of all rational financial innovation models is that if the innovation is not expected to be permanent, then prices will not respond to it. So all credible financial innovation models have to include exogenous and surprising reversals of the innovations to be consistent with both the real-world collapse in prices and their own internal logic.

A third point about financial liberalization models is empirical. To generate the massive increase in housing prices from 2002 to 2006, financial innovation models must assume that the market innovations were profound. To return to Favilukis, Ludvigson, and Van Nieuwerburgh (2010), these authors assume that in 2002 required down payments collapsed, falling from 25 percent to only 1 percent. To justify such a large change, the authors claim that "prior to the housing boom that ended in 2006, the combined LTV for first and second conventional mortgages (mortgages without mortgage insurance) was rarely if ever allowed to exceed 75 to 80 percent of the appraised value of the home" (Favilukis, Ludvigson, and Van Nieuwerburgh 2010, 42).

Facts 4 and 6 show that this statement is not even approximately true: a combined LTV of 100 percent was available in 1944, and the majority of borrowers borrowed more than 80 percent as far back as 1992. To make matters worse, figure 6.6 shows that, at least as far as down payments were concerned, there is no evidence of the exogenous reversal in lending standards needed to explain the house price decline. The share of borrowers putting less than 5 percent down in 2011 was higher than this share had been in any year prior to the crisis. In short, the data provide no foundation to believe either that a dramatic policy change occurred in 2002 or that any change was reversed in 2006, when house prices began to fall.

The fourth and final point about financial innovation is that financial market innovations are *exogenous* changes. Such changes can occur as consequences of new laws. For example, in the 1980s the federal government passed laws intended to address rising interest rate risk among lenders. Kristopher Gerardi, Harvey Rosen, and Paul Willen (2010) point out that these laws had the collateral effect of eliminating Depression-era limits on innovation in mortgage markets. The Monetary Control Act of 1980 allowed regulated lenders to make true adjustable rate mortgages, including option ARMs. The Secondary Mortgage Market Enhancement Act of 1984 and the 1986 Tax Act paved the way for private-label securitization. No comparable exogenous shocks occurred from 2002 to 2004. Ironically, as explained in fact 3, it was the 1980s innovations that made the more intensive use of alternative mortgage products possible in the 2000s. Researchers who argue that innovations occurred in the 2000s often point to the origination data in figure 6.3, which shows changes in the characteristics of underwritten loans—smaller down payments, more interest-only loans, less documentation—but these are all endogenous variables. Only if the option ARM had been invented in 2002 could one possibly argue that its growth was exogenous. But as we have seen, this loan had been around and widely used for twenty years prior to the boom.

Ultimately, the lesson of financial innovation models is that it is impossible to explain the dynamics of U.S. housing prices in the 2000s with a dynamic forward-looking general equilibrium model. Researchers should turn their attention to less-conventional approaches, such as those based on distorted beliefs.[37] We discuss those models next.

Theories Based on Bubbles and Distorted Beliefs

Economists have long been fascinated by bubbles. On a number of occasions, speculative fervor has gripped some asset, leading to prices that outstrip any realistic estimate of the future income that this asset could generate. When no more buyers for this asset are forthcoming—when the music stops—the prices crash. Bubbles and crashes commonly arise in the laboratories of experimental economists, where volunteer test subjects buy and sell simulated assets under controlled conditions.[38] Unfortunately, a comprehensive logical framework to analyze and explain bubbles continues to elude the economics profession. Models have been developed to explain why bubbles can persist for a long time, but as Markus Brunnermeier (2008, 14) notes, "We do not have many convincing models that explain when and why bubbles start."

Certainly, there is no general theoretical result linking bubbles to financial innovation. In fact, some theoretical results show just the opposite effect: financial innovation brings the asset price more in line with its fundamental value (see, for example, Miao and Wang 2012). A link between financial innovation and bubbles is also unsupported by the historical record. In the 1930s, many blamed the U.S. stock market bubble of the 1920s on financial innovations that allowed firms and individuals to increase leveraged positions in stocks. Consequently, the regulatory framework that emerged from the Great Depression placed severe limits on leverage in the equity market. But that regulation did not prevent the technology bubble of the 1990s, although it may have prevented the subsequent collapse in stock prices from causing a financial crisis. We will have more to say about the relationship between financial crises and asset price collapses in our concluding section.

If we are willing to accept that the U.S. housing market was in a bubble during the early to mid-2000s, then the decisions of both borrowers and lenders are understandable. To grasp the role of higher expected prices from an investor's perspective, return to table 6.3. First, high price expectations can explain why investors thought subprime mortgages were such a good investment. The average coupon on subprime adjustable rate mortgages was several hundred basis points above the comparable prime loan. And yet, if investors think that house prices can rise 11 percent per year, expected losses are minimal. This line of thought also illustrates why the envelope of available mortgage credit expanded to such a great extent. Zero-down loans, subprime mortgages, negative amortization, and reduced documentation all make sense if prices are expected to grow rapidly, since it is the value of the house—not the borrower's income—that guarantees repayment of the loan. A bubble also rationalizes the decisions of borrowers. All models of household portfolio choice generate a close relationship between the level of expected returns on risky assets and household leverage. If a risky asset (like a house) pays a return that exceeds the risk-free rate, then borrowing a dollar and investing in the risky asset is a better-than-fair bet. The higher the expected return, the more better-than-fair the bet is. In fact, standard models imply that the demand for the risky asset is linear in the difference between the expected return on it and the risk-free rate (see, for example, Merton 1969, equation 29). That means that if the mortgage interest rate is, say, 5 percent and the expected return on housing increases from 6 percent to 7 percent, then the demand for housing doubles.

Higher price expectations can also explain why so much mortgage credit was allocated to low-wealth households and why this allocation occurred through securitization. Higher price expectations encourage all households to increase their exposure to the housing market, but households with significant wealth can finance this increase by reducing their investment in bonds. Households with little or no wealth can finance an increase only through increased borrowing. Consequently, even the most basic portfolio choice model implies both the increase in mortgage debt and its distribution to low-wealth households.

The allocation of credit toward credit-constrained households also makes sense from the investor's point of view. High price expectations dramatically reduced the expected losses on subprime loans but had little effect on expected losses for prime loans, which were minimal to begin with owing to their much higher credit quality. Consequently, the statements like that in Rajan (2010, 130) claiming that there is "mounting evidence that much of the boom and bust was concentrated in low-income housing" in no way contradict the validity of the bubble explanation. To our knowledge, no one has disputed the fact that from 2002 to 2006 credit availability increased far more for subprime borrowers than for prime borrowers—this growth was widely discussed as it occurred.[39] These differential patterns in the credit expansion simply reflect a basic fact: relaxing a constraint affects only households that are constrained to begin with.

Finally, we have already seen that high prices can explain the growth of mortgage securitization. Because an individual borrower's characteristics no longer affect loss estimates as much when the underlying collateral is expected to rapidly appreciate, there is little incentive for the originator to gather information on these characteristics or, equivalently, for the investor to ask for it. As a result, the originator ends up with less private information relative to an environment in which expected price growth is lower. As Tri Dang, Gary Gorton, and Bengt Holmström (2010) point out, this "symmetric ignorance" actually facilitates trade.

It is important to stress that while we are deeply skeptical of the theory that securitization caused the crisis by introducing information asymmetries, we are sympathetic to the idea that securitization had some role in the financial crisis. Securitization cut out the middleman and allowed a direct link between borrowers and investors. Rather than depositing money in a financial institution that then had discretion over where to lend, securitization allowed investors to target their money directly to a specific market—housing, in this case. Under normal circumstances, this is a good thing. But in the housing mania of the mid-2000s, securitization worked like Othello loved—not wisely, but too well. Indeed, the inefficiency of a more traditional financial system might have proved a blessing during this time, as it could have prevented overly optimistic borrowers and investors from finding each other.

Of course, it is deeply unsatisfying to explain the bad decisions of both borrowers and lenders by citing a bubble without explaining how the bubble arose. One speculative story begins with the idea that some fundamental determinants of housing prices caused them to move higher early in the boom. Perhaps the accommodative monetary policy used to fight the 2001 recession, or higher savings rates among developing countries, pushed U.S. interest rates lower and thereby pushed U.S. housing prices higher. Additionally, after the steep stock market decline of the early 2000s, U.S. investors may have been attracted to real estate because it appeared to offer less risk. The decisions of Fannie Mae and Freddie Mac may have also played a role in supporting higher prices. Without speculating about the reasons for their investment decisions, it is beyond dispute that Fannie Mae and Freddie Mac were major players in the lending boom of the 2000s, even if much of this lending occurred outside of their traditional guarantee business. Specifically, both Fannie Mae and Freddie Mac indirectly invested heavily in risky mortgages by buying AAA tranches of subprime and Alt-A mortgage-backed securities and holding these securities in their retained portfolios. Figure 6.10 shows the aggregate amount of subprime and Alt-A MBSs that the GSEs purchased for their retained portfolios between 2000 and 2007. The GSEs absorbed between 30 and 40 percent of subprime MBSs and between 10 and 20 percent of Alt-A MBSs over the boom years, except for 2007, when the collapse of the market meant that the GSEs took almost

FIGURE 6.10 / Fannie Mae and Freddie Mac Investments in Subprime and Alt-A Residential Mortgage-Based Securities, 2000 to 2007

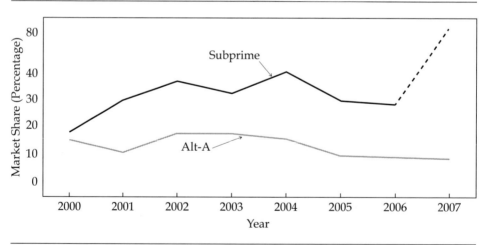

Source: Authors' compilation based on data from Thomas and Van Order (2011).

all the subprime issuance. The GSEs were limited to the AAA-rated portions of the deals. For subprime deals, about 80 percent of the security issuance by dollar value was typically rated AAA. This high percentage meant that in many of the boom years the GSEs accounted for half of the subprime AAA-rated securities.[40]

What we do not know is how any modest increases in house prices brought about by developments like these morphed into a full-blown housing bubble in which prices continued to rise under their own momentum to levels that far exceeded their fundamental values. Perhaps people simply noticed the original price increases and expected them to continue indefinitely. These optimistic price expectations encouraged buyers to offer high prices for houses, making the optimistic price expectations self-fulfilling—the hallmark of an asset bubble. Of course, the unanswered question is why this bubble occurred in the 2000s and not some other time. Unfortunately, the study of bubbles is too young to provide much guidance on this point. For now, we have no choice but to plead ignorance, and we believe that all honest economists should do the same. But acknowledging what we *do not* know should not blind us to what we *do* know: the bursting of a massive and unsustainable price bubble in the U.S. housing market caused the financial crisis.

POLICY IMPLICATIONS

Determining the origin of the financial crisis is not merely an idle academic pastime, because alternative explanations imply different policy responses. To illustrate the issues involved, consider the optimal policies related to two types of non-economic catastrophes: a malaria epidemic and an earthquake.

During the past 120 years, scientists have learned a lot about malaria. They know that malaria is caused by microscopic parasites—not "bad air," as originally thought—and they know that it is transmitted by mosquitoes. Armed with their empirically validated theories, public health officials can take steps to prevent the disease from spreading—for example, by eliminating pools of standing water where mosquitoes breed.[41] Earthquakes are another matter. Science has a theory of why earthquakes occur, but quakes strike without warning, and there is nothing we can do to prevent them. Even so, policymakers can mitigate their consequences. The Loma Prieta earthquake that hit San Francisco in 1989 and the Port-au-Prince quake of 2010 were of roughly the same magnitude. But while 200,000 people died in Haiti, only 60 died in San Francisco. The difference was that in San Francisco officials had created and enforced rigorous building codes. As geologists say, "Earthquakes don't kill people—buildings do" (Hough and Jones 2002).

For policymakers, the important question is whether the economic events of 2002 to 2008 were more like malaria or more like an earthquake. Was the crisis a "preventable disaster" (Warren 2010), resembling a disease whose pathology is well understood and for which we can administer an effective treatment? Or, to draw on the Nocera quotation from the beginning of the chapter, was the crisis instead caused by a poorly understood "mass delusion" that we can neither predict nor prevent? Proponents of the conventional wisdom on the financial crisis clearly view it as something like malaria. A great deal of policy since the crisis has focused on improving disclosure and changing incentives for financial intermediaries. But we are skeptical that this approach will work.

Consider the Dodd-Frank Act requirement that loan originators retain 5 percent of the credit risk of certain mortgages. During the housing boom, would this requirement have stopped lenders from making bad loans? In 2006 and 2007, lenders originated $791 billion subprime loans (Inside Mortgage Finance Publications 2011). Had Dodd-Frank existed, lenders would have retained 5 percent of that amount, or $40 billion of subprime credit. Overall loss rates of 35 percent would have saddled them with $14 billion in losses.[42]

Inspection of table 6.5 shows that mortgage-related losses exceeded that amount for no fewer than eight firms individually. In other words, if every one of those firms had followed the Dodd-Frank requirement and originated the *entire* subprime mortgage market, they would have suffered smaller losses than they actually did.

In addition, many analysts have argued that if the managers of financial institutions had had their own money at stake, they would have been more careful (Rajan 2010, 164–65). But the losses suffered by Jimmy Cayne and Richard Fuld, the CEOs of Bear Stearns and Lehman Brothers, respectively, dwarf by an order of magnitude any clawback provision contemplated so far. And further down the organization chart, Lehman staff owned nearly one-third of the company, so many managers obviously had significant skin in the game as well (Sorkin 2010, 294).[43]

Provisions to help borrowers understand their mortgages are also likely to be ineffective. The vast majority of borrowers who defaulted on their loans did so facing a payment amount that was the same as when they first got their mortgage, or even lower, so how could clearer terms have helped? Moreover, the idea that borrowers are the victims of confusing transactions is not remotely new—indeed, it was the premise behind the 1968 Truth in Lending Act as well as the 1974 Real Estate Settlement Procedures Act. Real estate regulators have been working on a "simple form that conveys all the relevant information" for more than forty years. Further, policymakers recognized the benefits of condensing all the costs of a financial product into a single number long before the emergence of behavioral economics, which is why the inscrutable annual percentage rate (APR) is now enshrined in law. Many people ridicule the APR—until they try to come up with something better.

If borrowers and investors made bad decisions owing to a collective belief that housing prices would rise rapidly and could never fall, then better disclosures, simpler products, and improved incentives for intermediaries would have made little difference. But that does not mean that policy is always ineffective. Even though scientists cannot predict or prevent earthquakes, robust building codes still prevent millions of deaths. How can we create a bubble-resistant financial system? Many new regulations, including some in Dodd-Frank, are designed to make the financial system more robust. We suggest three organizing principles for this type of policy going forward.

First, financial institutions must be able to withstand a serious house price shock. It is not unreasonable to argue that a financial institution should be able to withstand a 20 percent decline in house prices without any liquidity problems. In addition, regulators and financial institutions should ensure that the institutions can withstand such a fall no matter when it happens. For example, just because house prices have already fallen 20 percent does not mean they cannot fall another 20 percent. As table 6.4 illustrates, some analysts were convinced that a bottom had been reached for house prices in 2006. And after long periods of stability, even sophisticated analysts are tempted to declare that economic fluctuations are a thing of the past. Recall that in the mid-2000s economists were puzzling about what appeared to be a permanent reduction in macroeconomic volatility.

Second, borrowers must also be able to withstand a substantial fall in house prices. Elizabeth Warren and Amelia Tyagi (2004) argue that families should practice a "financial fire drill," which would ask how they would get by if one income-earner lost a job. We would argue that the fire drill should also include a scenario in which falling house prices prevent the family from selling their house for more than they owe on their mortgage. Effectively, such a fire drill would be similar to so-called stress tests that regulators conduct at financial institutions.

Third, if we are going to invest in financial education, we need to teach everyone—from first-time home buyers to Wall Street CEOs—that asset prices move in ways that we do not yet understand. Unfortunately, none of the new mortgage disclosure forms proposed by regulators includes the critical piece of information that borrowers need to know: there is a chance that the house they are buying will soon be worth substantially less than the outstanding balance on the mortgage. If this happens and the borrower does not have sufficient precautionary savings, then that borrower is one job loss or serious illness away from default.

Critics might contend that treating bubbles like earthquakes is reminiscent of a doctrine often associated with Alan Greenspan: policymakers should not try to stop bubbles, which are not easily identified, but should instead clean up the damage left behind when they burst. To some extent, we concur with this doctrine, because we believe that policymakers and regulators have little ability to identify or to burst bubbles in real time.[44] Yet this strategy works only when the financial system is robust to adverse shocks.

As we mentioned earlier, the reforms of the 1930s failed to prevent a bubble from forming in the stock market in the late 1990s. But the early 2000s stock market collapse did not lead to an economic crisis or to widespread financial problems among households. Why not? One possible explanation is that the reforms of the 1930s made the financial system "bubble-resistant," at least for equities. Our hope is that we can achieve something similar with housing in the future. But for that to happen, housing policy must be based on the facts.

Thanks to Alberto Bisin, Ryan Bubb, Scott Frame, Jeff Fuhrer, Andreas Fuster, Anil Kashyap, Andreas Lehnert, and Bob Triest for helpful discussions and comments. The opinions expressed herein are those of the authors and do not represent the official positions of the Federal Reserve Banks of Boston or Atlanta or the Federal Reserve System.

NOTES

1. Some examples of this work include Gennaioli and Shleifer (2010), Gennaioli, Shleifer, and Vishny (2012), Barberis (2011), Brunnermeier, Simsek, and Xiong (2011), Simsek (2012), Fuster, Laibson, and Mendel (2010), Geanakoplos (2009), Benabou (2012), and Burnside, Eichenbaum, and Rebelo (2011).

2. The classic reference on tulipmania is MacKay (1841/2003). A contrarian view on tulipmania is found in Garber (2000), which reviews data on tulip prices and argues that they can be justified by fundamentals during this period. The book takes a similar stance on other early bubbles, including the South Sea Bubble (1720) and the Mississippi Bubble (1719 to 1720).

3. Typically, the fully indexed rate was a fixed amount over some short-term rate—for example, six percentage points above the six-month LIBOR.

4. To some extent, this 5 percent difference understates the performance differential among subprime ARMs and FRMs because originations of subprime FRMs were concentrated in the later vintages of loans, which had the highest default rates. We comment on this concentration later. Also, a performance gap between subprime FRMs and ARMs is robust to a more sophisticated analysis that controls for observable characteristics (Foote et al. 2008).

5. The phrase "designed to fail" appears in speeches by presidential candidate Hillary Clinton and Senator Charles Schumer of New York and in press releases from prominent attorneys general, including Martha Coakley of Massachusetts and Catherine Cortez Masto of Nevada.

6. Our choice of the two-year period does not influence our results. Figure 6.2 shows that default rates on subprime loans did not spike after two years.

7. The balance of a traditional "amortizing" mortgage decreases over time because the borrower pays both interest and part of the outstanding principal each month.

8. One author's father took out an interest-only adjustable-rate, balloon-payment mortgage in 1967, but that was an exceptional situation.

9. Morgenson and Rosner (2011) go on to claim that requirements to verify income and demonstrate repayment ability were also reduced.

10. Combined LTV ratios, sometimes denoted as "CLTV ratios," include all mortgages taken out by the homeowner at the time of purchase, including so-called piggyback mortgages.

11. Public records do not allow us to know whether a purchase corresponds to a first-time home buyer. If it were possible to focus on those purchases alone, the average down payment would undoubtedly be even lower than the average that includes all purchases.

12. Edward Glaeser, Joshua Gottlieb, and Joseph Gyourko (2010) look at data for a broader set of cities and have similar results.

13. For a contemporary analysis of default rates on FHA, VA, and conventional mortgages, see Herzog and Earley (1970).

14. When recounting the history of the OTD model, it is important to distinguish between "mortgage brokers" and "mortgage bankers." Wei Jiang, Ashlyn Nelson, and

Edward Vytlacil (2011) claim that brokers "issue[d] loans on the bank's behalf for commissions but do not bear the long-term consequences of low-quality loans," but this statement is incorrect. Brokers, who often have specific knowledge of a local market, can help match borrowers with lenders, but they do not underwrite or fund mortgages. Rather, mortgage banks, which include mortgage companies and S&Ls, underwrite and fund loans. These lenders can choose to place a brokered loan in a security, sell it to another lender, or keep it on portfolio. In short, there is no necessary connection between brokers and the OTD model; the decision to extend a loan rests entirely with the lender, because the lender comes up with the money.

15. In the industry, bonds backed by subprime loans were considered asset-backed securities (ABSs) rather than MBSs, because subprime lending began as an alternative to unsecured credit for troubled borrowers. Thus, as an institutional matter, subprime lending was part of the consumer lending (ABS) market, not the mortgage (MBS) market.

16. The NINA loan is the basis for the apocryphal "NINJA" loan that is often used as an example of excesses in the boom-era mortgage market. NINJA supposedly stood for "no income/no job/no assets," but no such loan ever existed. Also, the NINA code, which did exist, did not signify a loan to a borrower with no income. Rather, the code signified that the lender had no information about the borrower's income.

17. Abacus was a deal arranged by Goldman Sachs in 2007 that largely amounted to a bet on whether a collection of BBB subprime securities would default. Hedge fund manager John Paulson took a short position in the deal while IKB and ABN Amro took long positions. The Securities and Exchange Commission (SEC) brought fraud charges against Goldman Sachs, alleging that it did not properly disclose the fact that Paulson played a role in choosing the specific securities that made up the deal.

18. A CUSIP is a nine-character code that identifies any North American security and is used to facilitate the clearing and settlement of financial trades.

19. The discussion of facts 8 and 9 is based on Gerardi et al. (2008). We direct interested readers to that paper for a more complete discussion of the issues.

20. The prime losses here refer to losses on non-agency ("jumbo") deals, which included mortgages that were too big to be securitized by Fannie Mae or Freddie Mac. For agency MBSs consisting of so-called conforming mortgages, credit risk was borne not by investors but by the agencies themselves.

21. Authors' calculations using FHFA national price index and the core PCE price index.

22. Along these lines, Ing-Haw Cheng, Sahil Raina, and Wei Xiong (2012) show that managers involved in the securitization process were no less likely to buy houses at the peak of the bubble than the population in general.

23. In taking on the question of why banks held so many risky subprime securities on their books and concluding that the best explanation is that they did so to signal the quality of the pools of loans, Isil Erel, Taylor Nadauld, and René Stulz (2011), in a sense, perfectly illustrate the arguments in Grossman and Hart (1980). Rather than withhold private information, agents have an important incentive to fully disclose information in order to obtain the best prices for their products.

24. These deals included subprime mortgages, Alt-A mortgages, and jumbo mortgages.

25. For a discussion of the link between CDOs and the underlying ABSs, see Ashcraft and Schuermann (2008).

26. When underwater owners who lose their jobs or suffer some other adverse life event are unable to sell their homes for enough to pay off their loans, foreclosure is often the only possible outcome. Alternatively, if their negative equity is large enough, underwater owners may simply walk away from their mortgage in a so-called ruthless or strategic default.

27. A better label for this type of analysis might be "semistructural," because it does not attempt to uncover deep parameters that are relevant to the default decision. For example, the analysis does not estimate the rate of time preference of individual homeowners, or how homeowners would value an extra dollar of wealth.

28. In the past, if the price of default insurance for two BBB tranches went up at the same time, the CDO analysts would infer that the default probabilities of the two tranches were positively correlated as well. Note that this inference could be made even if neither of the two tranches had ever defaulted. See Salmon (2009) for a discussion of a mathematical formula called the Gaussian copula that aided this calculation and Coval, Jurek, and Stafford (2009) for a more general discussion.

29. One of the authors of this chapter provides an example.

30. George Akerlof (1970) showed what happens when this result is carried out to a logical conclusion. If sellers of goods are unable to convey their quality to potential buyers, then the buyers assume that the quality of the goods being offered is low. Consequently, the buyers bid only low prices. These low prices encourage the sellers that really do have high-quality goods to pull them off the market, further depressing the average quality of goods offered for sale. Buyers then further reduce their offers. In equilibrium, trade can break down completely, so that welfare-improving exchanges between buyers and sellers do not occur.

31. In this case, the used-car analogy is especially appropriate, because the seller of the Ciera will not be responsible for any repair bills after he transfers title to the car.

32. In reality, a financially stressed mortgage borrower who had built up substantial positive equity would probably not default in the first place, because he could sell the house, pay off his mortgage, and still have money left over.

33. Indeed, investors often preferred reduced-documentation loans because of their superior prepayment properties. See Adelson (2003) for a more detailed discussion.

34. Ronel Elul (1997) shows that the folk theorem is not quite true. With sufficient market incompleteness, one can always find an innovation that raises asset prices. Yet the folk theorem remains valid for virtually all parameterized models in macroeconomics and finance.

35. Neither the word "unsustainable" nor any synonym appears in Cochrane (2005), for example.

36. The authors also show that a coincident inflow of foreign capital can keep interest rates low, as this financial liberalization raises the demand for loanable funds. "Without an infusion of foreign capital, any period of looser collateral requirements and lower housing transactions costs (such as that which characterized the period of rapid home price appreciation from 2000–2006) would be accompanied by an increase in equilibrium interest rates, as households endogenously respond to the improved risk-sharing opportunities afforded by a financial market liberalization by reducing precautionary saving" (Favilukis, Ludvigson, and Van Nieuwerburgh 2010, 3). The inflow of foreign capital plays only a small role, however, in generating higher housing prices.

37. For some examples of this type of research, see the citations in note 1.

38. For a classic early example of bubbles in a laboratory, see Smith, Suchanek, and Williams (1988). Looking back at the large literature that this study initiated, David Porter and Vernon Smith (2008, 247) note that bubbles and crashes are "standard fare" in lab experiments with inexperienced test subjects. Prices adhere more closely to fundamental values if subjects are allowed repeated opportunities to trade.

39. Additionally, the evidence that credit was expanding to low-income households was "mounting" as early as 2005. Simon (2005) and *National Mortgage News* (2005) are two of literally thousands of articles about the growth of subprime credit in 2005.

40. One popular perspective is that the purchases were driven primarily by the congressionally mandated affordable housing goals in the so-called GSE Act of 1992. This act, formally titled the Federal Housing Enterprises Financial Safety and Soundness Act, mandated that a proportion of each GSE's annual mortgage purchases come from low-income households and low-income and minority neighborhoods. However, the emerging empirical literature attempting to directly measure the impact of the GSE affordable housing goals on the volume of mortgage originations has, for the most part, found negligible effects (see Bhutta 2010; Moulten 2010; Ghent, Hernández-Murillo, and Owyang 2012).

41. See the description of how U.S. Army doctors attacked yellow fever and malaria during the construction of the Panama Canal in McCullough (1977).

42. The 35 percent figure is calculated using actual originations from Inside Mortgage Finance Publications (2008, table II.A.1), and cumulative losses for the relevant vintages were calculated using Jozoff et al. (2012).

43. See also the discussion in Fahlenbrach and Stulz (2011). Lucian Bebchuk, Alma Cohen, and Holger Spamann (2010) argue that managers did make large profits earlier, but they do not dispute that managers had large amounts of their own money at stake when the firms collapsed.

44. We know of no central bank that has successfully managed a bubble. In the early 1990s, the Japanese central bank was credited with engineering an end to the bubble in Japan, but few central bankers would use that as a model for policy today.

REFERENCES

Acharya, Viral V., and Matthew Richardson, eds. 2009. *Restoring Financial Stability: How to Repair a Failed System.* New York: John Wiley & Sons.

Adelino, Manuel, Kristopher Gerardi, and Paul S. Willen. 2009. "Why Don't Lenders Renegotiate More Home Mortgages? Redefaults, Self-Cures, and Securitization." Working Paper 15159. Cambridge, Mass.: National Bureau of Economic Research.

Adelson, Mark. 2003. "A Journey to the Alt-A Zone: A Brief Primer on Alt-A Mortgage Loans." *Nomura Fixed Income Research* (June 3).

Akerlof, George A. 1970. "The Market for 'Lemons': Quality Uncertainty and the Market Mechanism." *Quarterly Journal of Economics* 84(3): 488–500.

Arnold, Chris. 2009. "Forcing Banks to Put More 'Skin in the Game.'" National Public Radio, June 18. Available at: http://www.npr.org/templates/story/story.php?storyId=105558991 (accessed June 27, 2012).

Ashcraft, Adam B., and Til Schuermann. 2008. "Understanding the Securitization of Sub-prime Mortgage Credit." Staff Report 318. New York: Federal Reserve Bank of New York. Available at: http://www.newyorkfed.org/research/staff_reports/sr318.pdf (accessed June 27, 2012).

Bair, Sheila C. 2007. "Statement on Possible Responses to Rising Mortgage Foreclosures." Testimony before the House Financial Services Committee (April 17). Available at: http://www.fdic.gov/news/news/speeches/archives/2007/chairman/spapr1707.html (accessed June 27, 2012).

Barberis, Nicholas. 2011. "Psychology and the Financial Crisis of 2007–2008." Working paper. New Haven, Conn.: Yale University (August 1). Available at: SSRN: http://ssrn.com/abstract=1742463 or http://dx.doi.org/10.2139/ssrn.1742463 (accessed June 27, 2012).

Bebchuk, Lucian A., Alma Cohen, and Holger Spamann. 2010. "The Wages of Failure: Executive Compensation at Bear Stearns and Lehman, 2000–2008." *Yale Journal on Regulation* 27(2): 257–82.

Benabou, Roland. 2012. "Groupthink: Collective Delusions in Organizations and Markets." Princeton University Working Paper. Available at: http://www.princeton.edu/~rbenabou/papers/Groupthink%20IOM%202012_06_18_d%20paper.pdf (accessed June 29, 2012).

Bhutta, Neil. 2010. "GSE Activity and Mortgage Supply in Lower-Income and Minority Neighborhoods: The Effect of the Affordable Housing Goals." *Journal of Real Estate Finance and Economics* 45(1): 238–61.

Brunnermeier, Markus K. 2008. "Bubbles." In *The New Palgrave Dictionary of Economics*, 2nd ed., edited by Steven N. Durlauf and Lawrence E. Blume. Basingstoke, U.K.: Palgrave Macmillan. Available at: http://www.dictionaryofeconomics.com/article?id=pde2008_S000278 (accessed June 27, 2012).

Brunnermeier, Markus K., Alp Simsek, and Wei Xiong. 2011. "A Welfare Criterion for Models with Distorted Beliefs." Working paper. Princeton, N.J.: Princeton University (October). Available at: http://www.economics.harvard.edu/faculty/simsek/files/welfare8_g.pdf (accessed June 27, 2012).

Burnside, Craig, Martin Eichenbaum, and Sergio Rebelo. 2011. "Understanding Booms and Busts in Housing Markets." Working Paper 16734. Cambridge, Mass.: National Bureau of Economic Research.

Carter, Susan B., Scott S. Gartner, Michael R. Haines, Alan L. Olmstead, Richard Sutch, and Gavin Wright. 2006. *Historical Statistics of the United States: Millennial Edition*. Cambridge: Cambridge University Press.

Cheng, Ing-Haw, Sahil Raina, and Wei Xiong. 2012. "Wall Street and the Housing Bubble: Bad Incentives, Bad Models, or Bad Luck?" Working paper. Princeton, N.J.: Princeton University.

Cochrane, John H. 2005. *Asset Pricing*, rev. ed. Princeton, N.J.: Princeton University Press.

Cordell, Larry, Yilin Huang, and Meredith Williams. 2012. "Collateral Damage: Sizing and Assessing the Subprime CDO Crisis." Working Paper 11-30/R. Philadelphia: Federal Reserve Bank of Philadelphia. Available at: http://www.philadelphiafed.org/research-and-data/publications/working-papers/2011/wp11-30.pdf (accessed June 27, 2012).

CoreLogic, Inc. Various years. Loan-Level Mortgage Data. Proprietary data.

Coval, Joshua D., Jakub W. Jurek, and Erik Stafford. 2009. "The Economics of Structured Finance." *Journal of Economic Perspectives* 23(1): 3–25.

Dang, Tri V., Gary Gorton, and Bengt Holmström. 2010. "Financial Crises and the Optimality of Debt for Liquidity Provision." Working paper. New Haven, Conn.: Yale School of Management.

Dokko, Jane, Brian Doyle, Michael T. Kiley, Jinill Kim, Shane Sherlund, Jae Sim, and Skander Van den Heuvel. 2009. "Monetary Policy and the Housing Bubble." Finance and

Economics Discussion Series Papers 2009-49. Washington, D.C.: Board of Governors of the Federal Reserve System.

Eakes, Martin. 2007. "Evolution of an Economic Crisis? The Subprime Lending Disaster and the Threat to the Broader Economy." Testimony before Joint Economic Committee (September 19). Available at: http://www.responsiblelending.org/mortgage-lending/policy-legislation/congress/senate-sept-07-final.pdf (accessed June 27, 2012).

Elul, Ronel. 1997. "Financial Innovation, Precautionary Saving, and the Risk-Free Rate." *Journal of Mathematical Economics* 27(1): 113–31.

Erel, Isil, Taylor D. Nadauld, and René M. Stulz. 2011. "Why Did U.S. Banks Invest in Highly Rated Securitization Tranches?" Working Paper 17269. Cambridge, Mass.: National Bureau of Economic Research.

Fahlenbrach, Rüdiger, and René M. Stulz. 2011. "Bank CEO Incentives and the Credit Crisis." *Journal of Financial Economics* 99(1): 11–26.

Favilukis, Jack, Sydney C. Ludvigson, and Stijn Van Nieuwerburgh. 2010. "The Macroeconomic Effects of Housing Wealth, Housing Finance, and Limited Risk-Sharing in General Equilibrium." Working Paper 15988. Cambridge, Mass.: National Bureau of Economic Research.

Financial Crisis Inquiry Commission. 2010. "Credit Ratings and the Financial Crisis." Preliminary Staff Report (June 2). Available at: http://fcic-static.law.stanford.edu/cdn_media/fcic-reports/2010-0602-Credit-Ratings.pdf (accessed June 27, 2012).

———. 2011. *The Financial Crisis Inquiry Report: Final Report of the National Commission on the Causes of the Financial and Economic Crisis in the United States.* New York: Public Affairs.

Fishbein, Allen J. 2006. "Calculated Risk: Assessing Nontraditional Mortgage Products." Testimony before the Subcommittee on Housing and Transportation and the Subcommittee on Economic Policy of the Senate Committee on Banking, Housing, and Urban Affairs (September 20). Available at: http://www.consumerfed.org/elements/www.consumerfed.org/file/housing/Fishbein_Senate_Testimony_on_Non-Traditional_Mortgages092006.pdf (accessed June 27, 2012).

Flanagan, Christopher, Ting Ko, Seva Levitski, Chris Muth, and Amy Sze. 2006a. "February 2006 House Price Appreciation Update." JP Morgan Global Credit Research (April 11).

———. 2006b. "House Price Appreciation Update." JP Morgan Global Credit Research (various dates).

Foote, Christopher L., Kristopher Gerardi, Lorenz Goette, and Paul S. Willen. 2008. "Just the Facts: An Initial Analysis of Subprime's Role in the Housing Crisis." *Journal of Housing Economics* 17(4): 291–305.

Foote, Christopher L., Kristopher Gerardi, and Paul S. Willen. 2008. "Negative Equity and Foreclosure: Theory and Evidence." *Journal of Urban Economics* 64(2): 234–45.

Fuster, Andreas, David Laibson, and Brock Mendel. 2010. "Natural Expectations and Macroeconomic Fluctuations." *Journal of Economic Perspectives* 24(4): 67–84.

Garber, Peter M. 2000. *Famous First Bubbles: The Fundamentals of Early Manias.* Cambridge, Mass.: MIT Press.

Geanakoplos, John. 2009. "The Leverage Cycle." In *National Bureau of Economic Research Macroeconomics Annual 2009,* edited by Daron Acemoglu, Kenneth Rogoff, and Michael Woodford. Chicago: University of Chicago Press.

Gennaioli, Nicola, and Andrei Shleifer. 2010. "What Comes to Mind." *Quarterly Journal of Economics* 125(4): 1399–1433.

Gennaioli, Nicola, Andrei Shleifer, and Robert Vishny. 2012 "Neglected Risks, Financial Innovation, and Financial Fragility." *Journal of Financial Economics* 104(3): 452–68.

Gerardi, Kristopher S., Christopher L. Foote, and Paul S. Willen. 2011. "Reasonable People Did Disagree: Optimism and Pessimism About the U.S. Housing Market Before the Crash." In *Reinventing the American Mortgage System: Rethink, Recover, Rebuild*, edited by Marvin Smith and Susan M. Wachter. Philadelphia: University of Pennsylvania Press.

Gerardi, Kristopher, Andreas Lehnert, Shane M. Sherlund, and Paul S. Willen. 2008. "Making Sense of the Subprime Crisis." *Brookings Papers on Economic Activity* 2: 69–145.

Gerardi, Kristopher S., Harvey S. Rosen, and Paul S. Willen. 2010. "The Impact of Deregulation and Financial Innovation on Consumers: The Case of the Mortgage Market." *Journal of Finance* 65(1): 333–60.

Gerth, Jeff. 1981. "Savings Regulators End Mortgage Curb." *New York Times,* April 24.

Ghent, Andra C., Rubén Hernández-Murillo, and Michael T. Owyang. 2012. "Did Affordable Housing Legislation Contribute to the Subprime Securities Boom?" Working Paper 2012-005A. St. Louis: Federal Reserve Bank of St. Louis (March). Available at: http://research.stlouisfed.org/wp/2012/2012-005.pdf (accessed June 27, 2012).

Glaeser, Edward L., Joshua D. Gottlieb, and Joseph Gyourko. 2010. "Can Cheap Credit Explain the Housing Boom?" Working Paper 16230. Cambridge, Mass.: National Bureau of Economic Research.

Gorton, Gary. 2010. *Slapped by the Invisible Hand: The Panic of 2007.* New York: Oxford University Press.

Grossman, Sanford J., and Oliver D. Hart. 1980. "Disclosure Laws and Takeover Bids." *Journal of Finance* 35(2): 323–34.

Guttentag, Jack. 1984. "Recent Changes in the Primary Home Mortgage Market." *Housing Finance Review* 3: 221–54.

Harrigan, Susan. 1981. "Wachovia Has Other Bankers Taking Notice." *Wall Street Journal,* April 27.

Herzog, John P., and James S. Earley. 1970. "Home Mortgage Delinquency and Foreclosure." Cambridge, Mass.: National Bureau of Economic Research. Available at: www.nber.org/chapters/c3293.pdf (accessed September 5, 2012).

Hough, Susan, and Lucile Jones. 2002. "Earthquakes Don't Kill People, Buildings Do." *San Francisco Chronicle,* December 4. Available at: http://pasadena.wr.usgs.gov/office/hough/oped-sf.html (accessed June 27, 2012).

Inside Mortgage Finance Publications. 2008. *2008 Mortgage Market Statistical Annual.* Bethesda, Md.: Inside Mortgage Finance Publications.

———. 2011. *2011 Mortgage Market Statistical Annual.* Bethesda, Md.: Inside Mortgage Finance Publications.

Jiang, Wei, Ashlyn Nelson, and Edward Vytlacil. 2011. "Liar's Loan? Effects of Origination Channel and Information Falsification on Mortgage Delinquency." Working paper. New York: Columbia University Graduate School of Business. Available at: http://www.columbia.edu/~wj2006/liars_loan.pdf (accessed June 27, 2012).

Jozoff, Matthew, John Sim, Abhishek Mistry, Asif Sheikh, Robert Saltarelli, and Kaustub Samant. 2012. "MBS Credit Monthly, February." JPMorgan SPG Research (February 10).

Kashyap, Anil K. 2010. "Lessons from the Financial Crisis for Risk Management." Paper prepared for the Financial Crisis Inquiry Commission (February 27). Available at: http://faculty.chicagobooth.edu/anil.kashyap/research/papers/lesson_for_fcic.pdf (accessed June 27, 2012).

Klaman, Saul B. 1959. "The Postwar Rise of Mortgage Companies." Occasional Paper 60. New York: National Bureau of Economic Research.

Lender Processing Services, Inc. (LPS). Various years. Loan-Level Mortgage Data. Proprietary data.

Lewis, Michael. 2010. *The Big Short: Inside the Doomsday Machine.* New York: W. W. Norton & Co.

Liu, David. 2005. "Credit Performance of Option ARMs." U.S. Securitized Products Strategy Group Presentation (August 15).

MacKay, Charles. 2003. *Extraordinary Popular Delusions and the Madness of Crowds.* Hampshire, U.K.: Harriman House. (Originally published in 1841.)

Mago, Akhil, and Sihan Shu. 2005. "HEL Bond Profile Across HPA Scenarios." *U.S. ABS Weekly Outlook* (Lehman Brothers Fixed-Income Research), August 15.

McCullough, David. 1977. *The Path Between the Seas: The Creation of the Panama Canal, 1870–1914.* New York: Simon & Schuster.

Merton, Robert C. 1969. "Lifetime Portfolio Selection Under Uncertainty: The Continuous-Time Case." *Review of Economics and Statistics* 51(3): 247–57.

Mian, Atif, and Amir Sufi. 2009. "The Consequences of Mortgage Credit Expansion: Evidence from the U.S. Mortgage Default Crisis." *Quarterly Journal of Economics* 124(4): 1449–96.

Miao, Jianjun, and Pengfei Wang. 2012. "Bubbles and Credit Constraints." Working paper. Boston: Boston University (January 12). Available at: http://people.bu.edu/miaoj/Bubble.pdf (accessed June 27, 2012).

Morgenson, Gretchen, and Joshua Rosner. 2011. *Reckless Endangerment: How Outsized Ambition, Greed, and Corruption Led to Economic Armageddon.* New York: Times Books.

Moulten, Shawn. 2010. "The 1992 GSE Act and Loan Application Outcomes." Working paper. Notre Dame, Ind.: University of Notre Dame.

Muolo, Paul, and Mathew Padilla. 2010. *Chain of Blame: How Wall Street Caused the Mortgage and Credit Crisis.* New York: John Wiley & Sons.

National Mortgage News. 2005. "Subprime Growth Fueled $750 Billion in Third-Quarter Originations." *National Mortgage News,* October 24.

Nocera, Joe. 2011. "Inquiry Is Missing Bottom Line." *New York Times,* January 29. Available at: http://www.nytimes.com/2011/01/29/business/29nocera.html (accessed June 27, 2012).

Onaran, Yalman. 2008. "Subprime Losses Top $396 Billion on Brokers' Writedowns: Table." Bloomberg, June 18. Available at: http://www.bloomberg.com/apps/news?pid=newsarchive&sid=a5GaivCMZu_M (accessed June 27, 2012).

Porter, David, and Vernon L. Smith. 2008. "Price Bubbles." In *Handbook of Experimental Economics Results,* vol. 1, edited by Charles R. Plott and Vernon L. Smith. Amsterdam: Elsevier.

Rajan, Raghuram G. 2010. *Fault Lines: How Hidden Fractures Still Threaten the World Economy.* Princeton, N.J.: Princeton University Press.

Ranieri, Lewis S. 1996. "The Origins of Securitization, Sources of Its Growth, and Its Future Potential." In *A Primer on Securitization,* edited by Leon T. Kendall and Michael J. Fishman. Cambridge, Mass.: MIT Press.

Salmon, Felix. 2009. "Recipe for Disaster: The Formula That Killed Wall Street." *Wired,* February 23. Available at: http://www.wired.com/techbiz/it/magazine/17-03/wp_quant?currentPage=all (accessed June 27, 2012).

Savastano, Albert. 2005. "Basic Report: Golden West Financial." Philadelphia: Janney Montgomery Scott LLC (January 13).

Shiller, Robert J. 2005. *Irrational Exuberance.* 2nd ed. Princeton, N.J.: Princeton University Press.

Sichelman, Lew. 1990. "Fannie Mae Sets 30 Percent Down on Low-Doc Loan." *Chicago Tribune,* July 14. Available at: http://articles.chicagotribune.com/1990-07-14/news/9002270602_1_low-doc-loan-no-doc-loans-maximum-fha-loan (accessed June 27, 2012).

Simon, Ruth. 2005. "Mortgage Lenders Loosen Standards—Despite Growing Concerns, Banks Keep Relaxing Credit-Score, Income, and Debt-Loan Rules." *Wall Street Journal*, July 26.

Simon, Ruth, and James R. Hagerty. 2005. "How American Lenders Shelter Themselves." *Wall Street Journal*, September 22.

Simsek, Alp. 2012. "Belief Disagreements and Collateral Constraints." Working paper. Cambridge, Mass.: Harvard University (March 1). Available at: http://www.economics. harvard.edu/faculty/simsek/files/simsekBeliefDisagreementsCollateralConstraints7_ EMArevision.pdf (accessed June 27, 2012).

Smith, Vernon L., Gerry L. Suchanek, and Arlington W. Williams. 1988. "Bubbles, Crashes, and Endogenous Expectations in Experimental Spot Asset Markets." *Econometrica* 56(5): 1119–51.

Sorkin, Andrew Ross. 2010. *Too Big to Fail: The Inside Story of How Wall Street and Washington Fought to Save the Financial System—and Themselves*. New York: Penguin.

Stahl, David. 1996. "A COFI Break." *Mortgage Banking* 57(2).

Tett, Gillian. 2009. *Fool's Gold: How Unrestrained Greed Corrupted a Dream, Shattered Global Markets, and Unleashed a Catastrophe*. New York: Little, Brown.

Thomas, Jason, and Robert Van Order. 2011. "A Closer Look at Fannie Mae and Freddie Mac: What We Know, What We Think We Know, and What We Don't Know." Unpublished paper. Washington, D.C.: George Washington University, Department of Finance (March).

Warren, Elizabeth. 2010. "Priorities for the New Consumer Financial Protection Bureau." Speech delivered at the Consumer Federation of America Financial Services Conference (December 2). Available at: http://www.treasury.gov/press-center/press-releases/ Pages/tg987.aspx (accessed June 27, 2012).

Warren, Elizabeth, and Amelia W. Tyagi. 2004. *The Two-Income Trap: Why Middle-Class Parents Are Going Broke*. New York: Basic Books.

Warren Group, Inc. Various years. Public Records Data for Massachusetts. Proprietary data.

Zimmerman, Thomas. 2005. "Subprime Home Equities: It's (Almost) All About Home Prices" (conference call slide presentation), UBS U.S. Securitized Products Strategy Group (September 26).

Zuckerman, Gregory. 2010. *The Greatest Trade Ever: The Behind-the-Scenes Story of How John Paulson Defied Wall Street and Made Financial History*. New York: Crown Business.

Part III

Rethinking Financial Innovation

Chapter 7

Ratings, Mortgage Securitizations, and the Apparent Creation of Value

John Hull and Alan White

This chapter studies the criteria used by rating agencies when they rate structured products. The criterion used by Standard & Poor's (S&P) and Fitch aims to ensure that the probability of a loss on a structured product with a certain rating is similar to the probability of a loss on a corporate bond with the same rating. The criterion used by Moody's aims to ensure that the expected loss on a structured product with a certain rating is similar to the expected loss on a corporate bond with the same rating.

The rating of a structured product is in some sense a measure of quality. It is reasonable to assume that some investors assign a value to a structured product that increases as the credit rating improves. This raises the question of whether the ratings criteria permit arbitrage. Is it possible to improve the average perceived quality of a portfolio by restructuring it? We propose a *simple no-arbitrage condition that measures of credit quality should satisfy.* We show that the criterion used by Moody's does satisfy the condition whereas the criterion used by S&P and Fitch does not.

The traditional business of rating agencies is the rating of corporate and sovereign bonds. Between 2000 and 2007, another part of their business, the rating of structured products, grew very quickly, so much so that by the end of this period it was accounting for close to half of their revenues. This chapter examines whether the growth of the market for structured products was influenced by the rating criteria used by rating agencies. We do not examine whether the ratings criteria were correctly applied (this is considered in Hull and White 2010). Instead, we examine whether the ratings criteria, assuming that they were correctly applied, led to ratings arbitrage where investors were misled about the value of products.

This is an important public policy issue. Rating agencies have been widely criticized for their role in the credit crisis that started in 2007. Investors were prepared to buy the products that were created because rating agencies gave them AAA (Aaa) ratings. The products had complex, interdependent structures, and in many instances investors' reliance on ratings was so great that they did no analysis of their own. In the fall of 2007, many structured products were downgraded, which contributed to a panic in the market (for a discussion, see Gorton 2009).

In a securitization, a set of cash flows are repackaged to make them more attractive to the market. Franco Modigliani and Merton Miller (1958) argued that, in a perfect and complete market, it should not be possible to do this. A bundle of cash flows, whether from mortgages or other sources, should be worth the same regardless of how it is packaged. A securitization can be attractive only if it makes the market more complete or overcomes some market imperfection, such as taxes or regulation, and in doing so allows greater cash flows to be delivered to investors.

In practice, several factors influenced the development of the mortgage securitization market in the United States during the 2000 to 2007 period, including:

1. Banks were regulated in such a way that capital requirements for assets in the banking book were often greater than the capital requirements for equivalent-risk assets in the trading book.[1] A bank could therefore reduce its capital requirements by securitizing mortgages and holding equivalent-risk products in its trading book.

2. Although moving assets from the banking book to the trading book reduced capital to some extent, greater reductions could be achieved by removing the assets from the bank altogether. This led banks to use what is termed the "originate-to-distribute" model in which the banks originated loans and then eliminated their credit exposures through securitizations.

3. Arguably, markets were incomplete and securitization created products that were not otherwise available and for which there was unmet demand.

4. Structurers may have been able to take advantage of the methodologies used by rating agencies and the assumptions about ratings made by investors to create products that could be sold for considerably more than the value of the underlying assets.

It is this last point that is the focus of this chapter.

Michael Brennan, Julia Hein, and Ser-Huang Poon (2009) also consider the role of rating agencies in securitization. They argue that many arrangers of the securitizations of subprime mortgages were engaged in a form of ratings arbitrage. They consider a framework similar to Robert Merton's (1974), who bases the value of debt on the value of the underlying assets. In this context, the debt's rating is a property of the probability distribution of the underlying asset value at the debt maturity date. Two different underlying distributions may give rise to debt issues that have the same rating but different values. Our approach differs from that of Brennan and his colleagues in that we consider alternative debt structures based on the same underlying assets.

The research of Philippe Artzner and his colleagues (1999) is related to ours. Regulators have for many years used risk measures to determine capital requirements. These authors proposed four reasonable conditions that such risk measures should have. One of these conditions is subadditivity: if two portfolios are combined, the risk measure for the combined portfolio should not be greater than the sum of the risk measures for the individual portfolios. Diversification may cause the risk measure for the combined portfolio to be smaller than the sum of the risk measures for the individual portfolios, but there should never be a case in which the risks are somehow amplified. Artzner and his colleagues show that value at risk, which is the measure widely used by regulators, does not satisfy the subadditivity condition because the total value at risk sometimes increases when two portfolios are combined. Equivalently, value at risk sometimes decreases when portfolios are subdivided. In this chapter, we show that some of the criteria used by rating agencies lead to a similar phenomenon. When a portfolio is restructured, or split into a number of separate products, there is an apparent improvement in credit quality.

The research of Artzner and his colleagues (1999) emphasizes that risk measures are not necessarily concerned with value. Unless some sort of market imperfection is addressed, combining portfolios or subdividing a portfolio does not change total value. However, the total risk as quantified by some of the measures that are used may change. In this chapter, we show that, even when the restructuring of assets does not remove a market imperfection, restructuring can result in an apparent improvement in credit quality that leads to an increase in the value of the assets. To produce this result we make the plausible assumption that investors believe that, for all debt instruments with a certain life, the value as a percentage of the no-default value increases as the credit rating improves. Thus, if a five-year A-rated instrument sells for 95 percent of its no-default value, investors believe a similar AA-rated instrument should sell for more than 95 percent of its no-default value.[2]

Our results may explain some of the phenomena that were observed during the credit crisis and may have policy implications for the Securities and Exchange Commission (SEC) oversight of rating agencies that has been mandated by the Dodd-Frank legislation. They also raise some fundamental issues about what it is that ratings are trying to measure. If they are trying to measure value, some of the criteria are misguided. If they are trying to measure something else, it is important that this is made clear to the consumers of ratings.[3]

We begin this chapter by giving some background about rating agencies, subprime securitization, and the criteria used by rating agencies for structured products. We then propose a simple condition that any credit quality measure such as a rating should satisfy. We show that the probability of default does not satisfy this condition, whereas expected loss does. This leads us to conclude that in some cases the procedures used to rate structured products can create the illusion of a free lunch.

RATING AGENCIES

Rating agencies have a long and largely successful history in the United States. John Moody and Company first published *Moody's Manual*, which contained statistics and general information about stocks and bonds, in 1900. In 1909 it began publishing analytical information about railroad securities and in 1914 created Moody's Investors Service, which first provided ratings for government bonds and later for corporate bonds and commercial paper. Standard & Poor's (S&P) can trace its origins back to 1860, when Henry Varnum Poor began publishing a book, updated annually, on the financial and operational health of railroads. Standard Statistics was founded in 1906 to provide financial information on nonrailroad companies. Standard & Poor's was formed in 1941 from a merger of Standard Statistics and Poor's Publishing. The third major rating agency, Fitch, was formed in 1913 when John Knowles Fitch formed Fitch Publishing Company and published statistics via *The Fitch Stock and Bond Manual.*

S&P and Fitch use the rating categories AAA, AA, A, BBB, BB, B, CCC, CC, and C to describe bonds, while Moody's uses Aaa, Aa, A, Baa, Ba, B, Caa, Ca, and C. To create a finer gradation, S&P and Fitch divide all categories except AAA into three subcategories. For example, AA is divided into AA+, AA, and AA−; A is divided into A+, A, and A−; etc. Similarly, Moody's divides its rating categories into three subcategories: Aa is divided into Aa1, Aa2, and Aa3; A is divided into A1, A2, and A3; etc. The difference between adjacent subcategories is called a "notch." Thus, an A1 rating is one notch better than an A2 rating. It seems generally accepted by the market that there is equivalence between the rating systems of the three rating agencies. Thus, AA− from S&P is considered equivalent to AA− from Fitch and equivalent to Aa3 from Moody's.

Rating agencies use a "through-the-cycle" rather than a "point-in-time" approach to rating. This means that they try to consider only permanent changes in a company's health when changing the company's rating (for a discussion, see Altman and Rijken 2004). Problems faced by a company that are considered to be temporary (for example, poor economic conditions) do not usually lead to a rating change. This allows rating agencies to satisfy one of the requirements of investors: ratings stability. Ratings reversals (such as a downgrade followed by an upgrade) are avoided as far as possible. Richard Cantor and Chris Mann (2003) describe Moody's policy: "If over time new information reveals a potential change in an issuer's relative creditworthiness, Moody's considers whether or not to adjust the rating. It manages the tension between its dual objectives—accuracy and stability—by changing ratings only when it believes an issuer has experienced what is likely to be an enduring change in fundamental creditworthiness. For this reason ratings are said to 'look-through-the-cycle.'" Standard and Poor's (2010) states that it "incorporates credit stability as an important factor in our rating opinions."

Bond investors rely heavily on ratings.[4] Often the bonds that investment funds are allowed to invest in are determined by their ratings. For example, some funds are allowed to invest only in investment-grade bonds (those rated BBB [Baa] or better). If a bond is downgraded below investment grade, it must be sold. This is a simple governance tool that limits the activities of the fund manager. Without such a rule, the investors in the fund would have to monitor the fund's trading activities more closely to ensure that the fund is not taking undue risks. With such a rule, the monitoring role is effectively delegated to the rating agency. Investors assume that the bonds that are rated investment grade have an acceptably low level of risk.

A measure of the success of ratings is that they are used by more than just bond investors. Ratings are used by the Basel Committee in setting regulatory capital.[5]

Also, rating triggers are not uncommon in agreements for derivatives transactions between two parties. For example, an agreement might state that collateral has to be posted by a counterparty if its credit rating falls below a certain level. (A trigger of this type was involved in the government bailout of AIG.[6]) This is an example of how large financial institutions also delegate monitoring responsibility to the rating agencies.

Originally the credit rating agencies used a "user-pay" model. Ratings were published in books that were issued monthly and sold to users of ratings, such as investors. With the development of inexpensive photocopying in the 1970s, this business model was no longer viable, and the rating agencies switched to an "issuer-pay" model, in which the services of rating agencies are now paid for by the issuers of bonds, not by the investors and other market participants that use those services. This creates an obvious potential conflict of interest: the issuer may refuse to pay for a rating unless the rating is satisfactory to the issuer.

The main constraint on this potential conflict of interest is that the ratings business is a reputation-based business. The only reason investors rely on ratings is that the rating agencies have a long history of producing reasonably reliable ratings. As long as this reputation is maintained, the ratings business provides an ongoing stream of revenue from new ratings. (As a result, rating agencies have an incentive to avoid significant bias in the ratings.) Reputation also acts as a barrier to entry since new entrants would presumably have to operate at a loss for some time while developing their own reputation.

If the issuer decides not to pay, the agency may issue an unsolicited rating. Fearing that such an unsolicited rating would be worse than the solicited rating, issuers might then decide to pay for the rating. The evidence is that unsolicited ratings are most often issued for poorer-quality borrowers and so tend to be lower than average. There is also some evidence that unsolicited ratings are lower than solicited ratings for firms with similar financial statements (see Poon 2003; Poon and Firth 2005).

SUBPRIME SECURITIZATION

Asset-backed securities (ABSs) were first created in the late 1970s. In these securitizations, a special purpose vehicle (SPV) is created. The SPV is essentially a special type of corporation in which the assets of the corporation are a portfolio of debt instruments and the liabilities of the corporation are the securities issued to the investors. Unlike regular corporations—in which the types of financing are given names such as senior secured debt or equity and may receive different tax treatment—in an ABS the securities issued are referred to as "tranches," tend to receive the same tax treatment, and are usually just numbered. There are rules for determining how cash flows from the portfolio of debt instruments are distributed to the securities. The more senior a security is, the less likely it is to be affected by defaults on the debt instruments.

Figure 7.1 shows the structure of a very simple securitization. The most junior security, tranche 3, has a principal of $10 million, representing 10 percent of the

FIGURE 7.1   /   A Simple Example of a Mortgage Asset-Backed Security

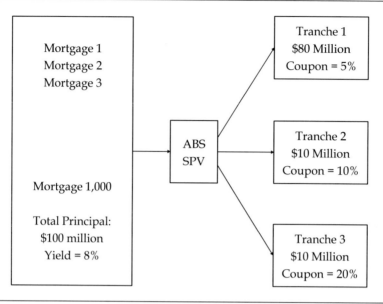

Source: Authors' figure.

total mortgage principal, and has a coupon rate of 20 percent. Investors in this tranche invest $10 million and are promised annual payments equal to $2 million per year plus the return of principal at maturity. As defaults occur in the mortgage portfolio, reducing the asset base, the principal of tranche 3 is reduced. This reduction in principal reduces the annual payments as well as the final repayment of principal. For example, if portfolio losses are $4 million, the remaining tranche 3 principal is $6 million and the annual interest payments are reduced to $1.2 million. If losses on the portfolio exceed $10 million—10 percent of the portfolio size—the tranche 3 principal is reduced to zero and the investors receive no further payments.[7] In a regular corporation, tranche 3 would be referred to as "equity." In an ABS, it is also often referred to as the "equity tranche." This tranche is quite risky, since a 4 percent loss in the mortgage portfolio ($4 million) would translate into a loss of 40 percent of the tranche 3 principal.

The next most junior security, tranche 2, has a principal of $10 million, representing 10 percent of the total bond principal, and has a coupon rate of 10 percent. Investors in this tranche invest $10 million and are promised annual payments of $1 million plus the return of principal at maturity. Default losses on the bond portfolio in excess of $10 million reduce the principal of tranche 2. This reduced principal size reduces the annual payments as well as the final repayment of principal. When losses on the portfolio exceed $20 million, the tranche 2 principal is reduced to zero and the investors receive no further payments. This tranche is often referred to as a "mezzanine tranche."

FIGURE 7.2 / New Tranches Rated by Standard & Poor's, 1990 to 2010

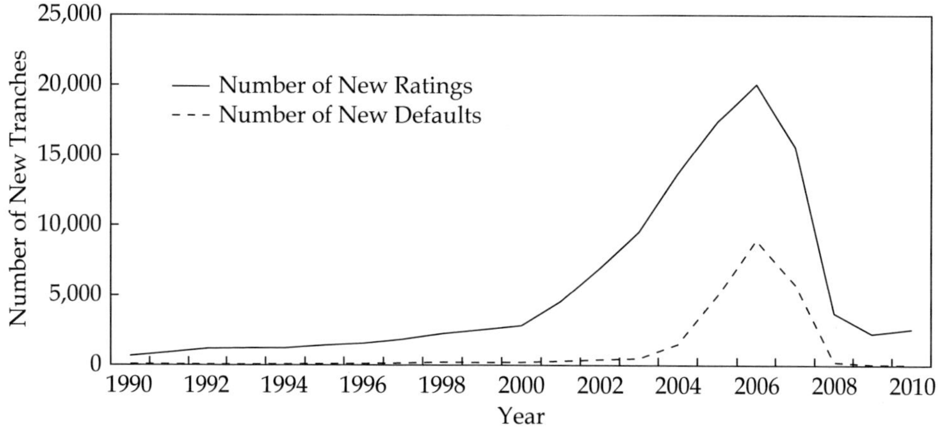

Source: Authors' compilation based on data from Standard & Poor's (2011b).

The most senior tranche, often called the "super-senior tranche," is treated in the same way as the mezzanine tranche. Investors in tranche 1 invest $80 million and are promised annual interest payments of $4 million. They are exposed to all losses on the bond portfolio in excess of $20 million. Tranche 1 is usually given a AAA rating. If we assume that, when a mortgage defaults, 30 percent of the value of the mortgage is lost,[8] more than 66.7 percent of the portfolio must default before the principal of tranche 1 is impaired.[9] If 100 percent of the mortgages default, the total loss on the mortgage portfolio is $30 million, of which only $10 million is borne by the tranche 1 investors.

The assets in an ABS do not have to be mortgages. They may be securities backed by auto loans, credit card receivables, student loans, manufactured housing loans, or nontraditional asset types such as mutual fund fees, tax liens, tobacco settlement payments, or intellectual property. In some cases, as we shall see, the assets in the portfolio may include tranches from other securitizations.

From its start in 1978, the securitization market grew steadily, but during the 2000 to 2007 period it underwent rapid growth largely as a result of growth in mortgage securitization. Between 1990 and 2000, the number of new tranches rated each year by S&P grew at a rate of about 16 percent per year. Between 2000 and 2006, however, the growth rate of new tranche ratings was about 39 percent per year. After 2006, the number of new tranches being rated declined, although the cumulative number of tranches rated by S&P continued to rise, peaking at 77,480 in 2008. The growth of the market is illustrated in figure 7.2, which shows the number of new tranches rated each year by S&P from 1990 to 2010 (see Standard & Poor's 2011b).

As of 2006,[10] the outstanding number of ABS tranches rated by Moody's was 37,035, of which 88 percent were rated investment grade and about 26 percent

FIGURE 7.3 / Example of Subprime Securitizations

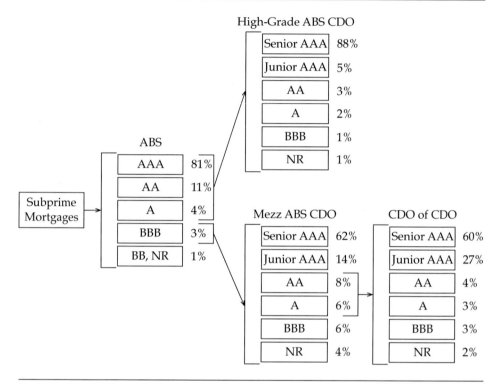

Source: Gorton (2009), reprinted with permission.

were rated Aaa (Moody's Investors Service 2007a). About 22 percent were U.S. residential mortgage-backed securities (RMBSs), 30 percent were U.S. home equity loans (HELs),[11] and about 12 percent were U.S. commercial mortgage-backed securities (CMBSs). By comparison, at the same time Moody's (2011) was rating 4,989 corporate bonds, of which 61.7 percent were rated investment grade and 2.7 percent were rated Aaa.

Market participants were very creative in how they used the ABS structure for subprime mortgages (see figure 7.1). An example is shown in figure 7.3. This figure is based on an illustration in Gorton (2009), which in turn is based on an article published by UBS. The ABS in figure 7.3 would typically be created from a portfolio of one thousand subprime mortgages, but the securitization did not end with this first step. BBB tranches created from the securitization of perhaps one hundred different subprime portfolios were resecuritized to create what is termed a "mezz ABS CDO." Similarly, AAA, AA, and A tranches created from multiple securitizations were resecuritized to form what is termed a "high-grade ABS CDO." Furthermore, as indicated in figure 7.3, there were re-re-securitizations because

AA and A tranches of mezz ABS CDOs were sometimes resecuritized to form what is termed a "CDO of CDO," or CDO-squared.

As we discuss later, the rating agencies used models to determine the ratings for tranches. The creators of the structure used their knowledge of the models used by rating agencies to ensure that they got the ratings they wanted. To avoid any uncertainty, they would typically present a proposed structure to a rating agency before actually creating it and ask how the tranches would be rated. If they did not get the ratings they wanted, they adjusted the design of the structure to achieve the desired ratings. This is an important difference between structured products and bonds. Structured products are designed to produce desired ratings. The company issuing a bond has no easy way of restructuring itself to change the rating assigned to a bond if it does not like the rating.

Securitization is profitable to the creators of tranches because the weighted average return paid to tranche holders is less than the weighted average return received from the mortgages. For example, in the structure illustrated in figure 7.1, the average interest rate on the mortgages is 8 percent. The weighted average interest rate on the three tranches issued is 7 percent. The difference between the interest rate earned on the mortgages and the rate paid on the tranches, 1 percent, is referred to as "excess spread." It is used to cover the cost of the securitization, provide extra security to the investors, and provide a profit to the creator of the structure. Profitability is maximized by making the ratings of the tranches as high as possible, because the higher rating of a tranche the lower the return the tranche holder is prepared to accept. Structurers therefore aim to make the percentage of AAA-rated products in a securitization as large as possible. If all securitizations had the characteristics of figure 7.3, 91.9 percent of the subprime mortgages fed into the securitization machines would eventually become AAA-rated securities.[12] Randall Dodd and Paul Mills (2008) suggest that the example shown in figure 7.3 is not atypical in this respect. They estimate that the total principal of the AAA-rated securities created from subprime mortgages was about 90 percent of the principal of the underlying mortgages.

RATINGS CRITERIA

The rating of bonds is based on a mixture of judgment and analysis. Rating agencies test whether the ratings are both reasonable and consistent over time. For example, they carry out annual cohort studies that measure the ex post realized default rates for all the securities they rate in each rating category. If the ratings are consistent over time, the realized default rate for each rating class does not change materially from year to year.

These cohort studies have become a rich source of default probability estimates. Table 7.1 shows a small excerpt taken from a Standard & Poor's (2011a) corporate bond cohort study. This table shows that of all bonds rated BBB in a particular year, on average 2.56 percent defaulted within the following five years while only 0.44 percent of AAA-rated companies defaulted within five years. Over time these

TABLE 7.1 / S&P Average Cumulative Default Rates, 1981 to 2010

Rating	One	Two	Three	Four	Five
			Time Horizon (Years)		
AAA	0.00%	0.04%	0.17%	0.30%	0.44%
AA	0.04	0.09	0.20	0.34	0.46
A	0.09	0.24	0.42	0.63	0.85
BBB	0.27	0.73	1.21	1.86	2.56
BB	1.00	3.02	5.47	7.77	9.80
B	4.77	10.67	15.78	19.79	22.84
CCC-C	28.31	39.25	45.51	49.42	52.35

Source: Authors' compilation of data from Standard & Poor's (2011a).

cohort studies (which are regularly published by the rating agencies) have led to a perception by market participants that the credit rating provides an estimate of the bond's probability of default.

When rating agencies started to rate structured products, their initial approach was similar to that used for bonds: judgment and analysis. However, because of the relatively simple nature of the structured products, over time the approach to rating structured products became more model-based.[13] The rating agencies are fairly open about the models they use. Two key inputs into their models are the probabilities of default for each of the assets underlying the securitization (derived from the cohort study results) and the expected losses given default for each asset (based on their historical experience). Default correlation also has to be quantified in some way.

We discuss the approach used by the rating agencies to assess the rating of a structured product in the context of the simplified structure illustrated in figure 7.1.[14] In assigning ratings to the tranches, the rating agency considers the historical behavior of the subprime mortgages. Experience has been that some subprime borrowers prepay their mortgages early, in order to borrow at a better interest rate, while other subprime borrowers default. As a result, although subprime mortgages are usually scheduled to last thirty years, in practice they have an average life of about five years. When determining the ratings of tranches created from subprime mortgages, it is therefore appropriate to compare their losses with the losses on bonds over a five-year period.

Suppose the historical experience has been that 10 percent of subprime borrowers default within five years of taking out the mortgage and that the losses due to default are 25 percent of the value of the outstanding mortgage.[15] If the future is the same as the past, this means that losses on the pool of mortgages in figure 7.1 will be $2.5 million, all of which will be borne by the tranche 3 investors. However, default rates in the future may be higher than in the past, and higher default rates will probably be associated with greater losses, since it will probably be more difficult to sell the repossessed house when there are many defaults. If more than 40 percent of subprime borrowers default within five years (more than four times the historic default rate) and losses due to default are 50 percent of the value of the outstanding mortgage (twice the historic experience), the total portfolio loss is over $20 million. This consumes the entire principal of tranches 2 and 3, and tranche 1 bears some loss. A rating agency that was matching the probability of tranche impairment to the historical bond default rates in table 7.1 would therefore give tranche 1 a rating of AAA if it believed that the probability that more than 40 percent of borrowers would default was less than 0.44 percent (which is the five-year AAA default rate for bonds in table 7.1).[16]

This procedure of assigning tranche ratings by comparing the estimated probability of tranche impairment to the historical realized probability of default for corporate bonds was used by Standard & Poor's and Fitch. The differences between the ratings assigned to a tranche by the two agencies were the result of different estimates of historical default behaviour and differences in the estimated probabilities of extreme default events.

Moody's assigned tranche ratings based on how much investors expected to lose on average as a result of defaults. The averaging was done over all possible outcomes. For example, suppose that Moody's estimated that 99 percent of the time the subprime default rate and the loss due to default would be sufficiently low that tranche 1 would suffer no loss, but that 1 percent of the time the total portfolio loss would be $40 million, so that the loss to tranche 1 would be $20 million (25 percent of its principal). In this case, the expected loss is

$$0.99 \times 0\% + 0.01 \times 25\%,$$

or 0.25 percent of the principal. This calculated expected loss would be compared with Moody's historical experience of the losses on bonds with different ratings. Table 7.2, taken from Moody's Investors Service (2007a), shows the relationship between ratings and expected loss. Based on the assumed outcomes, Moody's would give tranche 1 a rating of A, since the calculated expected five-year loss of 0.25 percent is smaller than the five-year idealized loss rate of 0.402 percent for A-rated bonds but larger than the loss rate for Aa-rated bonds.

TABLE 7.2 / Moody's Loss Rate Table

Rating	Time Horizon (Years)				
	One	Two	Three	Four	Five
Aaa	0.000%	0.000%	0.000%	0.001%	0.002%
Aa	0.002	0.011	0.033	0.056	0.078
A	0.021	0.083	0.198	0.297	0.402
Baa	0.231	0.578	0.941	1.309	1.678
Ba	1.546	3.031	4.329	5.385	6.523
B	6.391	9.136	11.57	13.22	14.88
Caa	28.04	31.35	34.35	36.43	38.40

Source: Authors' compilation of data from Moody's (2007a).

Because the rating agencies used different approaches for rating the tranches of structured products, it is liable to be the case that they would assign different ratings. This leads to the possibility of "ratings shopping," in which the issuer searches for the rating agency that gives the best rating (discussed further later in the chapter).[17] Whether expected loss or probability of default is used as the ratings criterion for bonds has not emerged as an important issue in the literature. This is probably partly because bond ratings are heavily dependent on judgment. However, we find that the criterion used is important in the rating of structured products. Specifically, the probability of default criterion fuels an illusion that restructuring the cash flows from securities can create value.

A NO-ARBITRAGE CONDITION FOR A CREDIT QUALITY MEASURE

In previous sections, we have described the nature of the securitizations that were created and the procedures used by rating agencies to rate them. In this section, we show that some rating approaches may lead to the appearance of securitization creating value. We suggest a simple no-arbitrage condition that a credit quality measure such as a credit rating should satisfy in order to avoid this problem.

Suppose that q is a measure of the credit quality of an asset that is subject to default risk, with the property that q increases as the credit quality decreases. As mentioned, the credit quality measure used by S&P and Fitch for structured products is the probability that the loss will be greater than zero, while that used by Moody's is the percentage expected loss. Both of these measures have the desired property: higher probability of default or higher expected loss due to default is associated with poorer credit quality.

The asset for which a credit quality measure is calculated can be a single asset, such as a bond or a portfolio of assets. For a portfolio, the credit quality can be measured either in terms of the single value of q corresponding to the whole portfolio or in terms of the frequency distribution of q's for the constituent assets. For example, suppose the portfolio contains four $100 bonds and our q-measure is the probability of default. One of the bonds has a default probability of 1 percent, one has a default probability of 2 percent, and two have a default probability of 5 percent. The q-measure for the entire portfolio is the probability that the portfolio suffers impairment due to default. This occurs if any bond in the portfolio defaults. (This q-measure is greater than 5 percent, the largest single bond default probability.) The frequency distribution of the q's is as follows:

25 percent of the portfolio has $q = 1$ percent

25 percent of the portfolio has $q = 2$ percent

50 percent of the portfolio has $q = 5$ percent

What we refer to as "credit quality dominance" is a concept that we define in terms of the frequency distribution of the q's for a portfolio. Portfolio Y dominates

TABLE 7.3 / Example Illustrating Credit Quality Dominance

	Portfolio A	Portfolio B	Portfolio C
Asset 1 ($q = 1$)	0%	80%	0%
Asset 2 ($q = 2$)	100	10	90
Asset 3 ($q = 3$)	0	10	10
Fraction with q equal to 1 or less	0	80	0
Fraction with q equal to 2 or less	100	90	90
Fraction with q equal to 3 or less	100	100	100

Source: Authors' table.

portfolio X if it gives an unambiguous better frequency distribution for the q's. The concept is best illustrated with an example. Suppose that there are three assets with q-values of 1, 2, and 3, respectively. Consider the three portfolios in table 7.3. The upper panel of table 7.3 shows the fraction of each portfolio invested in each asset. The lower panel (which is calculated from the upper panel) shows the fraction of each portfolio with q less than or equal to 1, 2, or 3. Portfolio B dominates portfolio C because it has a bigger percentage of assets for which q is 1 or less and the percentage of assets for which q is 2 or less or 3 or less is the same for both portfolios.[18] Also, portfolio A dominates portfolio C because they have the same percentage of assets for which q is 1 or less or 3 or less, but portfolio A has more assets for which q is 2 or less. There is no dominance between portfolio A and portfolio B.

We assume that some investors use the credit quality measure, q, as a guide to valuing a portfolio. More specifically, we assume that the value that some investors assign to a product with a certain life, as a percentage of its no-default value, increases as the credit quality measure improves. That is, assets with worse credit ratings (higher q) have lower value than otherwise similar assets with better credit ratings. This behavior is plausible and seems to be at the heart of the criticisms of the rating agencies.

We define a restructuring of a portfolio as a method by which all the cash flows generated by the assets in the portfolio are redistributed to create a new portfolio of assets. A credit quality arbitrage occurs when a portfolio can be restructured into a new portfolio that has a higher value for at least some market participants. Under our assumption about investor behavior in the previous paragraph, if the restructuring produces credit quality dominance it results in credit quality arbitrage.[19] It follows that:

A necessary condition for a credit quality measure to be arbitrage-free is that, for every portfolio X and every portfolio Y that can be restructured from X, there be no credit quality dominance between X and Y.

Probability of loss does not satisfy the no-arbitrage condition. To show this, define portfolio X as any portfolio that may be subject to losses due to default. (For example, portfolio X could be a single bond or a portfolio of bonds.) Define portfolio Y as a portfolio consisting of two securities (or tranches). The first security is responsible for all losses on portfolio X up to 50 percent of the principal of portfolio X; the second security is responsible for the remaining losses on portfolio X. Portfolio Y is a portfolio that can be costlessly created from portfolio X. The probability of loss for the first security of portfolio Y is the same as the probability of loss for portfolio X. In general, the second security in portfolio Y has a lower probability of loss than portfolio X.[20] As a result, the necessary condition for no arbitrage is violated. Part of portfolio Y has the same q-measure as portfolio X; the rest of the portfolio has a lower q-measure. If probability of loss is the credit quality measure used for X and Y, then Y will always be more valuable than X to some investors even though X can be costlessly converted into Y.

Now consider a third portfolio, Z, which consists of three tranches responsible for losses in the ranges of 0 to 25 percent, 25 to 50 percent, and 50 to 100 percent. Using arguments similar to those used in comparing portfolios Y and X, we can show that when probability of loss is used as a criterion, portfolio Z dominates portfolio Y even though portfolio Y can be costlessly converted into portfolio Z. It is easy to see how the probability of loss criterion encourages financial institutions to create multiple tranches from portfolios of loans. As more tranches are created, the violation of the no-arbitrage condition becomes greater.

It can be shown that the credit quality measure used by Moody's—percentage expected loss—always satisfies the no-arbitrage condition. To see this, suppose that the expected loss for portfolio X is 2 percent—that is, $q = 2$ percent. One of the properties of expected loss is that the weighted average of the tranche expected losses must equal the portfolio expected loss. Suppose that the EL for the two tranches of portfolio Y are 1 percent and 3 percent. The expected loss for the three tranches of portfolio Z might be 0.5 percent, 1.5 percent, and 3 percent. In each case, the weighted average of the tranche expected losses is 2 percent.[21] The frequency distribution of the q's for the three portfolios is shown in table 7.4. Portfolio X has a larger fraction than Y or Z for q less than or equal to 2 percent, but a smaller

TABLE 7.4 / Example Illustrating Expected Loss as a Credit Criterion

	Portfolio X	Portfolio Y	Portfolio Z
$q = 0.5$ percent	0%	0%	25%
$q = 1.0$ percent	0	50	0
$q = 1.5$ percent	0	0	25
$q = 2.0$ percent	100	0	0
$q = 3.0$ percent	0	50	50
Fraction with q equal to 0.5 percent or less	0	0	25
Fraction with q equal to 1.0 percent or less	0	50	25
Fraction with q equal to 1.5 percent or less	0	50	50
Fraction with q equal to 2.0 percent or less	100	50	50
Fraction with q equal to 3.0 percent or less	100	100	100

Source: Authors' table.

fraction for smaller q's. Thus, X does not dominate Y or Z, and they do not dominate X. Similarly, portfolio Y has a larger fraction than Z for q less than or equal to 1 percent, but a smaller fraction for smaller q's, so neither Y nor Z dominates.

THE SUBPRIME EXPERIENCE AND RATINGS SHOPPING

Even figure 7.3 is a simplification of the structures that were actually created. Typically, every single rating category was used so that the total number of tranches created in a securitization was about twenty. This is exactly what the probability of default criterion suggests should happen. Every time a new rating category is used, there is an apparent creation of value for investors who are using the S&P or Fitch ratings and who believe that ratings measure value.

The large number of ABS tranches created meant that many tranches were quite thin in the sense that they were responsible for a narrow range of losses. Consider the first level of securitization where an ABS is created. The AAA tranche is typically over 75 percent of the total principal. This means that the other tranches are on average about 1 percent wide. As a result, they tend to have "all-or-nothing" characteristics. They either experience no defaults or are completely wiped out.

For the AAA tranche, the expected loss given default is relatively low because, if it does experience loss, the loss will in most cases be small. By contrast, the all-or-nothing properties of the other tranches mean that the expected loss given default is high. The relation between the criteria used by rating agencies is:

$$\text{Expected Loss} = \text{Probability of Default} \times \text{Loss Given Default}$$

If the rating agencies agree on the probability of default, it is likely that Moody's will produce a lower rating for non-AAA tranches, because these tranches have a much higher loss given default than corporate bonds. A corporate bond that has the same expected loss as a non-AAA tranche is likely to have a lower rating than a corporate bond that has the same probability of default as the tranche.

There is evidence that this is the case. Moody's Investors Service (2007b) reports a comparison of Moody's ratings with the ratings of Fitch and Standard & Poor's for 59,547 tranches rated by Moody's and by one or more other rating agency as of January 31, 2007. The results of the comparison between the Moody's and S&P ratings are summarized in table 7.5, which is taken from the Moody's report.

The average gap in table 7.5 is the Moody's rating less the S&P rating, measured in notches. Negative values indicate that Moody's rating is lower. Table 7.5 shows that for tranches other than the Aaa-rated tranches, Moody's rating was about one-half of a notch lower than S&P's rating. Similar results are found in the comparison of Moody's and Fitch ratings. Table 7.5 includes tranches from all types of securitizations (ABS, RMBS, CMBS, and so on), but similar results are found for each individual type of securitization. This indicates that the difference is a result of Moody's methodology rather than the characteristics of a particular market. The positive average gap for the Aaa-rated tranches is an artifact of the

TABLE 7.5 / A Comparison of Moody's and S&P Ratings for Jointly Rated Tranches

Moody's Rating	Number of Tranches	Average Gap	Moody's Lower	Same	Moody's Higher
Aaa	29,687	0.03	0.0%	98.5%	1.5%
Aa	8,870	−0.16	29.8	60.3	9.9
A	8,408	−0.40	31.4	59.0	9.6
Baa	8,822	−0.45	31.1	61.6	7.2
Ba	2,837	−0.55	34.3	60.0	5.7
B	729	−0.49	26.1	65.8	8.1
Caa-below	194	−2.16	65.5	16.5	18.0

Source: Authors' compilation of data from Moody's (2007b).

calculation. Since it is the highest rating, S&P could not produce a higher rating that would produce a negative gap. The only possible differences are cases in which S&P has a lower rating.

The results reported in table 7.5 should be interpreted as a conservative estimate of the difference between Moody's ratings and the ratings of other agencies because of ratings shopping. Although multiple ratings are attractive to the underwriter, split ratings are not.[22] If one rating agency produced a lower rating for a tranche when a structure was being created, it was likely that they would not be asked to rate that tranche. As a result, almost all of the jointly rated tranches reported in table 7.5 had the same rating from both agencies at inception. The rating differences that subsequently evolved arose because the initial Moody's rating was closer to a downgrade.

It is likely that structurers recognized this. They could achieve the highest possible rating for each tranche by having Moody's rate the Aaa-rated tranches but not the lower-quality tranches. On the other hand, there may have been pressure from investors to have multiple ratings for tranches. The evidence is suggestive of these competing forces. Standard & Poor's (2011b) reports that of all RMBS tranches they rated issued between 1978 and 2010, when equivalent tranches are considered as a single tranche, about 20 percent were rated AAA at the time of issue. By comparison, Moody's Investor Services (2007a) reports that, of all the structured tranches being rated in 2006, about 26 percent were rated Aaa.[23] Although it appears that rather more of Moody's business was in rating Aaa-rated tranches, the difference is not large. At the same time, the results in table 7.5 suggest that the non-Aaa-rated tranches were structured in such a way as to just meet the Moody's criterion, resulting in more subsequent downgrades by Moody's.

The apparent creation of value happens when any portfolio of debtlike assets is securitized. It is therefore a potential explanation for the popularity of resecuritization and re-re-securitization. There is an apparent creation of value in figure 7.3 when the mezz ABS CDO is created from BBB-rated tranches, when the high-grade ABS CDO is created from AAA-, AA-, and A-rated tranches, and when the CDO of CDOs are created.

AAA RATINGS

The creation of tranches with AAA ratings was the key to the success of the securitization of subprime mortgages during the 2000 to 2006 period. Indeed, the profitability of a securitization to the structurer depended critically on the volume of AAA-rated tranches that were created. This helps to explain the popularity of resecuritizations and re-re-securitizations. In figure 7.3, without the re- and re-re-securitizations, 81 percent of mortgage portfolios became AAA-rated securities; with them, over 90 percent did so.

Pension funds, endowments, and other large investors typically establish rules governing how their assets can be invested. These rules often specify that the credit rating of instruments must be above a certain level and sometimes that the credit rating must be AAA. There is a limited supply of AAA-rated corporate and sovereign bonds in the world. The artificial creation of almost unlimited amounts of AAA-rated securities from the securitization of mortgages was therefore attractive to many fund managers.

Was a AAA-rated tranche equivalent to a AAA-rated bond? The answer should be clear from our analysis here. If the rating agencies applied their criteria appropriately, one dimension of the loss distribution of a AAA-rated tranche was the same as that of a AAA-rated corporate bond, but other aspects of the loss distribution were liable to be quite different. For example, if they have the same probability of suffering a loss, they are liable to have different expected losses. Consider a bond and a thin tranche, both rated BBB by S&P or Fitch. They will have approximately the same probability of default. In the case of the bond, however, the expected loss in the event of default is about 60 percent, whereas in the case of the tranche it is almost 100 percent.

There are other reasons why investors should have been wary of regarding a AAA bond as equivalent to a AAA tranche. As pointed out by Joshua Coval, Jakub Jurek, and Erik Stafford (2009), AAA-rated tranches have high systematic or market risk. They tend to lose money when the market as a whole performs very poorly and there are many defaults. AAA-rated bonds do not have as much systematic risk. The issuing firm may default because the market as a whole performs very poorly or for firm-specific reasons. Investors require compensation for bearing systematic risk. For this reason, even if the loss distribution for a AAA-rated bond and a AAA-rated tranche is exactly the same, the two securities would not be valued in the same way. The AAA-rated tranche would have a lower price and a higher rate of return.

Another difference concerns the probability of downgrade. As explained earlier, structurers knew the models used by rating agencies and were able to show proposed structures to rating agencies before creating them. As a result, it is likely that AAA-rated tranches had just made it to the AAA category. A structurer would not choose a AAA tranche to be 81 percent wide, as in figure 7.3, if a tranche that is 82 percent wide or 83 percent wide would also be rated AAA. If the tranche has just made it into the AAA category, then, assuming that the criterion applied by the rating agency does not change, any worsening of the portfolio underlying the structure leads to the tranche being downgraded, resulting in tranche downgrade rates that are much higher than bond downgrade rates. Rating agencies may counter this possibility by having more stringent conditions for initial tranche ratings than they do for ongoing ratings.

CONCLUSION

Rating agencies have come under criticism because of their role in the securitization of mortgages. We have argued in this chapter that the market may have been misled because of an ambiguity about what ratings were measuring. The probability of loss may be a satisfactory credit quality measure when used solely to characterize the credit quality of a single bond, but it permits arbitrage when it is used to rate portfolios of bonds or structured products.

The expected loss criterion does satisfy the basic no-arbitrage condition that we have proposed. However, this does not mean that it is correct to base a valuation solely on expected loss (or base it solely on a rating that is calculated from expected loss). Rating agencies calculate expected loss in the real world, not the risk-neutral world. As is well known, the discount rate that is appropriate for cash flows estimated in the real world is difficult to estimate and may be counterintuitive. Market participants that rely on the expected loss estimates of rating agencies are liable to be arbitraged by other market participants that employ more complete valuation methodologies.

The loss distributions for structured products are often quite different from those for bonds or portfolios of bonds. To provide a complete set of information to the users of ratings, it is tempting to propose a single measure that involves characteristics of the loss distribution other than its expected value. However, it is difficult to find a measure that does this and does not permit the basic arbitrage we have considered in this chapter. A better approach for rating agencies might be to provide multiple measures for structured products.

NOTES

1. The banking book consists of assets such as loans that are expected to be held to maturity. Unless severely impaired, these assets are usually recorded at historic cost plus accrued interest. The trading book consists of assets that are held for trading. These assets are recorded at current (mark-to-market) value.

2. Other similar simple assumptions about the way investors use ratings as a guide to valuation lead to the same results as those in this chapter.

3. Arguably, learning and competition should lead investors to understand the weaknesses of ratings over time. If this were the case, the regulation of rating agencies would seem to be unnecessary.

4. The National Association of Insurance Regulators (NAIC) implies that ratings are used to make investment decisions in its statement that, "unlike the ratings of nationally recognized statistical rating organizations, NAIC designations are *not* produced to aid

the investment decision making process." See NAIC and Center for Insurance Policy and Research, "Securities Valuations Office (SVO)," available at: http://www.naic.org/svo.htm (accessed September 14, 2011).

5. The Dodd-Frank Wall Street Reform and Consumer Protection Act of 2010 in the United States seeks to eliminate any reliance on external credit ratings and is therefore in conflict with Basel requirements.

6. In an August 6, 2008, regulatory filing, AIG revealed that a ratings cut might trigger more than $13 billion in collateral calls (Son 2008). Again in March 2009, AIG reported that another downgrade would result in $8 billion of collateral calls and termination payments (Barr 2009). A summary of the use of ratings in setting collateral can be found in International Swaps and Derivatives Association (2010).

7. This is a simplified description of events. In practice, losses due to default in the mortgage portfolio reduce the amount of income available to pay interest to the tranche investors. Any interest shortfall is borne by the tranche 3 investors first. The reduction of principal in the mortgage portfolio reduces the amount available to repay tranche investors when the mortgage portfolio is liquidated. Any principal repayment shortfall is borne by the tranche 3 investors first. Thus, it is as though losses due to default in the mortgage portfolio reduce the tranche 3 principal and the corresponding interest payments.

8. When a mortgagor defaults, the lender takes possession of the house and sells it. The loss represents the difference between the sale price of the house and the amount of the outstanding mortgage as well as the legal and other costs associated with the foreclosure and sale.

9. A tranche is said to be "impaired" if it has suffered any sort of loss due to default. The probability of impairment for a tranche is similar to the probability of default for a bond.

10. The Moody's results are reported for 2006 since this was the last year in which the two agencies counted tranches in the same way. Up until this time, pari passu and other equivalent tranches from the same securitization were counted as a single tranche. After 2006, Moody's counted all tranches separately. This led to an approximate doubling of the number of tranches reported. In 2006, S&P rated 50,899 tranches, about 37 percent more than Moody's.

11. Home equity loans include subprime mortgages, high loan-to-value loans, and home equity lines of credit.

12. This may overstate things a little, as there may be some overcollateralization in figure 7.3 where the total principal of the products used for the securitization created is slightly less than the principal of the products created.

13. It is much easier to understand the nature of the assets underlying a securitization and how these asset values may change than it is to understand how the value of the assets of a corporation may change.

14. In addition to the simplified structure, we ignore any excess spread or any prepayments of the mortgages being securitized.

15. These percentages are roughly consistent with subprime experience prior to 2005.

16. All of the complex default modeling undertaken by the rating agencies is related to determining the likelihood of high default rates and what the loss would be in such an environment.

17. For a discussion of the rating criteria and the potential for ratings shopping, see Fender and Kiff (2004).

18. The technical definition is: B dominates C if for each value of q the fraction of B with that q or smaller less the fraction of C with that q or less is either positive or zero and for at least one q it is positive.

19. This is intuitively obvious. It is proved formally in Hull and White (forthcoming).

20. This is always true providing there is some chance of losses less than 50 percent of the principal amount.

21. For portfolio Z, the weighted average is:

$$0.25 \times 0.5\% + 0.25 \times 1.5\% + 0.5 \times 3\% = 2\%$$

22. A split rating refers to the case in which different rating agencies assign different ratings to the same tranche.

23. These percentages are for the case in which pari passu and other equivalent tranches are considered to be a single tranche. The results in table 7.5 count every tranche separately.

REFERENCES

Altman, Edward, and Herbert Rijken. 2004. "How Rating Agencies Achieve Stability." *Journal of Banking and Finance* 28(12): 2679–2714.

Artzner, Philippe, Freddy Delbaen, Jean-Marc Eber, and David Heath. 1999. "Coherent Measures of Risk." *Mathematical Finance* 9(3): 203–28.

Barr, Alistair. 2009. "AIG Warns on Ratings, Collateral Calls, Solvency." *MarketWatch*, March 2.

Brennan, Michael J., Julia Hein, and Ser-Huang Poon. 2009. "Tranching and Rating." *European Financial Management Journal* 15(5, November): 891–922.

Cantor, Richard, and Chris Mann. 2003. "Are Corporate Bond Ratings Pro-Cyclical?" *Special Comment* (Moody's Investors Services) (October).

Coval, Joshua D., Jakub W. Jurek, and Erik Stafford. 2009. "Economic Catastrophe Bonds." *American Economic Review* 99(3): 628–66.

Dodd, Randall, and Paul Mills. 2008. "Outbreak: U.S. Subprime Contagion." *Finance and Development* 45(2): 14–18.

Fender, Ingo, and John Kiff. 2004. "CDO Rating Methodology: Some Thoughts on Model Risk and Its Implications." Working Paper 163. Basel: Bank for International Settlements (November).

Gorton, Gary. 2009. "The Subprime Panic." *European Financial Management* 15(1): 10–46.

Hull, John, and Alan White. 2010. "The Risk of Tranches Created from Mortgages." *Financial Analysts Journal* 66(5, September–October): 54–67.

———. Forthcoming. "Ratings Arbitrage and Structured Products." *Journal of Derivatives*.

International Swaps and Derivatives Association (ISDA). 2010. "Market Review of OTC Derivative Bilateral Collateralization Practices (2.0)." ISDA Collateral Steering Committee (March 1).

Merton, Robert. 1974. "On the Pricing of Corporate Debt: The Risk Structure of Interest Rates." *Journal of Finance* 29(2): 449–70.

Modigliani, Franco, and Merton H. Miller. 1958. "The Cost of Capital, Corporation Finance, and the Theory of Investment." *American Economic Review* 48(3): 261–97.

Moody's Investors Service. 2007a. "Default and Loss Rates of Structured Finance Securities: 1993–2006." *Special Comment* (April).

———. 2007b. "Comparing Ratings on Jointly Rated U.S. Structured Finance Securities: 2007 Update." *Structured Finance Special Report* (March 30).

———. 2008. "Default and Loss Rates of Structured Finance Securities: 1993–2007." *Special Comment* (July).

———. 2011. "Corporate Default and Recovery Rates, 1920–2010." *Special Comment* (February).

Poon, Winnie P. H. 2003. "Are Unsolicited Credit Ratings Downward Biased?" *Journal of Banking and Finance* 27: 593–614.

Poon, Winnie P. H., and Michael Firth. 2005. "Are Unsolicited Credit Ratings Lower? International Evidence from Bank Ratings." *Journal of Business Finance and Accounting* 32: 1741–71.

Son, Hugh. 2008. "AIG's Ratings Cut by S&P, Moody's, Threatening Fund Raising." *Bloomberg*, September 15.

Standard & Poor's. 2010. "General Criteria: Methodology: Credit Stability Criteria." May. Available by subscription at: http://www.standardandpoors.com/prot/ratings/articles/en/us/?assetID=1245211381919 (accessed September 14, 2011).

———. 2011a. "2010 Annual U.S. Corporate Default Study and Rating Transitions." March. Available by subscription at: http://www.standardandpoors.com/ratings/articles/en/us/?articleType=HTML&assetID=1245302234800#ID19071 (accessed September 14, 2011).

———. 2011b. "Default Study: Global Structured Finance Default Study—1978–2010: Credit Trends Started to Improve in 2010, but U.S. RMBS Faces Challenges." March. Available by subscription at: http://www.standardandpoors.com/prot/ratings/articles/en/us/?assetID=1245301718990#ID35314 (accessed September 14, 2011).

Chapter 8

The Role of ABSs, CDSs, and CDOs in the Credit Crisis and the Economy

Robert A. Jarrow

The credit derivatives—ABSs, CDSs, and CDOs—played a significant role in the financial crisis of 2007 to 2008, affecting both the financial and real economy. This chapter explains their economic roles, using the credit crisis as an illustration. It is argued that ABSs are beneficial in that they provide previously unavailable investment opportunities to market participants, facilitating the access to debt capital that spurs real economic growth. If properly collateralized, CDSs are also beneficial because they enable market participants to more easily short-sell debt, thereby increasing the informational efficiency of credit markets. And similar to mutual funds, CDOs provide investors with desired investments (cash flow streams) at reduced transaction costs. Prior to the credit crisis, CDOs were used to exploit market mispricings caused by the credit agencies' misratings of structured debt. These mispricings were persistent owing to both the complexity of the CDOs and the dysfunctional institutional and regulatory structures present in the economy. The regulatory reforms needed in this regard are herein discussed.

To understand the role of asset-backed securities (ABSs), credit default swaps (CDSs), and collatoralized debt obligations (CDOs) in the economy, one needs first to understand their role in the credit crisis. To help the reader follow the subsequent discussion, figure 8.1 provides a diagram of the credit crisis. In this respect, three issues and their relation to these credit derivatives need to be understood:

1. Incentive problems: agency problems in the management of various financial institutions and investment funds; the fee structure of the rating agencies; and the effect of ABSs and CDOs on the mortgage originators' lending standards.

2. Errors made by the credit rating agencies in rating both corporate debt and structured debt.[1]

3. Government regulation with respect to credit ratings and government policies with respect to the expansion of mortgage loans to low-income households.

FIGURE 8.1 / Diagram of the Credit Crisis of 2007 to 2008

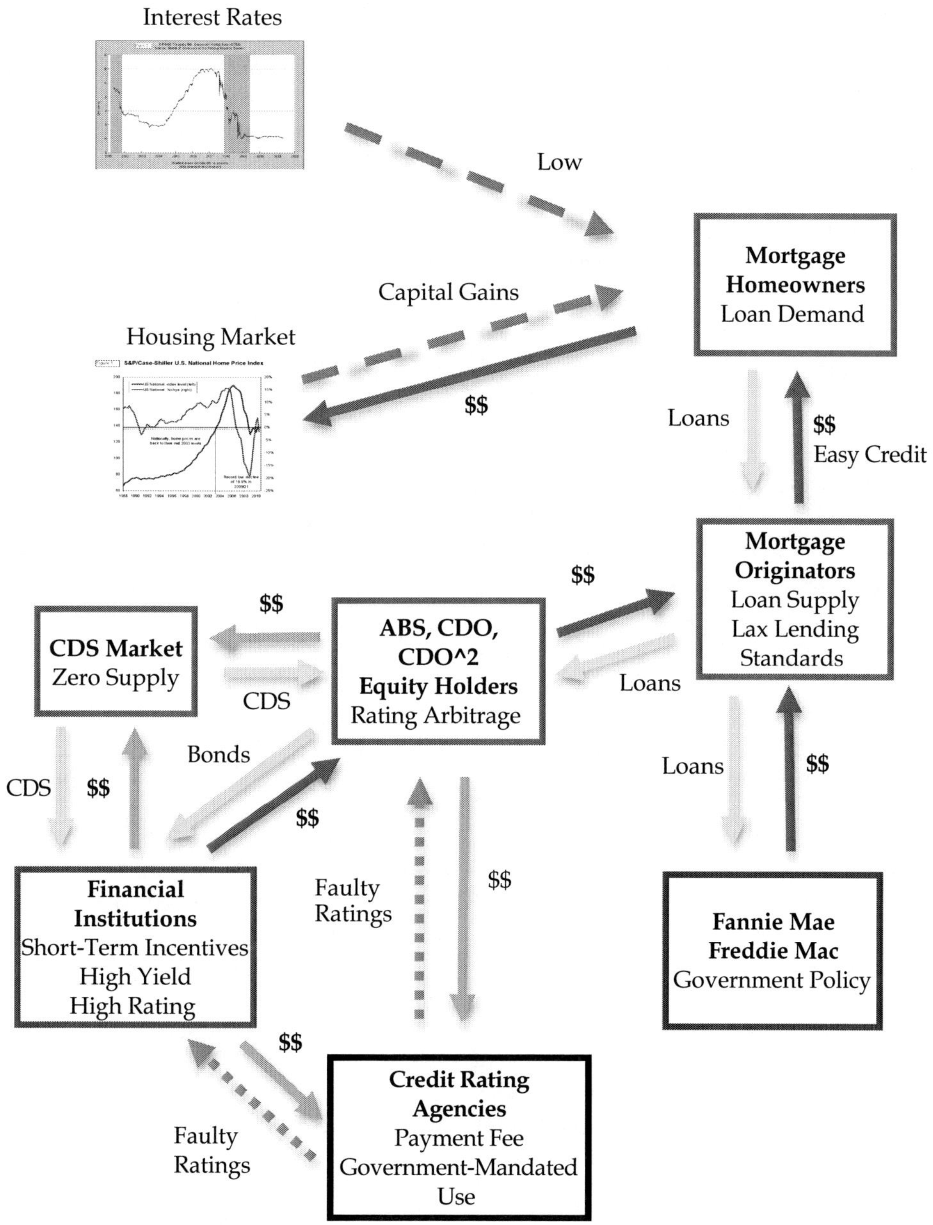

Interest Rates

Low

Capital Gains

Mortgage
Homeowners
Loan Demand

Housing Market

$$

Loans $$
             Easy Credit

$$

Mortgage
Originators
Loan Supply
Lax Lending
Standards

CDS Market
Zero Supply

$$

ABS, CDO,
CDO^2
Equity Holders
Rating Arbitrage

CDS

Loans

Bonds

CDS $$

$$

Loans $$

Financial
Institutions
Short-Term Incentives
High Yield
High Rating

Faulty
Ratings

$$

Fannie Mae
Freddie Mac
Government Policy

$$

Faulty
Ratings

Credit Rating
Agencies
Payment Fee
Government-Mandated
Use

Source: Author's figure.

Like a "perfect storm," these three forces interacted together to create the credit crisis. Incentive problems introduced by the creation of ABSs in mortgage origination as well as government policies regarding the desire to increase homeownership for low-income families led to lax lending standards by the mortgage originators. The lax lending standards of the mortgage originators and low interest rates created the excess demand for residential homeownership, fueling the housing price boom in the mid to late 2000s.

The capital for the growing volume of these subprime mortgage loans came from two sources: government-sponsored agencies and private industry. First, government policies designed to encourage homeownership by low-income families increased the supply of these loan funds from the government-sponsored enterprises (GSEs) Fannie Mae and Freddie Mac. Second, an increased supply of these loan funds was also generated by the sale of credit derivatives (ABSs, CDOs, CDO^2s) held by financial institutions.

An incentive problem created by the payment fee structure of the credit rating agencies and their use of poor models led to the misratings of both corporate and structured debt. Next, the government's mandated use of these ratings and the complexity of ABSs and CDOs led to their widespread use. Investment managers, maximizing their short-term bonuses and not shareholders' wealth, had an incentive not to do their own due diligence. These short-term incentives created an excess demand by financial institutions for investment-grade ABS and CDO bonds (in particular, the AAAs) with high yields. The result was that financial institutions' debt portfolios were exposed to more risk than the ratings of these ABS and CDO bonds implied.

Prior to the credit crisis, ABSs provided unavailable investment opportunities to market participants, facilitating the access to capital for mortgage loans and thereby spurring real economic growth. CDOs and CDO^2s were created to take advantage of market mispricings caused by the misratings of structured debt, called "rating arbitrage." The trading of these market mispricings should have increased the informational efficiency of debt markets, since the impact of the trades should have removed the arbitrage opportunities. But in this case, the institutional structures mentioned earlier enabled the mispricings to persist. As such, these securities facilitated a massive transfer of wealth from the financial institutions that overly relied on the credit ratings to the CDO and CDO^2 equity holders in hedge funds and investment banks.

CDSs enabled market participants more easily to short corporate and structured debt, thereby increasing the informational efficiency of the debt markets. Unfortunately, there was a problem with the usage of CDSs. Selling CDSs is analogous to selling insurance on a debt issue. For the "insurance" to provide protection, the sellers of the CDSs must be properly capitalized. This was not the case prior to the crisis. Owing to the misratings of financial institutions, little or no collateral was required for highly rated financial institutions when they sold CDSs. In addition, the poor modeling of mortgage default risk created the incorrect perception that CDS prices reflected an arbitrage opportunity. This created an excess supply of CDSs, resulting in the overselling of CDSs.

When the supply of available mortgage borrowers diminished, the housing boom started to end. The existing subprime mortgage holders, mostly holding adjustable rate mortgages (ARMs) with teaser rates, started to default on their loans as interest rates increased and oil prices rose. These mortgage defaults generated significant losses to credit derivatives, wiping out the capital of the financial institutions that held them. Financial institutions lost significant value from their investments in ABSs, CDSs, CDOs, and CDO^2s. The loss in aggregate wealth and the correlated failures of financial institutions froze financial markets, with severe negative consequences to the real economy: eventually rising unemployment and a deep recession set in.

This analysis of the credit crisis clarifies the role played by ABSs, CDSs, and CDOs in the financial and real economy. ABSs facilitate the access to capital for loans, thereby increasing economic efficiency and lowering the cost of equity capital, which has a correspondingly positive impact on the real economy. If properly collateralized, CDSs are also beneficial because they enable market participants to more easily short-sell debt, thereby increasing the informational efficiency of credit markets. And similar to mutual funds, CDOs provide investors with desired investments (cash flow streams) at reduced transaction costs.

To fully obtain the benefits of these credit derivatives, however, regulatory reforms are needed: first, to remove the misaligned incentives of the mortgage originators, financial institutions, and rating agencies (which should correct the debt misratings issued by the credit rating agencies), and second, to ensure better capitalization of those engaged in trading credit derivatives, to guarantee execution of the contracts. This can be accomplished through both increased exchange trading of various standardized credit derivatives and increased collateral requirements for customized credit derivatives trading in the over-the-counter (OTC) markets.

The remainder of the chapter explains these arguments in more detail, with particular emphasis on the role of ABSs, CDSs, and CDOs. The next section discusses the causes of the housing price boom, two of which were the short-term incentives of management in financial institutions and the credit rating agencies. These are discussed in greater depth in the next two sections. That discussion is followed by an analysis of the credit derivatives (ABSs, CDSs, CDOs, and CDO^2s) and their role in the crisis and the economy. After discussing the reasons why housing prices crashed, we conclude with a presentation of the regulatory reforms needed to avoid the problems associated with the trading of credit derivatives.

THE RESIDENTIAL HOUSING PRICE BOOM

The residential housing market and related construction industries are a large and important sector in the economy. In terms of a typical household's wealth, a home is one of the largest components. The recent credit crisis originated in the housing price boom and subsequent crash (see figure 8.2). This was alleged to be a bubble, but the proof is still lacking (see Jarrow, Kchia, and Protter 2011).

FIGURE 8.2 / S&P/Case-Shiller U.S. National Home Price Index, 1988 to 2010

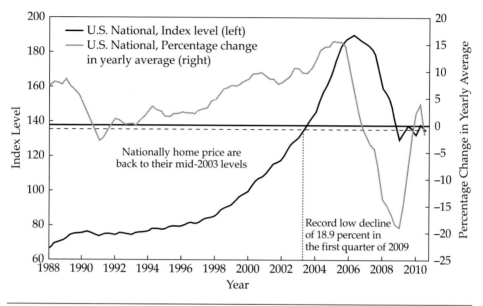

Source: Standard & Poor's (2011), reprinted with permission.

Note: Data through the third quarter of 2010.

To understand the cause of the credit crisis, one needs to start with an analysis of the boom and crash of residential housing prices. The key causes of the recent expansion in the housing price boom (from the early 2000s to the crash) were low interest rates and a shift toward lax mortgage lending standards and easy credit. The lax lending standards occurred in the mortgage loan origination process, or mortgage lending.

Mortgage Lending

The market for mortgage loans is characterized by asymmetric information between the borrowers, who know their financial situation, and the mortgage lenders, who have only incomplete information on the borrowers. Owing to this asymmetric information in issuing loans, the loan origination process involves significant fixed costs related to setting up the infrastructure necessary to evaluate loan applicants, issue loans, service payments, and handle the legal process if default occurs. Consequently, loan origination is performed by financial institutions with the necessary resources and expertise.

The loan originators finance the loans they issue with debt and equity. This is direct lending. To take advantage of the economies of scale in their infrastructure, however, the loan originators often sell these loans to third parties: the government-sponsored enterprises Fannie Mae and Freddie Mac, and the entities that issue credit derivatives (ABSs, CDOs, CDO^2s) (the details of mortgage-related credit derivatives are discussed later in the chapter). This indirect lending is called "securitization."

There is an incentive problem with originating loans if mortgage originators do not hold the loans in their inventory. If the loans default, the costs are not borne by the mortgage originators, but by third parties. When sold to third parties, the mortgage originators are only responsible for fraudulently issued loans. Hence, under the right circumstances, indirect lending has the potential to generate lax lending standards that result in loans being issued in vast quantities to borrowers who should not receive the loans.

That the lending standards became lax in the 2000s has been well documented in the financial press (see, for example, Bajaj 2008; Reckard 2008), the academic literature (see, for example, Demyanyk and Van Hemert 2011; Purnanandam 2011), and government reports (see U.S. Senate 2011). Traditionally, mortgage loans were issued only to good credit borrowers and required large down payments and a documentation of income. In contrast, in the late 1990s and 2000s, loans were given to borrowers who were higher credit risks, called "subprime borrowers," with little or no down payments required and often without an adequate documentation of income. Although there is no standard industry definition of "subprime," a working definition is a borrower who has a FICO (Fair Isaacs Corporation) score of 650 or less, a debt-to-income ratio of 40 percent or more, and a loan-to-value rate of 80 percent or more (see Nomura Fixed Income Research 2004a). Most subprime borrowers used adjustable rate mortgages in which the interest payments varied with short-term rates. Furthermore, to induce homeowners to borrow, mortgage originators commonly offered teaser rates and/or no principal prepayments for a couple of years. When the teaser period ended, as long as home values kept rising, the mortgage could be refinanced at new teaser rates, keeping the mortgage payments low and affordable.

The Excess Supply of Funds for Subprime Mortgages

The right circumstances for the lax lending standards were caused by the availability of an unusually large excess supply of funds for such mortgage loans in the 2000s. This excess supply of funds for subprime mortgage loans was generated by two interacting forces.

First was the introduction of government policies designed to encourage homeownership by low-income families. The American Dream Downpayment Act of 2003 provided financial assistance to lower-income and minority households in order to increase the homeownership rate.[2] This increased the supply of funds available from the government-sponsored enterprises Fannie Mae and Freddie Mac (Pinto 2009). Second, an unusual excess demand for subprime mortgage credit derivatives (ABSs, CDOs, CDO^2s) held by financial institutions and investment funds occurred. This excess demand generated, in turn, an increased supply of funds for subprime mortgages through the credit derivative creation process. (We discuss the process that generates these credit derivatives later in the chapter.)

TABLE 8.1 / U.S. Mortgage-Related Securities Outstanding (in Billions of U.S. Dollars), 2004 to 2010

Year	Agency RMBSs[a]	Non-Agency MBSs[b]	Total[c]	Agency Percentage
2004	$4,397.889	$1,532.6	$5,930.5	74.2%
2005	4,951.171	2,261.6	7,212.7	68.6
2006	5,713.094	2,922.3	8,635.4	66.2
2007	5,947.716	3,195.0	9,142.7	65.1
2008	6,383.726	2,718.2	9,101.9	70.1
2009	6,834.441	2,353.2	9,187.7	74.4
2010	6,839.955	2,071.6	8,911.5	76.8

Source: Author's compilation of data from SIFMA (various years).

[a] Includes Ginnie Mae, Fannie Mae, and Freddie Mac mortgage-backed securities and CMOs.

[b] Include both commercial and residential MBSs.

[c] Total does not account for the overlap of collateral.

Table 8.1 shows the total outstanding mortgage-backed ABSs, both agency and private, in billions of dollars, for the years 2004 to 2010. As shown, agency-related ABSs comprised the dominant percentage of this total, greater than 65 percent in all years. Also, note that the rate of increase in non-agency ABSs from 2004 to 2007 was greater than that of the agency-related ABSs. It is an open question whether the GSEs' or the private institutions' securitization had a larger impact on the housing boom and the lax credit standards (see Belsky and Richardson 2010).

There were two root causes for this excess demand for subprime mortgage-related credit derivatives by financial institutions and investment funds. One was the short-term incentives inherent in the compensation structures for the management of financial institutions and investment funds. The second was the incentive problems inherent in the way credit rating agencies are paid for their services. We discuss each of these causes in turn.

SHORT-TERM BONUS INCENTIVES

Proprietary trading group managers at financial institutions and investment fund managers receive a significant portion of their compensation through a yearly bonus based on their short-term trading performance. The wedge that this compensation scheme drives between the interests of the shareholders and those of the management is the "agency problem," so called because managers in their activities act as agents for the firm's shareholders. The managers in firms investing in investment-grade bonds sought the highest yield to maximize short-term profits.[3] The idea, of course, is that the credit ratings hold risk constant. Prior to the crash, AAA-rated ABS, CDO, and CDO^2 bonds were paying significantly higher yields than equivalent AAA-rated Treasuries. Consequently, AAA-rated ABS, CDO, and CDO^2 bonds were in great demand. In addition, as discussed in the next section, the Securities and Exchange Commission (SEC) and Labor Department "prudent man" rules limited acceptable investments by money market funds and pension funds, respectively, to investment-grade bonds, and banking regulators restricted some financial institutions from holding speculative-grade debt. These regulations artificially increased the excess demand for investment-grade ABSs.

Investment fund management depended on the rating agencies' ratings to judge the quality of the structured debt. They did this, partly, because the CDO and CDO^2 bonds had complex payoff structures that were difficult to understand and to model. Hence, the investment fund managers, motivated by their short-term bonuses, did not do their own due diligence. Nonetheless, they invested in these securities because the yields on AAA-rated ABS and CDO bonds exceeded those on similarly rated Treasuries. Although no one believed that they were of equal risk, the majority of the market did not comprehend that the risks were as different as they really were.[4]

Although proprietary trading groups at large financial institutions had more expertise available to evaluate the securities, they also invested heavily in the ABS and CDO bonds, motivated by their incentive structures; examples include Merrill Lynch and Bear Stearns.

A similar situation arose with the management of money market mutual funds, which invested in highly rated commercial paper issued by structured investment vehicles (SIVs). The SIVs were invested in ABS and CDO bonds, and many of these purchases were financed with short-term commercial paper. The money market funds were invested in higher-yielding SIV commercial paper to earn a spread above similar maturity Treasuries.

These investment strategies generated portfolios of bonds that were much riskier than portfolios of similarly rated maturity Treasuries. When the housing boom crashed and the underlying mortgage pools started defaulting, these bond portfolios lost significant value. If the portfolios had been in the similarly rated maturity Treasuries, no significant losses would have occurred.

THE CREDIT RATING AGENCIES

Credit rating agencies evaluate corporate and structured debt issues, assigning them ratings of their credit quality. Information on a borrower's creditworthiness is costly to obtain with economies of scale in its collection. Once obtained, however, there is little if any cost to disseminating this information. As such, this asymmetric information market structure provides a natural setting for the existence of credit rating agencies.

Government Regulations

In the United States, credit rating agencies are those firms designated by the SEC as "national statistical rating organizations," which include Moody's Investors Service, Standard & Poor's (S&P), and Fitch Investor Services, among others.

Across time, various government regulators have introduced rules that include credit ratings. For example, SEC regulations require the use of ratings in the issuance of certain types of debt. Both the SEC and the Labor Department have "prudent man" rules that limit acceptable investments by money market funds and pension funds to investment-grade bonds. Banking regulators (see the Basel I and II capital requirements) determine capital requirements for debt issues based on their ratings and enforce prohibitions on holding speculative-grade securities. This creates an artificial market segmentation in the financial institutions that can hold investment-grade versus speculative-grade debt. Ratings are also used to determine the eligibility of securities used as collateral for margin lending. These regulations mandating the use of credit ratings accentuate the importance of credit ratings in market activity. (For a more in-depth discussion of the credit rating industry, see Cantor and Packer 1994.)

Incentive Conflicts

Rating agencies are paid by the entities that issue the debt. This payment is not a onetime fee but is better characterized as a stream of future payments for continued credit evaluations. It is quite common, therefore, that borrowers choose among rating agencies based on the ratings they obtain (see Coval, Jurek, and Stafford 2009). This payment fee structure creates a conflict of interest for the rating agency between issuing accurate ratings and retaining business clients (see U.S. Senate 2011; for an economic model of this conflict of interest, see Jarrow and Xu 2010).

Misratings

The credit rating agencies misrated both corporate and structured debt prior to the credit crisis. The evidence of corporate debt misratings is found in the failures or near-failures (saved by government assistance) of the large investment and commercial banks Lehman Brothers, Merrill Lynch, and Citigroup, the insurance company AIG, and the government-sponsored enterprises Fannie Mae and Freddie Mac, among others (see table 8.2). The evidence of structured debt misratings is found in the massive downgrades of AAA-rated CDO debt to junk status in a couple of months during the midst of the credit crisis (Lowenstein 2008; Paley 2008; see also U.S. Senate 2011).

The rating agencies made these misratings both because of the conflict of interest and because they used poor models to estimate default risk (see Jarrow 2011b). In addition to the poor models, the parameters estimated in their structured debt models were based on historical data that did not include the changed and more lax lending standards discussed here. This fact was knowable but conveniently ignored by the rating agencies.

Given the importance of accurate credit ratings in the industry, these misratings resulted in excess demand for subprime mortgage credit derivatives. That excess

TABLE 8.2 / Corporate Failures and Ratings One Month Earlier, March to November 2008

Company	Distress Date	Ratings One Month Earlier		
		Moody's	S&P	Fitch
Bear Stearns	March 16, 2008	A2	A	A+
Fannie Mae	September 7, 2008	Aaa/B–	—	AAA
Freddie Mac	September 7, 2008	Aaa/B–	—	AAA
Lehman	September 15, 2008	A2	A	A+
AIG	September 15, 2008	Aa3	AA–	AA–
Merrill Lynch	September 15, 2008	A2	A	A+
WaMu	September 25, 2008	Baa3/D+	BBB–	BBB–
Wachovia Bank	September 29, 2008	Aa2/B	AA–	AA–
Fortis Finance	September 29, 2008	A1	A	AA–
Dexia	September 30, 2008	Aa2	AA	AA
Citigroup	November 23, 2008	Aa3	AA–	A+

Source: Jarrow (2009), reprinted with permission of *Canadian Investment Review.*

demand, in turn, led to investment funds having riskier portfolios than the ratings of the bonds indicated and financial institutions having insufficient capital to cover the losses eventually realized in their loan portfolios. The latter caused the failure of these financial institutions and the financial crisis.

CREDIT DERIVATIVES

To understand the economics of the credit derivatives used in the residential mortgage market—ABSs, CDSs, CDOs, and CDO^2s—we first consider an ideal debt market that satisfies the following "perfect market" assumptions:

1. Markets are frictionless (no transaction costs) and competitive (perfectly liquid).

2. There are no restrictions on trade, and in particular, shorting is allowed.

3. The market is complete.

4. There are no arbitrage opportunities.[5]

Frictionless markets and no short sale restrictions are self-explanatory. A complete market is one in which any cash flow pattern desired by an investor at a future date can be obtained by trading the available securities, perhaps in a dynamic fashion across time. For example, suppose an investor wants a cash flow of $1 in exactly one year if the three-month Treasury bill rate is between 50 and 100 basis points at that time. In a complete market, the investor can construct a portfolio of traded securities, perhaps changing its composition across time, that would generate such a cash flow. The debt market is therefore complete if any such debt-related cash flow at any future date can be so constructed by a dynamic trading strategy in the underlying debt issues.

An arbitrage opportunity is an investment portfolio that costs zero dollars to construct and never incurs losses, but with positive probability generates a positive cash flow at some future date. Such investment portfolios are "free-lunches" and, assuming no arbitrage opportunities, are consistent with a dynamic market where arbitrageurs quickly remove any such mispricings.

Under these perfect market assumptions, credit derivatives play no additional role in the economy, and there is no reason for them to exist. In such a setting, market completeness enables a trader to create any credit derivative desired by trading in the underlying debt. To understand the role played by each of these credit derivatives in actual markets, therefore, we need to understand the market imperfections that provide the economic rationale for their existence.

As is perhaps obvious, the perfect market assumptions are not satisfied by the debt markets under consideration. First, debt markets are certainly not frictionless. The markets are illiquid with significant transaction costs in terms of bid/ask spreads and a liquidity impact on the price from trading. Second, although not prohibited, this illiquidity makes short-selling a costly exercise. Third, asymmetric information, the variety of credit risks possible, and the lack of traded debt make the credit markets incomplete. Fourth, the misratings of structured debt by the credit rating agencies introduce arbitrage opportunities into the economy.

Interestingly, the imperfections that created the need for the different credit derivatives—the ABSs, CDSs, CDOs, and CDO^2s—differ. As we argue later in the chapter, ABSs exist to make the debt markets more complete. CDSs exist to facilitate the short-selling of corporate, sovereign, and structured debt. And CDOs and CDO^2s were created to exploit the "rating arbitrage" introduced by the credit rating agencies' misratings of structured debt.

As discussed previously, asymmetric information is a key characteristic of debt markets. Asymmetric information makes borrowing more costly for all participants, and also as noted earlier, it provides the economic rationale for the existence of credit rating agencies. The role of asymmetric information enters the discussion of credit derivatives by making equity capital costly. Equity capital is costly because in addition to the standard risk premiums for systematic risk (see Fama and French 2004), the expected return to capital includes a second component, another risk premium that compensates for the losses potentially generated by asymmetric information. Capital is costly to obtain (via debt or the issuance of equity shares), and the use of financial instruments to avoid the use of capital is an additional theme underlying our later discussion of each credit derivative.

Asset-Backed Securities

For the purposes of this chapter, we draw a distinction between ABSs (previously called "structured debt") and CDOs. ABSs hold untraded loans in their collateral pools, while CDOs hold traded ABS bonds. The distinction will become clear once the definitions are provided.

FIGURE 8.3 / Cash Flow and Waterfalls for an Asset-Backed Security

Assets	Liabilities	Waterfall	
	Senior bond tranches		
	Mezzanine bond tranches		
Collateral pool	Junior bond tranches	Cash flows ↓	Losses ↑
	Equity		

Source: Author's figure.

An ABS is best understood as a liability issued by a firm or corporation, although the legal structure of the entity issuing an ABS, usually a special purpose vehicle (SPV), is quite different from that of a typical corporation (see Fabozzi 2000). A firm's balance sheet consists of assets and liabilities. Liabilities are divided into debt and equity. Debts are loans, with interest paid for the use of the funds. Equity represents the ownership of the firm's residual cash flows after all debt obligations are paid.

The assets purchased by an SPV—called the "collateral pool"—are the collateral underlying the SPV's liabilities. The collateral pool usually consists of a collection of loans of a particular type—for example, auto loans, student loans, credit card loans, commercial real estate loans, or residential mortgages. When we discuss the credit crisis later, the ABSs of greatest interest will be those with residential mortgage loan collateral pools. The liabilities issued by these SPVs are often called RMBS (residential mortgage-backed securities). To simplify our terminology, however, we will still refer to these RMBSs as ABSs.

To help finance the purchase of the collateral pool, the SPV issues debt. The debt is issued in various tranches or "slices," from the senior bond tranches to the mezzanine to the junior bond tranches. These bond tranches have different claims to both the cash flows from the collateral pool and any losses realized on the collateral pool. The cash flows, consisting of interest and principal payments, are paid to the most senior bonds first, then to the mezzanine bonds, and then to the junior bonds, with the residual going to the equity (see figure 8.3). The cash flow and loss allocation across the various bond tranches is called the "waterfall." The losses are realized in the reverse order, starting with the equity first, moving to the junior, the mezzanine, then the senior bond tranches. As such, the senior bond tranches are the safest with respect to default risk, while the equity is the riskiest security in this regard.

Before issuing the various bond tranches in the market, because of the government regulations mentioned earlier, the ABS bond tranches need to be rated by at least one of the credit rating agencies, but more often by two. Because of the waterfall, the senior bond tranches are rated more highly than the mezzanine bond tranches, which in turn are rated more highly than the junior bond tranches, which may not even be rated. The SPV liability structure is constructed so that a large percentage of the liabilities that are senior bonds will be rated AAA. The percentage of bonds rated AAA is usually quite high (80 percent or more for CDOs; see Nomura 2004b). This is a key reason why certain ABSs, in particular CDOs and CDO^2s, are created.

To understand the economic role played by ABS in financial markets, we need briefly to return to the loan origination process. To take advantage of the economies of scale in the loan origination process, loan originators often sell the originated loans to third parties, the SPVs. The SPVs pay for these loans by issuing ABSs. For the loans sold to the SPVs, the originators service the loans with payments received for this servicing.

Also, as noted earlier, SPVs are legal entities created by their equity holders to purchase the assets in the collateral pool. Setting up a SPV is a costly exercise, with significant fixed costs paid to third parties (lawyers, rating agencies, and investment bankers). The assets—the loans—are purchased from the loan originators. Unless the loans are purchased below their "true" value and/or the SPVs sell their liabilities above their "true" value, setting up an SPV is a negative net present value activity and would not be done. The existence of SPVs, therefore, proves that there is value in the creation and selling of ABSs.

In terms of the perfect market assumptions discussed earlier, the value creation is obtained by the ABSs completing the market. The ABSs enable financial institutions and investment funds (hence, individuals in the economy) to invest indirectly in an alternative asset class—the loans. The financial institutions and investment funds could not invest in these loans directly owing to the fixed costs involved in the loan origination process.

In the real economy, ABSs decrease the cost of borrowing by making more capital available for issuing loans, thereby facilitating real economic activity related to the purpose of the loans. For example, the purpose of the loans could be homeownership, which increases activity in the construction industry. When the purpose of a loan is purchasing a car, activity in the auto industry is increased. The same applies for student loans, credit card loans, commercial real estate, and so on. The growth of the ABS market affected housing prices by facilitating the growth of the construction industry and the residential housing market, increasing the demand for housing and therefore housing prices.

The ABS creation process contributed to the housing price boom and the financial crisis by helping to provide the funds that fueled the unprecedented issuance of subprime mortgage loans. The incentive problems in the mortgage origination process we discussed earlier led to the lax lending standards and easy credit that generated the demand for the mortgage loans by homeowners. The demand for the ABS bonds was generated indirectly by the excess demand for CDO and CDO^2 AAA bonds by financial institutions and investment funds. The CDO and CDO^2 creation process required the ABS bonds. Before discussing CDOs and CDO^2s, however, we first need to understand CDSs.

Credit Default Swaps

Simply stated, credit default swaps are insurance contracts written between two counterparties insuring the face value of a particular corporate, sovereign, or structured debt issue for a fixed period of time. For selling the CDS, the insurer receives

FIGURE 8.4 / Payments to Corporate or Sovereign Credit Default Swaps

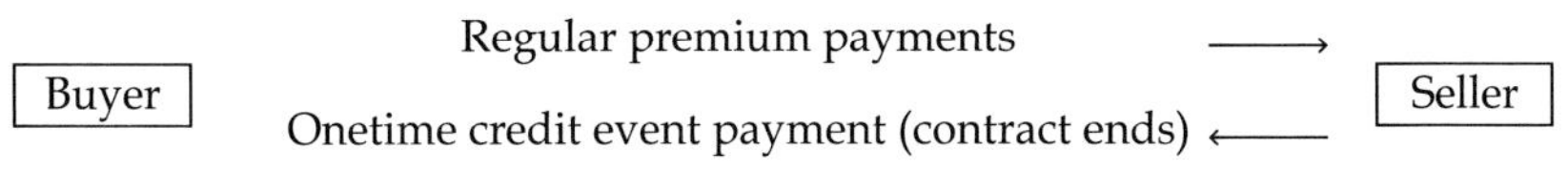

| | Regular premium payments | $\longrightarrow$ | |
| Buyer | Onetime credit event payment (contract ends) $\longleftarrow$ | | Seller |

Source: Author's figure.

premiums, paid regularly (usually quarterly) over the life of the CDS contract. Typical terms are one to five years. The premium payment is based on the notional value of the contract. The notional value of the contract is the aggregate dollar value of the insured bond. When a CDS is bought or sold at the market clearing spread, the value of the contract is zero.

For corporate or sovereign debt, if a default or credit event occurs, the contract terminates, and the seller of the CDS either pays the face value of the debt and receives the debt issue (if physical settlement) or pays the difference between the face value and market price of the debt (if cash settlement).[6] See figure 8.4 for the cash flows. Physical or cash settlement is specified in the contract terms. A credit event includes events such as a failure to pay or a change in the interest or principal, bankruptcy, and certain types of financial restructuring (see Berndt, Jarrow, and Kang 2007).

For structured debt, called "pay as you go" PAUG CDSs, or ABS CDSs, the events triggering a payment by the seller are different. For an ABS CDS, there are two types of events: credit and floating payment. For a credit or default event (similar to the standard CDS discussed earlier), the contract is terminated and the seller either pays the remaining principal value of the debt and receives the debt issue (if physical settlement) or pays the difference between the remaining principal value and market price of the debt (if cash settlement). A floating payment event occurs if the ABS bond incurs a principal write-down or a principal or interest shortfall. For a floating payment, the contract stays in force and is not terminated. These floating payment events are designed to mimic the cash flow risks embedded in an ABS due to its waterfall structure (see figure 8.5). It is possible, if a principal or

FIGURE 8.5 / Payments to ABS Credit Default Swaps

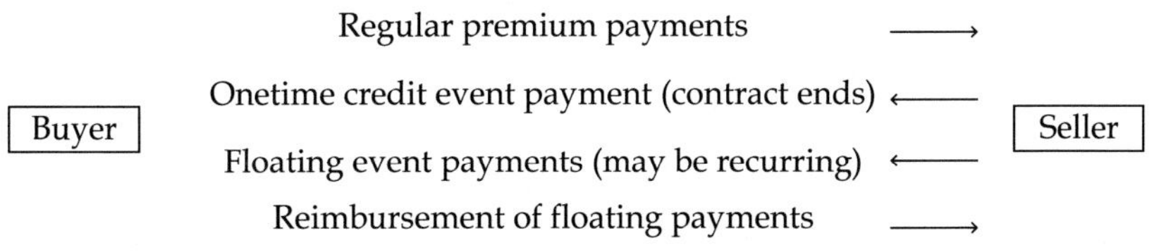

	Regular premium payments	$\longrightarrow$	
	Onetime credit event payment (contract ends) $\longleftarrow$		
Buyer	Floating event payments (may be recurring) $\longleftarrow$		Seller
	Reimbursement of floating payments	$\longrightarrow$	

Source: Author's figure.

interest shortfall is later returned to the underlying ABS, that the buyer needs to reimburse the seller for a previously paid floating payment (see Deutsche Bank 2005; Nomura 2005).

CDSs play an important economic role in financial markets. To understand their role, consider the liquidity of traded debt in the secondary debt markets. Debt markets are illiquid in general because debt holders (financial institutions and investment funds) tend to buy and hold debt in their inventories, trading it infrequently. This illiquidity makes it difficult to short-sell debt, because short-selling requires that the short-seller borrow the debt from a third party and sell it on the market. Borrowing debt for this purpose is difficult. Although repurchase agreements can be used to borrow debt, this alternative is costly, given the need to post collateral and roll over the repurchase agreements in order to keep the short position open.

In contrast, the buyer of a CDS is effectively shorting the credit (and floating payment) risks in the underlying debt instrument. If the buyer also adds a short position in the appropriate maturity Treasury security, the buyer's aggregate cash flows exactly match those from shorting the debt (see Jarrow 2011a). Hence, CDSs overcome a market imperfection by enabling market participants to more easily short corporate, sovereign, or ABS bonds. This market completion role of CDSs makes debt markets more informationally efficient with respect to default risk (see Jarrow and Larsson 2012). More efficient markets allocate capital to the appropriate uses, thereby facilitating economic growth.

A naked CDS trade occurs when the CDS buyer does not own the underlying debt issue. Concern has often been expressed in the financial press that the trading of naked CDSs is harmful to the economy because it distorts borrowing rates and increases the risk present in debt markets (see Jones 2011). In fact, quite the contrary is true. There are only two reasons why a naked CDS trades: the CDS buyer is trying to hedge a related security's risk, such as a long position in the equity of the firm issuing the debt, or the CDS buyer is trading on information—that is, speculating. Such speculation increases the informational efficiency of debt markets. But this is exactly the same market completion argument made in the preceding paragraph with respect to shorting debt.

There is a potential problem, however, with the trading of CDSs, one related to the risk of contract execution by the CDS seller. If insurance is written, but the seller does not have sufficient resources to guarantee execution of the contract (payment of the claims), then the risk of debt markets is increased, not decreased, by the trading of CDSs. Indeed, in this case payments are made for insurance that is worthless. To eliminate this problem, stronger collateral and capital requirements are needed for CDS traders. We return to this issue later when we discuss the financial crisis. Here it is important to recognize that this contract execution problem is orthogonal to the market completion role of CDSs and therefore does not invalidate any of our previous conclusions in this regard.

CDSs also serve a secondary role in financial markets. As noted previously, asymmetric information in loan markets makes capital costly to obtain. A highly rated financial institution currently can sell a CDS at zero value without posting any collateral. Hence, a financial institution can assume the credit risk in a bond without posting any additional equity capital to guarantee execution. In contrast, if the financial institution buys the bond instead, it needs to put up the present value of the principal. High leverage is an attractive feature of CDSs and one that played an important role in the construction of subprime CDOs.

CDSs also played a significant role in the housing price boom and the financial crisis. CDSs enabled financial institutions, especially insurance companies (for example, AIG), monoline insurers, and derivative product companies (DPs) to sell CDSs (in order to sell insurance) without posting sufficient collateral or equity capital. This inadequate posting of collateral and insufficient equity capital was partly caused by the misrating of the credit risk of these financial institutions. Highly rated financial institutions need not post collateral to trade in CDSs because the CDS market is part of the larger over-the-counter derivatives markets, which have been largely unregulated since their inception. In 1998 there was a push by the Commodity Futures Trading Commission's (CFTC) chairperson, Brooksley Born, to revise existing legislation to expand CFTC regulatory authority to include OTC swaps. Congress studied this proposal, but unified opposition to more regulation by Federal Reserve Board chairman Alan Greenspan and Treasury secretary Robert Rubin killed the proposal.[7]

The last cause of the inadequate posting of collateral and insufficient equity capital was the poor use of models by these financial institutions in measuring the risk of their CDS portfolios. The existing models caused these financial institutions to significantly underestimate the default risk of their portfolios (see Jarrow 2011b). In conjunction, the mis-estimation of risk in the CDSs combined with the lenient collateral requirements led to the incorrect perception that the pricing of CDSs reflected an arbitrage opportunity. This resulted in an excess supply of CDSs. Hence, when housing prices crashed and mortgages defaulted, there were unusually large positions in CDSs in numerous financial institutions and insufficient equity capital in these financial institutions to buffer the losses. Financial failures occurred. Since the reasons underlying the failures were the same, default contagion occurred, which resulted in the financial crisis.

Collateralized Debt Obligations

There are two types of CDOs: cash flow and synthetic. To be relevant to the credit crisis, the discussion in this section focuses on subprime residential mortgage ABSs. A subprime mortgage is one in which the underlying borrower is classified as subprime. As mentioned before, subprime borrowers are the riskiest in terms of default risk.

CASH FLOW CDOs AND CDO^2s A cash flow CDO is a type of ABS. The key difference between an ABS SPV and a CDO SPV is in the composition of the collateral pool. A subprime ABS has a majority of subprime residential mortgage loans in its collateral pool. In contrast, a subprime CDO has a majority of mezzanine ABS bonds, rated below AAA, in its collateral pool. The collateral pool of ABSs is

TABLE 8.3 / Global CDO Issuance (in Millions of U.S. Dollars), 2004 to 2010

Year	Cash Flow	Synthetic
2004	$0	$0
2005	206,224.0	44,421.2
2006	410,503.6	44,421.2
2007	340,375.8	88,842.4
2008	43,595.8	1,340.9
2009	2,560.9	254.3
2010	7,639.9	42.3

Source: Author's compilation of data from SIFMA (various years).

nontraded loans, while the collateral pool of CDOs is traded debt. Another minor difference is that CDO waterfalls can be more complex and have various triggers that redirect cash flows to more senior tranches if certain collaterization or interest coverage ratios are violated (see Lehman Brothers Fixed Income Research 1998).

Given the complexity of the collateral pool and waterfall rules, CDOs are complex securities. An additional difficulty in understanding CDOs is that each deal is slightly different in terms of its waterfalls, making modeling a tedious, deal-by-deal exercise. This complexity was a key reason why many financial institutions with limited research staffs depended solely on the credit agencies' ratings. In addition, this complexity combined with short-term compensation incentives to provide many financial institution managers with an excuse not to do their own due diligence.

CDO^2s are CDOs in which the collateral pool consists mainly of mezzanine tranche bonds, junior tranche bonds, or even the equity tranche bonds from subprime CDOs. Thus, a CDO^2 is a CDO whose collateral pool consists of other CDO bonds.

The economic role played by cash flow CDOs and CDO^2s is different than it was for either ABSs or CDSs. The market imperfection that enabled CDOs and CDO^2s to exist was a violation of the no-arbitrage assumption. Analogous to creating an ABS, it is quite costly to create a CDO, those costs including lawyer, rating, and investment banking fees. And the collateral pool's assets trade in the OTC market, unlike the collateral pool of ABSs (residential home mortgages). Therefore, CDOs do not help to complete the market, since the underlying collateral already trades. The CDO equity would have a negative value, and the CDOs would not be created, unless the ABS bonds in the collateral pool were undervalued and/or the CDO bonds issued were overvalued. CDOs were created in massive quantities before the crisis (see table 8.3), so one or both of these two possibilities were true.

Although government regulations have segmented the market for investment-grade versus speculative-grade bonds, there are still plenty of financial institutions that take advantage of this market segmentation and hold speculative-grade debt, for example, hedge funds and mutual funds. Consequently, it is unlikely that the mezzanine subprime ABS bonds were undervalued enough to justify the creation of CDOs. In contrast, as discussed earlier, there is significant evidence that the highly rated CDO bonds were misrated. Hence, it is reasonable to conclude that the CDO bonds issued were overvalued. This implies that CDOs were created in order to exploit the "rating arbitrage" that resulted from the rating agencies' misratings of the highly rated CDO bonds. That is, CDOs existed to transform "junk bonds" into "gold" (AAA-rated bonds with high yields).

Normally, we would believe that such arbitrage opportunities are short-lived, since the exploitation of an arbitrage usually hastens its removal as one side of the market loses wealth. But this need not be the case if the arbitrage's existence is due to institutional structures. Here the contributing institutional features for the "rating arbitrage" were the payment fee structures of the rating agencies and the short-term incentives of the managers within financial institutions. Before the crisis, financial institutions and investments funds were making unusual profits, even though they were overpaying for the highly rated bonds in their portfolios.

The economic role played by CDO^2s is similar. When the CDOs were created, there was not sufficient demand for the lower-rated bond tranches. Consequently, the equity holders of the CDOs had a difficult time placing these bonds. The solution, of course, was to create another type of CDO that included these bonds in their collateral pool—again turning "junk bonds" into "gold."

In fact, the demand for these AAA-rated CDO bonds was so great that there were too few ABS bonds available to fill the growing collateral pools. To help with this scarcity, ABS CDSs were used instead. Recall that an ABS CDS seller is taking a long position in the underlying ABS bond. In essence, an ABS CDS seller is creating a synthetic ABS bond that is absent the bond's principal. This use of ABS CDSs in the construction of the CDO collateral pool had the additional benefit that it required no equity capital. Consequently, it enabled the issuance of a super-senior bond tranche in CDOs that also required no up-front cash payment, in contrast to a typical bond purchase. Many super-senior bonds therefore had nearly "infinite leverage." The use of ABS CDSs in CDOs increased the correlated default risk across the ABS bonds and CDO bonds traded. The correlated defaults were generated by the same collection of mortgages in the collateral pools of the traded CDOs and many times leveraged.

Hence, the market imperfection that the cash flow CDOs and CDO^2s exploited was an institutional imperfection—"rating arbitrage." The CDO and CDO^2 equity holders were taking wealth away from financial institutions. Although the creation of CDOs increased the demand for speculative-grade ABSs, thereby indirectly increasing the capital available for mortgage loans, this increased demand was a result of a market misfunction—the misratings. Consequently, this indirect benefit of CDOs to the mortgage loan market disappears when the misratings disappear.

There is another argument that may justify the existence of cash flow CDOs. Given that it is costly for investors to create the CDO bond cash flows themselves, analogous to the reasons for the existence of electronic traded funds (ETFs) or mutual funds, CDOs may exist to provide these cash flows to investors in a way that minimizes transaction costs. Given the large fixed costs involved in creating the CDOs' SPV, it is an open question as to whether cash flow CDOs will provide enough value creation from minimizing transaction costs to justify their existence when rating arbitrage no longer exists.

Cash flow CDOs and CDO^2s played a key role in the housing price boom and the financial crisis. These securities were held by investment funds at financial institutions, pension funds, and retirement funds operated by corporations and government agencies. First, these funds overpaid for the bonds purchased, although they were making healthy profits prior to the crisis. Second, when housing prices crashed and mortgages defaulted, these CDO and CDO^2 bonds lost significant value. This value loss created severe hardships and/or failures of corporate pension funds (for example, General Motors), state government pension funds (as in California and New York), sovereign nations (Iceland), investment banks (Bear Stearns, Merrill Lynch), SIVs (Citigroup), and, indirectly, some money market funds (Reserve Primary Fund) (Condon 2008). The losses on these AAA-rated CDO bonds were unprecedented by comparison to historical losses of similarly AAA-rated debt issues. The reason for these unprecedented losses, of course, was the misrating of the structured debt from the beginning, for reasons we have previously discussed.

SYNTHETIC CDOS   A synthetic CDO is an ABS for which the underlying collateral pool consists entirely of ABS CDSs. No physical bonds are purchased for inclusion. The waterfall is therefore quite simple. It is arranged into a series of bond tranches, some of which are unfunded (require no initial purchase fee). The tranches have attachment and detachment points, which indicate the percentage of losses absorbed by the bond tranches' notional value. The notional value is the aggregate dollar amount that each bond tranche represents. The equity tranche is the lowest, taking losses from 0 percent to perhaps 5 percent. Then the next lowest tranche takes losses from 5 percent to perhaps 10 percent, and so forth. Since synthetic CDOs are based on a collateral pool of swap contracts, the cost of construction is smaller than that of a cash flow CDO.

Synthetic CDOs played three beneficial economic roles during the crisis, which will continue after the crisis is over. Cash flow CDOs trade in illiquid markets, as do all fixed income securities. Given the difficulty in modeling cash flow CDOs, when trading became sparse and marking-to-market unreliable, marking-to-model proved useless. In this circumstance, the first role of synthetic CDOs is to provide a more liquidly traded instrument that is easier to model and price based on the underlying CDSs. During the crisis, it provided more accurate market quotes for indexing the cash flow CDO prices. The second role of synthetic CDOs is to provide a more liquidly traded partial hedge for cash flow CDOs, reducing the transaction costs incurred in generating a particular exposure to a portfolio of mortgage-related ABSs. Because all of the ABS securities trade in the over-the-counter market, this same exposure could have been generated directly by trading in the underlying contracts, but greater transaction costs would have been incurred, owing to the market's illiquidity. The third role of synthetic CDOs is to provide a low-cost method of shorting the CDO bond tranches, thus avoiding the need to use repurchase agreements; synthetic CDOs are analogous in this regard to CDSs.

FIGURE 8.6 / Three-Month Treasury Bill: Secondary Market Rate (DTB3)

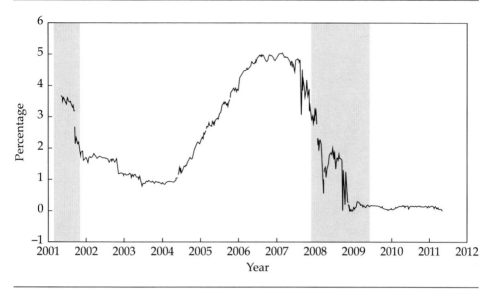

Source: Federal Reserve System Board of Governors (2011a).

Note: Shaded areas indicate U.S. recessions.

THE HOUSING PRICE CRASH

The housing price boom was too good to last. Housing prices crashed for three related reasons. First, the demand creating an upward trend in housing prices was eliminated when the supply of subprime home borrowers became exhausted. Second, interest rates started to rise owing to inflation worries brought on by increases in the federal budget deficit from the Iraq and Afghanistan Wars. And third, rising oil prices caused an increase in gas prices. These two price increases combined to put a damper on the ability of many subprime borrowers to meet their mortgage payments (see figures 8.6 and 8.7). Most subprime mortgage holders had adjustable rate mortgages whose interest payments varied with short-term rates. Furthermore, financial institutions induced homeowners to borrow by offering teaser rates and/or no principal prepayments for a couple of years. When teaser periods ended, as long as home values kept rising, mortgages could be refinanced at new teaser rates, keeping the mortgage payments low and affordable. When housing prices started to decline, such refinancing became impossible (see U.S. Senate 2011; see also Kirchhoff 2007). In conjunction, these economic forces caused an increased incidence of subprime mortgage defaults. Housing prices began to fall when mortgage defaults led to foreclosures. This, in turn, led to additional defaults for prime borrowers as well (see Ascheberg et al. 2010).

FIGURE 8.7 / Producer Price Index: Finished Energy Goods (PPIFEG)

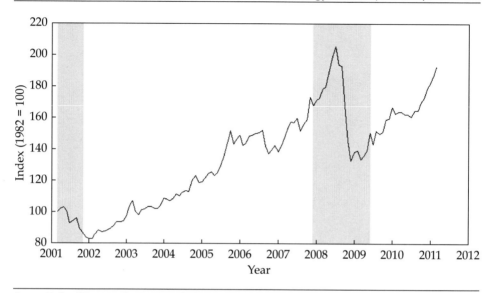

Source: Federal Reserve System Board of Governors (2011b).

Note: Shaded areas indicate U.S. recessions.

As mortgage defaults happened, the subprime residential mortgage ABS and CDO bond tranches lost value. The credit derivative losses eroded the capital of the financial institutions and investment funds that invested in these ABSs, CDSs, CDOs, and CDO^2s. This loss in aggregate wealth and the correlated failures of financial institutions froze financial markets, and the severe negative consequences to the real economy would culminate in the Great Recession.[8]

REGULATORY REFORMS

First, credit derivatives serve useful economic functions in financial markets. ABSs provide previously unavailable investment opportunities to market participants, facilitating the access to debt capital and spurring real economic growth through the increased financing for the underlying collateral pool. CDSs enable market participants to more easily short-sell debt, thereby increasing the informational efficiency of debt markets. CDOs and CDO^2s were created to take advantage of the debt market mispricings generated by the credit agencies' misratings of structured debt. It is an open question whether CDOs will continue to trade after the removal of the debt misratings, given the costs of constructing the CDOs' SPVs. Synthetic CDOs provide a transaction cost–minimizing method for investing in diversified pools of ABSs, and therefore they help to facilitate the efficient allocation of debt capital.

To correct the structural problems that created the misuse of credit derivatives (ABSs, CDSs, CDOs, CDO^2s), regulatory reforms need to be implemented. First and most important, it was the credit agencies' misratings that created the environment that facilitated the misuse of credit derivatives. Indeed, if the credit agencies' ratings had been correct, then even given the various misincentives, the market forces generating the misuses would have disappeared:

- Financial institutions and investment funds would not have invested in credit derivatives because the securities would have been considered too risky.

- The demand for indirect lending to subprime mortgages would have disappeared, except for the government-sponsored enterprise lending by Fannie Mae and Freddie Mac. This would have partially prevented the mortgage originators' lax lending standards from taking hold.

- The equity capital held in financial institutions would have been more appropriate since the regulators themselves would have had proper information regarding the likelihood and cost of financial institution failure.

The first reform needed to fix the credit agency misratings would be to change the payment structure of the credit rating agencies. The current payment structure of credit rating agencies being paid by those that are rated creates a severe incentive problem. Instead, we should return to the original payment fee structure of the rating agencies being paid by the users of the ratings (for a history of the credit rating agencies, see Sylla 2001). Since information once purchased is easily passed on at zero cost, for this proposal to be successful, the content of the credit rating agencies' information would need to be modified. The credit agencies would need to provide information that is dynamic and constantly updated, so that information becomes "stale" shortly after it is purchased. Although dramatic, this proposal is feasible because there are already such providers of debt market–related information in the financial markets.

Second, as correctly mandated by the Dodd-Frank Wall Street Reform and Consumer Protection Act of 2010, credit ratings should be removed from all government regulations, thereby removing the need for the designation of a "national statistical rating organization" as well as the market segmentation in the use of investment-grade versus speculative-grade bonds. The removal of this "barrier to entry," in turn, would open up the credit risk information markets to more competition. Credit risk information providers would then compete based on the accuracy of their information, and risk assessment would become more unbiased.

Next, to reduce the misuse of credit derivatives, the mis-incentive structures of the market participants need to be reformed. The compensation schemes of financial management need to be changed to be consistent with maximizing long-run performance and not short-term bonuses. This can be done by vesting or delaying payment of yearly bonuses over a multiple-year period or by implementing clawback provisions. And mortgage originators should be required to hold some percentage of their originated loans in inventory. A mechanism that prevents the "cherry-picking" of the best loans by mortgage originators also needs to be included.

Financial institutions' use of credit derivatives led to their failure because they had too little equity capital and collateral backing the buying and selling of these derivatives. Enough collateral and equity capital needs to be held by these institutions to guarantee execution of all contracts with a high degree of confidence. Various proposals have been made in this regard (see Jarrow 2011a). Good regulations are contained in the Dodd-Frank Act relating to the central clearing and exchange trading of these credit derivatives. Although not all credit derivatives can be traded on an exchange, owing to customization, it is important to exchange-trade as many of these credit derivatives as possible. Greater transparency in the trading of credit derivatives is also needed, which exchange trading would facilitate. Credit derivatives play a welfare-increasing role in the financial and real economy as long as they are properly capitalized. Regulatory reforms should ensure their proper capitalization, not their removal from trading.

Helpful comments from Alan Blinder, Andy Lo, Philip Protter, Robert Solow, and Sy Smidt are gratefully acknowledged.

NOTES

1. Structured debt is defined as debt issued as an ABS or CDO or CDO^2.

2. See U.S. Department of Housing and Urban Development, "American Dream Downpayment Initiative," available at: www.hud.gov/offices/cpd/affordablehousing/programs/home/addi/(accessed January 2011).

3. For Standard & Poor's (S&P) ratings, investment-grade bonds correspond to the ratings AAA, AA, A, and BBB. Speculative-grade or "junk bonds" are those rated BB, B, CCC, CC, and C. Default is rated D. Moody's ratings are investment-grade (Aaa, Aa, A, Baa) and junk bond (Ba, B, Caa, Ca, C). Fitch's ratings are investment-grade (AAA, AA, A, BBB), junk bond (BB, B, CCC, CC, C), restricted default (RD), and default (D). When we discuss ratings in the text, we use S&P ratings.

4. Of course, there were some market participants and hedge funds that did recognize these risk differences; see, for example, Crawshaw (2010).

5. There is a technical assumption that with the asymmetric information inherent in credit markets, all market participants must agree that the probability that a borrower will repay is either strictly positive or zero. If nonzero, participants do not need to agree on the magnitude of the probability. This reasonable assumption is imposed without further clarification.

6. If cash-settled, the procedure for determining the market price—usually an auction at a particular date after the credit event occurs—is also written into the contract.

7. For a more complete historical account of this event, see Goodman (2008).

8. As argued in Jarrow (2011b), the "best-practice" credit derivative models used by the industry did not accurately capture this increased correlation in defaults during times of financial stress (called "systemic risk").

REFERENCES

Ascheberg, Marius, Robert Jarrow, Holger Kraft, and Yildiray Yildirim. 2010. "Government Policies, Residential Mortgage Defaults, and the Boom and Bust Cycle of Housing Prices." Working paper. Ithaca, N.Y.: Cornell University.

Bajaj, Vikas. 2008. "Lax Lending Standards Led to IndyMac's Downfall." *New York Times,* July 29.

Belsky, Eric, and Nela Richardson. 2010. "Understanding the Boom and Bust in Nonprime Mortgage Lending." Working paper. Cambridge, Mass.: Harvard University.

Berndt, Antje, Robert Jarrow, and ChoongOh Kang. 2007. "Restructuring Risk in Credit Default Swaps: An Empirical Analysis." *Stochastic Processes and Their Applications* 117: 1724–49.

Cantor, Richard, and Frank Packer. 1994. "The Credit Rating Industry." *Federal Reserve Bank of New York Quarterly Review* (Summer–Fall): 1–26.

Condon, Christopher. 2008. "Reserve Primary Money Fund Falls Below $1 a Share." *Bloomberg News,* September 16.

Coval, Joshua, Jakub Jurek, and Erik Stafford. 2009. "Reexamining the Role of Rating Agencies: Lessons from Structured Finance." *Journal of Economic Perspectives* 23(1): 3–25.

Crawshaw, Julie. 2010. "Paulson's Hedge Fund Made Billions on Subprime Crisis." Moneynews.com, April 19. Available at: http://www.moneynews.com/StreetTalk/john-paulson-subprime-fund/2010/04/19/id/356122?s=al&promo_code=9CB5-1 (accessed July 10, 2012).

Demyanyk, Yuliya, and Otto Van Hemert. 2011. "Understanding the Subprime Mortgage Crisis." *Review of Financial Studies* 24(6): 1848–80.

Deutsche Bank. 2005. "Pay as You Go CDS and New Frontiers in ABS CDOs." June 9.

Fabozzi, Frank J. 2000. *Bond Markets, Analysis, and Strategies,* 4th ed. Englewood Cliffs, N.J.: Prentice-Hall.

Fama, Eugene F., and Kenneth R. French. 2004. "The Capital Asset Pricing Model: Theory and Evidence." *Journal of Economic Perspectives* 18(3): 25–46.

Federal Reserve System Board of Governors. 2011a. "3-Month Treasury Bill: Secondary Market Rate (DTB3)." Available at: http://research.stlouisfed.org/fred2/series/DTB3?cid=116 (accessed July 10, 2012).

———. 2011b. "Producer Price Index: Finished Energy Goods (PPIFEG)." Available at: http://research.stlouisfed.org/fred2/series/PPIFEG?cid=31 (accessed July 10, 2012).

Goodman, Peter. 2008. "The Reckoning: Taking a Hard New Look at a Greenspan Legacy." *New York Times,* October 9.

Jarrow, Robert. 2009. "An Expensive Education." *Canadian Investment Review* (Winter): 9–15.

———. 2011a. "The Economics of Credit Default Swaps." *Annual Review of Financial Economics* 3: 2.1–2.23.

———. 2011b. "Risk Management Models: Construction, Testing, Usage." *Journal of Derivatives* 18(4, Summer): 89–98.

Jarrow, Robert A., Younes Kchia, and Philip Protter. 2011. "How to Detect an Asset Bubble." *Society for Industrial and Applied Mathematics (SIAM) Journal on Financial Mathematics* 2: 839–65.

Jarrow, Robert, and Martin Larsson. 2012. "The Meaning of Market Efficiency." *Mathematical Finance* 22(1): 1–30.

Jarrow, Robert, and Liheng Xu. 2010. "Credit Rating Accuracy and Incentives." *Journal of Credit Risk* 6(3, Fall): 1–19.

Jones, Huw. 2011. "EU Markets Chief Questions Ban on Naked CDS Trade." Reuters, March 8.

Kirchhoff, Sue. 2007. "Mortgage Crisis: Home Loans Are Harder to Get." *USA Today,* August 6.

Lehman Brothers Fixed Income Research. 1998. "Collateralized Debt Obligations: Market, Structure, and Value." June.

Lowenstein, Roger. 2008. "Triple-A Failure." *New York Times,* April 27.

Nomura Fixed Income Research. 2004a. "Home Equity ABS Basics." November 1.

———. 2004b. "CDOs in Plain English." September 13.

———. 2005. "Synthetic ABS 101: PAUG and ABX.HE." March 7.

Paley, Amit. 2008. "Credit Rating Firms Grilled over Conflicts." *Washington Post,* October 23.

Pinto, Edward. 2009. "Acorn and the Housing Bubble." *Wall Street Journal,* November 12.

Purnanandam, Amiyatosh. 2011. "Originate-to-Distribute Model and the Subprime Mortgage Crisis." *Review of Financial Studies* 24(6): 1881–1915.

Reckard, E. Scott. 2008. "Countrywide Deal Will Pay Off, BofA's Top Exec Says." *Los Angeles Times,* July 10.

SIFMA. Various years. "Statistics database." Available at: http://www.sifma.org/research/statistics.aspx (accessed July 10, 2012).

Standard & Poor's. 2011. "S&P/Case-Shiller Home Price Indices." *S&P Indices: A Year in Review,* a white paper, January 2011.

Sylla, Richard. 2001. "A Historical Primer on the Business of Credit Ratings." Working paper. New York: New York University, Department of Economics.

U.S. Senate. Committee on Homeland Security and Governmental Affairs. Permanent Subcommittee on Investigations. 2011. "Wall Street and the Financial Crisis: Anatomy of a Financial Collapse." Majority and minority staff report. April 13.

Chapter 9

Finance Versus Wal-Mart: Why Are Financial Services So Expensive?

Thomas Philippon

Despite its fast computers and credit derivatives, the current financial system does not seem better at transferring funds from savers to borrowers than the financial system of 1910.

I would rather see Finance less proud and Industry more content.
— Winston Churchill, 1925

The role of the finance industry is to produce, trade, and settle financial contracts that can be used to pool funds, share risks, transfer resources, produce information, and provide incentives. Financial intermediaries are compensated for providing these services. Total compensation of financial intermediaries (profits, wages, salaries, and bonuses) as a fraction of gross domestic product (GDP) is at an all-time high, around 9 percent of GDP. What does society get in return? In other words, what does the finance industry produce?

I measure the output of the finance industry by looking at all issuances of bonds, loans, and stocks (initial public offerings [IPOs], seasoned equity offerings [SEOs]), as well as liquidity services to firms and households. The measured output of the financial sector is indeed higher than it has been in much of the past. But unlike the income earned by the sector, it is not unprecedentedly high.

Historically, the unit cost of intermediation has been somewhere between 1.3 percent and 2.3 percent of assets. However, this unit cost has been trending upward since 1970 and is now significantly higher than in the past. In other words, the finance industry of 1900 was just as able as the finance industry of 2010 to produce loans, bonds, and stocks, and it was certainly doing it more cheaply. This is counterintuitive, to say the least. How is it possible for today's finance industry not to be significantly more efficient than the finance industry of John Pierpont Morgan?

What happened? Why did we get the bloated finance industry of today instead of the lean and efficient Wal-Mart? Finance has obviously benefited from the information technology (IT) revolution, and this has certainly lowered the cost of retail finance. Yet even accounting for all the financial assets created in the United States,

/ 235

the cost of intermediation appears to have increased. So why is the nonfinancial sector transferring so much income to the financial sector?

One simple answer is that technological improvements in finance have mostly been used to increase secondary market activities—that is, trading. Trading activities are many times larger than at any time in previous history. Trading costs have decreased, but I find no evidence that increased liquidity has led to better (meaning more informative) prices or to more insurance.

MEASURING THE COST OF FINANCIAL INTERMEDIATION

The sum of all profits and wages paid to financial intermediaries represents the cost of financial intermediation. There are various ways to define the size of the financial sector. Conceptually, the measure is:

$$\text{Cost} = \text{Income of Finance Industry} / \text{Total Income}$$

The three most important issues are:

Definition of "finance": For the most part, financial activities are classified consistently over time (but subsectors within finance are not). The main issue is with real estate. The value added of the "real estate" industry includes rents and imputed rents for homeowners. Whenever possible, I exclude real estate. In my notations, all variables indexed with "fin" include finance and insurance and exclude real estate.

Definition of "income": The best conceptual measure is "value added." In this case, "cost" is the GDP of the finance industry over the GDP of the U.S. economy. However, this is only acceptable if we can exclude real estate, or at least imputed rents. When this is not possible, a good alternative is to use the compensation of employees. In this case, "cost" is the compensation of employees in finance over the total compensation of employees in the United States. For the postwar period, the two measures display the same trends, even though annual changes can differ. This simply means that, in the long run, the labor share of the finance industry is the same as the labor share of the rest of the economy. In the short run, of course, profit rates can vary.

Definition of "total income": During peacetime and without structural change, it would make sense to simply use GDP. World War I and World War II took resources away from the normal production of goods and services. Financial intermediation should be compared to the non-war-related GDP. To do so, I construct a measure of GDP excluding defense spending. This adjustment makes the series more stationary.

Measuring this cost from 1870 to 2010 as a share of GDP, I find large historical variations, as shown in figure 9.1. The first important point to notice is that the measures are qualitatively and quantitatively consistent. It is thus possible to create one "extended" series simply by appending the older data to the newer ones.

FIGURE 9.1 / GDP Share of Finance Industry, 1860 to 2010

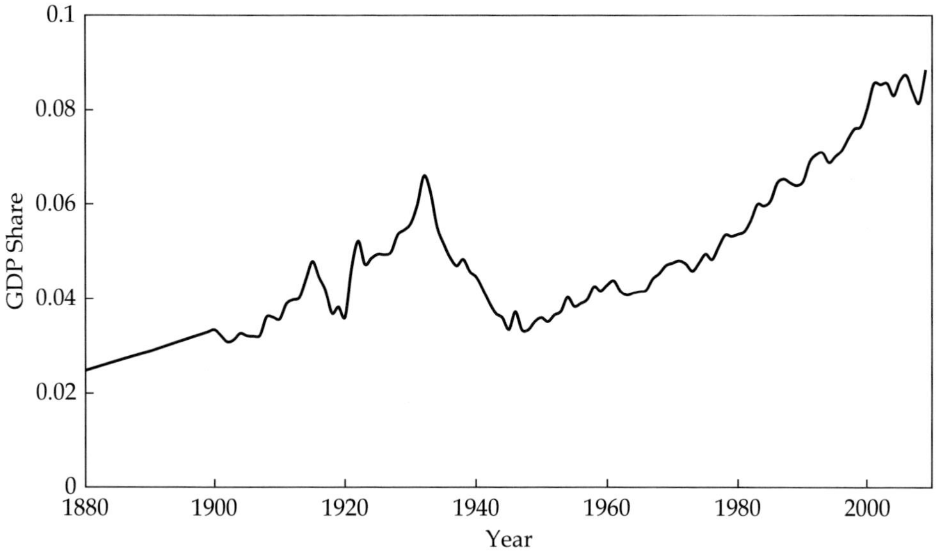

Source: Author's compilation based on data from Philippon (2011).

The cost of intermediation grows from 2 percent to 6 percent from 1870 to 1930. It shrinks to less than 4 percent in 1950, grows slowly to 5 percent in 1980, and then increases rapidly to almost 9 percent in 2010. This pattern is not driven by globalization or by structural changes in the economy. The pattern remains the same if finance is measured as a share of services, and if net financial exports are excluded (see Philippon 2011).

The second key point is that finance was smaller in 1980 than in 1925. Given the outstanding real growth over this period, it means that finance size is not simply driven by economic development.

MEASURING THE OUTPUT OF FINANCIAL INTERMEDIATION

Next comes the issue of measuring the output of the financial sector. Following Merton (1995) and Levine (2005), one can propose the following four categories of financial services or functions:

1. Provides means of payment (eases the exchange of goods and services)

2. Produces information about investment opportunities

3. Monitors investments and exerts corporate governance

4. Provides markets for insurance (diversification, risk management, liquidity)

These services are the output of the finance industry and its source of economic value. To the extent that this higher total cost is met with proportionally more output, the greater compensation of the sector should not be surprising.

These services are provided to both households and firms, and they facilitate the creation of financial assets. The most important contracts involve the credit markets. Measuring the production of credit separately for households, farms, nonfinancial corporate firms, financial firms, and the government, I show in Philippon (2011) that a simple benchmark can be constructed using the workhorse of modern macroeconomics: the neoclassical growth model. This benchmark is a weighted average of the financial assets created by the financial sector for the real economy.

The most important trends in recent years are the increases in household debt and in financial firms' debt. Household debt now exceeds 100 percent of GDP for the first time in history, while financial debt exceeds nonfinancial corporate debt for the first time. Surprisingly, the nonfinancial corporate credit market is smaller today than it was at its peak in the late 1920s.

For the corporate sector, we need to look at bonds and stocks, and for stocks, we want to distinguish seasoned equity offerings (SEOs) and initial public offerings (IPOs). We also need to look at the liquidity benefits of deposits and money market funds. When we put all the pieces together, we obtain a series for output for the finance industry. I then aggregate all types of nonfinancial credit, stock issuance, and liquidity services from deposits and money market funds.

I construct two series of output, as displayed in figure 9.2: one using the flows (gross issuances over GDP) and one using the levels (debt over GDP). Note that both are relevant in theory. Screening models apply to the flow of new issuances, while monitoring models apply to the stocks. Trading applies to both.

The production of financial services increased steadily until World War I, and then rapidly after 1919 until 1929. It collapsed during the Great Depression and World War II, increased steadily until 1975, then more randomly afterward. The flow and level measures share the same long-term trends, but are clear differences at medium frequencies. The flow variable was more stationary before World War I, suggesting a steady buildup of financial assets. The flow variable collapsed much faster during the Great Depression and the Great Recession. The level variable peaked in 1933 because of deflation and the need to deal with rising default rates.

THE DECREASING EFFICIENCY OF INTERMEDIATION IN THE UNITED STATES

These two output series enable me to estimate the cost of financial intermediation, defined as the value-added share divided by output series. The cost of intermediation in the United States (expressed as a share of outstanding assets) is between 1.3 percent and 2.3 percent (see figure 9.3). However, the cost of intermediation per dollar of assets created has increased over the past 130 years, and especially since the 1970s. In other words, according to this measure, the finance industry that sustained the expansion of the railroad, steel, and chemical industries and the

FIGURE 9.2 / Financial Intermediation Output, 1880 to 2010

Source: Author's compilation based on data from Philippon (2011).

FIGURE 9.3 / Financial Intermediation Unit Cost, 1880 to 2010

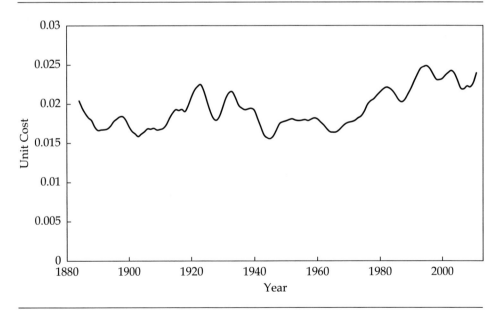

Source: Author's compilation based on data from Philippon (2011).

electricity and automobile revolutions was more efficient than the current finance industry.

This is counterintuitive. If anything, the technological development of the past forty years (and IT in particular) should have disproportionately increased efficiency in the finance industry. How is it possible for today's finance industry not to be significantly more efficient than the finance industry of John Pierpont Morgan?

It is important to understand that using the GDP share of finance to measure the costs of financial intermediation captures all fees and spreads, but ignores the hidden costs of systemic risk. The neoclassical benchmark also assumes that all agents borrow rationally ex ante. (Of course, that does not rule out the possibility that they will end up with too much debt ex post, but in that event, they have understood the risks involved and chosen to borrow.) We can debate this assumption, but the point I want to emphasize is that this provides an upper bound on financial efficiency. If anything, adding excessive risk-taking and overborrowing would decrease the risk-adjusted efficiency.[1]

INFORMATION TECHNOLOGIES: WHERE IS WAL-MART WHEN WE NEED IT?

An obvious driving force in financial intermediation is information technology. I often hear the argument that improvement in IT explains the increase in the share of finance. This argument, however, is either incomplete or misleading. One reason it is incomplete is simply that IT cannot explain the evolution of the GDP share of finance before 1970.

What makes the IT argument misleading is that it is far from clear why IT should increase the share of finance. The neoclassical growth model predicts that, in most cases, technological improvement will lower the share of GDP spent on financial intermediation. In particular, this prediction is unambiguous for most retail finance. Essentially, the physical transaction costs of buying and holding financial assets must have decreased because of IT. This effect must have lowered the amount spent on intermediation.

An apt analogy is with retail and wholesale trade, since these are also intermediation services.[2] As Olivier Jean Blanchard (2003, 68) explains in his discussion of Basu et al. (2003): "Fully one-third of the increase in TFP growth from the first to the second half of the 1990s in the United States came from the retail trade sector. For this reason, the general merchandising segment, which represents 20% of sales in the sector, was one of the sectors examined in a McKinsey study (McKinsey Global Institute 2001) aimed at understanding the factors behind U.S. TFP growth in the 1990s."

Figure 9.4 shows the evolution of GDP shares and IT investment in wholesale trade and retail trade.

Figure 9.5 shows this evolution for finance. The contrast is striking. Based on what we see in wholesale and retail trade, IT should have made finance smaller, not larger.

FIGURE 9.4 / IT Investment and GDP Shares of Retail and Wholesale Trade, 1970 to 2010

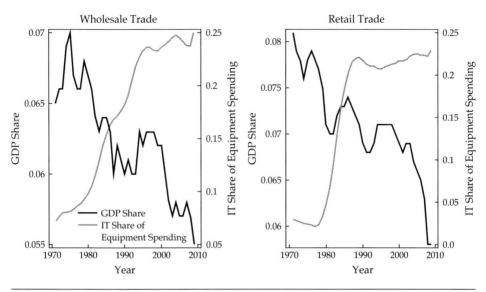

Source: Author's compilation based on data from Philippon (2011).

FIGURE 9.5 / IT and GDP Share in Finance, 1970 to 2010

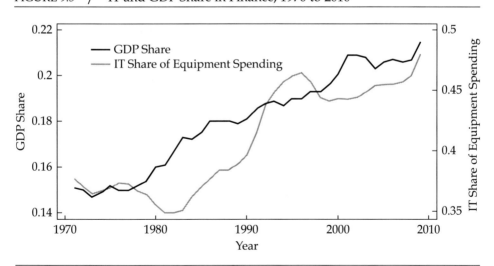

Source: Author's compilation based on data from Philippon (2011).

TRADING

As noted at the outset, the cost of intermediation appears to have increased, even accounting for all the financial assets created in the United States. So why is the nonfinancial sector transferring so much income to the financial sector?

As suggested earlier, one simple answer is that technological improvements in finance have mostly been used to increase trading. Figure 9.6 shows trading in the stock market from 1900 to 2010. Foreign exchange trading volumes are more than two hundred times larger today than in 1977. Finally, trading accounts for a large fraction of revenues for the largest banks.

Trading, of course, is neither a good nor a bad thing. It all depends on its impact on the real economy. The output measures developed here, however, capture only the production of financial assets (equity, bonds, money, and so on).[3] Two important functions of financial markets are not captured: the production of price information and the provision of insurance.

It is important now to ask the following question: if improvements in financial intermediation lead to more informative prices or better risk-sharing, where would these improvements be seen in equilibrium?

THE INFORMATIVENESS OF PRICES

In a model in which managers learn from prices, better prices should lead to better capital allocation and higher productivity. Are prices more informative about future income streams? Statistical analysis of the preliminary evidence in Bai, Philippon, and Savov (2012), who use a large panel of stock price data and ask whether a stock's price (relative to its assets) contains more information about future earnings growth today than it has in the past, suggest that the answer is no.

RISK-SHARING

Another benefit of financial intermediation is risk-sharing. Risk-sharing can affect both firms and households. At the firm level, risk-sharing is commonly called "risk management." In equilibrium, better risk management would mostly translate into a lower cost of funds, more issuances, and more investment. This first effect would be captured by my measures of debt and equity issuances. Better risk management could also increase total-factor productivity (TFP) if high-productivity projects are also riskier. I am not aware, however, of any evidence suggesting improvement in risk management. The most obvious index, that of precautionary savings by businesses, even suggests the opposite: corporate cash holdings have increased over the past thirty years. There is also no direct evidence of credit derivatives leading to better risk management, and it is commonly believed that hedging represents a small fraction of all trades in the credit default swap (CDS) market.

FIGURE 9.6   /   Equity Trading Volume over GDP, 1900 to 2010

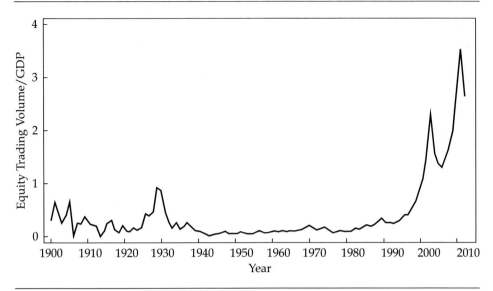

Source: Author's compilation based on data from Philippon (2011).

At the household level, better risk-sharing should lead to less consumption risk. Income inequality has increased dramatically in the United States over the past thirty years. If financial markets have improved risk-sharing, however, one would expect consumption inequality to have increased by less than income inequality. This is a controversial issue, but Mark Aguiar and Mark Bils (2011) find that consumption inequality has closely tracked income inequality over the period 1980 to 2007. It seems difficult to argue that the vast sums of money spent on intermediation are justified by better risk-sharing among households. It is also unclear that any of the main financial innovations of the past twenty years have improved risk-sharing opportunities.

One area where there is evidence of improved consumption smoothing is in the housing market. Kristopher Gerardi, Harvey Rosen, and Paul Willen (2010) find that the purchase price of a household's home predicts its future income. The link is stronger after 1985, which coincides with important innovations in the mortgage market. The increase in the relationship is more pronounced for households that are more likely to be credit-constrained. My model, however, captures this type of smoothing and is reflected as increased mortgage borrowing. Therefore, it does not bias my estimates.

FINANCIAL DERIVATIVES

Derivatives markets have grown enormously. As of June 2011, the notional amount of outstanding over-the-counter (OTC) contracts was $700 trillion (Bank for International Settlements [BIS] 2012), with interest rate contracts (mostly swaps) accounting for $550 trillion, and CDSs for $32 trillion. Measured at gross market values, the numbers are $20 trillion, $13 trillion, and $1.3 trillion, respectively.

These numbers are certainly impressive, but the relevant question is this: do they bear any connection to measures of market and economic efficiency? The short answer is no.

Most people are struck when they hear that the market for financial derivatives is $700 trillion, a number that is sometimes used to justify the costs of financial services. This is misleading. Derivatives are just the plumbing of the financial markets. End-users do not care about the plumbing, only about the quality of the service.

Another analogy comes to mind. Most people would probably be struck if they heard that each Airbus A380 contains 40,300 connectors and 100,000 wires that total 330 miles (530 kilometers) in length. The wires in a single airplane would stretch from Philadelphia to Boston, or from Paris to London or Frankfurt. Should we congratulate Airbus when it manages to increase the length of its wires? Or should we care more about the safety, comfort, speed, and fuel economy of the plane?

Similarly, suppose you were told that the inner workings of your computer had become more complex and interconnected. Would you pay for the pleasure of having a complex and interconnected computer, or would you only care about its speed, design, and battery life?

To understand better the relevance (or lack thereof) of financial derivatives, consider the following example. Corporation A needs a long-term fixed-interest loan. Making the loan would expose the lender to duration risk and to credit risk. How these risks are allocated, however, depends on the internal organization of the finance industry. Consider two polar cases. Suppose first that the loan is made and retained by bank B. Bank B must be compensated for bearing duration and credit risks. For instance, bank B must monitor its credit exposure and maintain a buffer of equity against credit risk. Bank B must also monitor and hedge its interest rate risk. These activities are costly, and the costs are passed through to the borrowers through spreads and fees.

Assume now that bank B can transfer credit risk to fund C using a CDS. Fund C now bears the credit risk, while bank B retains the duration risk. Bank B and fund C must be compensated accordingly. The key point is that bank B and fund C together hold exactly the same risk as bank B in the earlier example. Absent other frictions, the two examples are exactly equivalent in terms of economic efficiency. Comparing the two polar cases, one can see that the size of the CDS market bears no connection to any measure of efficiency.

Let us now extend the example. In terms of economic theory, derivatives can add real value in one of two ways: through risk-sharing and through price discovery. Risk-sharing among intermediaries would not, however, create a bias in my measurements. To see why, let us go back to the simple example. Suppose there are frictions that rationalize why bank B and fund C should be separate entities and why they gain from trading with each other—that is, bank B has a comparative advantage at managing duration risk, and fund C has such an advantage at managing credit risk.

Thus, the existence of CDS contracts can improve risk-sharing among intermediaries, lower the risk premia, and lead to a decrease in the borrowing costs of corporation A. With free entry, the total income going to the intermediaries $\{B + C\}$ would decrease. The unit cost measure developed earlier would correctly capture these effects: either borrowing costs would go down or borrowing volumes would go up, or both. In all cases, my approach would register an increase in efficiency.

Therefore, the only bias from derivative contracts must come from better risk-sharing or price discovery among nonfinancial borrowers. The correct way to measure the value added of derivatives is to directly measure the informativeness of prices, or the welfare gains from risk-sharing among nonfinancial firms and households. As explained earlier, however, I am not aware of any evidence suggesting better risk-sharing or better prices.

CONCLUSION

The finance industry of 1900 was just as capable as the finance industry of 2000 of producing bonds and stocks, and it certainly did so more cheaply. Today levels of trading activities are at least three times larger than at any time in history, and though trading costs have decreased (Hasbrouck 2009), the costs of active fund management are large. Kenneth French (2008) estimates that investors spend 0.67 percent of asset value trying (in vain, by definition) to beat the market.

In the absence of evidence that increased trading leads to either better prices or better risk-sharing, I must conclude that the finance industry's share of GDP is about two percentage points higher than it needs to be and that this represents an annual misallocation of resources of about $280 billion for the United States alone.

NOTES

1. For insightful discussions, see Haldane and Madouros (2011), Popov and Smets (2011), and Arcand, Berkes, and Panizza (2011).

2. For instance, one can compare retail finance and retail trade. Households go to grocery stores, not because they derive utility from doing so, but rather to have access to groceries. Similarly, households use financial intermediaries to gain access to the financial products that they need.

3. Note that the impact on average user costs is already taken into account. If trading lowers borrowing costs, firms can borrow more and invest more. This would be captured by the previous measures.

REFERENCES

Aguiar, Mark, and Mark Bils. 2011. "Has Consumption Inequality Mirrored Income Inequality?" Working paper. Rochester, N.Y.: University of Rochester.

Arcand, Jean-Louis, Enrico Berkes, and Ugo Panizza. 2011. "Too Much Finance?" VoxEU (April 7). Available at: http://www.voxeu.org/index.php?q=node/6328 (accessed September 2011).

Bai, Jennie, Thomas Philippon, and Alexi Savov. 2012. "Have Financial Prices Become More Informative?" Working paper. New York: NYU Stern School of Business.

Bank for International Settlements. 2012. "Semiannual OTC Derivatives Statistics at End-December 2011." Available at: http://www.bis.org/statistics/derstats.htm (accessed June 2012).

Basu, Susanto, John G. Fernald, Nicholas Oulton, and Sylaja Srinivasan. 2003. "The Case of the Missing Productivity Growth." In *NBER Macroeconomics Annual*, vol. 18, edited by Mark Gertler and Kenneth Rogoff. Cambridge, Mass.: MIT Press.

Blanchard, Olivier Jean. 2003. "Comment on Basu et al." In *NBER Macroeconomics Annual*, vol. 18, edited by Mark Gertler and Kenneth Rogoff. Cambridge, Mass.: MIT Press.

French, Kenneth R. 2008. "Presidential Address: The Cost of Active Investing." *Journal of Finance* 63(4): 1537–73.

Gerardi, Kristopher S., Harvey S. Rosen, and Paul S. Willen. 2010. "The Impact of Deregulation and Financial Innovation on Consumers: The Case of the Mortgage Market." *Journal of Finance* 65(1): 333–60.

Haldane, Andrew G., and Vasileios Madouros. 2011. "What Is the Contribution of the Financial Sector?" VoxEU (November 22). Available at: http://www.voxeu.org/index.php?q=node/7314 (accessed September 2011).

Hasbrouck, Joel. 2009. "Trading Costs and Returns for U.S. Equities: Estimating Effective Costs from Daily Data." *Journal of Finance* 64(3): 1445–77.

Levine, Ross. 2005. "Finance and Growth: Theory and Evidence." In *Handbook of Economic Growth*, vol. 1A, edited by Philippe Aghion and Steven Durlauf. Amsterdam: Elsevier.

McKinsey Global Institute. 2001. "U.S. Productivity Growth, 1995–2000: Understanding the Contribution of Information Technology Relative to Other Factors." Washington, D.C.: McKinsey Global Institute.

Merton, Robert C. 1995. "A Functional Perspective of Financial Intermediation." *Financial Management* 24(2): 23–41.

Philippon, Thomas. 2011. "Has the U.S. Finance Industry Become Less Efficient?" Unpublished paper. New York: New York University.

Popov, Alexander, and Frank Smets. 2011. "On the Tradeoff Between Growth and Stability: The Role of Financial Markets." VoxEU (November 3). Available at: http://voxeu.org/index.php?q=node/7208 (accessed September 2011).

Chapter 10

Shadow Finance

Patrick Bolton, Tano Santos, and José A. Scheinkman

Shadow finance refers to all financial transactions that take place outside regulated and transparent financial markets. We emphasize one important reason why a shadow financial sector exists: to prevent the dissemination of valuable information about asset values and to "cream-skim" the most valuable assets away from public, transparent exchanges. We highlight one important negative externality on organized markets from the migration of financial transactions to the shadow finance sector—the reduced access of retail investors to the most lucrative investments. We argue that existing exemptions from securities regulations for "qualified investors" in the shadow finance sector facilitate cream-skimming and thereby undermine public markets.

Is finance a game, or is it much more important than that? It should be something else entirely. Finance ought to provide an economy with an efficient means of allocating capital. It should provide a means of price discovery of assets, whether real or financial. It should provide a safe and reliable payments system. Financial innovations are worthwhile if, and only if, they help in those areas. All too often, players see financial innovations as providing ways to manipulate the system and make money off less savvy traders.
—Floyd Norris (2011)

One of the most important functions of financial markets is indeed to provide "a means of price discovery of assets." This is an essential step in the process of capital allocation, risk-sharing, and the provision of liquidity. But price discovery—the determination of an asset's value—requires skill, talent, and information, which are all in scarce supply. Implicit in Floyd Norris's analysis is the view that price discovery ought to be a public good provided by financial markets. This is consistent with a long tradition in finance scholarship that holds that financial markets are on average "informationally efficient." That is, equilibrium asset prices on average reflect assets' true (risk-adjusted) fundamental value and thus allow investors to discover assets' true prices (see, for example, Fama 1970). More precisely, the "efficient-market hypothesis" holds that competitive financial markets produce "publicly quoted equilibrium asset prices" that on average accurately convey information about fundamental asset values to all. In essence, according to this hypothesis, financial markets essentially are somehow able to overcome a private provision of public goods problem and provide a valuable public service of price discovery.

As Sanford Grossman and Joseph Stiglitz (1980) pointed out in their classic article, this hypothesis is just too good to be true and violates the basic economic tenet that "there is no such thing as a free lunch." When information about fundamental asset values is costly to produce, they argued, it cannot all be accurately reflected in equilibrium prices, for then no one would have an incentive to produce this costly information and every investor would simply "free-ride" by obtaining the valuable information from quoted prices. The producer of costly information has to be adequately rewarded for this valuable economic activity. In competitive financial markets with publicly quoted prices, they suggested, this can come only in the form of "insider trading," whereby the informed investor is able to trade and thus make a capital gain before her information is entirely revealed to other investors (or is never revealed at all). What Grossman and Stiglitz had in mind was not the illegal and socially wasteful practice of trading on the inside information of others, but the perfectly legal and socially valuable practice of generating costly information to be able to make better investment decisions.

As Grossman and Stiglitz (and other scholars) also pointed out, to the extent that costly, privately produced information can easily leak out in the process of trading, there may be too little information produced by "insiders." The amount of information produced is directly related to insiders' ability to profit from insider trading, which itself is related to how easily "insiders" can "make money off less savvy traders." Paradoxically, the better financial markets are at publicly disseminating information the fairer the trading system is, and the better protected the less savvy traders are the less reliable are the valuations produced by financial markets, as they rest on less information.

Insider trading is one mechanism for eliciting the production of costly information. Another equally important mechanism (which we focus on in Bolton, Santos, and Scheinkman 2011) is to avoid the public disclosure of prices or to trade bespoke securities at negotiated prices, which are difficult to compare to other securities. This is accomplished by trading in non-organized, less regulated, opaque markets—what we refer to here as the "shadow finance sector." In this sector, costly private information can be produced and its value can be largely appropriated by limiting its dissemination to the wider investing public. While transactions in this sector often serve an efficiency-enhancing purpose by eliciting better information, more accurate valuations, and value-improving financial innovation, they also impose a negative externality on organized markets by diverting the influx of certain investments from organized markets, which is the only place where the investing public at large can invest. The types of assets and deals that are likely to take place in the shadow finance sector involve investments that are most sensitive to information that can be acquired only by skilled investors. These are the investments that are most likely to be undervalued by retail investors in organized markets and that require the most input from financiers with special valuation skills and information. This is why we refer to the diversion of these transactions to the shadow finance sector as a form of "cream-skimming."

Interestingly, transactions in the shadow finance sector between highly sophisticated parties satisfy Floyd Norris's basic test for socially valuable financial innovations: they benefit all parties to the deal, rest on better price discovery, and maximize the surplus from trade through customization of the deal to the parties' needs. In particular, the value of these deals does not rest—at least not directly—on any exploitation of less savvy investors, in contrast to the "insider trading" in organized markets, which can only come at the expense of uninformed investors. It would thus seem that the growth of the shadow finance sector in the past three decades is a welcome development, reflecting mainly the greater efficiency of modern finance. This is indeed the perspective underlying much of the regulatory approach to the shadow finance sector, hedge funds, private equity funds, private placement, and over-the-counter (OTC) markets. As we explain later, this sector remains largely unregulated on the theory that the main actors in it are sophisticated players who do not need any regulatory protection. Indeed, players in this sector mainly view regulatory intervention as counterproductive, as it limits the freedom of contracting. We argue, however, that the fact that all parties to a transaction (in the shadow finance sector) gain from a deal does not imply that society at large gains, nor that overall welfare is increased. To the extent that the shadow finance sector enhances cream-skimming, it may undermine both resource allocation and the welfare of retail investors who have access only to less valuable investments in organized markets.

In Bolton, Santos, and Scheinkman (2011), we analyze a model with a three-period structure. In the first period, agents face an occupational choice between entrepreneurship in the real sector and a career in finance. Those who choose to become entrepreneurs then proceed to set up a business, and those who choose to become financiers invest in human capital and information to be able to value assets for sale by entrepreneurs in the second period. When an entrepreneur needs to raise funding in the second period by selling assets (or a stake in her business), she can turn to either organized and transparent exchanges or to private placement markets. In organized exchanges, entrepreneurs sell primarily to retail investors, who do not have any special valuation skills or information. Assets therefore tend to sell at their average estimated value, which means that high-value assets tend to sell at a discount in these markets. This is why entrepreneurs attempt to sell to informed financiers (or "qualified investors") in private placement markets in the hope that their asset will be found to be of high value. Should entrepreneurs indeed have above-average value assets to sell, these assets are likely to be identified by informed investors and therefore to sell for a higher-than-average price. This is why in equilibrium a shadow finance sector generally exists alongside organized, transparent and regulated exchanges. Although entrepreneurs with above-average value assets benefit from trading in the shadow finance sector, they are unable to appropriate the full value of the asset because of a lack of competition in the shadow finance sector. The informational rent that financiers are able to extract in the shadow finance sector is due to both the *opacity* of the shadow finance sector and the *scarcity* of valuation skills in the economy.[1] In the last period of the model, returns from production in the real sector are realized, distributed to their owners, and consumed.

In sum, financiers with high valuation skills operating in the shadow finance sector offer a valuation service at a premium to entrepreneurs with high-value assets, thereby cream-skimming the most valuable assets away from organized, regulated, and transparent markets. This cream-skimming imposes a negative externality on these markets and ultimately allows for excessive informational rent extraction by financiers in the shadow finance sector. This happens because prices in organized markets, which offer a lower bound to entrepreneurs seeking to raise funding, are lowered by cream-skimming: those prices reflect the average value of the assets placed in organized markets, and that value is lower the more high-value assets are placed privately in the shadow finance sector. The rent that informed financiers can extract in the shadow finance sector is increased in proportion to the reduction in the "reserve price" that entrepreneurs can get in organized markets. In Bolton, Santos, and Scheinkman (2011), we focus on an occupational choice inefficiency resulting from the informational rent extraction in the shadow finance sector: because more rents can be extracted in this sector, too many talented agents are attracted by a more lucrative career in the shadow finance sector and choose it over entrepreneurship.[2]

In this chapter, we focus on a different aspect of cream-skimming, namely, that investment returns in organized, regulated, markets—the main source of returns available to retail investors—are eroded as a result of the cream-skimming of assets to the shadow finance sector. To highlight this effect we provide here a simplified treatment of the analytical framework in Bolton, Santos, and Scheinkman (2011) by suppressing the occupational choice problem in the first period. In this simple analytical framework, we show that when the shadow finance sector grows relative to the organized, transparent sector, the equilibrium investment returns of retail investors are reduced and those of professional or "qualified investors" increase. Thus, in this adaptation of our model, the cream-skimming by the shadow finance sector is at the expense of retail investors, while in Bolton, Santos, and Scheinkman (2011) it is at the expense of entrepreneurs.

The observation that the growth of the shadow finance sector results in simultaneously lower returns for retail investors in organized, regulated markets and higher returns for professional investors in the shadow finance sector is broadly consistent with observed realized returns over the past decade. As one of the most successful professional investors, David Swensen (2005), forcefully argues in his book on personal investing, the high-return investments that professional investment teams have access to are simply out of reach for ordinary investors. And while a typical 401(k) investment portfolio in U.S. stocks and bonds has languished over the past decade, hedge fund returns (to the extent that they can be measured) have generally outperformed the S&P 500 index on a risk-adjusted basis (see, for example, Agarwal and Naik 2004; Kosowski, Naik, and Teo 2007).[3] In any case, one is more likely to find sophisticated investors *running* hedge funds than simply investing in them, so that the returns of hedge funds underestimate the returns to their managers.

In the aftermath of the financial crisis of 2008, many commentators have raised concerns about the opacity of the shadow finance sector as a hidden source of systemic risk. The main worry is that risky positions could build up in the shadow finance sector in the hands of a few institutions, unbeknownst to regulators, and thus pose a systemic risk. This is largely the reason why the Dodd-Frank Wall Street Reform and Consumer Protection Act of 2010 opens the way to regulations requiring greater reporting of positions in OTC swaps markets, a major segment of the shadow finance sector. Under the act, the Commodity Futures Trading Commission (CFTC) and the Securities and Exchange Commission (SEC) have a broad mandate to require the registration of swaps dealers, capital requirements for certain swaps dealers, and the trading of standardized swaps on organized exchanges with a central clearing platform (CCP). As we discuss later, the financial industry has put up considerable resistance to the introduction of these regulations. Although some concessions have been obtained relatively easily, such as the creation of CCPs, others, such as the implementation of greater transparency for swaps prices and quotes, are being fought over bitterly.

The Dodd-Frank Act also considers tighter regulation of hedge funds, calling for more transparency in the form of registration and greater disclosure requirements for advisers. Moreover, the act sets out further criteria that "qualified investors" must meet, essentially raising the bar on retail investors for access to the shadow finance sector. All in all, while the new regulations may help reduce the likelihood of the buildup of systemic risk in the shadow finance sector, they also make this sector less accessible to retail investors. As we elaborate later, an unintended consequence of these regulations may thus be to further increase inequality between retail and qualified investors.

A SIMPLE ANALYTICAL FRAMEWORK

We begin our discussion by describing the simplified analytical framework of Bolton, Santos, and Scheinkman (2011), without occupational choice and with "cash-in-the-market pricing." In the appendix to this chapter, we give a detailed exposition of the formal model underpinning our analytical framework and state our main proposition on cream-skimming in the shadow finance sector and the welfare consequences for retail investors. By cash-in-the-market pricing—a term first coined by Franklin Allen and Douglas Gale (1998)—we mean that average equilibrium asset prices in the organized exchange are given by the ratio of total cash in the hands of market investors divided by total assets for sale. When cash-in-the-market prevails, asset prices can be below the present value of the exchange's cash flows; this reflects frictions that prevent investors from borrowing to finance all of their investment opportunities.[4]

We divide time into three critical phases. In the initial phase, entrepreneurs make their investments. In the interim phase, the assets created through these investments may be sold so as to allow the entrepreneurs who wish to do so to exit their investments. The assets originated by entrepreneurs may be of high or low value. The true value of the originated assets is difficult to ascertain, and both entrepreneurs and retail investors can only determine the likely average value of an asset for sale. There are, however, financiers who specialize in valuing assets and are able to distinguish the valuable assets from the other ones. These financiers operate mainly in the opaque, dealer-based shadow finance sector, where they can single out the best assets and acquire them at some price, which we denote by p_d.[5] Skilled financiers operate mainly in this sector because they are better able to protect their informational rent in this market: other investors cannot infer their information from their quoted prices, which remain hidden. In contrast, in the organized, regulated, and centralized market, where buyers are required to disclose their bids, it is much harder for informed financiers to protect their informational rent. Accordingly, in the centralized market there are mainly retail and uninformed institutional investors, who are ready to buy any asset up for sale at some price p. We refer to this centralized market in what follows as an "exchange" and to the dealer-based market as a "private market." In the final phase all asset returns are realized and consumed by investors and financiers.

Another key distinction between the private market and the exchange is the customization and complexity of financial transactions. On the private market, assets can be customized for the special needs of a particular entrepreneur. This tends to enhance the value of the transaction. In contrast, only standardized financial assets, such as stocks, bonds, and futures, are traded on the exchange, making relative comparisons between two assets easier and enhancing competition. The dark side of customization in the private market is complexity and opacity. Customized financial assets are unique and therefore harder to value by referring to the value of comparable assets. Thus, customization, while creating higher added value, also facilitates extraction of this value by informed financiers. It also produces greater complexity and a greater risk of unintended consequences with respect to the buildup of systemic risk.

Three classes of agents operate in our stylized economy: entrepreneurs, who originate assets; financiers or financial intermediaries, who are able to value assets; and uninformed retail investors, who invest in assets sold on the exchange. Since compensation for holding risky assets is not essential to our analysis, we assume that all agents are risk-neutral. The assets originated by entrepreneurs yield a return or payoff in the third and last phase of our model, but to capture trading in assets after they have been originated and before they have matured, we shall assume that all entrepreneurs are eager to realize their investments and that they start consuming their accumulated wealth in the interim phase.[6]

Financiers stand ready to value and purchase assets for sale in the interim period, but they have limited wealth and cannot absorb all assets that are up for sale at a reasonable price. For simplicity, we assume that each financier can purchase at most one asset and—as is empirically plausible—that there are fewer financiers in the economy than entrepreneurs. The remainder of the assets that cannot be purchased by financiers are absorbed by retail investors in the exchange. An important assumption in our analytical framework is that there is no overall excess savings, or "savings glut," in our economy. In other words, there is a relative abundance of assets originated by entrepreneurs that can serve as savings vehicles for retail investors. This ensures that in equilibrium the return on investment for retail investors will be strictly positive.

What determines whether an asset is traded on the private market or on the exchange? A first factor, of course, is whether financiers identify the asset as valuable.

If in their assessment the asset is only average or below average, then they do not seek to purchase it. Accordingly, all average or below-average assets end up being traded on the exchange. If the asset value in their estimate is above average, then financiers seek to purchase it at a competitive price, which would be the price the asset is expected to fetch on the exchange. This is how informed and skilled financiers are able to extract an informational rent in the private market: they are able to acquire an asset with above-average value at a price that is close to the average value of the assets that are traded on the exchange. What fraction of above-average value assets are thus traded on the private exchange? Essentially, as many as financiers can afford to buy. To the extent that their financial capacity is limited, they have to turn down some attractive deals, which then take place on the exchange.

Cream-Skimming and the Welfare of Retail Investors

What is the effect of an increase in the number of financiers or in the capacity of financiers to absorb valuable assets for sale in the interim period? Basically, as the number of financiers increases, the fraction of valuable assets that are cream-skimmed by the private market increases. This means, first, that retail investors have access to fewer valuable investments on the exchange. Thus, other things being equal, the expected return of assets open to retail investors decreases as fewer assets are available to them as savings vehicles and the average quality of the assets sold on the exchange decreases. Second, the expected return obtained by financiers in the private market increases as the proportion of high-quality assets traded in the private market increases, because financiers get to purchase the valuable asset at the competitive price, which is the price quoted on the exchange. But to the extent that this price declines to reflect a worsening of the average quality of the assets sold on the exchange, financiers are able to purchase assets on more favorable terms. This is the fundamental cream-skimming externality imposed by the shadow finance sector on the exchange and on retail investors, as emphasized in our analysis. Commentators on the financial crisis have focused on the externality in the shadow finance sector in the form of accumulation of hidden systemic risks. We add to that the externality of cream-skimming, which would remain even if adequate reporting of positions in the shadow finance sector reduced or eliminated the systemic risk.

The Credit Boom Through the Lens of the Model

One way in which the shadow finance sector can grow is for the number of financiers operating in that sector to grow. But an equally plausible way in which this sector can grow is if existing financiers are able to borrow more or (more generally) obtain more financing from retail investors to acquire more assets. This channel of growth of the private market induces the same negative externality in terms of cream-skimming on the exchange, and on top of that it is the source of a major systemic risk: through a lending boom-and-bust cycle, initially greater leverage enables financiers to boost their returns, but eventually excessive expansion of the private market results in too much money chasing too few valuable assets, overleverage, and a crash.

To see this, consider the following dynamic extension of our analytical framework: we simply paste a sequence of economies, like the one described here, one after the other. In every period t, there is then the same population of entrepreneurs originating assets as described earlier. In the interim phase $t+\Delta$, these entrepreneurs then sell their assets, which mature in the final phase, $t+T$, where $\Delta \geq 1$ and $T > \Delta$.

Moreover, in every period t a population of long-lived retail investors enters the exchange and provides liquidity in this market. After they acquire the assets sold by entrepreneurs in period $t+\Delta$, they simply hold them until maturity in period $t+T$. There is also a date-specific group of financiers, μ_t, that enters the $(t+\Delta)$– period private market. As with the retail investors just described, financiers can participate only in the private market that is open in their period. Once they have acquired their assets, they also hold them until maturity at date $t+T$. In sum, financiers and retail investors are, as a simplifying assumption, buy-and-hold investors.

Before we discuss the effects of a gradual increase in the size of the private market through leverage, we first consider the simpler scenario in which the private market grows as a result of an increase in the group of financiers over time, that is, $\mu_{t+1} > \mu_t$. Then it is easy to see what this dynamic version of our framework can deliver. First, notice that because the group of financiers is increasing over time, so is the amount of cream-skimming. As a result, the quality of the "vintage" of assets in the hands of retail investors deteriorates progressively, as reflected in the expected payoff for each of the vintages.

At the same time, consider what happens with equilibrium prices in the exchange. As long as cash-in-the-market pricing prevails, the price of the average asset traded in the exchange goes up on account of the lower volume of assets flowing into it: $p_{t+1} > p_t$. It follows that for any retail investor, the "realized" return between two periods (other than the maturity date) is always strictly positive and given by:

$$R_{t,t+1} = \frac{p_{t+1} - p_t}{p_t} \tag{10.1}$$

Notice that this is the case even though in every period the expected rate of return of an asset acquired in the exchange is lower than in the previous period.

Thus, in this economy the quality of vintages in the hands of retail investors deteriorates over time, but the quality of vintages in the hands of financiers remains constant, as they acquire only the best assets. Also, as long as cash-in-the-market pricing prevails, every cohort of retail investors enjoys positive capital gains, even though the difference between the expected rate of return (see appendix 10.7) and the return on the safe technology, which is normalized here to 1, goes down. This simple model thus can explain the stylized patterns observed in the mortgage market throughout the real estate bubble.

The evolution of prices in this dynamic model is also revealing (see figure 10.1). Recall that we are assuming that all investors are buy-and-hold investors, so that

FIGURE 10.1 / Prices for Cash-in-the-Market Pricing Versus Discounted
Cash-Flow Region

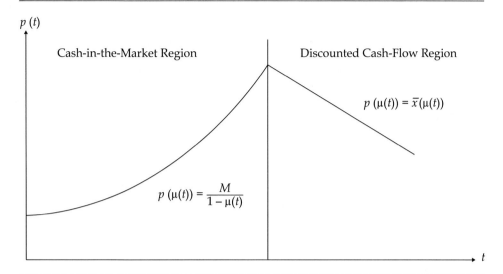

$p(t)$

Cash-in-the-Market Region

Discounted Cash-Flow Region

$p(\mu(t)) = \bar{x}(\mu(t))$

$p(\mu(t)) = \dfrac{M}{1-\mu(t)}$

t

Source: Author's figure.

by assumption we eliminate, again, the possibility of reselling the asset at some later date. Figure 10.1 shows how prices evolve in this model over time. As long as cash-in-the-market pricing holds, the increase in the group of financiers is reducing the volume of the assets flowing into the exchange and thus increasing the prices paid by retail investors. Moreover, prices are "convex" in the amount of cream-skimming, so that the realized returns are increasing every period. At some point, however, cream-skimming catches up with the economy and the quality of vintages is so low that retail investors are not willing to pay more than the expected payoff for the asset. After that, further cream-skimming only lowers this expected payoff and thus the prices of the assets flowing into the exchange. Notice also that the incentives to purchase assets do not disappear. Early retail investors enjoy large expected returns in their hold-to-maturity portfolios, whereas late retail investors—those arriving to the market in the discounted cash-flow region—capture only the risk-free rate when holding their assets to maturity.

Needless to say, many elements are missing from this simple story. For one, the supply of assets has been kept constant every period, although in practice there was a notable increase in the issuance of mortgage bonds during the credit boom. Another pre-crisis phenomenon that this simple story does not capture is the increase in the number of uninformed funds available waiting to buy (dollar assets): these were in shorter supply after the burst of the dot-com bubble and the corporate governance scandals following the collapse of Enron, which depressed the initial public offering (IPO) market for a decade and spurred a wave of de-listings through leveraged buyouts.

Consider now the scenario where the private sector grows through leverage. When financiers (or, now, financial intermediaries) can borrow, an increase in the size of the private sector has two distinct effects when cash-in-the-market pricing prevails. First, financial intermediaries' returns may go down because, as intermediaries buy more projects, they increase the cash-in-the-market price of assets in the exchange and therefore the price at which they themselves can acquire assets. Second, financial intermediaries' returns increase because some of the cash owned by retail investors is loaned to intermediaries, depressing the cash-in-the-market price in the exchange. It is intuitive that as long as leverage requires that some capital of intermediaries be used in each purchase, this latter effect will be dominated by the first—less money is withdrawn from the exchange than the value of assets bought by the uninformed. In this case, our general conclusion still holds: an increase in the size of the private market decreases the welfare of retail investors. In addition, to the extent that leverage makes it possible for the private market to grow to the point where all valuable assets are cream-skimmed by the private market, this market could grow too large; consequently, some overleveraged financial intermediaries, unable to repay all their debts, would go bust.

IMPLICATIONS

The Regulation of Hedge Funds

The Dodd-Frank Act mostly reinforces the existing regulatory approach to hedge funds, which is built around several exemptions from the much tighter regulations that apply to mutual funds under the Securities Act of 1933 and the Investment Company Act of 1940. The justification for these exemptions is that as long as hedge funds target only "accredited investors" and "qualified purchasers," there is no need to provide regulatory protection to these investors, as they are sophisticated enough to be able to fend for themselves. The Dodd-Frank Act calls for a strengthening of the criteria for eligibility as an "accredited investor," thus raising the barrier to entry to these investments. A possible unintended consequence of the new proposed rules is that it makes it even harder for retail investors to benefit from the superior returns offered by these funds. Some commentators have argued that this approach to the regulation of hedge funds may therefore be counterproductive and that access should be made easier, not harder (see, for example, Edwards 2004).

In terms of our analysis, one difficulty with relaxing the criteria for eligibility as an "accredited investor" is that investors who lack the necessary valuation skills may be left unprotected and may not be able to generate higher returns for their investments. They may simply be easy targets for charlatan investment advisers. The challenge is not so much to give greater access to the hedge funds as to allow greater dissemination of the price discovery service these hedge funds provide. Thus, greater disclosure would be beneficial not only because it would improve the monitoring of risk concentration but also because it would make hedge funds' price discovery service available to a wider investment public.

The Regulation of Private Placements

Private placement markets grew substantially following the adoption by the SEC of rule 144A in 1990.[7] Under this new rule, so-called "qualified institutional investors" are exempt from registration requirements under the Securities Act of 1933 for transactions exceeding $500,000. As Geraldine Lambe (2007) and Vicki Wei Tang (2007) have documented, the relaxation of registration requirements under rule 144A has substantially increased the secondary market liquidity of this segment of the shadow finance sector, making it a much more attractive source of capital for corporations. In 2006 more equity capital was raised via rule 144A private placements ($162 billion) than in IPOs in Amex, NASDAQ, and NYSE (which totaled $154 billion).[8] Financial intermediaries rushed to design proprietary platforms where qualified institutional buyers (QIBs) trade rule 144A shares. Goldman Sachs created the Goldman Sachs tradable unregistered equity (GSTrUE) platform; Citi, Lehman, Merrill Lynch, Bank of New York, and Morgan Stanley created Opus-5; and NASDAQ followed suit with Portal. An important milestone in the development of this market was the sale by Oaktree Capital Management LLC of an equity stake for $800 million.[9]

There are many reasons for the success of private equity placements. Escaping the regulatory burdens associated with the Sarbanes-Oxley Act of 2002 is an important factor, but in addition, there is some evidence that higher-quality issuers are flocking to rule 144A rather than public offerings (Lambe 2007).[10] The evidence on private investments in public equity (PIPEs), which are private equity offerings by public firms, also points in the same direction. PIPEs increased from $4 billion in 1996 to $56 billion in 2007. To get a sense of the orders of magnitude, this compares with a total of capital raised through seasoned equity offerings (SEOs) of $75 billion in 2007. This trend in private placements has led some to argue that exchanges run the risk of being deprived of high-quality issues. For instance, Roger Ehrenberg, former CEO of Deutsche Bank's hedge fund platform DB Advisors, has argued that rule 144A equity issuances "will quickly detract from the Nasdaq, NYSE and Amex. These private exchanges will effectively *skim the cream off the market*. The very highest quality issuers will forgo the public markets to issue on the private exchanges" (quoted in Lambe 2007, 42, emphasis added).

More recently, this tendency to shun public equity offers has even reached highly successful new ventures, such as Facebook, Twitter, and Zynga, which traditionally would have sought an IPO on NASDAQ but now are instead seeking to first raise capital through private placements (see Eaglesham 2011). One of the regulatory hurdles these companies face is being subject to much more stringent disclosure requirements once they pass the threshold of five hundred shareholders,[11] but in response to calls by some investors and representatives in Congress, the SEC has recently announced that it may consider raising this ceiling.[12] Interestingly, one of the main concerns about this limit voiced by U.S. investors is that the five-hundred-shareholder ceiling can be evaded by "raising money from investors overseas, denying U.S. citizens a chance to buy stakes" (Eaglesham 2011).

In terms of our analysis, an increase in the five-hundred-shareholder ceiling—or more generally, any weakening of the disclosure requirements for private placements—would probably result in more cream-skimming, *thus denying retail investors access to the privately placed stocks.* An alternative response to concerns that some large U.S. investors may be denied access to these ventures would be to apply the five-hundred-shareholder limit to any shareholder, regardless of nationality and place of issue, and to tighten the application of the ceiling so that it applies to the number of ultimate shareholders and not just to the number of shell corporations investing directly in ownership blocks.

Over-the-Counter Derivatives Markets

OTC derivatives markets emerged as a response to hedgers' and insurers' demands for customized insurance contracts, and over time they have grown into an enormous and highly lucrative shadow financial sector. To give a sense of the orders of magnitude, figure 10.2 shows the growth of the interest rate derivatives markets in exchanges versus OTC markets. The growth in OTC markets dwarfs that of exchanges by several orders of magnitude.

Clearly, these markets create value not just by cream-skimming the most valuable deals away from organized exchanges but also through contractual innovation and customization. Nowadays, however, many of the derivatives contracts that are traded in these markets are highly standardized, and the initial justification for trading these contracts in unregulated OTC markets has largely disappeared. Under the Dodd-Frank Act, the CFTC has a broad mandate to extend prudential regulation to these markets and to induce the trading of standardized swaps to migrate onto organized exchanges.

As the chairman of the CFTC, Gary Gensler (2010), recently emphasized, the purpose of moving the trading of standardized derivatives and swaps onto organized exchanges is not just to forestall the buildup of systemically risky positions in these markets, by requiring central clearing, but also to

> shift the information advantage from a small group of derivative dealers on Wall Street to the broader market. It is only Wall Street that benefits by keeping trades bilateral, where derivatives dealers internalize the transaction information. That means one corporation could get an entirely different price on a derivative than another. Wall Street profits from access to trading information while businesses, municipalities, consumers and others pay the costs. In the securities markets, this would be like putting 100 shares of a stock into your 401k with no knowledge of where the market prices the stocks. We should require that standardized derivatives be traded on regulated trading venues where all market participants get to see the pricing.

The OTC markets' response to these regulatory moves has largely been to give in on the central clearing requirements, but to resist greater transparency for the

FIGURE 10.2 / Interest Rate Derivatives: Over-the-Counter Markets Versus Exchanges, 1998 to 2011

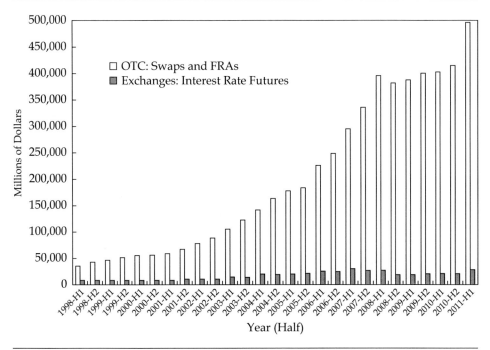

Source: Author's compilation based on Bank for International Settlements (2011).

Notes: OTC: notional values in millions of U.S. dollars of interest rate swaps and forward rate agreements (FRAs); exchanges: notional value in billions of interest rate futures.

new exchanges (see, for example, Leising 2009; Morgenson 2010; Scannell 2009; Tett 2010). For example, when Citadel, the Chicago-based hedge fund, tried to set up an electronic trading system that would display prices for credit default swaps (CDSs), it met with stiff resistance from the leading Wall Street banks. Similarly, when the leading banks in the OTC swaps and derivatives markets decided to set up clearinghouses like the InterContinentalExchange (ICE) under their control, they tried to protect their oligopoly rents by keeping out even well-established potential entrants like the Bank of New York. They also put in place rules giving exclusive access to market data to Markit (see Story 2010).

CONCLUSION

The main goal of securities regulation is to protect less savvy investors from financial sharks. This is why public markets, where retail investors put most of their money, are overseen by regulatory agencies charged with protecting investors, and come with strict disclosure rules and other regulations limiting investors' risk exposure as well as promoters' ability to take advantage of unsuspecting investors. In private markets, on the other hand, retail investors' access is restricted and there are virtually no regulatory agencies protecting investors and hardly any regulations. Only sophisticated investors are meant to be present in private markets, and the thinking is that not only are these investors able to fend for themselves, but regulation would mostly be harmful to the contracting parties, as it would impede freedom of contracting in these markets.

We have argued that there is a fallacy in this simple distinction between public markets (open to small investors) and private markets (open to qualified investors), namely, that it rests on the implicit assumption that the investments on offer in both markets provide more or less the same risk-adjusted return to investors. The reality, however, is that private markets offer sophisticated investors unique access to more lucrative investment opportunities. Moreover, as these private markets grow, they tend to cream-skim the best investment opportunities away from public markets. The end result is that retail investors, while for the most part adequately protected for the less juicy investments offered to them in public markets, are denied access to the more lucrative investment opportunities in private markets. When public and private markets coexist, the problem of underprovision of price discovery takes not only the form of underinvestment in costly information acquisition in public markets but also the form of underdiffusion of the information acquired in private markets, which in turn may give rise to too much information production in private markets.

Although the new regulations of the shadow finance sector called for by the Dodd-Frank Act may help redress some of the currently unbalanced approach to securities regulation, a more fundamental revision of the basic approach to securities regulation may be necessary, as indicated by the SEC's recent decision to consider relaxing the rules limiting private placements. There has to be a more systematic recognition of the fact that any expansion of the shadow finance sector imposes negative externalities on retail investors by making it harder for them to gain access to better investment opportunities.

APPENDIX: A SIMPLE MODEL

Preliminaries

We consider three dates. At $t = 0$, entrepreneurs make an investment. The projects that are the product of these investment decisions are sold at $t = 1$, and at $t = 2$ these projects' payoffs are realized. The payoffs can be high or low. At $t = 1$, there are two markets for projects. One is an opaque, dealer-based market where financial intermediaries identify the best projects and acquire them at a price, p_d. The second market is a centralized market where a class of uninformed agents supplies liquidity, obtaining projects for a price p. We assume that there is a storage technology by which all agents can transfer their endowment from one period to the next costlessly.

Agents

There are three types of agents, all risk-neutral: entrepreneurs, financial intermediaries, and uninformed investors. We normalize the measure of entrepreneurs to 1. Each entrepreneur starts a project that will result in time $t = 2$ consumption goods, but only values consumption at time $t = 1$. For this reason, entrepreneurs will sell their projects at time 1. The project payoff is x_h with probability π and $x_l < x_h$ with probability $1 - \pi$.

Financial intermediaries are endowed with k units of period 1 consumption good and are indifferent between consuming at time $t = 1$ or $t = 2$. They are also endowed with a technology that allows them to identify good projects (those with payoff x_h). We make two simplifying assumptions for now: first, we assume that each financial intermediary can find only one good project, and that the measure μ of financial intermediaries satisfies $\mu < \pi$; second, we assume that $k \geq x_h$. These two assumptions guarantee that each financial intermediary has enough resources to acquire the one good project that it is able to identify and that financial intermediaries collectively are not able to acquire all good projects available at $t = 1$. Both of these assumptions can be relaxed, and the model can be generalized to allow for leverage by financial intermediaries. Later in the appendix, we briefly discuss the implications of introducing leverage, but a full analysis of leverage is beyond the scope of this chapter.

Uninformed investors have a total capital of M and are indifferent between consumption at date $t = 1$ or $t = 2$.

Markets

PRIVATE MARKET. On the private market, financial intermediaries identify good projects and acquire them from entrepreneurs. Since we have assumed that each financial intermediary can identify only a single project, the volume v of good projects transacted on the private market is at most μ, the measure of financial intermediaries.

EXCHANGE. On the organized exchange, uninformed agents supply liquidity competitively to acquire the projects that are not placed on the private market. Because entrepreneurs need to sell their projects at $t = 1$, the total supply of projects on the uninformed exchange is given by

$$\pi - v + (1 - \pi) = 1 - v \tag{10.2}$$

Thus, the expected value of the projects traded in the uninformed exchange is given by

$$\bar{x}(v) = \frac{(\pi - v)x_h + (1 - \pi)x_l}{1 - v} \tag{10.3}$$

given that all agents are risk-neutral. In the absence of financial constraints, the price of assets on the uninformed exchange would be given by equation 10.3; instead, because the amount of capital in the hands of uninformed investors is limited to M, the price of the asset in the uninformed exchange is given by

$$p(v) = \min\left\{\bar{x}(v), \frac{M}{1-v}\right\}$$

(10.4)

Following the terminology introduced by Allen and Gale (1998), when $p = M/1 - v$, we say that cash-in-the-market pricing obtains on the exchange.

BARGAINING BETWEEN INTERMEDIARIES AND ENTREPRENEURS.   Since there are $\pi > \mu$ good projects available, we assume that all the bargaining power rests with the short side of the market, financial intermediaries, who thus pay the minimum price acceptable to entrepreneurs.[13] Since entrepreneurs want to consume at time $t = 1$, they would accept any price greater than or equal to the price they can obtain on the exchange, $p(v) < x_h \leq k$. Since intermediaries buy projects that are certain to yield x_h, they obtain a rate of return that exceeds 1 by paying $p(v)$. Hence, at prices $p(v)$, all intermediaries would acquire a project, and thus, in equilibrium, $v = \mu$, and intermediaries pay $p(\mu)$ for the (good) projects they acquire.

Cream-Skimming

Given the equilibrium price $p(\mu)$ and volume of trade $v = \mu$ on the private market, it follows that each financial intermediary has in equilibrium utility of

$$U^{fi} = k + x_h - p(\mu),$$

(10.5)

and uninformed investors have an aggregate expected payoff of

$$V(\mu) = M + (\pi - \mu)x_h + (1 - \pi)x_l - (1 - \mu)p(\mu)$$

(10.6)

The following proposition immediately follows from these observations:

Proposition 1: (a) There exists a measure of financial intermediaries $0 \leq \bar{\mu} \leq \pi$ such that cash-in-the-market holds if and only if $\mu \leq \bar{\mu}$.

(b) If cash-in-the-market-pricing prevails in the exchange, then an increase in the number of financial intermediaries (μ) decreases the aggregate utility of uninformed investors.

If cash-in-the-market pricing prevails, uninformed investors obtain a net surplus from their investments. When μ increases, this surplus diminishes for two reasons. First, the same cash is chasing fewer projects. Second, the quality of the average project bought by uninformed investors in the exchange declines. Notice as well the effect that an increase in the number of financial intermediaries has on the price and returns faced by uninformed investors. First, the returns faced by uninformed investors are given by

$$\bar{R}(\mu) = \frac{\bar{x}(\mu)}{p(\mu)} \geq 1 \tag{10.7}$$

They are strictly greater than 1 whenever cash-in-the-market prevails. In this domain, as the number of financial intermediaries increases, the expected rate of return decreases, $R_\mu < 0$, both on account of the lower expected payoff, as $\bar{x}_\mu < 0$ and on account of the price increase, $p_\mu > 0$, that results from the smaller supply of assets to the exchange. Notice that there are thus two effects associated with an increase in the number of financial intermediaries. First, an increase in the number of financial intermediaries translates into an increase in the cream-skimming taking place in the private market, which lowers the quality of the assets flowing into the uninformed exchange. Second, the overall quantity of assets flowing into the uninformed exchange also goes down, producing an upward pressure on prices.

NOTES

1. For a related theory of informational rent extraction in bargaining, see Glode, Green, and Lowery (2010).

2. William Baumol (1990) and Kevin Murphy, Andrei Shleifer, and Robert Vishny (1991) also consider the question of whether the financial sector attracts too much talent. Their theories, however, do not distinguish between an organized, regulated, and transparent sector and a shadow finance sector.

3. For a dissenting view on hedge fund performance, see Malkiel and Saha (2005).

4. This is a simple way of modeling a downward-sloping demand curve for financial assets. Cross-sectional dispersion in risk aversion among potential buyers of the assets is another.

5. The subscript $_d$ refers to the price of assets in the dealer market (the shadow finance sector).

6. We could have allowed entrepreneurs in need of liquidity to borrow against their projects instead of selling them, but as we argue in Bolton, Santos, and Scheinkman (2011), they would weakly prefer to sell them outright.

7. William Sjostrom (2008) and Kellye Testy (1990) provide a detailed analysis of rule 144A and its ramifications.

8. See Lambe (2007, 40) and Tang (2007, figure 1) for a figure showing private equity capital issuance compared to IPO issuance for the period 2002 to 2006.

9. See Sjostrom (2008) for a description of this deal as well as a discussion of rule 144A in general. For a legal analysis that is contemporaneous with the 1990 adoption of rule 144A, see Testy (1990).

10. A significant fraction of rule 144A issues come from reputable foreign issuers. In addition, the probability of issuing under rule 144A is inversely related to the size of the issuing firm. It is also worth noting that many rule 144A equity issues came from real estate investment trusts (REITs) over the period covered by Tang (2007).

11. However, this limit can be circumvented through institutional investment pools that purchase a single block of shares.

12. As Jean Eaglesham (2011) notes, the American Bankers Association has called for an increase of the ceiling from five hundred to two thousand.

13. As in Bolton, Santos, and Scheinkman (2010), we could assume more generally that some of the bargaining power rests with the entrepreneur and thus that the price paid by intermediaries would be a weighted average of $p(v)$ and x_h.

REFERENCES

Agarwal, Vikas, and Narayan Y. Naik. 2004. "Risks and Portfolio Decisions Involving Hedge Funds." *Review of Financial Studies* 17(1): 63–98.

Allen, Franklin, and Douglas Gale. 1998. "Optimal Financial Crisis." *Journal of Finance* 53(4): 1245–84.

Bank for International Settlements. 2011. "Semiannual Over-The-Counter (OTC) Derivatives Markets Statistics of the Bank of International Settlements." *BIS Quarterly Review*, December. Data available at: http://www.bis.org/statistics/derstats.htm (accessed July 13, 2012).

Baumol, William J. 1990. "Entrepreneurship: Productive, Unproductive, and Destructive." *Journal of Political Economy* 98(5): 893–921.

Bolton, Patrick, Tano Santos, and Jose A. Scheinkman. 2011. "Cream Skimming in Financial Markets." Working Paper 16804. Cambridge, Mass.: National Bureau of Economic Research. Available at: http://papers.ssrn.com/sol3/papers.cfm?abstract_id=1770065 (accessed February 2011).

Eaglesham, Jean. 2011. "U.S. Eyes New Stock Rules: Regulators Move Toward Relaxing Limits on Shareholders in Private Companies." *Wall Street Journal*, April 8.

Edwards, Franklin R. 2004. "New Proposals to Regulate Hedge Funds: SEC Rule 203(b)(3)-2." Working paper. New York: Columbia University Business School. Available at: http://www0.gsb.columbia.edu/faculty/fedwards/papers/New%20Prop%20to%20Reg%20Hedge%20Funds%2001.pdf (accessed August 22, 2012).

Fama, Eugene. 1970. "Efficient Capital Markets: A Review of Theory and Empirical Work." *Journal of Finance* 25(2): 383–417.

Gensler, Gary. 2010. Remarks on OTC Derivatives Reform, delivered at Fordham University College of Business Administration, January 27. Available at: http://www.cftc.gov/PressRoom/SpeechesTestimony/opagensler-25.html (accessed August 22, 2012).

Glode, Vincent, Richard Green, and Richard Lowery. 2010. "Financial Expertise as an Arms' Race." Working paper. Philadelphia: University of Pennsylvania, Wharton School.

Grossman, Sanford, and Joseph Stiglitz. 1980. "On the Impossibility of Informationally Efficient Markets." *American Economic Review* 70(3): 393–408.

Kosowski, Robert, Narayan Y. Naik, and Melvyn Teo. 2007. "Do Hedge Funds Deliver Alpha? A Bayesian and Bootstrap Analysis." *Journal of Financial Economics* 84(1): 229–64.

Lambe, Geraldine. 2007. "Public Versus Private Equity Markets." *The Banker* (September).

Leising, Matthew. 2009. "ISDA Hires Rosen to Fight Obama OTC Derivatives Plan." Bloomberg, July 10.

Malkiel, Burton, and Atanu Saha. 2005. "Hedge Funds: Risk and Return." *Financial Analysts Journal* 61(6): 80–88.

Morgenson, Gretchen. 2010. "Fair Game: It's Not Over Until It's in the Rules." *New York Times,* August 29.

Murphy, Kevin, Andrei Shleifer, and Robert Vishny. 1991. "The Allocation of Talent: Implications for Growth." *Quarterly Journal of Economics* 106(2): 503–30.

Norris, Floyd. 2011. "In Korea, the Game of Trading Has Rules." *New York Times,* August 26.

Scannell, Kara. 2009. "Big Companies Go to Washington to Fight Regulations on Fancy Derivatives." *Wall Street Journal,* July 10.

Sjostrom, William K., Jr. 2008. "The Birth of Rule 144A Equity Offerings." *UCLA Law Journal* 56(2): 409–49.

Story, Louise. 2010. "A Secretive Banking Elite Rules Trading in Derivatives." *New York Times,* December 11.

Swensen, David F. 2005. *Unconventional Success: A Fundamental Approach to Personal Investment.* New York: Free Press.

Tang, Vicki Wei. 2007. "Economic Consequences of Mandatory Disclosure Regulation: Evidence from Rule 144A Equity Private Placements." Working paper. Georgetown University, McDonough School of Business.

Testy, Kellye Y. 1990. "The Capital Markets in Transition: A Response to New SEC Rule 144A." *Indiana Law Journal* 66(1): 233–71.

Tett, Gillian. 2010. "Calls for Radical Rethink of Derivatives Body." *Financial Times,* August 26.

Part IV

Rethinking Financial Regulation

Chapter 11

The Political Economy of Financial Regulation after the Crisis

Robert E. Litan

The 2007 to 2008 financial crisis has spawned a vast and growing literature. This chapter tackles an aspect of the crisis—the political economy of financial regulation before and since the crisis—that up to now has not been extensively discussed.

First, I identify and briefly discuss in broad outlines the many asserted causes of the crisis and the role that regulatory failure played. The chapter argues that several types of regulatory failure—the de facto loosening of capital or leverage standards for banks and the formerly independent investment banks, the inability or unwillingness of the Fed and Congress to regulate subprime lending primarily by state-chartered lenders, and the excessive reliance by regulators on credit ratings—were central "but for" causes, even if one accepts the view that Fed monetary policy was excessively loose in the years running up to the crisis or that federal housing policy excessively promoted home ownership (primarily through the increase in the GSE's affordable housing targets)

Second, the chapter assesses the causes of these regulatory failures: capture or interest group pressures (notably from large banks and the housing industry), ideology, incompetence, or honest mistakes.

Third, the chapter assesses various ideas that have been advanced for improving financial regulation, given the central role it has been given by Dodd-Frank in fixing what went wrong, and in light of the constraints under which regulators necessarily must operate.

The chapter predicts that the next crisis in the United States, if one occurs, is most likely to be triggered by concerns over government deficits, not weakness in the financial sector, though the latter could aggravate any crises triggered by other factors. The chapter was written before the European sovereign debt and banking crises and thus could not take into account those events as they have unfolded during the spring of 2012 and later. Meanwhile, although memories of the 2007 to 2008 financial crisis will fade and financial regulation will continue to be imperfect, Dodd-Frank on the whole was a useful response to a major breakdown in market and regulatory discipline that required correction.

There are so many alleged "causes" of the great financial crisis of 2007 to 2008 that it is easy to lose count. The official body charged with explaining how the crisis happened, the Financial Crisis Inquiry Commission (FCIC), was specifically instructed by the Congress that created it to investigate at least eighteen causes. The final report of the commission did not disappoint.

But this should not be surprising because, in fact, like the multiple culprits in Agatha Christie's *Murder on the Orient Express*, there actually were many "but for" causes of the financial crisis. (That is, "but for" each particular factor, the crisis would not have not occurred or would not have been nearly as severe.) Among these causes were the low interest rate policy of the Federal Reserve, steadily higher "affordable housing" mandates for the two dominant housing government-sponsored enterprises (GSEs), Fannie Mae and Freddie Mac, and greatly mistaken ratings of securities backed by subprime mortgages, to name just a prominent few.

The "but for" cause addressed in this chapter is massive regulatory failure: the weak and weakly enforced capital standards for commercial banks and the formerly independent investment banks, and the essentially nonexistent regulation of subprime mortgage origination by nonbank mortgage lenders.[1] Even with loose monetary policy, aggressive purchases by Fannie and Freddie of subprime mortgage securities, or lax screening by the rating agencies, the crisis either might not have occurred or clearly would have been much less severe if regulators had implemented and enforced much tighter mortgage underwriting standards (so that there would have been far fewer subprime mortgage originations and "synthetic" mortgage securities) or had maintained and enforced sound bank capital standards (so that at least the banking system would have been far less leveraged).

Although I will do a bit of rehashing of the past, my main purpose here is to look ahead and to address a seemingly simple, but actually quite complex, question: From what we know about regulation generally, and about financial regulation in particular, is the broad reregulation mandated by the legislation enacted to prevent future crises, the Dodd-Frank Wall Street Reform and Consumer Protection Act of 2010, likely to "work"? Or is it doomed, like many previous regulatory efforts in finance, to "fail"? This is not strictly speaking a question about economics but essentially a question about political economy, which requires informed guesses about the future behavior of regulators postcrisis based on what is known about their behavior after similar episodes in the past as well as in more normal times.

I concentrate what I hope are plausible guesses primarily about the United States because that is where the crisis began and it is the country I know best. But many, if not most, of the observations I advance here could apply equally well to financial regulation in other countries.

To cut to the chase, even at this writing, roughly two years after the Dodd-Frank Act was passed, it is difficult to provide a definitive answer to the question of whether the broad reregulation mandated by Dodd-Frank will achieve its aims, not only because the future is inherently difficult to predict but because most of the rules mandated by the legislation have yet to be implemented. Nonetheless, I will defend several broad observations.

First, Dodd-Frank will not prevent all future financial crises. As the masterful and deservedly admired survey by Kenneth Rogoff and Carmen Reinhardt (2010) amply documents, financial crises have a long history in a wide variety of economic settings, and it would be foolish to claim that one bill or set of regulations will end the speculative boom-and-bust cycles that lead to them. Instead, the act should be judged in the future by whether it reduces the frequency and severity of financial crises, and if so, whether these benefits outweigh the costs of complying with the act's many regulatory mandates and any reduction in productive financial innovation that these regulations may cause. A related standard is whether a beneficial outcome apparently induced by Dodd-Frank or a similar policy intervention would have occurred anyhow—or would have emerged in a different and better form—through the evolution of market activity.

Second, I believe, and will argue here, that there is a reasonable prospect by the time all of the regulations mandated by the Dodd-Frank Act are written and implemented that under either or both standards, the act will have had a net positive impact on the financial system and the economy. This will be true, in my view, even if, as many suspect and fear, the United States suffers its next (or a future) financial crisis owing to loss of faith by creditors in the ability of the U.S. government to rein in spiraling deficits. Should that happen, the U.S. financial system will be more resilient on account of a number of the major reforms mandated by Dodd-Frank that would not have been generated by market developments alone. Indeed, the added resilience of the banking industry in particular has no doubt cushioned the impact of the weak economy in 2011 on the U.S. financial system.

Nonetheless, the extent to which this relatively sanguine view of Dodd-Frank is borne out depends heavily on the political economy of the behavior of regulators and the entities they regulate—which is the subject of this chapter. To explore it, I begin by briefly summarizing the major theories in the academic literature about why regulation in general exists and some of the features unique to financial regulation. This introductory material sets up the main part of the chapter: an application of these observations to project how the major regulatory mandates embodied in the Dodd-Frank legislation are likely to be set and implemented over time. Where relevant, I also discuss the political economy of the failures in regulation and public policies that led to some of these new mandates.

THE POLITICAL ECONOMY OF REGULATION: A BROAD OVERVIEW

Three broad theories of regulation can be found in the academic literature. Each has a certain bearing on financial regulation, although, as I argue in the next section, other considerations as well figure importantly into the nature and timing of regulation of the financial sector.

The first theory of regulation is the classic one taught in textbooks—that it is invoked and required to fix some "market failure" in the economy and is therefore pursued in the "public interest." Examples include externalities such as pollution, asymmetries in information between buyers and sellers, and monopoly power. In the real world, however, government does not always fix these externalities, or its attempts to do so are not always optimal. The reasons are found in political economy. If the costs of regulating are imposed on a concentrated few, those parties have much greater incentive to resist regulation than do the multitudes of beneficiaries, each of whom may benefit from correcting the market failure by only a tiny amount. The failure by various government agencies to prevent the explosion of securities backed by subprime mortgages that should not have been constructed and sold and whose subsequent defaults imposed huge external costs on the entire economy provides a classic illustration of this problem. Going forward, it will be a challenge for some form of the somewhat discredited "public interest" model of financial regulation to resurface and actually work—that is, for regulators to give consumer and taxpayer interests much more weight and as the economy recovers and risk-taking in multiple forms again becomes the norm, to make rational decisions that pass a benefit-cost test.

A second theory of regulation is that it happens because regulated firms actually want it, largely as a way to raise barriers to others entering their lines of business and thus providing additional competition.[2] This "public choice" theory explained the longtime opposition of the nonbanking industries, especially the securities industry, to increased competition in securities underwriting, which eventually was provided by the elimination of the barriers to bank entry into that activity imposed by the Glass-Steagall Act. The process was launched by the Fed in the late 1980s, continued in the 1990s, and then completed by the passage of the Gramm-Leach-Bliley Act of 1999, but it has been incorrectly blamed by some for the financial crisis eight years later. As the facts clearly show, most subprime mortgages were originated by nonbank mortgage lenders or by investment banks without any connection to commercial banks before the crisis (such as Lehman Brothers, Bear Stearns, Goldman Sachs, Merrill Lynch, and Morgan Stanley). Likewise, commercial banks with no links to investment banks were just as eager to package and underwrite mortgage securities as the few "one-stop shops" (such as Citibank and Bank of America) that were allowed to operate that way after 1999.

The public choice theory, however, fails to explain other aspects of financial regulation because the industry now and always has been very heterogeneous, made up of firms in very different lines of business, of different sizes, and with very different interests. Financial regulators are thus often put in the position of having to mediate these varying interests, as well as those of consumers. The Dodd-Frank rules offer many illustrations of regulators having to play this role.

Third, a close cousin of the public choice model of regulation is the notion of "regulatory capture," which holds that regulated parties strongly influence and even determine how regulators behave toward them. Regulators are susceptible to capture for various reasons: many of them eventually want to work in the industries they oversee, so they do not want to make enemies; regulating is hard work (especially in finance, which is growing increasingly complex); regulated firms have the best information about how they operate; and regulators tend to see employees and representatives of the firms they regulate more frequently than they do consumers or those who purport to represent them. Regulatory capture provides a plausible explanation of why bank supervisors, for example, failed effectively to enforce bank capital standards, as will be elaborated shortly. Avoiding or limiting regulatory capture in the future will be a huge challenge for the regulators charged with writing and enforcing the rules mandated by Dodd-Frank.

SPECIAL FEATURES OF FINANCIAL REGULATION AND THE MOTIVES BEHIND IT

Thirty years ago, former Federal Reserve Bank of New York president (and at the time president of the Federal Reserve Bank of Minneapolis) E. Gerald Corrigan (1982) penned a highly influential piece entitled "Are Banks Special?" For the purposes of this chapter, it is useful to rephrase this question: what makes *financial regulation* (not just banking regulation) special? Two features of financial regulation that are largely independent of the forces affecting regulation more generally deserve mention.

One factor is that because the health of the financial system is inextricably linked with the health of the real sector of the economy, regulators and policymakers are acutely sensitive to how the regulation and supervision of financial institutions at any point affect the real economy. This is not to say that other types of regulation do not have economic effects (good or unwelcome), which is surely true, but only to note that the financial sector (and banking in particular) is especially important, which gives its regulation special importance. It is hard to imagine, for example, that the failure of regulation of any other sector of the economy would have contributed to an economic calamity of the magnitude of the 2007 to 2008 financial crisis and subsequent recession.

Second, unlike environmental, occupational, and other forms of regulation, the failure of financial regulation can cost the government, and thus ultimately taxpayers, money—lots of it. The cost of cleaning up the savings and loan mess during the 1980s, for example, was roughly $150 billion. The ultimate direct cost to the government of the 2008 financial crisis may not be much larger, but when we add in the much more extensive costs borne by the entire economy and the millions of people who lost their jobs as a result of the recession triggered by the crisis, then the cost of this second crisis (including the loss in government tax receipts from reduced economic activity) is really quite staggering.

These two features of financial regulation in particular—the interconnection between finance and the real sector, and the fiscal penalties for getting it wrong—have several noteworthy implications for how financial policymakers and regulators behave.

First, when the financial system gets into trouble, especially depository institutions, policymakers' first impulse typically is to hope and pray that whatever caused the problem—a spike in interest rates, the popping of an asset bubble, a drop in GDP, or any combination of these—will reverse itself and that the problem will be solved without the need for any kind of government funding. In the mid-1980s, for example, U.S. regulators of both the banking and thrift industries exercised massive "regulatory forbearance"—looking the other way when losses on loans and asset holdings were clearly evident to all—in order to avoid lending or adding to the government deposit insurance funds for each industry and using the money to close down, force the merger of, or recapitalize the struggling or failed institutions. Japanese banking regulators did the same thing in the 1990s. And throughout 2010 and 2011, European policymakers and bank regulators also followed the same strategy, until that course became untenable and European leaders agreed in the fall of 2011 on a comprehensive strategy for haircutting Greek sovereign debt, while shoring up the capital positions of weakened European banks. At this writing (August 2012), it is not clear whether these steps will be enough to forestall haircuts on the sovereign debt of other Eurozone countries, or even whether the Eurozone will continue in its present form.

It is not difficult to explain the impulse toward regulatory forbearance. Elected government officials are understandably reluctant to explain to voters the need to pay for the crises in some way, and so delay comes naturally. The storm of protest following the U.S. government's Troubled Asset Relief Program (TARP), which quickly morphed into a massive recapitalization of hundreds of banks during the height of the 2008 financial crisis, clearly validated why regulators would rather hope and pray than confront and pay for cleaning up the financial sector when it runs into trouble. Indeed, the backlash against the perceived "bailout of the banks" (actually their creditors) has been so great (and, at least to this author, somewhat surprising) that policymakers now and in the future are unlikely to forget it.

Second, whether or not government funds have been used in some manner to avert a financial crisis or to diminish its impact, there is a natural tendency for policymakers (by law or by regulation) to tighten regulation and supervision *after* a crisis and to proclaim that such actions will ensure that crises like it "will never happen again." In effect, this is the public policy version of the financial theories associated with the late Hyman Minsky, who noted the tendency of bankers and other private-sector actors to ignore the warning signs of a potential crash in boom times and then to become excessively cautious thereafter (see, for example, Minsky 1978).

We have encountered this pendulum idea in regulation many times, and it is one that I will expand on shortly. The U.S. financial regulatory landscape certainly reflects this impulse to legislate and regulate after crises. The Federal Reserve System was created in 1913 as a direct response to the financial panic of 1907. Many regulatory statutes, including one establishing federal deposit insurance, were enacted after the stock market crash of 1929 and the thousands of bank failures that followed during the Great Depression. New minimum capital standards for depository institutions were legislated after the thrift and banking crises of the 1980s and early 1990s. New financial reporting and corporate governance requirements were added in the Sarbanes-Oxley Act of 2002 after the disclosure of financial scandals at a number of large publicly traded companies. And a sweeping bill like Dodd-Frank, with its numerous regulatory mandates, was a predictable response to the financial crisis of 2008 and the specific and more general government bailouts and rescues mounted thereafter. At each point, some policymakers claimed that these fixes would prevent future reoccurrences of the events that had just occurred. But as Rogoff and Reinhardt (2010) remind us, such claims are never borne out. Still, that does not mean that new rules or institutions cannot delay future crises or reduce their severity, and there is a case to be made that in each of the foregoing examples, that is exactly what happened.

Third, financial actors, usually aided by their attorneys, nonetheless often eventually find their way around the new, more restrictive rules or find clever ways to live with and exploit them. Such never-ending games of "regulatory cat and mouse"—or as Sam Peltzman has called it in a more general context, "progress strikes back"—are not necessarily bad, but they can be counter-productive if the new rules go too far.[3] A well-known historical example is the Depression-era limit on interest paid on bank deposits, a rule that later contributed to the initial thrift crisis of the early 1980s when market interest rates soared and regulation-bound thrifts ("banks" that specialized in extending mortgage loans) faced the loss of much of their deposit funding.

On other occasions, however, financial innovations spawned by efforts to circumvent the effects of regulation that are taken too far and not stopped or slowed by regulators themselves can cause great damage and later help bring about a crisis that leads to another round of even more restrictive regulation. The securitization of subprime mortgages and the eventual adoption of Dodd-Frank is a prime example.

Although securitization of prime mortgages was launched by the federal government and later the two housing government-sponsored enterprises, Fannie Mae and Freddie Mac, the idea was extended in the 1990s and especially during the next decade to subprime mortgages, pushed both by congressionally mandated higher "affordable housing" goals for the GSEs and by aggressive "private-label" securities developed by mortgage lenders and commercial and investment banks. For banks in particular, the ability to package large pools of mortgages and use them to back new kinds of securities (especially collateralized debt obligations, or CDOs) was a way of originating more loans and generating more fees with a given amount of required capital than was possible by simply holding the mortgages in their portfolios. The subprime mortgage process was turbocharged by yet another financial innovation—the ostensibly off-balance-sheet "structured investment vehicle" (SIV) that warehoused these new subprime mortgage securities until they were sold and that was an even bolder and more explicit attempt by commercial banks to avoid the binding effects of bank capital regulation. Along with the ill-advised blessings of the rating agencies that made all these maneuvers possible, these excessively innovative mortgage securitizations led to disastrous results, which in turn led to Dodd-Frank (and thus eventually, surely, to another round of financial innovation, whose developments regulators must closely monitor, of which more will be said shortly).

Fourth, totally apart from whether new rules are written after a crisis, regulators of banks and any other relevant financial institutions, at least for some time, become substantially more risk-averse and thus intensify their supervision. This is the other side of the "policy pendulum" I referred to earlier, and it should not be surprising, for it reflects human nature. When you burn your hand on the stove, you are likely to be much more careful approaching it again. Moreover, regulators typically have longer time horizons than elected officials and thus face the prospect of being blamed by their overseers, a future body of Congress, if they are perceived to have fallen down on the job. (Although when many other things go wrong all at the same time, as they did in the run-up to the 2007 to 2008 financial crisis, regulators can escape much deserved criticism.)

Fifth, intensified financial regulation and supervisory scrutiny nonetheless can later lead to a backlash or regret if economic performance, either in the aggregate or in a specific sector, is widely viewed to be unsatisfactory and regulatory arbitrage has not yet undone the effects of the new regulatory regime. As an example of the former, consider the continuing debate over the wisdom of the Sarbanes-Oxley Act of 2002, enacted to clean up and prevent the kinds of corporate financial reporting scandals typified by Enron and Worldcom. Criticism of the act, especially regarding the more costly than expected auditing requirements in section 404 relating to public firms' "internal controls," began almost as soon as the ink was dry on the bill, and it intensified during the rest of the decade, even through and after the subsequent financial crisis. Responding to concerns about the significant drop-off in initial public offerings (IPOs) in the United States but not elsewhere (notably in Asia) after Sarbanes-Oxley was enacted, the Securities and Exchange Commission (SEC) provided a series of temporary exemptions from section 404 compliance by firms with market capitalizations under $75 million, which Dodd-Frank made permanent. In April 2012, Congress went further by enacting the "JOBS" Act, which among other things, relaxed the SOX exemption for "emerging public companies" with sales less than $1 billion.

Elected officials and political appointees also are tempted to blame sluggish macroeconomic performance on excessively tight bank supervision, even though loan demand typically plummets during recessions or sluggish growth. So far, however, in the two recent episodes when such attacks have been mounted, during the 1991 to 1992 recession and its aftermath and in the several years since the great contraction of 2008 to 2009, bank regulators and their staffs have not buckled. To the contrary, anecdotally one hears complaints from bankers that supervisors have become excessively cautious, which would be consistent with the "pendulum" behavior in both markets and public officialdom. At the same time, when it comes to the tightening of the rules on a *forward-looking basis*—notably the rewriting of the Basel Capital Accord (the main international bank regulatory mechanism, which has been in place since 1989) after the crisis—the pace of the pendulum was explicitly taken into account. The policymakers who negotiated the new Basel standards (who also had supervisory duties) did factor in the weakness of the economy by providing for a lengthy (many academic observers thought too lengthy) transition period before the new standards were to become fully effective.

Sixth, if regulators are going to relax their guard, it is far more likely that they will do so when times are good than when they are bad. This reflects the opposite of the "hot stove" reaction. Again, it is human nature to want to go along for the ride when the economy is humming and to avoid being blamed for taking the pro-verbial "punch bowl away from the party" just when it is in full swing. Of course, this is the primary job of central bankers, and most of them in most countries over the past several decades have tightened when necessary. (Although, again, crit-ics often charge that they are late to do so, since monetary policy authorities also understandably do not want to cause or be blamed for recessions.) But central banks are aided in three very important respects in carrying out their counter-cyclical duties: they typically have a clear legislative or organizational mandate to keep inflation in check, they are generally independent of any elected branch of government (that is certainly true in the United States), and there are clear and well-recognized measures of inflation by which all can judge their success or need to act.

In contrast, there is as yet no such well-recognized "asset bubble" measure or indicator for regulators who since the crisis have been charged (in different ways in different countries) with monitoring and avoiding systemic risk. In theory, the presence of a bubble should be reflected in a high and rising ratio of price to some measure of income, such as housing prices to average incomes, or stock prices in relation to earnings, and so forth. The higher the price or the growth rate in prices relative to some measure of income, presumably the greater the risk that a bubble is forming and the lower the risk of a "false positive"—taking action to "pop" a presumed bubble that is no such thing. Although, as I discuss later in connec-tion with the systemic-risk responsibilities under Dodd-Frank, I support the pub-lication of price-to-income ratios (levels and rates of change) and measures of leverage, among other indicators of bubbles in formation and thus systemic risk,[4] such measures will never establish as much certainty of a systemic problem in the making as an inflation statistic, which is an explicit target of monetary policy and an indicator widely agreed to be best held in check.

Finally—and this is a point I cannot overemphasize—until the financial cri-sis, supporting homeownership and extending it to low- and moderate-income families, many of them minorities, was as close to a national secular religion as America has had. Owning one's own home is almost the essence of the American dream. Raghuram Rajan (2010) also has argued persuasively that policies aimed at raising the homeownership rate, especially those enabling low- and moderate-income families to buy homes with little or no down payments, were ways of off-setting growing income inequalities during the 1990s and the following decade. Hindsight critics of legislators and regulators who made the laundry list of mis-takes that led up to the crisis sometimes overlook how deeply rooted the support for homeownership (including mortgage refinancing) was in Congress and by successive presidents from both political parties, and thus how much political fortitude any of the responsible regulators would have had to display had they taken the housing punch bowl away even as the party was clearly getting out of control.

THE POLITICAL ECONOMY OF REGULATION
UNDER THE DODD-FRANK ACT

It is now time to apply the foregoing general and finance-specific insights about the political economy of regulation to questions surrounding the content of the many rules mandated by Dodd-Frank and, perhaps more important, how they are likely to be enforced over time. In addition, these insights can help explain some of the "but for" causes of the crisis itself.

It is useful to begin by framing these observations in a broader context. The policy debate after the great financial crisis of 2007 to 2008 largely centered on two broad but very different views of the crisis and how to respond to it, which divided almost exactly along party lines in Congress but were also reflected in academic and popular discussions of what happened.

Democrats basically believed that the crisis was due to a combination of failed market discipline (by shareholders, debt holders, management, and rating agencies) and a massive failure in offsetting government regulation of financial institutions—principally banks but also the "shadow banking system" of nonbank mortgage originators, investment banks, money market funds, and insurer hedge funds (such as AIG). The largely Democratic response to these failures was to direct various federal financial regulatory agencies to write a comprehensive set of new rules to prevent all actors in the system from again taking such huge risks.

Republicans, in contrast, argued that market-based governance of finance had not failed, but was hugely distorted by government in at least two major respects. Policymakers in both parties took homeownership too far, in this view, especially by requiring Fannie Mae and Freddie Mac to purchase ever-larger amounts of mortgages extended to increasingly unqualified borrowers. In addition, critics (not just Republicans) aimed their fire at the Federal Reserve for maintaining excessively loose monetary policy, which fueled the demand for housing and created a bubble that eventually popped. The low-interest policy also encouraged investors to search for yield, which they found in CDOs, a new form of mortgage-backed securities (MBSs) backed by subprime loans that were given safe ratings (unwisely) by the rating agencies. On the Republican view, the fixes for the future lay in withdrawing or significantly cutting back housing mandates and subsidies, coupled with monetary policies that would avoid the creation of future bubbles, not with more regulation and supervision by the same regulators who (they agreed here with the Democratic view) failed so badly in the run-up to the crisis.

Although the Democratic narrative of the crisis prevailed in the legislative debate that led to the enactment of Dodd-Frank, the debate between the two views goes on. After the midterm 2010 congressional elections, Republicans took control of the House and gained a large enough minority in the Senate to prevent cloture on debate under the Senate's sixty-vote majority rule. They have used that new power to hold down appropriations and intensify oversight of the federal financial regulatory agencies charged with writing the more than 240 rules mandated by Dodd-Frank. This strategy has contributed to the delayed issuance of most of these rules (which, to be fair, were so numerous and complex that they would have been late in any event, though the shortage of money has made the problem worse).

In what follows I provide a brief synopsis of the major regulatory mandates of Dodd-Frank, including their rationale for being in the bill and the design and implementation issues that the affected parties, the media, the Congress, and perhaps a future administration will continue to debate. Readers interested in further details can consult other chapters in this volume and excellent summaries elsewhere.[5] After the description of each regulatory mandate, I hazard some guesses, informed by the prior discussion about the political economy of regulation in general and about finance in particular, as to how well each component of Dodd-Frank is likely to perform, and for how long. Along the way, where relevant, I apply some of the insights advanced earlier in the chapter to help explain the problems that led to each particular new mandate.

Bank Capital Rules

The cornerstone of any sound financial regulatory system is effective minimum standards for bank capital, since shareholders must have their own "skin in the game" to have incentives to deter excessive risk-taking by bank managers, while the government, as insurer of last resort, must know that banks have a cushion to absorb losses.[6] The U.S. and international bank standards failed miserably, however, to prevent banks both from originating unsound mortgages and, more importantly, packaging them into complex securities and selling them to other investors, including some of the largest banks' own ostensibly off-balance affiliates. In the run-up to the crisis, the banks felt compelled for reputational and legal reasons to rescue these affiliates and thus absorb their losses, which contributed significantly to the banks' own capital shortfalls. Likewise, securities regulators permitted investment banks during this period to increase their leverage, which put these institutions at greater risk of failure (as shareholders of Bear Stearns and Lehman Brothers learned to their dismay when the first was forced into the arms of JPMorgan and the second was permitted to fail) as the subprime mortgage crisis unfolded later in the decade.

What accounts for these massive failures in regulation? Complacency and misplaced trust in private-sector bank management certainly played a large part. The strengthened bank capital rules after the banking debacles of the 1980s and early 1990s worked for a long time: bank failures stayed low, and reported bank capital ratios kept increasing. Given these trends, bank regulators not surprisingly gave the benefit of the doubt to the banks they regulated; securities regulators acted in the same way when they permitted investment banks to escalate their leverage ratios in 2004.

As for the foray of the large banks into the subprime mortgage business, it was primarily done indirectly—through loans to nonbank mortgage originators that later had to be rescued or went out of business, or through the creation of the SIVs that were ostensibly off the banks' balance sheets. Only a thorough history yet to be written will uncover how much and when regulators knew of the SIVs and the circumvention of the capital rules they represented (illustrating the classic "cat and mouse" problem in finance referred to earlier). Furthermore, as long as the economy was expanding, virtually everyone, including regulators, bankers, and investors, was seduced into believing that residential real estate price inflation, which made the subprime mortgage bubble possible, would continue at some pace. Hardly anyone believed that home prices would eventually plunge as rapidly, deeply, and broadly throughout the country as began to happen in 2006. As George Akerlof and Robert Shiller (2009) have described it so well, it is consensus views like these that have created bubbles in the past and that account for the real estate bubble that led to the crisis.

When the bubble popped, of course, it turned out that much of the reported bank capital was illusory (for those banks that had large commitments to their SIVs) or insufficient (especially in the case of investment banks). Dodd-Frank responded to the bank capital problem, in particular, by requiring federal banking regulators to set new, higher capital standards, which the relevant agencies have since done, in coordination with other advanced countries that are party to the Basel Capital Accord. Roughly speaking, the new standards require three times as much capital as was required by the ones they replaced, but this requirement is to be formally phased in over an eight-year period (and thus is not fully effective until 2019). U.S. regulators, however, have effectively already implemented the new standards by making clear to the largest U.S. banks that they cannot pay dividends unless they can prove that they will be in compliance with the Basel rules by 2013.[7]

It is safe to say that higher bank capital requirements would not have occurred through market pressure alone or without action by the Basel Committee (which, given the magnitude of the crisis, would have acted whether or not Dodd-Frank was enacted). I can write this with confidence because of the vigorous objections mounted by the banking industry to the higher standards, which confirms that bank managements were not being pressed after the crisis by their shareholders or creditors to enlarge their capital cushions.

Although the Basel standards also call for additional capital to be maintained by "systemically important" banks, this term has not been standardized across countries. (Dodd-Frank set the threshold at $50 billion in assets for U.S. banks.) Nor is there a uniform number for this capital surcharge or add-on, but rather a favored range of 1 percent to 2.5 percent of risk-weighted assets.[8] The largest U.S. banks strongly opposed application of the systemic-risk surcharge by U.S. bank regulators given the other measures in Dodd-Frank aimed at ending taxpayer bailouts in the future (and discussed further later in the chapter), but ultimately the Basel Committee rejected the banks' views and agreed on the 1 to 2.5 percent range in the late fall of 2011.

In my view, the large banks should count themselves lucky. The systemic-risk surcharge can be viewed as a tax on the externalities imposed on the rest of the financial system (and potentially taxpayers if orderly liquidation mechanisms in the act do not work as planned) caused by the failure of large and/or highly interconnected banks. A number of prominent analysts, including former Fed chairman

Alan Greenspan, urged during the debate on Dodd-Frank that the largest banks be broken up to solve this problem (see also Johnson and Kwak 2011). Calls for the breakup of the largest banks—surprisingly, from elected officials or those seeking election in both political parties—continue at this writing. The large banks and their supporters in Congress (and the administration) had sufficient clout to resist any efforts at immediate breakup through legislative fiat, although Dodd-Frank gave regulators that power under the "living will" provisions of the act (to be discussed shortly), largely because supporters of the final bill could point to the systemic-risk charge as a substitute for breakup. Without a meaningful surcharge in place, large U.S. banks would have had a more difficult time convincing legislators to resist calls for breakups.

Ultimately, even more important than the specific capital standards themselves is how they will be enforced over time. For example, will regulators be able to thwart banks from coming up with variations of the SIVs that were used to warehouse CDOs but that eventually they felt compelled to absorb? So far the evidence suggests a positive answer to this question, but we are only a few years out from the crisis. We know from Minsky's pendulum theory of finance that memories are short, especially as new people come into organizations that got burned in the last crisis. The same is true for regulators, who will have to be highly vigilant in the years ahead to prevent dangerous SIV-like financial innovations, as well as new games that surely will be played with the new Basel bank standards.

A related challenging question is whether regulators will consistently compel banks to set aside realistic provisions for future losses on their loans and other assets that are charged against capital. As suggested earlier, recent financial history does not provide a lot of comfort that this posture can be maintained indefinitely, especially when the financial system suffers shocks from the real economy or asset markets. Indeed, European banking regulators, despite adopting new "stress tests" for their banks, have gone easy on their banks during the sovereign debt crisis afflicting Greece and other (mostly southern) European countries. Once the European sovereign debt crisis is resolved, and if the U.S. economy can avoid another major recession or asset bubble during at least the phase-in of the new Basel standards, perhaps the larger capital cushions mandated by those standards will reduce the likelihood that regulators will have to return to the time-honored practice of forbearance for some time thereafter (though most assuredly, not likely forever). But this may also be wishful thinking.

Systemic-Risk Regulation

Until the recent financial crisis, all bank safety and soundness regulation in all countries was directed at ensuring the financial health of individual banks rather than the financial system as a whole. In theory, central banks (including the Federal Reserve Board in the United States) had responsibility for the latter through their mandate to provide liquidity to banks and nonbanks in temporary financial distress. But no central bank, to my knowledge, nor any other regulatory agency of the U.S. government, had any direct authority to set rules to prevent events that could lead to systemwide distress.

Dodd-Frank changes that by establishing a new federal interagency body, the Financial Stability Oversight Council (FSOC), to monitor systemic risk and to recommend rules to minimize it. The FSOC is also charged with designating nonbank systemically important financial institutions (SIFIs), a designation that banking organizations with over $50 billion in assets are given by Dodd-Frank itself. With input from the Fed, the FSOC is supposed to define what additional capital any SIFI (bank or nonbank) is required to have (presumably, but not necessarily, to be consistent with the Basel standards at least with respect to banks). The FSOC also should be aided by the analytical capabilities of the new Office of Financial Research (OFR), which Dodd-Frank established within the Treasury Department.

Although there was broad support among Dodd-Frank advocates for charging some new entity explicitly with systemic-risk monitoring and prevention responsibilities, there was much debate over which governmental body should be given this authority. Initially, there was some support for making the Fed responsible, given its large staff and lender-of-last-resort tools, but as the debate over the bill wore on, the Fed's reputation was somewhat tarnished by its own admitted regulatory lapses in the run-up to the crisis and by the controversy over the Fed's participation in (or even orchestration of) the bailouts of the creditors of large, troubled financial institutions. In the end, the decision was made, driven by supporters and even ultimately some opponents of Dodd-Frank, to lodge the systemic-risk authority instead in an interagency body composed of all the key federal financial regulators, a representative of state insurance regulators, and the chairman of the Federal Reserve, with the FSOC chair occupied by the secretary of Treasury. As a practical matter, however, because of its large staff and expertise, the Fed is likely to be the primary or lead agency on the FSOC.

It has already become evident that the new FSOC will be slowed in reaching decisions by turf battles among its regulator-members. (I initially preferred giving the Fed systemic-risk responsibility in order to avoid this precise problem, despite the Fed's prior regulatory failures, and I question whether any new, truly independent systemic-risk monitor would have been given the resources and could have had the stature to carry out this function.) At this writing, although regulators have set forth the criteria for determining which nonbanks should be on the SIFI list, the actual names of the institutions have not yet been announced. Nor is it clear how much additional information from nonbanks the FSOC, through its regulator-members, will require or what, if any, countercyclical regulatory measures it will adopt. There also remains great skepticism about the ability of the FSOC and its two analytical arms (the new Office of Financial Research and the Fed) to identify bubbles in formation and then to "prick them" in a timely and least-cost manner.

Perhaps an even more fundamental problem is that the FSOC, like any body given such a charge, has the inherent problem of proving its worth. The FSOC never will be able to convincingly identify systemic crises that its actions avoided or reduced in severity in the same way that the Department of Homeland Security

(DHS) theoretically can disclose (though perhaps in confidence) the potential terrorist acts that it has prevented. To make matters worse, if future systemic crises do arise, requiring future bailouts (despite the best efforts of regulators to prevent them), it is virtually certain that Congress will blame the FSOC for not being sufficiently proactive.

This inherent public relations problem is a severe one, and it makes the job of the FSOC much more difficult than pursuing countercyclical monetary policy (specifically, raising interest rates to combat inflationary pressure). Earlier I suggested that the only way I know of to minimize this problem is for the FSOC to agree upon and publish "bubble indicators"—the more the better—that are meant to highlight, *in a probabilistic fashion only,* the potential danger of a future systemic event caused by increases in asset prices or credit aggregates (in relation to measures of income) above historical norms. Publishing such indicators at least should help make transparent the decisions that the FSOC may take to reduce potential systemic risks—such as raising capital standards, margin requirements, or minimum loan-to-value (LTV) ratios—that inevitably will be resisted by the financial sector and by borrowers.

To be sure, no single systemic-risk indicator or set of indicators will be perfect, and for that reason the FSOC and its members will need to apply some judgment. Inevitably, there will be false positives—that is, actions that would slow down the economy and might not, in retrospect, be justified. In addition, in light of the huge costs of the 2007 to 2008 crisis, it may be more difficult for the FSOC to *lower* capital requirements or LTV ratios in a weak economy—for fear of being blamed for thereby having contributed to a subsequent crisis—than to raise those standards. Nonetheless, precisely because of the scale of the costs of the 2007 to 2008 crisis, I believe that the benefits of averting such events in the future are likely to exceed these very real costs and risks. It is better that some body (even one divided by turf battles) be given the chance—indeed, the responsibility—to try to monitor and help avert those outcomes than to have no entity charged with these duties at all.

Financial Derivatives, Clearinghouses, and Quasi-Exchanges

Arguably among the most important provisions of Dodd-Frank are those aimed at pushing financial derivatives previously traded off exchanges (over-the-counter [OTC]) onto more organized trading platforms and through central clearinghouses. The opaque nature of the credit default swap (CDS) market in particular, and the fact that such instruments were "cleared" bilaterally solely between the two parties involved (buyer and seller), were the features that led the Treasury and the Fed to bail out the creditors of AIG, whose derivatives subsidiary could not honor the hundreds of billions of dollars of CDS commitments it had made after Lehman Brothers was permitted to fail in September 2008. The authorities feared that creditor or counterparty losses from an AIG failure could have caused financial havoc.

The New York Fed, at the urging of then Fed chairman Greenspan, began working in 2005 on ways to reduce systemic risks in OTC derivatives markets, first by requiring the major dealers to clean up their disheveled paper-based methods of keeping track of trades, and later by urging the creation of a clearinghouse for such trades, the use of which was voluntary. AIG did not use the facility, nor did many of the dealers, and it is not difficult to understand why: they were making more by not having to post margin to a third party. In addition, the major dealers had no interest in seeing their bids and asks, which were communicated in private over the phone, made public, although they did see some benefit in having actual transaction prices reported after the fact (typically a day late) so that market participants would have at least some benchmark for conducting deals. On the whole, however, the New York Fed apparently believed that it lacked the power to mandate clearing or pre- and post-trade transparency, while the handful of bank dealers in these markets had no financial incentive to make them more transparent. They were making too much money from opacity (see Litan 2010).

In principle, the clearinghouse mandate for standardized derivatives in Dodd-Frank, coupled with requirements that trades be conducted in more transparent, exchange-like venues ("swaps execution facilities" [SEFs] under the act), should make an AIG-like episode—a derivatives counterparty with huge obligations it cannot honor—far less likely in the future. In addition, the Commodity Futures Trading Commission (CFTC) is charged under the act with making sure that the clearinghouses set adequate capital requirements for clearing members and margin or collateral requirements for trading parties, whether or not their instruments are sufficiently standardized to be cleared centrally. The CFTC also is charged with setting rules for how the SEFs will operate—specifically, the extent to which derivatives bids (offers to buy) and asks (offers to sell) can or must be posted electronically on some type of platform or can continue to be relayed over the telephone between the parties (as is the case now) and how transactions will be reported (more frequently than is now the case would be preferable).

These technical rules are crucially important because they will have a large impact on what up to now has been a highly profitable business in a highly concentrated market dominated by only a handful of major bank dealers. Moves toward transparency and central clearing will squeeze some, if not much, of the "spread" between the bids and asks and thus reduce dealers' profits. Little wonder, then, that the major dealer banks have been fighting and urging their allies in Congress to combat and slow down the issuance of any new derivatives rules, including those that might restrict the ability of dealer banks to control the clearinghouses, through voting or governance. Likewise, "end-users" of financial derivatives that use them primarily for hedging purposes were able to convince Congress to carve out an exemption for them from margin and other rules, and they have continued their campaign to convince regulators who must write the specs on the exemption to keep it as wide as possible. All of this opposition clearly and directly contradicts the public choice notion that regulated parties want regulation, though it is consistent with the view that they want to "capture" the agencies by delaying or substantially watering down the content of the rules.

Regulators acknowledge a further complication: U.S. authorities are constrained by how other countries attempt to achieve the same derivatives goals embodied in Dodd-Frank—that is, moving more of them on exchanges and through central clearinghouses. If U.S. rules make derivatives trading more difficult or more expensive, counterparties will gravitate to offshore markets in Europe and Asia to conduct these trades. Overall financial risk will have been shifted, not reduced. Mindful of this problem, U.S. regulators have been negotiating with their counterparts abroad to harmonize or achieve rough parity in the rules. As a practical matter, however, since other countries historically have looked to the United States to lead, it is likely (though not a sure thing) that once U.S. regulators set rules, other key nations will follow.

Harmonized rules will not prevent the proliferation of national or at least multiple clearinghouses for different kinds of financial derivatives originated in different geographic markets. National pride and an eagerness to capture clearing business motivate the formation of multiple clearinghouses, and competition among them can be healthy, up to a point, because it encourages efficiencies and innovation in clearing services. Nonetheless, multiple clearinghouses make derivatives clearing more expensive, since parties doing business through one clearinghouse are unable to set off their trade obligations (at least not with current technologies and under current rules) against obligations originating in other venues. In addition, multiple clearinghouses may compete with one another through the laxity of their credit terms, which may not be caught by vigilant regulators monitoring margin requirements. There still is some optimal number of clearinghouses greater than one that will both encourage competition yet afford parties cost savings by consolidating their clearing through just a few venues. Although it is extremely unlikely that governments will be able to agree to stop the proliferation of national or even subnational clearinghouses, over time economic forces will drive consolidation for cost reasons, just as has happened with exchanges.[9]

And so, in the end, the derivatives reforms mandated by Dodd-Frank eventually should make the derivatives market safer, more transparent, and less susceptible in the future to events like the collapse of AIG. Indeed, as of August 2011, there was already some evidence that derivatives markets had moved in the right direction since Dodd-Frank, reflected in $14 billion of new collateral pledged to back up CDS transactions in particular (Leising 2011). More progress will depend on the content and timing of the various new rules the CFTC is charged with issuing. Already the agency has been delayed twice in issuing its main body of new rules, which at this writing are not expected to be issued until late 2012.

There are two further caveats that should be noted. One is that because they concentrate risk in themselves, clearinghouses need to be closely watched and regulated—specifically, to ensure that they have adequate capital and liquidity and loss-sharing, features that Dodd-Frank charges the CFTC with overseeing. As has been commonly quipped, when you put all your eggs in one basket, you need to watch that basket very carefully. The importance of this challenge was underscored in November 2011 by the failure of MF Global, which required the Chicago Mercantile Exchange (CME) to cover much of that institution's clearing losses. Nonetheless, I believe this is a manageable issue. Clearinghouses for banks, stock exchanges, and futures and options exchanges have long existed. Adding derivatives clearinghouses to the list, which the FSOC has done, should not pose an exceptional challenge for regulators.

Second, the clearing and quasi-exchange requirements of Dodd-Frank apply only to "standardized" derivatives, which should cover a healthy majority of interest rate, foreign currency, and credit default swaps (assuming that foreign currency swaps are included in any final rules, which at this point is uncertain). Dealers and private actors can still engage in customized or "bespoke" transactions outside of these requirements, although the CFTC does have authority to set margin requirements for these deals. Given the opportunity cost of posting margin (the interest forgone on the securities eligible for collateral), end-users and dealers will continue pressing the commission to keep these margin requirements low. Depending on how this dynamic plays out, the margins could be set high enough to discourage the proliferation of customized derivatives (not necessarily a bad thing), or so low that such proliferation happens and leads to future AIGs. Only time will tell.

Finally, the whole debate over derivatives regulation raises a fundamental question: Are these financial products even desirable? Do they not legitimate a casino-like activity that simply moves money from one set of parties to another set, with the "house" (the dealers through whom these deals are currently arranged) collecting the equivalent of vigorish (the "vig") in the process? I am not that cynical, though I certainly recognize that betting can get out of control and is socially dangerous if the bettors do not have the means to honor their debts and if cumulatively those debts (which may be leveraged) are large.

Derivatives—financial instruments whose values are "derived" from some other underlying assets, such as futures contracts—have been around for several centuries, and they arose for very good economic reasons. In a world of uncertainty, some actors (farmers, for example) wanted to lock in the prices they would get in the future for their crops or what they would have to pay for their supplies. More recent financial derivatives perform similar functions, allowing different parties to "hedge" against price fluctuations in an underlying asset. This is true even of the infamous (in some quarters) credit default swaps. These instruments permitted holders of bonds to hedge their bets, though they also gave other parties the ability to gamble on the possibility that bondholders would go bankrupt. CDS prices have performed a very valuable function: providing additional signals of financial distress that *may* be more accurate than the thinly traded bonds underlying these particular derivatives.[10]

Still, many raise questions about the social desirability of letting parties who do not actually *own the underlying assets* bet on their value, or their demise. As some have put, CDSs are the equivalent of insurance policies on other people's houses. We do not let people do that, presumably because it would give insurance holders incentives to commit arson. Why allow its equivalent in the financial world?

I see CDS speculators no differently than speculators in other kinds of financial instruments, such as stocks (where short sellers, for example, often do not own the stocks they are selling but instead borrow them temporarily from someone else). The fact is that hedging markets do not work as well without speculators as with them. Unless speculators are willing to take the other side of trades, hedgers may not have anyone to deal with, or at least fewer parties to deal with. Speculators, who do not always take one side of a trade or the other, add much liquidity to derivatives markets, which narrows spreads and makes it easier for the true hedgers to conduct their trades. In turn, hedging, like insurance, serves an important social function by reducing financial risks for those engaged in hedging (much like limited liability reduces risks for entrepreneurs).

A major social problem arises, however, when speculators or hedgers cannot pay off. That is the central lesson of AIG, and Dodd-Frank applies it by mandating central clearing, backed by regulation of the margins and capital of the parties, where the contracts are standardized. This, to me, is the right answer, although I would hope that regulators eventually require more pre- and post-trade transparency and actual exchange trading of these same instruments. Precisely because these moves will reduce the "vig" collected by the major dealers, these moves no doubt will be strongly resisted. We will learn in the coming years whether the public interest theory or the capture theory of regulation of these markets better explains what eventually happens.

A final complex question turns on the use of derivatives to create "synthetic products," such as collateralized debt obligations, which were really bundles of derivatives rather than of mortgages. Derivatives therefore in this instance became the underlying instruments that helped inflate a bubble in securities that should not have occurred. Since the crisis, the market for these synthetic instruments has collapsed, but the fact that derivatives were used in a way that contributed to the crisis provides yet another illustration of the importance of regulators keeping a vigilant eye out for potentially dangerous financial innovations that can turn out to be destructive.[11]

Failure Resolution and Living Wills

To the general public not well tuned in to the fine points of financial regulation, clearly the most disturbing part of the financial crisis was the government bailout of the creditors of large "too big to fail" financial institutions—nonbanks (especially AIG but also Fannie Mae and Freddie Mac) even more so than banks. The authorities who mounted these bailouts clearly did not like what they were doing but felt it necessary to protect these creditors in order to prevent a wider financial panic. The only exception to the pattern was the refusal of the Fed and the Treasury to protect the creditors of Lehman Brothers, a decision that was much criticized for aggravating the crisis at its most sensitive time (mid-September 2008).

So when legislators turned to writing a reform package, a top priority was finding a way to make it much more difficult to grant such bailouts again—to make bailouts the rule rather than the exception. After much wrangling, the solution they came to was to provide a banklike resolution process for nonbanks; they even gave authority for executing it to the Federal Deposit Insurance Corporation (FDIC), which has long been charged with "resolving" problems with troubled banks (forcing their merger, their recapitalization, or their liquidation) at "least cost" to the bank deposit insurance fund.

In brief, Dodd-Frank gives the Treasury secretary, with the approval of two-thirds of the members of the Federal Reserve Board and two-thirds of the directors of the FDIC, the authority to appoint the FDIC as the receiver for *any* troubled non-bank financial institution (not just those deemed by the FSOC to be systemically important). Among other things, the deciding authorities must determine that undertaking such action "would avoid or mitigate serious adverse effects on the financial stability or economic conditions of the United States." Unless the board of the troubled entity consents, the Treasury secretary must gain approval, under an expedited process, for the receivership from the federal district court in the District of Columbia. The FDIC nonetheless is instructed to resolve the institution under a *presumption* that priority claims under the bankruptcy code apply, which means that all unsecured creditors *except derivatives counterparties* can be expected to suffer some loss. The FDIC also has the authority to recover (or "claw back") pay from the senior executives and directors who were "substantially responsible" for the failure of the institution. In sum, then, Dodd-Frank puts all unsecured creditors (except derivatives counterparties) and management of all large, important financial institutions, bank and nonbank, at risk if the institution fails.[12]

There is another escape hatch, but it is a narrow one. The act gives the FDIC the authority to provide a wide variety of temporary or up-front financial assistance to the troubled entity, in order to ease its resolution, and if necessary to borrow from the Treasury, but unsecured creditors still can receive no more than they have a right to under liquidation, while management must be removed. The secretary of the Treasury can establish a resolution fund to pay for any borrowings the FDIC might need, financed by assessments on large banks and systemically important financial institutions. Meanwhile, the Fed is prohibited under the act from using its lender-of-last-resort authority under section 13(3) of the Federal Reserve Act to bail out any specific institutions or their creditors. In combination, these provisions should prevent any *taxpayer* bailouts of individual institutions or their creditors in the future. (It is quite possible, however, that some creditors may be better protected by the resolution fund than they would be in bankruptcy.) Whether all of this will work as designed cannot be known until the process is tested in a future crisis, but it is about as airtight as could be constructed while giving federal authorities at least some flexibility to use cash, as needed, to ease any temporary liquidity problems associated with the resolution of a large troubled financial institution.

Will all these anti-bailout provisions allow a future financial crisis to get out of hand? Again, we cannot know until the process is tested, but the Fed still can provide generalized liquidity to the market if it sees a panic developing. My hunch is that this will be sufficient, but I cannot know this with certainty—and neither can anyone else.

Dodd-Frank also anticipates future financial troubles by requiring all systemically important financial institutions to have resolution plans, or "living wills," that enable a receiver or trustee to dismantle or liquidate them at least cost. This provision is especially important to provide a guide to resolving financial troubles at large, complex financial organizations that have hundreds, if not thousands, of subsidiaries and affiliates, often domiciled in different countries. The FDIC approved its living will rule in September 2011, but no rule in this area can become final until the Federal Reserve Board also acts. The FDIC rule phases in its requirement, beginning with the largest banks, effective July 2012 and requires annual updating of the plans (plus updates within forty-five days of any material changes in bank operations).

Although no one should be under the illusion that the presence of a living will eliminates all creditor disputes over priority in claims, the mere act of having such a document prepared—as well as signed off on regularly by both the board of the holding company or top-level legal entity in charge of the organization and the appropriate regulators—helps to focus attention on legal structures that clearly delineate creditor priority.[13] Simply having to go through the exercise could help reduce the costs of resolving the institution in the event of failure.

As already noted, the living will provisions give the regulators the "nuclear option" of forcing the organization to divest certain operations or even break up entirely if the resolution plan is not deemed satisfactory. To be sure, it is doubtful that regulators would ever take such a step. Nonetheless, the mere threat that they could roll out this weapon gives the authorities powerful leverage to force large, highly interconnected entities either to reduce their complexity (often constructed for tax reasons) or at least to provide clearer guidance to a future receiver or trustee in bankruptcy.

Large financial institutions surely had mixed motives in the debate about all these provisions. Those that were currently well managed did not want ever to be in the position of having to pay in the future for the mistakes of their competitors. In addition, large financial institutions could not have been happy about the compliance costs associated with the living will requirements in particular. Given the public furor over the creditor bailouts during the financial crisis, this is one instance in which philosophical objections to future bailouts and wider public revulsion about that prospect were the deciding factors. Elected officials and regulators clearly wanted to be able to say there would be "no more bailouts" in the future, though regulators and financial policymakers still wanted the ability to tap some source of cash assistance to douse any financial fires if necessary. In the end, everyone got what they wanted (although those who voted against the bill wanted to eliminate any possibility of cash-assisted resolutions of any nonbank financial enterprise).

Rating Agency Reform

The three major credit rating agencies—Standard & Poor's, Moody's, and Fitch—were high on the list of villains in the financial crisis, and deservedly so. CDOs and the subprime mortgage-backed securities collateralizing them would never have been sold in the massive volumes they were—if at all—without the AAA blessings conferred on them (unwisely, given the absence of sufficient historical data to justify such a high rating) by the rating agencies. In turn, without buyers of the securities, subprime mortgages would not have been originated in the first place.

There are no easy answers to fixing the rating agency problem, however, since in principle, investors want due diligence performed by third parties but have been reluctant to pay for ratings information that, in an age of instant communication, is quickly disseminated to the public. As a result, the agencies have for several decades charged the issuers of securities for ratings and continue to do so. Despite the previous efforts and the new mandates (under Dodd-Frank) to erect and maintain Chinese walls between their sales and rating staffs, the agencies still inevitably have major conflicts of interest, since they make more money the more securities they rate; in particular their high ratings facilitated the issuance of large volumes of securities backed by subprime mortgages.

Dodd-Frank nonetheless contains several constructive policy changes that could improve matters going forward. First, the act authorizes suits against the rating agencies for reckless ratings, under the same standards that have been in place for investor suits against accounting firms or securities analysts. Up to now, the rating agencies have been insulated from suit by court rulings validating their claims that ratings are opinions or speech protected by the First Amendment. It may take the courts some time to sort out whether the new liability provisions of Dodd-Frank are constitutionally permissible, but if they are, liability exposure should induce the agencies to be far more careful (though it also may drive them to be excessively cautious).

Second, the act charges the SEC with issuing rules that require the rating agencies to provide users with more information about the methods and data they use to generate their ratings and to satisfy the SEC that they have adhered to the methodologies they claim to use. In addition, the SEC must issue rules directing the agencies to regularly publish the performance of their ratings. Collectively, these provisions better arm users of ratings with useful information about them, which can only improve the efficiency of the markets for rated securities. So far there appears to be no resistance, even by the agencies, to any of these reforms.

What is proving to be more controversial, however, at least among regulators, is a third set of reforms: the provisions requiring the removal of federal statutory and regulatory mandates that ratings be used as a standard of creditworthiness and that an alternative standard (not specified in the act) be substituted. Thus, for example, federal rules limit money market funds to investing only in investment-grade securities, while the Basel bank capital standards for years have based (and continue to base) their risk weightings for most banks on ratings assigned to their loans and securities.[14] In the years preceding the crisis, the ratings mandates were criticized by a number of scholars for artificially boosting the demand for ratings, while giving investors a false sense of comfort that the ratings made additional due diligence unnecessary before purchasing (or selling) the rated securities. But as the proposed rules to implement these provisions have been made public, banking regulators have expressed reservations, unsure of what alternatives to put in the place of the ratings. Somewhat surprisingly, the rating agencies themselves have not opposed the removal of the mandates; so far, having been chastened by their role in the crisis, they seem willing to compete to prove their usefulness going forward.

They are likely to get the chance. The agencies' prominent role in the ratings of sovereign debt of both the troubled European economies and of the United States during the summer 2011 debate over raising the U.S. debt ceiling—and especially the downgrade of U.S. Treasury debt by S&P immediately after a ten-year $2.1 billion deficit reduction package was enacted—has provoked a backlash at least in the United States against the agencies that should put a stop to any efforts to roll back the Dodd-Frank requirements that ratings be deemphasized by the regulatory agencies. The swift and negative reaction to the S&P downgrade certainly disproves the claim by some that, in the wake of the agencies' failures during the mortgage crisis, they have become irrelevant. To the contrary, investors at least initially treated the S&P action as quite serious, as U.S. equities fell roughly 5 percent on the Monday following the downgrade; equity prices recovered quickly by the end of that week (though they would be falling the next), while the yields on Treasuries actually *fell* as scared investors ran to the safest asset they could find, even one that had just been downgraded. How the agencies would react to the failure in late November 2011 of the congressional "Super-Committee" to come up with $1.2 trillion in ten-year deficit reduction was also very much in the news around the time of this event. In any event, S&P and the other agencies seem to be betting that investors will continue to want their ratings, although the agencies still will probably have to rely on the "issuer-pays" business model to stay in business.

There is, of course, one final nagging question about the rating agencies: why did market participants or regulators not scrutinize their ratings of securities based on subprime mortgages more closely in the run-up to the crisis? For investors, the answer is easy: they simply assumed that the agencies knew what they were doing and they saw no need to pay for their own due diligence. Regulators at the SEC almost surely believed the same thing, but even if they had not, the SEC was spread thin—it was trying to execute its many other responsibilities, and not so well, as the Madoff affair certainly showed—and in any event, the SEC was specifically prohibited from being substantively involved in the ratings process. Even so, surely few, if any, at the SEC believed that they had the knowledge to second-guess what the rating firms were doing, especially as long as real estate prices were rising and mortgage default rates were low. What is more troubling is that banking regulators around the world continue to mandate the use of ratings under the Basel capital standards, even though regulators have to know that ratings of mortgage securities in particular are based on sample periods without significant housing deflation.

Consumer Financial Protection

One of the sharpest dividing lines between supporters and opponents of Dodd-Frank centered on the question of whether many subprime borrowers were duped by unscrupulous, predatory lenders or brought their troubles on themselves—and by implication the rest of the financial system—by borrowing far too much for houses they could not afford. In the end, the first view prevailed and culminated in the establishment of the new Consumer Financial Protection Bureau (CFPB), charged with reducing the complexity of consumer protection rules for virtually all financial products (except insurance, securities, and derivatives products regulated by other state or federal agencies) and with enforcing federal financial protection laws. In a nod to the tougher antipredatory laws in some states that federal authorities had sought to preempt before the crisis, Dodd-Frank generally did not give preemption authority to the new bureau; thus, with some exceptions, states are now free to adopt even tougher financial consumer protection laws. Most unusually and controversially, the act located the new agency within the Federal Reserve but gave it budgetary independence from Congress by funding it from earnings of the Fed. The CFPB director also sits on the potentially powerful FSOC, which retains authority, by a two-thirds vote, to set aside any rule established by the bureau.

The bureau has been the flashpoint of continuing controversy from the day Dodd-Frank became law (July 21, 2011), but especially after Republican gains in the 2010 midterm elections. The banking industry, especially the larger banks with multistate operations, has been very wary of having its consumer functions regulated both by a potentially aggressive federal regulator and by fifty separate state regulators. The creation of the CFPB thus does not fit well with the public choice theory of regulation, although eventually it could be captured by a more industry-friendly director. Republicans generally have continued to oppose the creation of the bureau on philosophical grounds, and they have been especially critical of its structure (a single director rather than a multimember commission) and its exemption from the normal congressional appropriations process. Indeed, through the fall of 2011, Republican leaders in the Senate had refused to confirm as bureau director the Obama administration's proposed nominee until and unless the structure of the new agency was changed. Eventually the president's nominee for the position, Richard Cordray, was placed in the job, in January 2012, as a recess appointee.

Even when it was operating without a director, the bureau had a substantial budget. Since Cordray's appointment, the bureau has followed through on its widely expected plans to simplify mortgage and other credit disclosures. How aggressive it will be in the future is likely to depend heavily on the outcome of future presidential and congressional elections. Nonetheless, unless this part of Dodd-Frank is altered, the new Consumer Financial Protection Bureau *could* be a powerful agency that significantly affects the nature of and disclosures relating to banking products and services for the indefinite future.

As to why regulators, federal and state, were not more aggressive in policing subprime mortgage originations—especially those with no money down and low initial teaser rates—the reasons are well known. Fed chairman Greenspan has confessed to mistakes in trusting market forces, although it still is not clear (at least to this author) whether the Fed had the legal authority to crack down on the nonbank lenders that originated most of the questionable mortgages. But even if the Fed did not have this ability, it could have requested such authority from Congress. In addition, the Fed and other federal banking regulators, as well as their state counterparts, could have more closely scrutinized bank lending to the most aggressive nonbank subprime mortgage originators. That they did not reflects a combination of complacency and an unwillingness to take the punch bowl away from the "housing party" that was being widely enjoyed by the public and their elected representatives, as noted earlier in this chapter.

New Securitization Rules

Although there are large differences of opinion over the wisdom of many of the provisions in Dodd-Frank, there seems to be a consensus that one significant factor contributing to the crisis that led to passage of the bill was that the commercial and investment banks that securitized subprime loans had insufficient incentives to encourage sound underwriting of those loans in the first place. As long as the mortgage securities could be sold to an all-too-willing investor community, why bother looking at the collateral and borrower incomes that were supposed to support them?

The Dodd-Frank fix for this problem is to require loan originators and/or securitizers of asset-backed securitized instruments to retain at least a 5 percent equity or at-risk *unhedged* interest in the underlying loans or the securities packages sold to investors. Regulators are directed to determine the allocation of the 5 percent risk retention requirement between originators and securitizers, as well as to permit an exemption for "qualified residential mortgages," a term left to the banking, housing, and securities regulators to define. These regulators have since proposed a rule requiring that originators and/or securitizers bear the entire 5 percent requirement, which is not to be applied to securities backed by prime mortgages (essentially those with at least a 20 percent down payment).

The carve-out for prime mortgages has taken much of the sting out of the criticism of the risk retention rule. The continuing problem in implementing the requirement for other securities is that regulators have not yet defined what an "unhedged" position is and found a way to monitor it. Clearly, a very specific hedge, such as a credit default swap taken out on the security, would qualify. But it is much more difficult to police a reasonable practice of portfolio diversification, which can hedge at least some of the retained risk. Moreover, even though a risk retention or "skin in the game" requirement seems entirely plausible, critics point to the fact that many banks that engaged in securitizing CDOs also held open positions in these or similar assets and this did not stop them from taking the risks they did, so a new risk retention rule should have very little effect going forward. My response to this line of argument is that we now know that much of the large banks' *subprime* mortgage exposure was farmed out to their ostensibly off-balance sheet SIVs, for which bank managements may have been deluded into thinking they would never be responsible. To the extent that this is true, the new risk retention rules, however limited they may be, are a step in the right direction.

We will not know for sure for some time, however, because at this writing the market for mortgage securities is essentially dead, as it has been since the onset of the crisis. Although some may blame the risk retention rule for delaying a comeback in this market, the better explanation is the continuing poor state of the housing market and much tougher bank supervision, a combination that almost surely would have kept a lid on subprime mortgage origination and securitization even in the absence of any new risk retention requirement. In addition, the fact that subprime mortgages in their previous incarnation have not returned to the marketplace is not a bad outcome. If policymakers want to assist low- and moderate-income householders to buy homes, they are likely in the future to have to come up with much more transparent and on-budget means of subsidy for these borrowers.[15]

The Volcker Rule

Like much legislation that makes its way through Congress, Dodd-Frank had Christmas tree elements to it—namely, provisions that had little or nothing to do with rectifying the causes of the crisis that preceded it but nonetheless were politically useful in one manner or another in attracting support for the overall bill and for punishing the large banks at the center of the financial storm. The so-called Volcker rule is one such provision. Although simple to state, it has subsequently proven devilishly difficult for regulators to implement and, I predict, could easily be one of many targets in the bill for regulatory arbitrage or circumvention at some point in the future.

With some exceptions, and subject to a transition period, the Volcker rule prohibits any bank or thrift institution, or a bank or thrift holding company, from engaging in "proprietary trading." The Volcker rule was not in the initial drafts of what became Dodd-Frank; it was added several months later when President Obama endorsed the idea, at the behest of Paul Volcker, the chair of his outside economic advisory board, the former distinguished chairman of the Federal Reserve Board, and a longtime critic of bank speculative activities.

Given the lack of evidence that bank proprietary trading (much of which centered on the trading of stocks, bonds, and currencies) played a significant role in causing the crisis, the best that can be said for the Volcker rule is that proprietary trading arguably is not the kind of activity that should be supported or subsidized by deposit insurance and that prohibiting it could contribute to preventing a *future* crisis. At the same time, however, to the extent that such trading has been profitable for banks, denying them the ability to pursue it could detract from their safety and soundness. This last point is not contradicted by the exceptional, widely publicized trading loss posted by J. P. Morgan in the spring of 2012. At this writing, it is not clear that the Volker rule drafted by the regulatory agencies (described shortly) would have prohibited the derivatives transactions that led to J. P. Morgan's trading loss.

As the J. P. Morgan episode illustrates, the practical question relates to how the rule is actually implemented by financial regulators. But the term "proprietary trading," which the statutory rule would ban, is inherently difficult to define. Some activities, such as running an internal hedge fund, are clearly off limits and easily stopped. Indeed, even in advance of a final rule from the regulators implementing the Volcker provision, virtually all banks affected by it had divested themselves of any hedge fund activities.

Drawing a sharp line between permissible hedging of customer transactions and conducting trades for the banks' own accounts, however, is difficult and fraught with the potential for negative unintended consequences (see, for example, Government Accountability Office 2011). In early November 2011, federal banking regulators released a three-hundred-page proposal that attempts to flesh out the legislative language, an effort that Volker himself criticized for being too complicated and reflecting lobbying by the banking industry (quoted in Reuters 2011). In my view, Volcker is certainly right about the influence of the banking industry on the regulatory process (see the foregoing discussion of the derivatives rules under Dodd-Frank), but the complexity of the implementing rules for the Volcker provisions was entirely predictable. As a practical matter, the real implementation will have to done by banking supervisors on a case-by-case basis, which will mean uncertainty for some period of time. Depending on how strictly regulators enforce the proposal, the Volcker rule could significantly diminish liquidity in the trading of financial instruments, imposing a social cost on the markets that could outweigh any benefits of risk reduction that it is meant to achieve.

In any event, given the way that banks, or any financial institutions, historically have behaved, it will not be surprising if the banks affected by the rule continue to push the envelope if they believe it requires pushing. If U.S. regulators push back too hard, U.S. banks are likely to move any potentially questionable trading activities offshore. In the end, it is the opinion of this author that the Volcker rule, however it is finally implemented, will do little to enhance the safety and soundness of the banking or the financial system.

The Lincoln (or "Swaps Push-out") Rule

Another antibank rule that made it into the Dodd-Frank bill was the "swaps push-out" or the "Lincoln rule," named after its sponsor, former senator Blanche Lincoln.[16] Briefly summarized, this provision denies Federal Reserve loans to support a "swaps entity," or any organization, including a bank, that "regularly enters into swaps with counterparties as an ordinary course of business for its own account." Like the customer exception in the Volcker rule, the Lincoln rule exempts banks that enter into swaps in connection with loans to customers or that limit their swaps activities to hedging.

Regulators will have difficulty over time enforcing a strict line between customer- or hedging-related swaps transactions and all others that the Lincoln rule is meant to cover. These difficulties are likely to surface most pointedly during a financial crisis when the Fed is trying to decide whether it can extend a loan to a troubled bank that, like many banks, engages in swaps transactions. The Fed takes a political risk if it construes the Lincoln prohibition too liberally, but an economic risk to the financial system if it construes the prohibition too strictly. I cannot predict in which direction the Fed is most likely to err.

Unlike banks' ability to circumvent the Volcker rule by moving otherwise prohibited activities offshore, there is no profit for U.S. banks (including subsidiaries or branches of foreign banks) subject to the Lincoln rule in moving swaps activities to non-U.S. locations, unless they have the prospect of receiving crisis support from central banks in those jurisdictions. But precisely because the home offices or holding companies of these banks would be in the United States, such assistance is not likely to be forthcoming, or at least it cannot be counted on. So U.S. banks' only countermeasures are likely to consist of ongoing pushback against pre-crisis attempts by regulators to cover swaps activities within the scope of the Lincoln prohibition. In response, banks will have incentives to find creative ways to avoid such measures by constructing their swaps operations so that they fit within the statutory or regulatory exceptions to the rule.

Compensation Rules

Another factor that probably contributed to the 2007 to 2008 financial crisis was the short-term nature of many compensation packages, not only for bank and financial executives but for more junior personnel, such as loan officers. To the extent that any of these individuals were paid on loan volume originated or processed, for example, these compensation arrangements weakened their incentives to pay attention to sound underwriting and banking practices, especially when the loans were simply sold to another entity for securitization.

Dodd-Frank seeks to end these practices by requiring federal banking regulators to issue regulations aimed at encouraging the use of compensation arrangements that discourage excessive risk-taking, which as a practical matter means the use of long-term bonus arrangements and/or salaries rather than compensation tied to short-run targets. In fact, the banking regulatory agencies issued proposed guidance on bank compensation arrangements in 2009, as Dodd-Frank was being debated, and finalized these rules in June 2010, before it was enacted. These rules require that compensation for many bank employees (not just executives) be consistent with safe and sound banking practices and that banks have monitoring arrangements to see whether these arrangements are successful in balancing risks against potential rewards.[17]

These rules pushed banks in a direction they were already going after the crisis: shifting the composition of their compensation packages more toward restricted stock or longer-term bonus arrangements. Banks did this not only to comply with the new rules but also to respond to the pressure from shareholders and the wider public to achieve a better alignment of incentives and risk. So it is not clear how much incremental effect Dodd-Frank has had or will have in the future in this regard. And even under Dodd-Frank and the prior compensation rules, there is nothing to prevent financial institutions from raising base-level salaries as a means of recruiting or retaining highly talented individuals, as some institutions already have done.

No Provisions for the Future of Fannie Mae and Freddie Mac

The one glaring omission in the "comprehensive" financial reform embodied in Dodd-Frank, of course, was the failure to define the future role, if any, for the two housing GSEs, Fannie Mae and Freddie Mac. At one level, this is surprising and disappointing, because the final taxpayer bill for rescuing their creditors is already above $100 billion and thus will be the most costly (on a net basis, after recoupment from asset sales or refloating of shares) budgetary component of the overall financial rescue. At another, more political level, the omission is more readily understood. Fannie and Freddie were two of the largest engines of public policy (along with the mortgage interest tax deduction) favoring homeownership since their creation many decades ago, and both institutions, even in conservatorship, had continued through 2011 to buy virtually all of the residential mortgages securitized in the United States since the crisis. In light of the extremely weak housing market that has persisted once real estate prices topped out in 2006, it is little wonder that elected officials have been reluctant to tamper with two of the only institutions that have kept the market from being even worse than it already has been.

At the same time, there is widespread postcrisis recognition that the quasi-public, quasi-private nature of Fannie and Freddie should not and cannot be permanently maintained. Given the complex politics surrounding not only these two GSEs but housing policy in general, it is virtually certain that the final fate of Fannie and Freddie will not be determined until after the 2012 presidential election.

At this writing, there are two main competing ideas about what to do with the two entities: either to phase them out over some gradual period (most likely by lowering the "conforming limit" of mortgages they can purchase or guarantee) or to explicitly make them government entities subject to stricter safety and soundness oversight. If the latter route is chosen, the regulatory dynamics are likely to be similar to those for banks: initial tough scrutiny by regulators who would have the political freedom to act that way during some postcrisis "honeymoon period," followed by a tendency to relax their guard if and when the economy, and especially the housing market, recovers.

CONCLUSION

If there is one safe prediction about how Dodd-Frank and its implementation will play out, it is this: the debate over the law and the rules set under it will continue for some time. Because the law was passed by a partisan vote, its legitimacy will continue to be in question. But because it takes sixty votes in the Senate to stop debate on any bill, it is unlikely for the foreseeable future that the law will be dismantled or changed in a fundamental way. If statutory alterations are made, they are likely to be of an incremental nature (similar to the slight easing of the Sarbanes-Oxley Act requirements for smaller and newer public companies written into the Dodd-Frank Act itself).

The major caveat to this forecast is that it could change significantly if another financial crisis materializes in the United States that has a major impact on U.S. financial institutions. (At this writing in August 2012, the U.S. economy is growing weakly; European government debt and banking markets are in crisis mode, but the impact on the U.S. financial sector so far has been modest.) If the projections here are correct, even with the controversy over the law and its implementation, Dodd-Frank is likely to delay the onset of a U.S. crisis centered in the financial sector in particular and to reduce the severity of such a crisis when it occurs. But if history is any guide, there will be no way to completely avoid another crisis.[18] When it comes, history also suggests the nature of any legislative and regulatory response: yet another ratcheting-up of regulation and supervision and, most likely, an attempt to close whatever loopholes in Dodd-Frank are discovered by clever financial institutions and their attorneys in the years to come. Indeed, if large banks have anything to do with the next crisis, or if they require more bailouts, then the voices for the breakup of the largest institutions may yet prevail, for then they will have "proof" that regulation alone could not stop the damage. Whether a system of ten to twenty $100 billion banks will be safer than the more concentrated banking system we now have (and have had in the wake of the 2007 to 2008 financial crisis) surely will be the subject of future papers and books of this kind.

As for Dodd-Frank on the merits, I take a cautiously positive view, recognizing that the law, like most laws, is far from perfect and that its regulatory implementation will continue to be plagued by the political economy issues identified in this chapter. As noted earlier, the crisis and the subsequent period of recession and slow growth that it triggered have entailed trillions of dollars of costs to the United States and other economies. Even if the law has the effect of slowing future growth by 0.1 or 0.2 percentage points, preventing for some significant period a repetition of the events of the last crisis or at least significantly reducing the costs of a future crisis, as I believe this law broadly will do, the act, even with its warts, will be justified. A challenge for quantitatively oriented economists in the future will be to shed more detailed light on this judgment, as well as on ways to improve the benefit-cost ratio of any future financial regulation.

Finally, what do the academic theories have to say about Dodd-Frank? The overriding conclusion here is that the act generally is not consistent with the public choice model of regulation; the regulated institutions clearly did not want most of this act, and many of them are fighting and will continue to fight its implementation. The more interesting question is whether in the future regulators carrying out the act's many mandates will act in the public interest or whether they will eventually be captured by the institutions they regulate. The answer will help determine the timing and severity of the next financial crisis.

For conversations about the topics discussed in this chapter, I am grateful to my Brookings colleagues Martin Baily, Doug Elliott, and Donald Kohn, as well as for comments provided by Kim Shafer and the volume editors and other chapter authors on earlier drafts of this chapter. In the interest of full disclosure, during the course of my career, in addition to serving in three positions in the federal government, I have consulted or served as an expert witness for several financial institutions in various litigations, and I have consulted and written papers for different financial trade associations on various financial matters. I have also consulted or written papers on financial issues for the House Banking Committee, the U.S. Treasury Department, the Federal Home Loan Bank of San Francisco, and the Monetary Authority of Singapore, and I have served on the Ahead of the Curve advisory panel for FINRA (Financial Industry Regulatory Authority). In addition, I was a member of the Presidential-Congressional Commission on the Causes of the Savings and Loan Crisis. I previously served on the International Advisory Board of the Principal Financial Group and the research advisory boards of the Center for Audit Quality and the Committee for Economic Development.

NOTES

1. For a searing indictment of U.S. financial regulatory failure on many fronts, see Barth, Caprio, and Levine (2012).

2. The seminal article on the public choice theory of regulation is Stigler (1971).

3. One of the first economists to identify the "cat and mouse" feature of financial regulation was Ed Kane (1988). For the more general point about market circumvention of rules, see Peltzman (2004).

4. For a more thorough defense of this measure, see Borio and Drehmann (2009).

5. See, for example, the excellent provision-by-provision summary by the law firm of Davis Polk and Wardwell of New York, available at: http://www.davispolk.com/dodd-frank/ (accessed April 2012).

6. Technically, the Federal Deposit Insurance Corporation (FDIC) is operated in such a way that only insured banks cover the costs of failed banks. But in a major crisis such as the one that occurred in 2007 to 2008, the FDIC can become short of funds and needs to borrow from the Treasury, which in fact was done during that episode.

7. One disappointment in the new Basel rules is that the Basel Committee rejected contingent capital instruments (or "Cocos") as counting for part of required equity capital. Cocos normally count as debt but automatically convert to equity upon some triggered event, such as a decline in the bank's measured capital ratio below some minimum threshold. One advantage of Cocos is that the newly converted equity provides an additional cushion to absorb losses when it is most needed—that is, when the bank is in trouble. Furthermore, the prospect that the holder of the instrument will have its debt converted into equity, without a stated right to an interest payment, should give Coco buyers strong incentives to monitor and discourage excessive risk-taking by bank management. It is to be hoped that U.S. regulators will take a kinder view of Cocos in implementing any supplemental capital rules, especially for systemically important banks.

8. The standards also allow, but do not require, member countries to assess a third "countercyclical" capital surcharge of up to 2 percent of risk-weighted assets that would not have to apply during times of economic stress. Having such a surcharge in place, in theory, should help smooth out national economic cycles.

9. For an excellent analysis of the market structure issues in derivatives markets, see Duffie and Zhu (2011).

10. This statement is the conventional view, which I admit may not be correct. In September 2011, two journalists from the *Wall Street Journal* published a revealing article indicating that CDS trading is a lot thinner than widely believed, perhaps even thinner than bond trading (see Mollenkamp and Ng 2011). To the extent that this result is validated, it calls into question, or at least reduces the social benefits from, the "single name" CDS market (contracts written on the possibility of default of bonds issued by individual companies).

11. I am indebted to Kim Shafer, who worked on the staff of the Financial Crisis Inquiry Commission, for making this point.

12. The fact that derivatives counterparties still may be protected in full under the Dodd-Frank resolution process is no different from the bankruptcy code. That code presumably treats derivatives contracts differently because derivatives counterparties are in a position to immediately seize the collateral backing their contracts and so they can make themselves whole. For a thoughtful critique of this exemption, see Roe (2011).

13. It is important that regulators insist on regular sign-offs; otherwise, the living will becomes stale and likely to be ignored.

14. For a fuller discussion of this topic, see White (2010).

15. One additional potential problem with the risk retention rule, taken alone, is that unless the managers of the financial institutions involved have some of their own skin in the game, any risk retention requirement imposed on the institutions may have something less than the desired effect on the behavior of the managers or loan officers. One way to address this problem would be to require that any loan origination or securitization fee be payable over time and be subordinate to the revenues earned by the financial institution on the transaction. In this way, managers and loan/securitization personnel would have some personal stake in how well the transactions perform after they are completed. For an elaboration of this suggestion, see Shafer (2011).

16. I omit discussion of yet another antibank provision, the "Durbin amendment"—which directed the Federal Reserve to put limits on the debit interchange fees that banks above $10 billion in assets charge retail merchants (eventually the Fed did so, after a notice-and-comment procedure in early 2011)—because this provision was clearly unrelated to any of the causes of the financial crisis. Given the strong opposition to these limits of the banking industry (even smaller community banks, formally exempted in the amendment, were opposed), this provision clearly is not consistent with the public choice theory of regulation (except to the extent that it favored merchants, who wanted the limits but were not subject to them). It is also far from clear that it is consistent with the public interest theory, since banks have been raising other fees or changing the way they charge for debit transactions to offset the per-transaction limits required by the amendment. It should be noted that I coauthored (with David Evans and Richard Schmalensee) comments to the Fed on behalf of a select group of banks in the Federal Reserve's rulemaking. These comments opposed the Fed's proposed twelve-cent-per-transaction limit on debit transaction fees, which the Fed raised to twenty-one cents in its final rule implementing the Durbin amendment.

17. More generally, Dodd-Frank also stipulates that the SEC will issue rules requiring, among other things, that publicly traded companies disclose relationships between their executives' compensation and the firms' financial performance and provide shareholders at least once every three years with an opportunity to have a nonbinding vote on executive compensation (the "say on pay" provision).

18. I am putting aside for this purpose the possibility of a crisis triggered by the failure of Congress and the administration to materially reduce fiscal deficits at some point in the future when their magnitude triggers another round of political brinksmanship of the kind put on display over the acrimonious debate to lift the federal debt ceiling during the summer of 2011.

REFERENCES

Akerlof, George A., and Robert J. Shiller. 2009. *Animal Spirits: How Human Psychology Drives the Markets, and Why It Matters.* Princeton, N.J.: Princeton University Press.

Barth, James R., Gerard Caprio Jr., and Ross Levine. 2012. *The Guardians of Finance: Making Them Work for Us.* Cambridge, Mass.: MIT Press.

Borio, Claudio E. V., and Mathias Drehmann. 2009. "Assessing the Risk of Banking Crises— Revisited (March 2, 2009)." *BIS Quarterly Review* (March). Available at: http://ssrn.com/abstract=1513316 (accessed September 2011).

Corrigan, E. Gerald. 1982. "Are Banks Special?" (1982 annual report). Minneapolis: Federal Reserve Bank of Minneapolis.

Duffie, Darrell, and Haoxiang Zhu. 2011. "Does a Central Counterparty Reduce Counterparty Risk?" Working Paper 46. Palo Alto, Calif.: Stanford University, Rock Center for Corporate Governance. Also available as Research Paper 2022, Stanford University Graduate School of Business. Available at SSRN: http://ssrn.com/abstract=1348343 (accessed September 2011).

Government Accountability Office (GAO). 2011. *Proprietary Trading: Regulators Will Need More Comprehensive Information to Fully Monitor Compliance with Restrictions When Implemented.* Washington: GAO (July). Available at: http://www.gao.gov/Products/GAO-11-529 (accessed September 2011).

Johnson, Simon, and James Kwak. 2011. *Thirteen Bankers: The Wall Street Takeover and the Next Financial Meltdown.* New York: Vintage.

Kane, Edward J. 1988. "The Interaction of Financial and Regulatory Innovation." *American Economic Review* 78(2, May): 328–34.

Leising, Matthew. 2011. "Credit Seen Safest Since 2008 as Clearinghouses Control Swaps." Bloomberg, August 4.

Litan, Robert E. 2010. "The Derivatives Dealers' Club and Derivatives Markets Reform: A Guide for Policy Makers, Citizens, and Other Interested Parties." Washington, D.C.: Brookings Institution (April 7). Available at: www.brookings.edu/papers/2010/0407_derivatives_litan.aspx (accessed September 2011).

Minsky, Hyman P. 1978. "The Financial Instability Hypothesis: A Restatement." Thames Papers in Political Economy. London: Northeast London Polytechnic, School of Social Sciences of Thames Polytechnic. Available at: http://digitalcommons.bard.edu/hm_archive/180/ (accessed September 2011).

Mollenkamp, Carrick, and Serena Ng. 2011. "A Fear Gauge Comes Up Short." *Wall Street Journal,* September 28.

Peltzman, Sam. 2004. "Regulation and the Natural Progress of Opulence." 2004 Distinguished Lecture. American Enterprise Institute–Brookings Joint Center for Regulatory Studies Distinguished Lecture. Washington, D.C.: AEI-Brookings (September 8).

Rajan, Raghuram. 2010. *Fault Lines: How Hidden Fractures Threaten the World Economy.* Princeton, N.J.: Princeton University Press.

Reuters. 2011. "Paul Volcker Says Volcker Rule Too Complicated." Reuters, November 9. Available at: http://jp.reuters.com/article/newsOne/idUSTRE7A83KN20111109 (accessed September 2011).

Roe, Mark J. 2011. "Bankruptcy's Financial Crisis Accelerator: The Derivatives Players' Priorities in Chapter 11." Working Paper 153/2010. Brussels: European Corporate Governance Institute (ECGI); also available as Harvard Public Law Working Paper 10-17 and in *Stanford Law Review* (forthcoming). Available at SSRN: http://ssrn.com/abstract=1567075 (accessed September 2011).

Rogoff, Kenneth, and Carmen Reinhardt. 2010. *This Time Is Different.* Princeton, N.J.: Princeton University Press.

Shafer, Kim Leslie. 2011. "Risk Retention for CLOs: Achieving Its Objectives." New York: Center for Financial Stability (July 29). Available at: www.centerforfinancialstability.org/oped/Comments_080111.pdf (accessed September 2011).

Stigler, George. 1971. "The Theory of Economic Regulation." *Bell Journal of Economics and Management Science* 2(1, Spring): 3–21.

White, Lawrence J. 2010. "Markets: The Credit Rating Agencies." *Journal of Economic Perspectives* 24(2): 211–26.

Chapter 12

Pay, Politics, and the Financial Crisis

Kevin J. Murphy

The Wall Street bonus culture—coupled with suspicions that the culture facilitated excessive risk-taking—led to an effective prohibition on cash bonuses for participants in the government's Troubled Asset Relief Program (TARP) and to more sweeping regulation of executive compensation as part of the July 2010 Dodd-Frank Wall Street Reform and Consumer Protection Act. This chapter explores the banking bonus culture, its role in inducing risk-taking, and the appropriateness of the regulatory response. While I find little evidence that the pay structures provided incentives for risk-taking among top-level banking executives, there is some evidence of value-destroying performance measurement problems for lower-level traders, brokers, and loan officers. The regulatory reforms imposed in TARP and Dodd-Frank have largely focused on punishing perceived excesses in top-level executive pay and have not served to reduce risk, improve pay, or protect taxpayers. Overall, while incentives for bankers can clearly be improved through well-functioning corporate governance, further government intervention is likely to be counterproductive for the interests of both shareholders and taxpayers.

In early 2009, with the United States still enmeshed in the financial crisis and reeling from the government bailouts to the banking sector, Congress shifted its attention to the critical task of finding someone (or something) to blame.[1] The most obvious culprit—or perhaps scapegoat—was the "Wall Street bonus culture," the tradition in which traders, brokers, and executives receive most of their compensation not in base salaries but rather in bonuses paid at the end of the fiscal year. Since this tradition rewards success but (allegedly) imposes no real penalties for failure, the Wall Street culture (allegedly) provides incentives for excessive risk-taking of the sort that facilitated the crisis.

Public anger over banking bonuses surfaced in January 2009 amid reports that Wall Street bankers were set to receive nearly $20 billion in bonuses for their 2008 performance (White 2009),[2] and it heightened with revelations that bailout recipient Merrill Lynch paid nearly $4 billion in year-end bonuses just prior to completion of its acquisition by Bank of America (Farrell and MacIntosh 2009).[3] Outrage further intensified following the March 2009 revelation that American International Group (AIG) was in the process of paying $168 million in "retention bonuses" to its executives. Revelations that bankers were receiving bonuses when their firms were obviously failing—coupled with the belief that the bonuses were a root cause of the crisis—led to an effective prohibition on cash bonuses for participants in the government's Troubled Asset Relief Program (TARP) and to more sweeping regulation of executive compensation as part of the July 2010 Dodd-Frank Wall Street Reform and Consumer Protection Act. In 2011 public anger over Wall Street pay and calls to reform it became major rallying points in the populist "Occupy Wall Street" movement.

In this chapter, I explore how the recent financial crisis has affected executive compensation in financial services firms. I show that many of the changes in compensation have been made in direct response to new rules and regulations. However, in tracing the evolution of the new rules and regulations, an obvious tension emerges between shareholders and taxpayers who want to solve legitimate problems with the banking bonus culture, on the one hand, and politicians or populists who want to punish executives in the companies perceived to be responsible for the global meltdown, on the other.

I begin by describing the Wall Street bonus culture and documenting differences in the level and structure of pay and incentives for executives in broker-dealer firms compared to traditional banks and industrial firms. In particular, I show that the Wall Street bonus culture is indeed a Wall Street phenomenon that prevails in broker-dealer firms (especially large ones) and not in other financial services firms. In addition, I show that the Wall Street bonus culture is an equity culture: until the market collapse during the financial crisis, equity incentives and equity ownership were substantially higher for broker-dealer executives than for their counterparts in banking and industry.

Next, I review how banking bonuses—or incentive compensation more broadly—can create incentives for excessive risk-taking, through two channels: asymmetric rewards and penalties, and performance measures that reward risky behavior. I conclude that both of these channels may have contributed to excessive risk-taking among lower-level traders and brokers. In contrast, I find no evidence that compensation structures provided such incentives for top-level banking executives.

I then analyze the regulatory responses to perceived excesses in banking bonuses, beginning with the original restrictions on TARP recipients through the ongoing implementation of the Dodd-Frank Act. I show that the responses (and the rhetoric behind the responses) were not intended to reduce risk, improve pay, or protect taxpayers, but rather to attack perceived excesses in pay for top-level executives and to destroy the Wall Street banking culture.

I then address four key questions:

1. Did banking bonuses cause or contribute to the financial crisis?

2. Were the regulators responding to "excessive risk" or "excessive pay"?

3. Are banking bonuses excessive?

4. Should banking bonuses be regulated?

Finally, while identifying several ways in which compensation structures could be improved through better corporate governance, I conclude that further government intervention will be counterproductive to both shareholders' and taxpayers' interest.

THE WALL STREET BONUS CULTURE

Heavy reliance on bonuses has been a defining feature of Wall Street compensation for decades, going back to the days when investment banks were privately held partnerships. Such firms kept fixed costs under control by keeping base salaries low and paying most of the compensation in the form of cash bonuses that varied with profitability. This basic structure remained intact when the investment banks went public, but the cash bonuses were replaced with a combination of cash, restricted stock, and stock options.

In contrast to nonfinancial firms—where significant bonus opportunities are limited to relatively senior managers and executives—Wall Street firms offer compensation primarily in the form of bonuses for virtually all professional staff, including entry-level positions (for example, analysts hired after receiving an undergraduate degree or associates hired after receiving an MBA). One closely watched source of trends in bonuses is the annual analysis conducted by the New York State Comptroller (DiNapoli 2011), which is based on personal income tax withholding collections and industry revenue and expense data. Figure 12.1 shows the evolution of average bonuses from 1985 to 2008 for New York City–based employees working in the securities industry (NAICS 523), drawn from state comptroller estimates. Between 1985 and 2006, average bonuses increased from $28,000 (in 2010-constant dollars) to over $200,000, falling to "only" $102,000 in 2008 and rebounding to $129,000 in 2010.

The average bonuses illustrated in figure 12.1 mask the important "skewness" in the distribution of Wall Street bonuses: a relatively small number of traders and executives often receive a disproportionate share of the bonus pool. While details on the compensation of the chief executive officer (CEO), chief financial officer (CFO), and the three other highest-paid executive officers are publicly disclosed and widely available, banks have historically been highly secretive about the magnitude and distribution of bonuses for their traders and investment bankers. Indeed, since the Securities and Exchange Commission (SEC) disclosure rules apply only to *executive officers,* the banks can have non-officer employees making significantly more than the highest-paid officers. Following the Merrill Lynch and AIG revelations, New York attorney general Andrew Cuomo subpoenaed bonus records from the nine original TARP recipients, arguing that New York law allows creditors to challenge any payment by a company if the company did not get adequate value in return. His report, published in late July 2009, was provocatively titled "No Rhyme or Reason: The 'Heads I Win, Tails You Lose' Bank Bonus Culture."

Table 12.1 summarizes the distribution of bonuses for the nine original TARP recipients, based on data from the Cuomo (2009) report. The table shows, for example, that 738 Citigroup employees received bonuses over $1 million and 124 received over $3 million in a year when the bank lost nearly $30 billion. The percentage

FIGURE 12.1 / Estimated Average Bonuses on Wall Street, 1985 to 2010

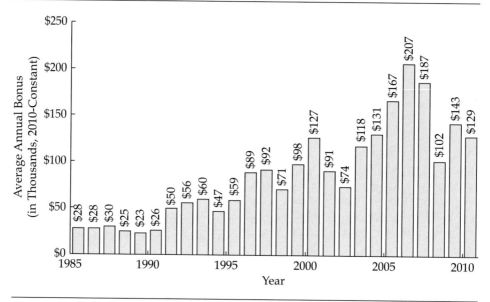

Source: Author's compilation of data from N.Y. Office of the State Comptroller (2011).

Note: Average bonuses estimated by DiNapoli (2011) based on personal income tax withholding collections and industry revenue and expense data for New York City-based employees working in the securities industry (NAICS 523). Dollar amounts in the original report are converted to 2010-constant dollars using the consumer price index.

TABLE 12.1 / Earnings and Bonus Pools for Nine Original TARP Recipients, 2008

Corporation	2008 Earnings (Losses) (Billions)	2008 Bonus Pool (Billions)	Number of Employees	Number of Employees Receiving Bonuses Exceeding: $3 Million	$2 Million	$1 Million
Bank of America	$4.0	$3.3	243,000	28	65	172
Bank of NY Mellon	$1.4	$0.9	42,900	12	22	74
Citigroup	($27.7)	$5.3	322,800	124	176	738
Goldman Sachs	$2.3	$4.8	30,067	212	391	953
JPMorgan Chase	$5.6	$8.7	224,961	>200	—	1,626
Merrill Lynch	($27.6)	$3.6	59,000	149	—	696
Morgan Stanley	$1.7	$4.5	46,964	101	189	428
State Street Corp.	$1.8	$0.5	28,475	3	8	44
Wells Fargo & Co.	($42.9)	$1.0	281,000	7	22	62

Source: Author's compilation of data from Cuomo (2009).

Note: Wells Fargo losses include losses from Wachovia (acquired in December 2008).

FIGURE 12.2 / Median Realized Compensation for CEOs in S&P 500 Broker-Dealers, Banks, and Industrials, 1970 to 2010

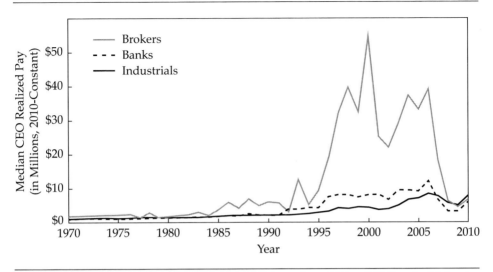

Source: Author's compilation of Forbes (1970–1991) and ExecuComp 1992 to 2010 (Standard & Poor's, various years).

Note: Dollar amounts are converted to 2010-constant dollars using the consumer price index.

of employees receiving bonuses above $1 million was especially high in the three broker-dealer firms: Goldman Sachs (5.2 percent), Morgan Stanley (1.5 percent), and Merrill Lynch (1.4 percent).[4] The 2008 bonus pools exceeded annual earnings in six of the nine banks; in aggregate the banks paid $32.6 billion in bonuses while losing $81.4 billion in earnings. Not surprisingly, the Cuomo report further fueled outrage over Wall Street bonuses on both Main Street and in Washington.

Figure 12.2 compares 1970 to 2010 time trends in the median realized compensation for CEOs in Standard & Poor's (S&P) 500 broker-dealer firms (primary SIC codes 6200 to 6212), banks (SIC codes 6000 to 6199), and industrials (SIC below 6000 and above 7000, excluding utilities [4900 to 4999] and financial services [6000 to 6999]). Realized pay includes salaries, bonuses, payouts from long-term incentive plans (and other non-equity plans), gains from exercising stock options, and the vesting value of restricted shares.[5] Data from 1970 to 1991 are from the annual *Forbes* surveys of executive compensation, while data from 1992 to 2010 are from S&P's ExecuComp database.

As shown in figure 12.2, realized pay in broker-dealer firms closely tracked pay in banks and industrials until the mid-1980s, when several privately held partnerships went public (for example, Bear Stearns in 1985 and Morgan Stanley in 1986) and as traditional banks began competing for investment banking talent. In the peak year of 2000—propelled by trading profits associated with the Internet bubble and revenues from work related to mergers, acquisitions, and IPOs—the median CEO in the 5 S&P 500 broker-dealer firms took home $54.7 million, almost

FIGURE 12.3 / Median Realized Pay for the "Average" Top Five Executives in Broker-Dealers, Banks, and Industrials, 1992 to 2010

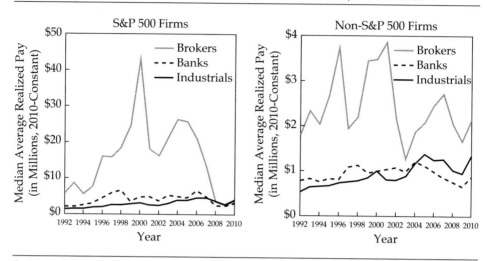

Source: Author's compilation of data from ExecuComp (Standard & Poor's, various years) 1992 to 2010.

seven times the median pay in 39 S&P 500 banks ($8.1 million) and more than twelve times the median pay in 371 S&P 500 industrials ($4.4 million).[6] Median realized CEO pay in S&P 500 broker-dealer firms plummeted 84 percent between 2006 ($39.2 million) and 2008 ($6.3 million). By 2010, median CEO pay in S&P 500 broker-dealer firms ($6.8 million) had fallen to a position between banks ($5.8 million) and industrials ($7.7 million).

The escalation in realized pay in broker-dealer firms was not limited to the CEOs, nor did it happen only at the largest Wall Street firms. The left-hand panel of figure 12.3 shows the median of the average realized pay received by the top five executives in S&P 500 firms.[7] In the 2000 peak year, the median S&P 500 broker-dealer firm paid its top five executives an average of $43 million, compared to $4.7 million and $3.2 million for S&P 500 banks and industrials, respectively. The right-hand panel of figure 12.3 replicates the analysis for firms not in the S&P 500.[8] While the basic pattern remains (broker-dealer executives earning more than their banking and industrial counterparts), the most striking difference between the two panels is the scale: companies below the S&P 500 pay considerably less than companies in the S&P 500, regardless of sector.

The volatility of pay for broker-dealer executives suggested by figures 12.2 and 12.3 reflects the Wall Street culture of coupling low (and relatively stable) base salaries with variable pay tied to the profitability of the enterprise. For example, since going public in 1985 and through 2005, base salaries for partners at Bear Stearns were limited to $200,000 annually; base salaries were raised to $250,000 in 2006, but in most years base pay still constituted only about 1 percent of the realized compensation for Bear Stearns's CEO. Similarly, in 2007 (largely before the

FIGURE 12.4 / Average Ratio of Salary to Total Realized Pay for the Top Five Executives in S&P Broker-Dealers, Banks, and Industrials, 1992 to 2010

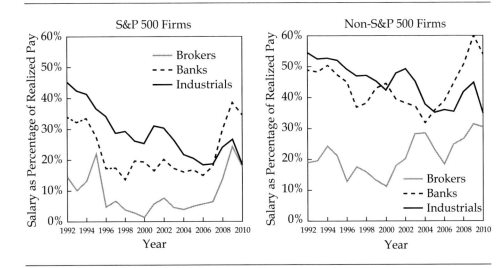

Source: Author's compilation of data from ExecuComp 1992 to 2010 (Standard and Poor's, various years).

market crash), Goldman Sachs paid CEO Lloyd Blankfein a salary of $600,000 and a bonus of $67.9 million, for a total of $68.5 million; his salary accounted for less than 1 percent of his total compensation.

Figure 12.4 shows the average ratio of base salary to total realized compensation for the top five executives in broker-dealer firms, banks, and industrials. (The ratio for each firm is calculated by dividing the sum of base salaries for the top five executives by the sum of their realized pay.) The left-hand panel shows the average ratio for S&P 500 firms; the right-hand panel shows firms below the S&P 500. For both sets of firms, base salaries constituted a modest fraction of total realized compensation for executives in broker-dealer firms compared to their counterparts in banks and industrials.

In contrast to the cash bonuses traditionally paid in other sectors, executives in broker-dealer firms routinely receive bonuses in a combination of cash, unvested stock awards, and unexercisable stock options. For example, in addition to his $250,000 salary in 2006, Bear Stearns's CEO James Cayne received a bonus of $33.6 million, comprising cash ($17 million), restricted shares ($14.8 million), and stock options ($1.7 million). By the time of the company's collapse in March 2008 and the "fire sale" to JPMorgan Chase for $10 a share, the (not yet vested) stock that Cayne had received as part of his 2006 bonus was worth only 6 percent of its grant-date value, and his options expired worthless. Similarly, only $26.8 million of Lloyd Blankfein's $67.9 million 2007 bonus from Goldman Sachs was paid in cash; the rest was paid in restricted stock units ($24.66 million) or options ($16.44 million).[9] By January 2011 (when the stock vested and options became exercisable),

FIGURE 12.5 / Median Effective Percentage Ownership and Equity at Stake
for the Top Five Executives in S&P Broker-Dealers, Banks,
and Industrials, 1992 to 2010

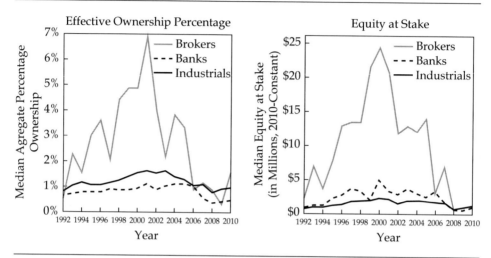

Source: Author's compilation of data from ExecuComp 1992 to 2010 (Standard & Poor's, various years).

Note: Dollar amounts are converted to 2010-constant dollars using the consumer price index.

Blankfein's 2007 options were underwater, and the restricted stock was worth
about 80 percent of its grant-date value.

As illustrated by the Bear Stearns and Goldman Sachs examples, paying bonuses
in the form of equity strengthens the pay-performance relation, since the ultimate
bonus depends on subsequent performance. With no single way to measure the
incentives from equity ownership, time-series and cross-sector patterns are two
widely used measures of equity incentives: the effective ownership percentage
and the "equity at stake" (see figure 12.5). The effective ownership percentage
in the left-hand panel (which is essentially Jensen and Murphy [1990b]'s "pay-
performance sensitivity") is defined as the change in the value of the executive's
wealth for an incremental change in shareholder value and is calculated as:

$$\left(\begin{array}{c}\text{Effective}\\\text{Ownership Percentage}\end{array}\right) = \frac{\begin{array}{c}\text{Restricted and Unrestricted Shares}\\+\left(\text{Delta-Weighted}\right)\text{Options}\end{array}}{\text{Common Shares Outstanding}}$$

In constructing an aggregate measure of CEO incentives, I weight each option
by the "option delta," defined as the change in the value of a stock option for
an incremental change in the stock price. Option deltas range from near-zero (for
deep out-of-the-money options) to near-one (for deep in-the-money options on
nondividend paying stock).[10] I call this measure the "effective ownership percentage" to distinguish it from the actual ownership percentage based only on stock
(and not option) holdings.

FIGURE 12.6 / Median Aggregate Value of Options and Equity Held by the Top Five Executives in S&P Broker-Dealers, Banks, and Industrials, 1992 to 2010

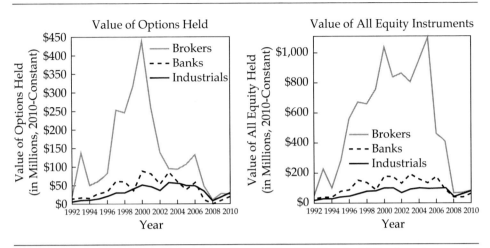

Source: Author's compilation of data from ExecuComp 1992 to 2010 (Standard & Poor's, various years).

Note: Dollar amounts are converted to 2010-constant dollars using the consumer price index.

As shown in the left-hand panel of figure 12.5, the aggregate effective owner-ship percentage for broker-dealer executives (calculated by summing individual ownership percentages across the top five executives) peaked in 2000 and was substantially above the ownership percentage for executives in banks and indus-trials for all years except 1992 and 2006. The decline in effective ownership since 2001 primarily reflects a decline in option deltas (as options fell out of the money) and not massive stock sales.

An alternative measure of executive incentives—introduced by Brian Hall and Jeffrey Liebman (1998) and explored theoretically by George Baker and Hall (2004)—is the change in executive wealth for a 1 percent change in the value of the firm. The left-hand panel of figure 12.5 shows the evolution of the Hall-Liebman measure—what Carola Frydman and Dirk Jenter (2010) call "equity at stake"—from 1992 to 2010. The equity-at-stake measure is calculated as 1 percent of the effective owner-ship percentage multiplied by the firm's market capitalization.[11] In 1999 each 1 per-cent change in shareholder wealth resulted in a $25.7 million change in wealth for the median executive team in S&P 500 broker-dealer firms, compared to only about a $2 million change for executive teams in banks and industrials.

Finally, figure 12.6 shows the median year-end value of options (left-hand panel) and equity (right-hand panel) held (in aggregate) by the top five execu-tives in S&P 500 firms, by sector. The value of the options held by broker-dealer executives declined dramatically after 2000, reflecting both the stock market crash (associated with the burst of the Internet bubble in 2000 and exacerbated by the terrorist attacks on the World Trade Center in 2001) and the shift toward restricted stock. Until stock prices collapsed in 2008, the median value of all equity held by broker-dealer executives remained substantially above the value of equity held by executives in banks and industrials.

To summarize, the purpose of this section has been to provide a background on the Wall Street bonus culture to use when discussing the culpability of banking bonuses in the financial crisis and the ongoing regulatory responses. For data reasons, most of the focus has been on the top executives, not on lower-level traders and managers. Nonetheless, several results emerge:

- Although the regulatory responses have been broadly applied to all financial institutions, the Wall Street bonus culture is indeed a Wall Street phenomenon that prevails in broker-dealer firms (especially large ones) and not in commercial banks and savings institutions.

- In fact, traditional banks are more similar to industrial firms in pay levels, equity incentives, and equity ownership than to broker-dealer firms.

- Relative to executive pay in banking and industrials, realized compensation for Wall Street executives (who receive most of their pay in the form of bonuses paid in cash, stock, and options) increased in the late 1980s and exploded in the mid-1990s.

- The Wall Street bonus culture is, at least for top-level executives, a Wall Street *equity* culture: until the market collapse during the financial crisis, equity incentives and equity ownership were substantially higher for broker-dealer executives than for their counterparts in banking and industry.

- Although realized pay, equity incentives, and the value of equity ownership plummeted during the financial crisis across all sectors, the decline was especially pronounced for executives in broker-dealer firms.

- In the aftermath of the crisis, and at least through 2010, the realized pay, the equity incentives, and the value of equity ownership for executives in large broker-dealer firms have largely converged to general industry practices.

BANKING BONUSES, RISK-TAKING, AND THE FINANCIAL CRISIS

The public and political anger over Wall Street bonuses arguably reflects two primary factors. The first factor is outrage (or incredulity) that the banks would pay *any* bonuses at all given their objective failure and their reliance on government bailouts. Indeed, the bonuses to bankers in bailed-out firms were perceived by many to be an undeserved direct transfer of wealth from taxpayers to already-wealthy bankers. The second factor is the belief that the bonus culture provided incentives to take excessive risks that ultimately caused the crisis. In this section, I analyze the economic incentives to take risks and ask whether the Wall Street culture provided such incentives.

Bonus plans can provide incentives to take risks through two channels: asymmetric rewards and penalties, and performance measures that reward risky behavior. I

FIGURE 12.7 / Typical Compensation Structure with Asymmetric Rewards and Penalties

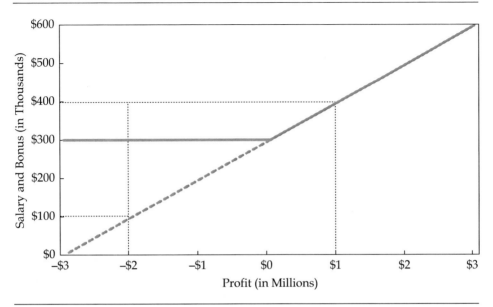

Source: Author's figure.

Note: Figure shows the (hypothetical) compensation for a trader with a base salary of $300,000 and a bonus of 10 percent of (positive) profits.

conclude that both of these channels may have contributed to excessive risk-taking among lower-level traders and brokers. In contrast, I find no evidence that compensation structures provided such incentives for top-level banking executives.

Asymmetric Rewards and Penalties

When executives (or traders or brokers) receive rewards for upside risk but are not penalized for downside risk, they will naturally take greater risks than if they faced symmetric consequences in both directions. The classic example of asymmetries (or what economists call "convexities") lies in the pay-performance relation implicit in stock options, which provide rewards for stock-price appreciation above the exercise price but impose no penalties (below zero) for stock-price depreciation below the exercise price. Executives with options that are out of the money and close to expiration have strong incentives to gamble with shareholder money; executives with options that are well in the money have fewer such incentives.

To show how asymmetries in rewards and penalties can cause excessive risk-taking, the solid line in figure 12.7 depicts the compensation structure for a hypothetical trader with a base salary of $300,000 and a cash bonus equal to 10 percent of his (positive) trading profits. Suppose the trader is considering a trade that will generate $1 million in profits with 50 percent probability, and $2 million in *losses* with 50 percent probability. This trade has an expected value of –$500,000; it is clearly a bad gamble. But since the trader gets a bonus of $100,000 when profits are $1 million (total compensation $400,000) and no bonus when profits are –$2 million (total compensation $300,000), his expected bonus is +$50,000, and it is a good gamble from his perspective.

CREATING LINEAR BONUS PLANS   The obvious solution (at least conceptually) to the dilemma in figure 12.7 is to extend the "bonus line" so that the trader is punished for negative profits (as well as rewarded for positive profits). The dashed line in the figure shows his potential compensation when his bonus is set to 10 percent of both positive and negative profits. In this case, the trader gets a "bonus" (actually a penalty) of –$200,000 when profits are –$2 million (total compensation $100,000). His expected bonus is –$50,000, and the trade is a bad gamble from his perspective. By making his bonus schedule linear for both positive and negative outcomes, we have eliminated the asymmetric rewards and penalties, thereby eliminating his incentives to take excessive risks.

While the solution in figure 12.7 is obvious in theory, it is difficult to implement in practice because it effectively requires paying (or charging) "negative bonuses" when there are bad outcomes. Conceptually, negative bonuses can be implemented by asking the executive to write a check back to the company in bad years, but this scheme is difficult to implement, especially after the executive has paid taxes on the bonuses. A more palatable way of achieving negative bonuses is through deferred bonuses that are subject to partial or full forfeiture if performance deteriorates. For example, "bonus banks" can be structured so that a positive bonus is not paid out entirely in cash each period but rather is deposited into the trader's bonus bank account. The trader receives a cash distribution equal to a fixed fraction of the account balance each year, while the remaining balance is "at risk" to fund negative bonuses in future years.

Another indirect way to impose negative bonuses is by reducing base salaries and offering enhanced bonus opportunities (through reduced bonus thresholds). For example, suppose the trader's base salary in figure 12.7 is reduced from $300,000 to $100,000, and suppose that he starts earning his 10 percent bonus for profits in excess of –$2 million (instead of profits in excess of zero). The new contract generates the same total payments for profits above zero, but the second contract (depicted by the dotted line) provides *higher* bonuses and *lower* total compensation for operating income below zero.

It probably seems counterintuitive to characterize enhanced bonus opportunities as a negative bonus, but consider the following. For each $1 million reduction in profit below zero, the trader paid under the second contract (with the $100,000 salary) receives $10,000 *less* than he would have received under the first contract (with the $300,000 salary). Although payments for performance between a $2 million loss and zero are reported as bonuses, in fact they are negative bonuses compared to the original contract.

THE AGENCY COST OF DEBT AND "TOO BIG TO FAIL" GUARANTEES As emphasized earlier, the Wall Street bonus culture was largely a Wall Street equity culture: top banking executives had large equity stakes in their companies and strong incentives to increase shareholder value. However, for leveraged firms, excessive focus on shareholder value can lead to inappropriate risk-taking. The asymmetry comes from the fact that the shareholders receive all the upside of investments with positive realizations, but can lose at most the value of their equity for negative realizations: any loss greater than the value of equity is borne by debt-holders.

The potential conflict of interest between a company's shareholders and its debt-holders was identified by Michael Jensen and William Meckling (1976) as the "agency cost of debt": shareholders in a leveraged firm prefer riskier investments than those that would maximize firm value, while debt-holders prefer safer investments than those that would maximize firm value. While the agency cost of debt is clearly valid conceptually, there is very little empirical evidence that leverage in fact leads to excessive risk-taking, for several reasons. First, precisely because the shareholder–debt-holder conflicts are well understood, the potential problem is mitigated through debt covenants and constraints on how the proceeds from debt financing can be used. Moreover, since the problem is "priced" into the terms of the debt (with debt-holders charging higher interest rates in situations where executives have incentives to take higher risks), firms anticipating repeat trips to the bond market are directly punished for their risky behavior.

The potential for shareholder–debt-holder conflicts are exacerbated, however, when the debt-holders (or other fixed claimants, such as depositors) are protected against losses by the government. Such government guarantees can be explicit (such as FDIC insurance on deposits) or implicit (such as "too big to fail" guarantees). In these situations, the debt-holders (or depositors) have little incentive to monitor management or enforce debt covenants, since the government is rationally expected to cover losses.

Lucian Bebchuk and Holger Spamann (2010) cite the typical leverage structure of banks as prima facie evidence of risk-taking incentives, particularly for executives narrowly focused on shareholder value. However, what is important for risk-taking is not the *fraction* of equity in the capital structure, but rather the *value* of the equity relative to the downside of potential bets. For example, consider two banks, both with $5 billion in equity, one with $20 billion in debt and deposits, and the other with $50 billion. The potential problems in both banks arise in bets with a downside loss exceeding $5 billion; the risk-taking is not expected to be more severe in the more highly levered bank (the one with $50 billion in debt and deposits). Therefore, the shareholder preferences for risky gambles decline with the value of their equity, because shareholders as a group have more to lose from unlucky outcomes. Similarly, holding the value of shareholder equity constant, executives with higher-valued equity positions will also have more to lose from unlucky outcomes and are therefore less likely to pursue risky bets.

Concerns about leveraged-induced risk-taking also led the influential Squam Lake Working Group on Financial Regulation (French et al. 2010) to recommend that deferred banking bonuses "not take the form of stock or stock options," but rather be a "fixed dollar amount" that would be forfeited if the bank "goes bank-rupt or receives extraordinary government assistance." The motivation for this recommendation is that holding deferred compensation in the form of a fixed but unsecured claim mitigates equity-based incentives for excessive risk-taking by aligning the interests of managers and unsecured creditors. However, given the dearth of evidence that the "problem" addressed by the Squam Lake proposal actually exists (that is, that risk-taking in leveraged firms is excessive because the executives own too much equity), coupled with the acknowledged incentive ben-efits of equity ownership (namely, incentives to pursue value-creating projects and avoid value-destroying projects), requiring deferred pay to be a fixed dollar amount rather than stock reflects a wasted opportunity.

Performance Metrics That Reward Risk-Taking

REWARDING QUANTITY RATHER THAN QUALITY   Incentive compensation can create incentives for risk-taking when bonuses are paid out based on performance mea-sures that reward risky behavior. For example, in the years leading up to its dramatic collapse and acquisition by JPMorgan Chase at fire-sale prices, mortgage brokers at Washington Mutual ("WaMu") were rewarded for writing loans with little or no verification of the borrower's assets or income, and they received especially high commissions when selling more profitable adjustable rate (as opposed to fixed rate) mortgages (Goodman and Morgenson 2008). The basic incentive problem at WaMu was a culture and reward system that paid people to write loans rather than to write "good" loans—that is, loans with a decent chance of actually being paid back. In the end, WaMu got what it paid for: bad loans. Similar scenarios were played out at Countrywide Finance, Wachovia, and scores of smaller lenders that collectively were not overly concerned about default risk as long as home prices kept increasing. But home prices could not continue to increase when prices were being artificially bid up by borrowers who could not realistically qualify for or repay their loans.

In the current antibanker environment, it has become fashionable to charac-terize plans such as those at WaMu as promoting excessive risk-taking. But the problems with paying loan officers for the quantity rather than the quality of their loans is conceptually identical to the well-known problem of paying a piece-rate worker based on the quantity rather than the quality of output. Put simply, these are performance measurement problems, not risk-taking problems, and character-izing them as the latter leads to the impression that they are somehow unique or more important in the banking sector, when in fact they are universal.

Financial innovation contributed to performance measurement problems for loan officers. In the early 2000s, mortgages were increasingly pooled together and sold as mortgaged-back securities. Although such "securitization" can provide for efficient ex post risk allocation, it creates ex ante "moral hazard" problems, since the loan offi-cer will care only about (and be rewarded only on) the quantitative measures of cred-itworthiness required for securitization and will ignore important qualitative aspects that would be considered important if the bank were intending to hold the loan in its own portfolio.[12] The loan officer was even further removed from the ultimate repayment when the mortgage-backed securities were restructured as collateralized debt obligations (CDOs) and sold to investors in difference tranches according to their purported risk.

REWARDING SHORT-TERM RATHER THAN LONG-TERM RESULTS Paying executives (or traders or investment bankers) for short-term rather than long-term results leads to a related set of performance measurement issues. For example, bankers trading in illiquid assets might be rewarded on the estimated appreciation of the assets on the bonus payment date, which may bear little resemblance to the gain (or loss) ultimately realized. If the traders are not held accountable for the long-run value consequences of their actions, they will predictably focus on the quick (if illusionary) profit.

Focusing on short-run profit rather than long-run value is a performance measurement problem and not a risk-taking problem; indeed, trades that generate profits in the short run are likely to be less risky than trades generating profits only in the longer run. Nonetheless, rewarding short-run profit can easily destroy long-run value. These problems are exacerbated when the traders have inside information that the trades or deals are likely to go sour after bonuses are paid.

More broadly, basing bonuses on short-run results can often lead to paying "too much" in a prior year, owing to revisions in performance data that are not apparent until after the bonus has been paid. Such revisions include, but are not limited to, formal restatements of accounting numbers, such as earnings or revenues, due to mistakes; over-optimistic assumptions; "managed earnings"; and outright fraud or short-term-oriented decisions that generated profits in an earlier period but led to substantial long-run value destruction.

SOLVING PERFORMANCE MEASUREMENT PROBLEMS For top-level banking executives whose actions directly affect company stock prices, performance measurement problems can be mitigated by paying bonuses partially in stock or options that vest long after the actions generating the bonuses have been taken. Executives who take actions that increase short-run profit at the expense of long-run value will be punished through lower stock-price valuations, while those who increase long-run value will be rewarded through higher valuations. Forcing executives to hold large unvested equity positions also protects debt-holders, depositors, and taxpayers from excessive risk-taking, since risk-averse executives are less likely to gamble when they personally have more to lose.

The solution to many performance measurement problems—loan officers being rewarded for writing too many mortgages, traders being rewarded for short-term results—is to design pay plans that hold employees accountable for the long-run consequences of their actions. Such solutions can be difficult, however, to implement: consider, for example, that it might take thirty years for a broker to know whether a mortgage was actually repaid. But at the very least brokers and traders should be held accountable for results beyond the first year.

When traders, brokers, or banking executives receive bonuses based on performance measures that are subsequently revised downward, the bank must reserve the right to recover the ill-gained rewards. These ex post adjustments to already paid bonuses have become known as "clawbacks," since the company is "clawing back" rewards it had already paid out. Clawbacks were introduced in the 2002 Sarbanes-Oxley Act, significantly expanded for TARP recipients in 2009, and expanded more broadly in the 2010 Dodd-Frank Act. In practice, clawbacks have proven to be hard and costly to enforce, especially for executives who have paid taxes on (or otherwise spent) erroneously awarded bonuses or who may have left the firm.

As an alternative to clawbacks, the ill-gained reward can be deducted from deferred compensation accounts, nonqualified retirement benefits, restricted stock or option holdings, or other funds under the control of the company. Bonus banks, described earlier as a palatable way of achieving negative bonuses, can also be used as a funding mechanism for bonus recoveries.[13]

Did Banking Bonuses Encourage Excessive Risk-Taking?

TOP-LEVEL BANKING EXECUTIVES   As discussed earlier, the primary way in which compensation structures can encourage excessive risk-taking is through asymmetric rewards and penalties—that is, high rewards for superior performance but no real penalties for failure. Financial services firms (and especially broker-dealer firms) provide significant penalties for failure in their cash bonus plans by keeping salaries below competitive market levels, so that earning a zero bonus represents a penalty. Put differently, in comparison to other sectors, the bonus plans for top Wall Street executives are effectively linear, which should mitigate rather than exacerbate incentives to take risk.

A second way in which compensation structures might encourage excessive risk-taking is through faulty performance measures. However, at least for top-level banking executives, these potential problems are mitigated by paying a large fraction of the bonus in unvested stock or unexercisable options. As documented earlier, until the market collapse during the financial crisis, equity incentives and equity ownership were substantially higher for broker-dealer executives than for their counterparts in banking and industry.

Banking executives' substantial equity holdings also mitigate potential conflicts between shareholders and debt-holders or taxpayers. In particular, concerns over excessive, leverage-induced risk-taking arise when the total value of the equity held by executives (that is, the maximum amount of downside exposure) is small relative to the upside potential of the risky projects being considered. As shown in figure 12.6, the median top management team in broker-dealers held over $1 billion in equity instruments in 2005, more than five times the median equity for executives in commercial banks and ten times the median equity for executives in industrials. In order for these structures to provide disproportionate incentives for broker-dealer executives to take excessive risks, the upside potential for broker-dealer "bets" would need to be in excess of five and ten times the upside potential in commercial banks and industrials, respectively.

A heavy reliance on options (rather than restricted stock) can indeed provide incentives for risk-taking. The pay-performance relation implicit in stock options

FIGURE 12.8 / Median Aggregate Option Vega and Vega Elasticity for the Top Five Executives in S&P Broker-Dealers, Banks, and Industrials, 1992 to 2010

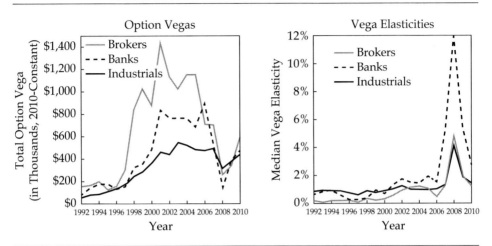

Source: Author's compilation of data from ExecuComp 1992 to 2010 (Standard & Poor's, various years).

Note: Dollar amounts are converted to 2010-constant dollars using the consumer price index.

is inherently convex, since executives receive gains when stock prices exceed the exercise price, but their losses when the price falls below the exercise price are capped at zero. Thus, the value of a stock option increases monotonically with stock-price volatilities, providing an incentive for executives to take risks that increase such volatilities. However, compared to their counterparts in banking and industrials, broker-dealer firms have long favored restricted stock over options.

There is no accepted methodology on measuring incentives for risk in executive option portfolios, or in executive contracts more generally. However, following Rudiger Fahlenbrach and René Stulz's (2011) analysis of executive compensation and the financial crisis, I computed two option-based measures for incentives to increase stock-price volatilities:

Total option vega = Change in value of outstanding options held by the top five executives for a one-percentage-point increase in volatility

Vega elasticity = Percentage change in the value of the outstanding options held by the top five executives for a one-percentage-point increase in volatility

Figure 12.8 shows the time-series and cross-sector patterns of the two measures of pay-volatility sensitivities for the median executive team in S&P 500 firms from 1992 to 2010. As shown in the left-hand panel, the total option vega in broker-dealer firms was generally higher than the corresponding measure in banks and industrial firms for most of the pre-crisis period (although total option vegas for banks and broker-dealers were virtually identical after 2005). In the 2001 peak year, each one-percentage-point increase in volatility increased option values by $1.4 million for the median executive team in broker-dealer firms, compared to $833,000 and $460,000 for the median executive teams in banks and industrials, respectively. However, total realized compensation for the median broker-dealer firm in 2001 was triple that in banks, and seven times that in industrials (see figure 12.3). Therefore, as a percentage of total compensation, the total option vega was lower in broker-dealer firms.

The right-hand panel of figure 12.8 shows that, when measured as an elasticity, risk-taking incentives were typically lower in broker-dealer firms than in other sectors in the pre-crisis years. In addition, the figure shows inconsistencies in the two measures of risk-taking incentives: total option vegas plummeted in 2008, while vega elasticities spiked. The differences in the two measures reflect the effect of stock market movements and, in particular, the market crash at the end of 2008 and the partial rebound by 2010. When stock prices fell (as they did abruptly in 2008, across all sectors of the economy), the options fell out of the money, which implies that the option vega for each option became smaller. (Option vegas are typically highest when the stock price is close to the exercise price.) But it turns out that, as stock prices fall, the value of the options held fall even faster than the option vega. As a result, the value of options that are out of the money increases more in percentage terms (but less in dollar terms) as volatility increases. More generally, the two vega measures—both legitimate measures for risk-taking incentives—predictably move in opposite directions in market downturns.

Overall, the data in figure 12.8 do not support the hypothesis that compensation in broker-dealer firms provided incentives to take excessive risks. While the total option vegas for broker-dealer firms were generally higher in broker-dealer firms, this result is reversed after dividing by total compensation or by the value of outstanding options (in other words, the vega elasticity).

In summary, when compared to bonus plans in other sectors, bonuses for Wall Street executives are effectively linear with (relatively) small salaries, low bonus thresholds, and no caps. Moreover, a major part of the bonuses are paid in the form of unvested stock or unexercisable stock options, which effectively reduces the value of bonuses based on subsequent performance. This culture, with these plans, in general creates incentives to focus on long-run value creation rather than short-run gains. In addition, the primary way in which compensation structures might encourage excessive risk-taking is through asymmetric rewards and penalties—high rewards for superior performance but no real penalties for failure. Financial services firms provide significant penalties for failure in their cash bonus plans by keeping salaries below competitive market levels, so that earning a zero bonus represents a penalty. These plans reduce (rather than increase) incentives for risk-taking.

THE TROUBLE WITH TRADERS   Although I find little evidence of risk-taking incentives for top-level banking executives, this conclusion cannot necessarily be extrapolated to traders, loan officers, and other lower-level banking employees whose business activities could subject the institution to large losses. For example, my conclusion relies on evidence of large stock and options holdings that would be decimated following a bad gamble: lower-level employees would have less accumulated wealth and therefore less to lose. In addition, though it is sensible to tie incentive pay for top-level executives to changes in the overall value of the firm, bonuses for lower-level employees are inherently based on shorter-term measures of individual performance.

LIMITS TO LINEARITY   To fully mitigate excessive risk-taking, the compensation structure must be linear across the full range of outcomes, including large losses. Given prohibitions against servitude, torture, and murder—coupled with individual-friendly bankruptcy protection—the penalties that can be imposed on bankers for huge losses are largely limited to loss of employment, reputation, and existing wealth (including bonus banks, deferred accounts, unvested benefits, and stock holdings). For top-level executives with substantial stock holdings and legacy concerns, the potential losses in personal wealth are arguably sufficient to mitigate incentives for excessive risk-taking. However, for younger traders with less accumulated wealth in the company, the potential gains from excessive risk-taking might seem attractive relative to the limited downside.

It is therefore not surprising that many so-called rogue traders are relatively young low-level traders with less wealth to lose. For example, UBS's Kweku Adoboli was only thirty-one years old when his unauthorized unhedged trades in various S&P 500, DAX, and EuroStoxx index futures in 2011 resulted in a loss to UBS of $2.4 billion (Cimilluca, Ball, and Mollenkamp 2011). Similarly, Société Générale's Jérôme Kerviel was thirty-one years old when his unauthorized unhedged trades on stock-index futures in 2006 and 2007 resulted in a loss of $7.2 billion. As an exception that proves the rule, the "limits to linearity" are obvious in the October 2010 judgment against Kerviel: in addition to serving three years in prison, the judge ordered Kerviel to repay his former employer *$6.7 billion*. News accounts at the time noted that it would take him 180,000 years to pay back this sum at his current salary (Gauthier-Villars, Mollenkamp, and MacDonald 2008).

In both the UBS and Société Générale cases, the traders were charged with criminal fraud and taking unauthorized actions that violated company policy (although there is some evidence in both cases that monitoring was lax). The larger point is that no bonus system in the world can adequately punish a trader (or any employee) for generating billions of dollars in losses (Gauthier-Villars 2010). This fact, however, does not justify a condemnation of the banking bonus culture, but rather emphasizes that high-powered incentives must always be coupled with continuous monitoring systems and risk-control systems to ensure that outsized bets are never allowed to occur and that measured and rewarded performance reflects actions that create rather than destroy value.

RISK LOVERS LOVE HIGH-POWERED INCENTIVES   Individuals with a larger appetite for risk are naturally attracted to firms with higher-powered incentives, even with fully linear bonus plans offering symmetric rewards and penalties. For example, suppose that one bank offers its traders a bonus of 1 percent of individual prof-its (positive or negative), while a second, otherwise identical bank offers 10 per-cent. Assuming that the "expected total pay" is similar across the two banks, more risk-averse employees will be attracted to the bank with the 1 percent bonus pool, while more risk-loving traders will prefer the 10 percent bonus pool.

Therefore, while the Wall Street bonus culture does not necessarily provide incentives for excessive risk-taking, the culture predictably attracts a disproportionate share of risk-takers. For similar reasons, the culture also attracts a disproportionate share of high-ability, highly motivated, and highly confident individuals, including the best and the brightest from the top undergraduate and MBA programs.

UNDETECTED SHORT-TERM CHEATING Trades or deals that look good when bonuses are paid might fall apart before performance is actually realized. When traders are rewarded based on short-run profits, they have incentives to not only pursue projects that will look good in the short run but also to take deliberate (and often illegal) actions to make the projects look better (or less risky) than they are. For example, Société Générale's Kerviel and UBS's Adoboli were both traders who were supposed to take offsetting bets on European stock futures (Kerviel) and exchange-traded funds (ETFs) (Adoboli); these strategies were designed as low-risk ways to make a small profit. Instead, both made unhedged bets only in one direction and created fake trades in the opposite direction to hide the real risk they were taking (MacDonald and Abboud 2008; Gauthier-Villars and Mollenkamp 2008; Cimilluca et al. 2011). The real and fictitious trades balanced out within the traders' risk limits, and everything looked relatively normal in the short run.

CLIENTS VERSUS COUNTERPARTIES A final—albeit more speculative—trouble with traders is that they grow up to be executives, taking with them a distorted view of the fiduciary duties owed to their stakeholders.[14] In particular, instead of having customers or clients, the traders have "counterparties" (that is, the parties on the other side of the transaction). The formal commitments that traders make to their counterparties are minimal, often amounting to little more than a commitment to provide "best execution" of their trades.

The conflict of interest between traders and their counterparties is well understood: the objective of each party is to make a profit at the expense of the other, though not by doing something so blatant or opportunistic that it would jeopardize the future relationship. When the clients and customers of the advisory business are treated like counterparties, the reputation of the entire firm is at risk, which in turn jeopardizes shareholders, debt-holders, and (possibly) taxpayers. This cultural difference between the advisory and trading sides of the business is a very serious and potentially damaging source of conflict inside the firm.

Consider, for example, the involvement of Goldman Sachs in the Abacus synthetic collateralized debt obligation (CDO), which ultimately imposed massive losses on its investors, resulted in a record $550 million fine to settle SEC fraud charges, and severely (and perhaps irreparably) damaged the firm's once-sterling reputation. According to the complaint filed by the SEC in April 2010, hedge fund manager John Paulson approached Goldman Sachs in January 2007 seeking counterparties and mechanisms that would allow him to "short" various residential mortgage-backed securities (RMBSs) that he believed were overvalued and would default in the near future. Working with Goldman's thirty-one-year-old vice president, Fabrice Tourre, Paulson helped select a list of RMBS candidates. Tourre and Goldman then approached ACA Management, LLC, to serve as the "portfolio selection agent" for the $2 billion CDO, telling ACA about Paulson's involvement but suggesting that Paulson would be investing $200 million in a long (rather than short) position. Goldman and ACA then marketed the CDO to clients without revealing that Paulson (and his company) was involved in selecting the initial set of securities in the portfolio (paying Goldman $15 million for the privilege) and that he intended to sell the Abacus CDO short. Moreover, all this was being done in a context in which Goldman as a whole was betting that home mortgages would decline in value— what was known within the firm as the "big short" (Goldfarb 2010).

Goldman's involvement in the Abacus deal violated its own guiding principle that "our clients' interests always come first," unless it was viewing its client as Paulson and not the buyers of the CDO. Determining why Goldman risked its reputation in the deal will be debated for years, but meanwhile, Michael Jensen and I (Murphy and Jensen 2011) have speculated that the root causes involve Goldman's 1999 going-public decision and the more recent shift of power from its advisory services to its traders. After Goldman became a publicly held corporation in 1999, its access to large amounts of outside capital enabled its traders to significantly expand their operations and generate substantial profits. These trading activities now are the major source of Goldman's profits, and Goldman is now essentially run by the traders; the CEO, Lloyd Blankfein, is a trader. When Goldman collaborated in the creation and sale of the Abacus securities without notifying its clients that it was shorting the subprime market, it was treating the buyers of those securities as if they were counterparties rather than clients or customers and thus violating its core business principle.

Importantly, there is no evidence that Goldman's involvement can be explained by the incentives provided by its executive bonus system. Bonuses were paid in stock and options (as well as cash), and all the senior executives held huge ownership positions in Goldman equity. For example, by year-end 2007, the five named executives in Goldman's proxy statement held illiquid equity and options on Goldman Sachs with a total value of $1.8 billion. Therefore, those executives on balance had no monetary incentives to take actions that would increase Goldman's short-term earnings at the expense of its long-term equity value. More broadly, it is difficult to find any short-term monetary gains for these executives that would cause them to rationally choose the actions taken by their firm in the Abacus deal. The cautionary conclusion is that bonus plans cannot be blamed for, and cannot solve, all internal organizational problems.

REGULATORY RESPONSES TO "OBSCENE" BONUSES

Overall, there is little evidence that the Wall Street bonus culture provided incentives for risk-taking among top-level banking executives; indeed, the general structure of compensation, coupled with substantial equity holdings, should mitigate excessive risk-taking. Nonetheless, the banking bonus culture came under attack in 2009, reflecting in part the (largely uncorroborated) suspicion that banking bonuses created incentives for excessive risk-taking that led to the meltdown of world financial markets.

In this section, I analyze the regulatory responses to perceived excesses in banking bonuses, beginning with the original restrictions on TARP recipients through the ongoing implementation of the Dodd-Frank Act. I conclude that the responses (and the rhetoric behind them) were not intended to reduce risk, improve pay, or protect taxpayers, but rather to attack perceived excesses in pay levels and destroy the Wall Street banking culture.

The Emergency Economic Stabilization Act

On September 19, 2008—at the end of a tumultuous week on Wall Street that included the Lehman Brothers bankruptcy and the hastily arranged marriage of Bank of America and Merrill Lynch—Treasury secretary Paulson asked Congress to approve the Bush administration's plan to use taxpayers' money to purchase "hundreds of billions" in illiquid assets from U.S. financial institutions (Solomon and Paletta 2008). Paulson's proposal contained no constraints on executive compensation, since the fear was that restrictions would discourage firms from selling potentially valuable assets to the government at relatively bargain prices (Hulse and Herszenhorn 2008). Limiting executive pay, however, had long been a top priority for Democrats and some Republican congress people, who viewed the "Wall Street bonus culture" as a root cause of the financial crisis. Congress rejected the bailout bill on September 30, but reconsidered three days later after a record one-day point loss in the Dow Jones industrial average and strong bipartisan Senate support. The Emergency Economic Stabilization Act (EESA) was passed by Congress on October 3 and signed into law by President George Bush the same day.

The original TARP bailout bill included what at the time seemed like serious restrictions on executive pay. For example, while section 304 of the 2002 Sarbanes-Oxley Act (SOX) required clawbacks of certain executive ill-gotten incentive payments, SOX covered only the chief executive officer and chief financial officer and was also limited to accounting restatements. Although it applied only to TARP recipients (SOX applied to all firms), the October 2008 EESA covered the top five executives (not just the CEO and CFO) as well as a much broader set of material inaccuracies in performance metrics. In addition, EESA lowered the IRS cap on deductibility for the top five executives from $1 million to $500,000 and applied this limit to all forms of compensation (not just non-performance-based pay). EESA also prohibited new severance agreements for the top five executives and limited payments under existing plans to 300 percent of the executives' average taxable compensation over the prior five years. When Treasury invited (or, in some cases, coerced) the first eight banks to participate in TARP, a critical hurdle involved getting the CEOs and other top executives to waive their rights under their existing compensation plans.

The American Reinvestment and Recovery Act amends EESA

In January 2009, reports began surfacing that Merrill Lynch had distributed $3.6 billion in bonuses to its 36,000 employees just before the completion of the merger with Bank of America: the top 14 bonus recipients received a combined $250 million, while the top 149 received $858 million (Cuomo 2009). The CEOs of Bank of America and the former Merrill Lynch (neither of whom received a bonus for 2008) were quickly hauled before congressional panels outraged by the payments, and the attorney general of New York launched an investigation to determine if shareholders voting on the merger were misled about both the bonuses and Merrill's true financial condition. The SEC joined in with its own civil complaint, suing the Bank of America but not its individual executives, and the bank agreed to settle for $33 million. A few weeks later, however, a federal judge threw out the proposed settlement, insisting that individual executives be charged and claiming that the settlement did not comport with the most elementary notions of justice and morality (Scannell, Rappaport, and Bravin 2009). In February 2010, the judge relented and reluctantly approved the settlement after it had been increased to $150 million (Fitzpatrick, Scannell, and Bray 2010).

By the time the Merrill Lynch bonuses were revealed, the United States had a new president, a new Congress, and new political resolve to punish the executives in the companies perceived to be responsible for the global meltdown. Indicative of the mood in Washington, Senator Claire McCaskill (D-MO) introduced a bill in January 2009 that would limit total compensation for executives at bailed-out firms to $400,000, calling Wall Street executives "a bunch of idiots" who were "kicking sand in the face of the American taxpayer" (Andrews and Bajaj 2009, p. A20).

On February 4, 2009, President Barack Obama's administration responded with its own proposal for executive pay restrictions that distinguished between failing firms requiring exceptional assistance and relatively healthy firms participating in TARP's Capital Purchase Program. Most importantly, the Obama proposal for exceptional assistance firms (which specifically identified AIG, Bank of America, and Citigroup) capped annual compensation for senior executives at $500,000, except for restricted stock awards (which were not limited, but could not be sold until the government was repaid in full, with interest). In addition, for exceptional assistance firms the number of executives subject to clawback provisions would be increased from five under EESA to twenty, and the number of executives with prohibited golden parachutes would be increased from five to ten. In addition, the next twenty-five highest-paid executives would be prohibited from parachute payments that exceeded one year's compensation.

Moreover, in response to reports of office renovations at Merrill Lynch, corporate jet orders by Citigroup, and corporate retreats by AIG, the Obama proposal stipulated that all TARP recipients adopt formal policies on luxury expenditures. Finally, the Obama proposal required all TARP recipients to fully disclose their compensation policies and allow nonbinding "say on pay" shareholder resolutions.[15]

In mid-February 2009, separate bills proposing amendments to EESA had been passed by both the House and Senate, and it was up to a small conference committee to propose a compromise set of amendments that could be passed in both chambers. On February 13—as a last-minute addition to the amendments—the conference chairman (Senator Chris Dodd [D-CT]) inserted a new section imposing restrictions on executive compensation that were opposed by the Obama administration and were severe relative to both the limitations in the October 2008 version and the February 2009 Obama proposal. Nonetheless, the compromise was quickly passed in both chambers with little debate and signed into law as the American Recovery and Reinvestment Act (ARRA) by President Obama on February 17, 2009.

Table 12.2 compares the pay restrictions under the original 2008 EESA bill, the 2009 Obama proposal, and the 2009 ARRA (which amended section 111 of the 2008 EESA). While the clawback provisions under the original EESA covered only the top five executives (up from only two under Sarbanes-Oxley), the Dodd amendments extended these provisions to twenty-five executives and applied them retroactively.[16] In addition, while the original EESA disallowed severance payments in excess of 300 percent of base pay for the top five executives, the Dodd amendments covered the top ten executives and disallowed *all* payments (not just those exceeding 300 percent of base). The Dodd amendments also retroactively extended the deductibility restrictions to the top twenty-five executives (not just the top five). Most importantly, the Dodd amendments allowed only two types of compensation: base salaries (which were not restricted in magnitude) and restricted stock (limited to grant-date values no more than half of base salaries). The forms of compensation explicitly prohibited under the Dodd amendments for TARP recipients include performance-based bonuses, retention bonuses, signing bonuses, severance pay, and all forms of stock options.

Finally, the Dodd amendments imposed mandatory "say on pay" resolutions for all TARP recipients. (The requirements were extended to all publicly traded firms under the 2010 Dodd-Frank Act, to be discussed later.) In early 2009—not long after the Dow Jones industrial average hit its crisis minimum at about 6500—shareholders had an opportunity to provide a nonbinding vote of approval on the 2008 compensation received by the top executives at the TARP recipients (in other words, the compensation for the year when these firms allegedly dragged the economy into a financial crisis). As an interesting historical footnote, none of the TARP recipients received a majority vote against its executive compensation levels and policies.

There is another interesting historical footnote: while almost all attempts to regulate executive compensation have produced negative unintended side effects, the Dodd amendments produced a positive one. In particular, many TARP recipients found the draconian pay restrictions sufficiently onerous that they hurried to pay back the government in time to receive year-end bonuses.

As draconian as the Dodd amendments (triggered by the Merrill Lynch payments) were, things were about to get worse. The next flash point for outrage over bonuses involved insurance giant American International Group (AIG), which had received over $170 billion in government bailout funds, in large part to offset over $40 billion in credit default swap losses from its financial products unit. In March 2009, AIG reported that it was about to pay $168 million as the second installment of $450 million in contractually obligated retention bonuses to employees

TABLE 12.2 / Comparison of Pay Restrictions in EESA (2008),
Obama Proposal (2009), and ARRA (2009)

Legislation or Proposal	Restrictions on Executive Compensation
Limits on Pay Levels and Deductibility	
Pre-EESA (IRS §162[m], 1994)	Limits deductibility of top five executives' pay to $1 million, with exceptions for performance-based pay
EESA (2008): all TARP recipients	Limits deductibility of top five executives' pay to $500,000, with no exceptions for performance-based pay
Obama proposal (2009): exceptional assistance firms	In addition to deductibility limits, cash pay is capped at $500,000; additional amounts can be paid in restricted shares vesting after the government is paid back
Obama proposal (2009): other TARP recipients	Same as exceptional assistance firms, but pay caps can be waived if firm offers full disclosure of pay policies and a nonbinding "say on pay" vote
ARRA (2009): all TARP recipients	In addition to deductibility limits, disallows all incentive payments, except for restricted stock capped at no more than one-half base salary; no caps on salary
Golden Parachutes	
Pre-EESA (IRS §280[g], 1986)	Tax penalties for change-in-control-related payments exceeding three times base pay
EESA (2008): Auction Program	No new severance agreements for top five executives
EESA (2008): Capital Purchase Program	No new severance agreements for top five executives, and no payments for top five executives under existing plans exceeding three times base pay
Obama proposal (2009): exceptional assistance firms	No payments for top ten executives; next twenty-five executives limited to one times base pay
Obama proposal (2009): other TARP recipients	No payments for top five executives under existing plans exceeding one times base pay
ARRA (2009): all TARP recipients	No payments for top ten executives; disallows all payments (not just excess payments)
Clawbacks	
Pre-EESA (Sarbanes-Oxley, 2002)	Covers CEO and CFO of publicly traded firms following restatements
EESA (2008): Auction Program	No new provisions
EESA (2008): Capital Purchase Program	Covers top five executives; applies to public and private firms; not exclusively triggered by restatement; no limits on recovery period; covers broad material inaccuracies (not just accounting restatements)
Obama proposal (2009): all TARP recipients	Same as terms of Capital Purchase Program, but covers twenty executives
ARRA (2009): all TARP recipients	Covers twenty-five executives for all TARP participants, retroactively

Source: Author's compilation.

in the troubled unit. (The public outrage intensified after revelations that most of AIG's bailout money had gone directly to its trading partners, including Goldman Sachs [$13 billion], Germany's Deutsche Bank [$12 billion], and France's Société Générale [$12 billion].) The political fallout was swift and furious: in the week following the revelations, seven bills were introduced in the House and Senate aimed specifically at the bonuses paid by AIG and other firms bailed out through Treasury's Troubled Asset Relief Program:

- The Bailout Bonus Tax Bracket Act of 2009 (H.R. 1518) imposed a 100 percent tax on bonuses over $100,000.

- H.R. 1527 imposed an additional 60 percent tax (on top of the 35 percent ordinary income tax) on bonuses exceeding $100,000 paid to employees of businesses in which the federal government had an ownership interest of 79 percent or more. (Not coincidentally, the government owned 80 percent of AIG when the bill was introduced.)

- The End Government Reimbursement of Excessive Executive Disbursements Act (the "End GREED" Act, H.R. 1575) authorized the attorney general to seek recovery of and limit excessive compensation.

- The AIG Bonus Payment Bill (H.R. 1577) required the secretary of Treasury to implement a plan within two weeks to thwart the payment of the AIG bonuses and required Treasury approval of any future bonuses by any TARP recipient.

- H.R. 1586 sought to impose a 90 percent income tax on bonuses paid by TARP recipients; employees would be exempt from the tax if they returned the bonus in the year received.

- The Compensation Fairness Act of 2009 (S. 651) imposed a 70 percent excise tax (half paid by the employee and half by the employer) on any bonus over $50,000 paid by a TARP firm.

- The Pay for Performance Act of 2009 (H.R. 1664) prohibited any compensation payment (under existing as well as new plans) if such compensation was deemed unreasonable or excessive by the secretary of the Treasury and included bonuses or retention payments not directly based on approved performance measures. The bill also created a Commission on Executive Compensation to study and report to the president and Congress on the compensation arrangements at TARP firms.

H.R. 1518, 1527, 1575, and 1577 and S. 651 were either stalled in committees or failed in a vote. However, H.R. 1586 and H.R. 1664 (the Pay for Performance Act of 2009) were passed by the House and sent to the Senate. H.R. 1586 was ultimately passed after being stripped of the executive compensation provisions, while the main features of H.R. 1664 were incorporated into the July 2010 Dodd-Frank Wall Street Reform and Consumer Protection Act.[17] Although ultimately only H.R. 1664 had any relevance to policy, I list them all here as evidence of congressional outrage and political resolve to punish Wall Street for its bonus practices.

Treasury Issues Final Rules and Appoints a Pay Czar

The Dodd amendments were signed into law with the understanding that the U.S. Treasury would work out the implementation details. In June 2009, Treasury issued its rulings and simultaneously created the Office of the Special Master of Executive Compensation. The special master (colloquially known as "the pay czar") had wide-ranging authority over all TARP recipients, but was particularly responsible for all compensation paid to the top twenty-five executives in the seven firms deemed to have required exceptional assistance from the U.S. government: Bank of America, Citigroup, AIG, General Motors, Chrysler, and the financing arms of GM and Chrysler.[18]

Since taxpayers had become the major stakeholder in the seven exceptional assistance firms, the government arguably had a legitimate interest in these firms' compensation policies. One could imagine, for example, embracing an objective of maximizing shareholder value while protecting taxpayers, or perhaps maximizing taxpayer return on investment. However, Treasury instructed the special master to make pay determinations using the "public interest standard," an ill-defined concept that allows too much discretion and destroys accountability for those exercising the discretion. For example, applying the public interest standard allows Congress to limit compensation that it perceives as excessive, without evidence or accountability for the consequences. Similarly, invoking the public interest standard forced the special master to navigate between the conflicting demands of politicians (who were insisting on punishments) and taxpayers and shareholders (who were concerned with attracting, retaining, and motivating executives and employees).

Ultimately, the special master catered to prevailing political and public sentiment and severely penalized the executives in firms viewed as responsible for the meltdown by drastically reducing their cash compensation. As shown in table 12.3, 2009 cash compensation at the three banks regulated by the special master was cut by an average of 94 percent, while total compensation was cut by an average of 64 percent.

As an example of how the public interest standard can lead to punitive pay cuts, consider the case of Bank of America's Ken Lewis, who as recently as December 2008 was named *American Banker*'s "Banker of the Year" for his firm's rescue of Merrill Lynch (Fitzpatrick and Scannell 2009). In October 2009, Lewis announced that he would step down at the end of the year and indicated that he would forgo his 2009 bonus and the remainder of his 2009 salary. The special master decided that was not enough and demanded that Lewis return *all* the salary already earned for services rendered that year or risk a determination that his contractual pension benefits were contrary to the public interest (and therefore subject to renegotiation) (Story 2009). It is difficult to view this decision as anything other than punitive and a misuse of the public interest standard, since Lewis had clearly rendered services on behalf of Bank of America during 2009 and should clearly have been compensated for that service.

TABLE 12.3 / Changes in Pay Imposed by the U.S. Treasury's Special Master
for Seven U.S. Firms Requiring Exceptional Assistance

Corporation	Percentage Change in Pay from 2008 Levels		Percentage Change in Pay from 2007 Levels		Number of Executives in Top Twenty-Five
	Cash	Total	Cash	Total	
AIG	−90.8%	−57.8%	−89.2%	−55.7%	13
Bank of America	−94.5	−65.5	−92.2	−63.3	13
Citigroup	−96.4	−69.7	−78.4	−89.6	21
General Motors	−31.0	−24.7	−46.0	−16.9	20
Chrysler	−17.9	+24.2	+14.0	+72.3	25
GMAC	−50.2	−85.6	−42.5	−78.2	22
Chrysler Financial	−29.9	−56.0	n.a.	n.a.	22

Source: Author's compilation of data from U.S. Department of the Treasury (2009).

The Dodd-Frank Wall Street Reform and Consumer Protection Act (2010–2011)

PAY RESTRICTIONS FOR FINANCIAL INSTITUTIONS   In July 2010, President Obama signed
into law the Dodd-Frank Wall Street Reform and Consumer Protection Act, which
was the culmination of controversial and wide-ranging efforts on the part of both
the president and Congress to regulate the financial services industry. While the
pay restrictions in the TARP legislation apply only to banks receiving government
assistance, the Dodd-Frank Act goes much further by regulating pay for all financial institutions: TARP recipients and nonrecipients; both public and private institutions, including Fannie Mae and Freddie Mac; and U.S.-based operations of foreign
banks. Specifically, part (a) of section 956 of the Dodd-Frank Act requires all financial
institutions to identify and disclose (to their relevant regulator) any incentive-based
compensation arrangements that could lead to material financial loss to the covered
financial institution or that provide an executive officer, employee, director, or principal shareholder of the covered financial institution with excessive compensation,
fees, or benefits. In addition, part (b) of section 956 prohibits financial institutions
from adopting any incentive plan that in the determination of regulators encourages inappropriate risks by (1) providing an executive officer, employee, director, or
principal shareholder with excessive compensation, fees, or benefits; or (2) raising
the possibility of material financial loss to the financial institution.

The responsibility for implementing section 956 of the Dodd-Frank Act fell
jointly to seven agencies: the Securities and Exchange Commission (SEC), the
Federal Reserve System, the Office of the Comptroller of the Currency (OCC), the
Office of Thrift Supervision (OTS), the Federal Deposit Insurance Corporation
(FDIC), the National Credit Union Administration (NCUA), and the Federal
Housing Finance Agency (FHFA). In March 2011, the seven agencies issued a joint
proposal for public comment, modeled in part on section 39 of the Federal Deposit
Insurance Act of 1950. Although the proposal stops short of explicitly limiting the

level of executive compensation, it prohibits compensation that is unreasonable or disproportionate to the amount, nature, quality, and scope of the services performed. In addition, the proposal calls on firms to identify the individuals who could expose the firm to substantial risk, and for the larger institutions, it demands that such individuals have at least 50 percent of their bonuses deferred for at least three years; deferred amounts would be subject to forfeiture if subsequent performance deteriorates. Final rules are expected in 2012.

PAY AND GOVERNANCE REFORMS FOR ALL PUBLICLY TRADED COMPANIES   Although they ostensibly were focused on regulating firms in the financial services industry, the authors of the Dodd-Frank Act seized the opportunity to pass a sweeping reform of executive compensation and corporate governance and impose it on all large publicly traded U.S. firms across all industries. The new rules include:

"Say on pay": Shareholders are to be asked to approve the company's executive compensation practices in a nonbinding vote at least every three years (with an additional vote the first year and every six years thereafter to determine whether the "say on pay" votes will occur every one, two, or three years). In addition, companies are required to disclose, and shareholders are asked to approve (again, in a nonbinding vote), any "golden parachute" payments in connection with mergers, tender offers, or going-private transactions. In January 2011—and effective for the 2011 proxy season—the SEC adopted rules concerning shareholder approval of executive compensation and "golden parachute" compensation arrangements. Shareholders of 98.5 percent of the 2,532 companies reporting by July 2011 approved the pay plans; over 70 percent of the companies received more than 90 percent favorable support (Holzer 2011b).

Clawbacks: Companies must implement and report policies for recouping payments to executives based on financial statements that are subsequently restated. The rule applies to any current or former executive officer (an expansion of Sarbanes-Oxley, under which only the CEO and CFO are subject to clawbacks) and applies to any payments made in the three-year period preceding the restatement. (Sarbanes-Oxley applies only for the twelve months following the filing of the inaccurate statement.) The SEC intends to propose rules regarding the recovery of executive compensation by late 2012.

Compensation committee independence: Following Sarbanes-Oxley requirements for audit committees, publicly traded companies are required to have compensation committees comprising solely outside independent directors (the determination of their independence taking into account any financial ties they might have with the firm). In March 2011, the SEC proposed listing standards relating to the independence of the members on a compensation committee, the committee's authority to retain compensation advisers, and the committee's responsibility for the appointment, compensation, and work of any compensation adviser. Once an exchange's new listing standards are in effect, a listed company must meet these standards in order for its shares to continue trading on that exchange for compensation committees. Final rules were issued in June 2012.

Proxy access: The Dodd-Frank Act authorized the SEC to issue rules allowing certain shareholders to nominate their own director candidates in the company's annual proxy statements. The SEC issued its rules on proxy access in August 2010, but delayed implementation after lawsuits by the Business Roundtable and the U.S. Chamber of Commerce claimed that the rules would distract management and advance special-interest agendas. In July 2011, the U.S. Circuit Court of Appeals (Washington, D.C.) ruled in favor of the business groups and issued a sharp rebuke to the SEC, saying that the SEC had failed in analyzing the cost that the rule would impose on companies and in supporting its claim that the rule would improve shareholder value and board performance (Holzer 2011a).

It is too early to assess the ultimate effect of Dodd-Frank on executive compensation, since many of the rules have just been implemented or are still being written. Indeed, attorneys at DavisPolk (2010) calculate that the act requires regulators to create 243 new rules, conduct 67 studies, and issue 22 periodic reports. Without question, the Dodd-Frank Act as ultimately implemented will provide financial economists with research fodder for years to come.

ASSESSMENTS

The public and political outrage over banking bonuses reflects perceptions that such bonuses are excessive and were a contributing factor to the financial crisis. In this final section, I provide my assessments of whether banking bonuses indeed caused the final crisis, whether such bonuses are excessive (and how we might define "excessive" in this context), whether the political responses serve to mitigate excessive risk taking, and whether banking bonuses should (or even can) be further regulated.

Did Banking Bonuses Cause the Financial Crisis?

The hypothesis that compensation arrangements at financial institutions precipitated the financial crisis has gained considerable political and popular appeal. Certain facts—that the financial meltdown involved banks, that banks rely heavily on bonuses, and that pay levels in banks are high—have led many in the political sector or popular press to presume that banking bonuses must have caused the crisis and thus need to be reformed. However, "connecting the dots" is not an accepted way to pursue a scientific inquiry, and the empirical evidence in support of such claims is currently not overwhelming.

The emerging academic evidence on banking bonuses and the financial crisis is largely consistent with the findings documented in this chapter: there is little evidence that the Wall Street bonus culture provided incentives for risk-taking, at least among top-level banking executives. After investigating ninety-five banks from 2006 through December 2008, Fahlenbrach and Stulz (2011) reject the hypothesis that compensation arrangements at banks were fundamentally flawed. They find that CEOs with incentives that were better aligned to shareholders actually performed worse in the crisis. CEOs took decisions they felt would be profitable for shareholders ex ante, but ultimately these turned out to perform badly ex post. If CEOs had advance knowledge that their decisions would not optimize shareholder value, then they would have taken actions to insulate their own personal wealth from adverse price movements. However, Fahlenbrach and Stulz find no evidence of unusual share selling or other hedging activity by bank executives in advance of the crisis. They also show that CEOs' aggregate stock and option holdings was more than eight times the value of their annual compensation. The amount of CEO wealth at risk prior to the financial crisis makes it improbable that any rational CEO knew of an impending financial crash or knowingly engaged in excessively risky behavior.

Similarly, I have documented elsewhere (Murphy 2009) that executives in banks participating in the TARP program had "more to lose" (they faced larger downside risks) than did executives in banks not participating (or executives outside of the banking sector). Again, if those bank executives had known about an impending crash, then one would have expected to observe them engaging in hedging activities to mitigate such risk—there is no systematic evidence that they did so. Other data are consistent with this conclusion. Ing-Haw Cheng, Harrison Hong, and José Scheinkman (2009) find that executives with better incentives (which they define based on residuals from annual compensation regressions) have higher capital asset pricing model (CAPM) betas and higher return volatilities and are more likely to be in the tails of performance (with especially high pre-crisis performance and especially low performance during the crash). Renee Adams (2009) compares nonfinancial to financial firms from 1996 to 2007. She finds that governance arrangements in financial firms are typically no worse than in nonfinancial firms. Interestingly, she finds that, controlling for firm size, the level of CEO pay and the fraction of equity-based pay was actually lower in banks, even in 2007. Also, banks receiving bailout money had boards that were more independent than boards of other banks. Outside of the United States, Ken Bechmann and Johannes Raaballe (2009) analyze CEO pay and performance in a sample of Danish banks and also find that CEOs with more incentive-based compensation (and thus more to lose from poor performance) performed worse than CEOs at other banks during the crisis. Therefore, while there appears to be a correlation between compensation structures and performance during the crisis, the companies faring the worst in the crisis were those with better (and not worse) executive incentives.

In contrast, Lucian Bebchuk, Alma Cohen, and Holger Spamann (2010) and Sanjai Bhagat and Brian Bolton (2011) conclude that top-level banking executives had incentives to take excessive risks, based on the finding that the amount of cash the executives extracted from their firms between 2000 and 2008 (from salaries, nondeferred cash bonuses, and stock sales) was often more than the losses realized during the crisis. The underlying (though largely unstated) theory is that executives pursued investments they knew would deliver short-run gains but long-term losses and that they were willing to do this because they could extract enough cash in the short run to make the bad investments worthwhile. As discussed earlier, the underlying theory is not about risk-taking at all, but rather about rewarding short-term rather than long-term results. Moreover, the authors present no evidence that the executives knew that their investments would ultimately fail, and they do not explain why the executives were so inept at cashing out: when the crisis hit, the executives were left with large holdings of vested stock and exercisable options that would presumably have been sold (or exercised and then sold) if they had truly known that the "long term" had arrived.

In January 2011, the Financial Crisis Inquiry Commission (FCIC) issued its report on the causes of the financial crisis (Angelides et al. 2011). The commission's final report was over six hundred pages long, containing twenty-two chapters and supporting material. While providing no direct evidence that pay practices were complicit in the crisis, the report takes a "guilt by association" approach, showing a widening pay gap between bankers and nonbankers and generally criticizing banking bonuses for being too short-term-oriented. Six of the ten commission members voted to accept the report, and four members dissented; the disagreement was serious enough for two dissenting reports to be issued. The first dissenting report (Hennessey, Holtz-Eakin, and Thomas 2011) identified ten factors that caused the crisis: a credit bubble, a housing bubble, nontraditional mortgages, credit rating and securitization, financial institutions' correlated risk, leverage and liquidity risk, risks of contagion, common macroeconomic shocks, a severe financial shock, and the financial shock causing the economic crisis in the real economy. Executive and other compensation practices did not figure as a major part of the problem. The second dissenting report (Wallison 2011) argued that "Wall Street greed and compensation polices" were at most trivial contributions to the crisis compared to the growth in nontraditional mortgages.

The precise causes of the global financial crisis will be debated for decades (just as the precise causes of the 1930s depression are still being debated). However, the evolving consensus suggests that the risk-taking that contributed to the crisis reflected a combination of factors, including social policies on homeownership, loose monetary policies, "too big to fail" guarantees, and poorly implemented financial innovations such as exotic mortgages, securitization, and collateralized debt obligations. These different factors, however, have nothing (or little) to do with the Wall Street bonus culture.

Are Regulators Responding to "Excessive Risk" or "Excessive Pay"?

Once taxpayers became a major stakeholder in the TARP recipients (and especially in the seven recipients requiring "exceptional assistance"), the government arguably had a legitimate interest in the firms' compensation policies. For example, compensation policies should clearly avoid providing incentives to take excessive risks with taxpayer money. More generally, one could imagine embracing an objective of "maximizing shareholder value while protecting taxpayers," or perhaps "maximizing taxpayer return on investment."

Similarly, the government arguably has a legitimate interest in banks protected by FDIC insurance, since shareholders receive all of the upside rewards from risky activities, while taxpayers share in the downside. The government may also have an interest in firms protected by vague and undefined "too big to fail" guarantees for roughly the same reason, though the legitimacy of the interest here is a bit more dubious and difficult to quantify.

However, in retrospect, the apparent intent of the pay restrictions in TARP and Dodd-Frank is not to reduce risk, improve pay, or protect taxpayers, but rather to attack perceived excesses in pay levels and destroy the Wall Street banking culture. Beyond generic demands that pay not provide incentives to take unnecessary or excessive risk (offered without defining excessive risk or suggesting how boards might distinguish between excessive and normal risks), the pay restrictions in EESA, ARRA, and Dodd-Frank offer no obvious protections for taxpayers.

For example, when ARRA with the Dodd amendments was enacted in February 2009, Congress and the general public were angry at Wall Street and its bonus culture and suspicious that this culture was a root cause of the financial crisis. By limiting compensation to uncapped base salaries coupled with modest amounts of restricted stock, the Dodd amendments completely upended the traditional Wall Street model of low base salaries coupled with high bonuses paid in a combination of cash, restricted stock, and stock options. A charitable interpretation is that Congress decided that banking compensation was sufficiently out of control that the only way to save Wall Street was to destroy its bonus culture. More plausibly, Congress's intention was to punish the executives and firms allegedly responsible for the crisis.

In return for the TARP investments, the government typically received a combination of preferred stock and warrants to purchase common equity at a predetermined market price. Taxpayers therefore want executive compensation to be tied to the contractual dividend payments on (or repurchases of) the preferred stock and on the appreciation of the common stock. Most compensation consultants and practitioners working on behalf of taxpayers would have recommended low base salaries coupled with bonuses tied to company operating performance (most likely based on cash flows available for preferred dividends) and stock options, restricted stock, and other plans tied to shareholder-value creation. Taxpayers would also be in favor of firms being able to pay reasonable signing bonuses to attract executive talent into the company and to pay reasonable severance to ease the transition of executives leaving the company.

In contrast, the ARRA allowed exactly two forms of compensation (base salary and restricted stock) and put no limits on the amount of base salary, but limited restricted stock to no more than one-half of base salary (that is, no more than one-third of total compensation). The legislation prohibited signing bonuses, incentive bonuses, severance bonuses, stock options, performance shares, fringe benefits, and other common components of well-designed compensation plans. The pay restrictions in the legislation were destructive and ultimately harmful for both taxpayers and shareholders.

The attack on perceived excesses in compensation continued under the 2010 Dodd-Frank Act. Since at least the early 1990s, there has always been a tension between shareholders (a firm's legal owners) concerned about CEO incentives and third parties (such as politicians and labor unions) concerned about high levels of pay. After the TARP bailouts in the financial crisis, the analogous tension was between taxpayers (who wanted to be protected from excessive risks while receiving an appropriate return on their investment) and politicians who were outraged about perceived excesses in banking bonuses. Section 956 of the Dodd-Frank Act deliberately conflated these tensions by explicitly defining "excessive compensation, fees, or benefits" as an inappropriate risk. Moreover, the act required banks to inform their regulators of compensation plans that provide excessive compensation, delegating to the regulators the Herculean task of defining what compensation is excessive (or, indeed, which risks are inappropriate).

Are Banking Bonuses Excessive?

When executive compensation is described as "excessive" (or "inappropriate" or "unwarranted"), the individual offering the description usually means one of three things. First, the term might refer to cases where compensation is determined not by competitive market forces but rather by captive board members catering to rent-seeking entrenched executives.[19] Second, the term might refer to concerns about the misallocation of resources, such as a belief that top executives should not earn that much more than teachers because teachers are more important to society. Finally, although generally not acknowledged by the participants in these often frenzied debates, the term might reflect one of the least attractive aspects of human beings: jealousy and envy.

Without question, the highest-paid employees in financial services firms are paid more than their counterparts in other industries. The rewards available to top performers have attracted the best and brightest college, MBA, and PhD graduates into financial services. Although some might argue that it would be better to have the best and brightest graduates become doctors or public servants, a general advantage of a capitalist free-market economy is its propensity to move resources to higher-valued uses.

The fact that pay is *high* does not, however, imply that pay is *excessive* in the sense of not being determined by competitive market forces. Even the most vocal advocates of the view that powerful CEOs effectively set their own salaries rarely apply the view to executives and employees below the very top. The highest-paid employees in financial services firms typically have scarce and highly specialized skills that are specific to their industry but not necessarily to their employer. As a result, employees in financial services are remarkably mobile, both domestically and internationally, compared to employees in virtually any other sector in the economy. When the Dodd amendments were enacted in February 2009, the entire global financial system was in crisis and there was a belief that pay could be cut "across the board" since, after all, there was nowhere else for financial services employees to go. However, even by the time the special master made his pay determinations in October 2009, the world had changed: most formerly constrained recipients had repaid their TARP obligations, were actively hiring, and were competing with unconstrained hedge funds and private equity funds for top financial talent.

As evidence of the mobility of financial service executives, consider the following result from table 12.3: of the seventy-five highest-paid executives at AIG, Bank of America, and Citigroup in 2008, only forty-seven (62 percent) had remained with their firms through October 2009 (and were thus subject to pay approval by the special master). Although the twenty-eight departures were not all "regretted resignations" (they included several former Merrill Lynch traders and some resignations encouraged by the special master), the departures did include several high-performing executives and traders. For example, Andrew J. Hall, the head of Phibro, Citigroup's profitable energy-trading division, was set to receive $100 million in bonuses for 2009. Although Citigroup maintained that these bonuses should be exempt from the special master's scrutiny because they were based on a contract that predated TARP, the special master contended that the contract could be voided because it promoted excessive risk-taking and ran counter to the public interest (Dash and Healy 2009). To avoid the conflict, Citigroup sold the Phibro unit at approximately its book value to Occidental Petroleum, which in turn promptly (and happily) paid Hall his contractual bonus. The Phibro divestiture deprived taxpayers of approximately $400 million in annual net cash flow that would have been available to pay dividends or retire preferred stock.

Assuming (with good evidence) that banking bonuses are the result of competitive market forces, and assuming (also with good evidence) that a capitalist free-market economy is relatively efficient in moving resources to higher-valued uses, the most consistent interpretation of the continued outrage over banking bonuses is that the parties making the attacks are opposed to high banking bonuses per se and that their outrage appears to go far beyond concerns that such bonuses motivated excessive risk-taking.

Should Banking Bonuses Be Regulated?

Compensation practices in financial services can certainly be improved. For example, cash bonus plans in financial services can be improved by extending and enforcing bonus banks or clawback provisions for the recovery of rewards if and when there is future revision of the critical indicators on which the rewards were based or received. Indeed, in the wake of the financial crisis in late 2008 (and before the 2010 Dodd-Frank Act), several financial institutions introduced clawback provisions allowing the firm to recover bonuses paid to traders and other employees on profits that subsequently proved to be incorrect. In November 2008, UBS introduced a "bonus malus" system in which at least two-thirds of senior managers' bonuses in good years are "banked" to offset possible losses in subsequent bad years (Associated Press 2008). In December 2008, Morgan Stanley introduced a clawback feature to its bonuses for seven thousand executives and employees that enabled the company to recover a portion of bonuses for employees who caused "a restatement of results, a significant financial loss or other reputational harm to the firm" (Farrell and Guerra 2008). In January 2009, Credit Suisse began paying bonuses in illiquid risky securities that lose value in bad years and can be forfeited if employees quit their job or are fired (Harrington 2009). These moves represent a good start toward a general adoption of clawback provisions.

Bonus plans in financial services can also be improved by ensuring that bonuses are based on value creation rather than on the volume of transactions without regard to the quality of transactions. Measuring value creation is inherently subjective, and such plans will necessarily involve discretionary payments based on subjective assessments of performance.

Compensation practices in financial services can undoubtedly be improved through government oversight focused on rewarding value creation and punishing value destruction. However, it is highly unlikely that compensation practices can be improved through increased government rules and regulations. Indeed, as I emphasize in Murphy (2011a) and Murphy (2011b), the U.S. government has a long history of attempts to regulate executive pay that systematically created unanticipated side effects that generally led to higher pay levels and less efficient incentives.

Part of the problem with governmental regulation of pay is that such interventions, even when well intended, always create unintended (and usually costly) side effects. For example, laws introduced in 1984 to reduce "golden parachute" payments led to a proliferation of change-in-control arrangements, employment contracts, and tax gross-ups. Similarly, a variety of rules implemented in the early 1990s are largely responsible for fueling the escalation in pay levels and option grants in the 1990s, and the enhanced disclosure of perquisites in the 1970s is generally credited with fueling an explosion in the breadth of benefits offered to executives. More recently, the Dodd-Frank–inspired rules mandating deferral of bonuses has resulted in large increases in base salaries among financial firms.[20]

In addition, efficient compensation practices inherently vary across time, sector, and the unique economic circumstances facing individual firms and executives. In contrast, government regulation inherently imposes one-size-fits-all rules to disparate organizations. For example, the seven government agencies charged with implementing section 956 of Dodd-Frank are attempting to impose a one-size-fits-all model on broker-dealers, commercial banks, investment banks, credit unions, savings associations, domestic branches of foreign banks, and investment advisers.

More importantly, regulation is often designed to be punitive rather than constructive and is inherently driven by politicians more interested in pursuing their political agendas than creating shareholder value. For example, the draconian restrictions on pay for TARP recipients are clearly punitive and politically motivated. Similarly, the provision in the Dodd-Frank Act requiring firms to report the ratio of CEO pay to the pay for the median worker at the firm reflects a political agenda to reduce levels of pay rather than a shareholder agenda to improve pay.

It is important to recognize that the outrage over banking bonuses is emanating not from shareholders but from politicians, labor unions, and the general public. Although such outrage is understandable—especially toward banks paying bonuses after being bailed out by taxpayers—it is often driven by jealousy and envy, not by concerns about maximizing value or even protecting taxpayer interests in the future. Moreover, even for those who believe that CEOs can effectively set their own salaries, there is no credible evidence that the compensation arrangements for lower-level bankers, traders, underwriters, and brokers are set in anything other than a highly competitive market for talent. For better or worse, there is an extremely scarce supply of individuals with the highly specialized skills required to understand and trade in increasingly complex derivative instruments, and the market for such individuals is global, with little respect for international boundaries. Restricting banking bonuses for TARP recipients led to a drain of talent from those banks to private equity and unrestricted banks (including those banks that quickly paid the money back). Similarly, punitive restrictions on financial institutions will lead to both costly circumvention and a drain of talent from restricted to unrestricted sectors.

To summarize, pay practices in the financial services sector can clearly be improved, and many of the largest banks have made significant changes in their plans in anticipation of, or perhaps to preempt, government intervention. Ultimately, the question is not whether banking compensation should be reformed, but whether the government is the efficient agent of reform. The best improvements in executive compensation will emanate from stronger corporate governance, not from direct government intervention.

NOTES

1. This chapter draws in part from Murphy (2009, 2010, 2012), Murphy and Jensen (2011), and Conyon et al. (2011).

2. The $18.4 billion payout was estimated by the New York State comptroller based on personal income tax collections.

3. The $10 billion bailout to Merrill Lynch in October 2008 was ultimately delayed (pending the merger) and then completed on January 9, 2009.

4. In contrast, the percentage of employees with million-dollar bonuses in the more traditional banks was 0.3 percent or less.

5. Realized pay under the pre-2006 disclosure rules includes the grant-date rather than the vesting value of restricted shares.

6. Realized 2000 CEO pay in the S&P 500 broker-dealer firms included $93.8 million for Philip Purcell (Morgan Stanley), $83.6 million for Richard Fuld (Lehman Brothers), $54.7 million for James Cayne (Bear Stearns), $49.6 million for David Komansky (Merrill Lynch), and $35.5 million for Charles Schwab Jr. (Charles Schwab).

7. Following SEC disclosure rules, the CEO and, after 2006, the CFO are included among the top five executives even if their compensation is less than that of other executive officers. In cases where firms disclose pay for more than five executives, I use the five highest-paid executives based on grant-date values for stock and options.

8. ExecuComp tracks firms in the S&P 500, S&P MidCap 400, and S&P SmallCap 600, along with a modest number of additional firms that are included in various S&P indices (or firms that dropped out of one of the major indices).

9. These figures are taken from Goldman Sachs 2008 and 2009 proxy statements. Blankfein's actual cash bonus was a bit lower, and his stock grant a bit higher, because he voluntarily elected to receive additional shares (at a discount) in lieu of cash compensation. Because of a quirk in SEC reporting rules, bonuses that were paid in cash for 2007 performance and received after fiscal closing are reported as 2007 compensation in the 2008 proxy statement, but bonuses that were paid in stock or options for 2007 performance and received after fiscal closing are considered 2008 compensation and reported in the 2009 proxy statement.

10. The percentage option holdings multiplied by the option delta is a measure of the change in CEO option-related wealth corresponding to a change in shareholder wealth. More formally, suppose that the CEO holds N options, and suppose that shareholder wealth increases by \$1. If there are S total shares outstanding, the share price P will increase by $\Delta P = \$1/S$, and the value of the CEO's options will increase by $N\Delta P(\partial V/\partial P)$, where V is the Black-Scholes value of each option, and $(\partial V/\partial P)$ is the option delta (Black and Scholes 1973). Substituting for ΔP, the CEO's share of the value increase is given by $(N/S)(\partial V/\partial P)$, or the CEO's options held as a fraction of total shares outstanding multiplied by the "slope" of the Black-Scholes valuation. For examples of this approach, see Jensen and Murphy (1990a), Yermack (1995), and Murphy (1999). Brian Hall and I (Hall and Murphy 2002) offer a modified approach to measure the pay-for-performance incentives of risk-averse undiversified executives. An alternative approach, adopted in Jensen and Murphy (1990b), involves estimating the option pay-performance sensitivity as the coefficient from a regression of the change in option value on the change in shareholder wealth.

11. Suppose that the CEO holds M shares and N options, and suppose that the share price P increases by 1 percent. If there are S total shares outstanding, the value of the CEO's portfolio will increase by $.01P(M + N(\partial V/\partial P))$, or $.01(PS)[(M + N(\partial V/\partial P))/S]$, where PS is the firm's market capitalization and the quantity in the square brackets is the equation for the CEO's effective ownership percentage.

12. The moral hazard problem in securitization is limited by "early pay default" clauses, which require originators to repurchase loans that become delinquent within ninety days of securitization (Piskorski, Seru, and Vig 2010). I also note that mortgage lenders such as Countrywide kept most of their mortgages in their own portfolios, and that CDO underwriters such as Merrill Lynch held on to a large portion of their own mortgage-backed CDOs.

13. There is a subtle but important difference between "negative bonuses" and "clawbacks." The former occur when the performance metrics appropriately indicate that bonuses should be negative instead of positive. The latter refer to the recovery of bonuses paid based on performance data that were subsequently revised. Deferred bonuses and bonus banks can address both situations.

14. This section draws heavily from Murphy and Jensen (2011).

15. TARP recipients not considered exceptional assistance firms could waive the disclosure and "say on pay" requirements, but would then be subject to the \$500,000 limit on compensation (excluding restricted stock).

16. The number of executives covered by the Dodd amendments varied by the size of the TARP bailout, with the maximum number effective for TARP investments exceeding \$500 million. As a point of reference, the average TARP firm among the original eight recipients received an average of \$20 *billion* in funding, and virtually all of the outrage

over banking bonuses has involved banks taking well over $500 million in government funds. Therefore, we report results assuming that firms are in the top group of recipients.

17. Without trying to explain (because it is beyond my comprehension), H.R. 1586 was ultimately passed and signed into law as the FAA Air Transportation Modernization and Safety Improvement Act, stripped of any mention of executive bonuses and TARP recipients.

18. For the record, I (along with Lucian Bebchuk from Harvard) served as an academic adviser to Kenneth Feinberg, the special master. However, the fact that advice was given does not imply that it was followed.

19. See, for example, the "managerial power" views advanced by Bebchuk and Fried (2003, 2004a, 2004b), Bebchuk, Grinstein, and Peyer (2010), Bebchuk, Fried, and Walker (2002), and Fried (1998, 2008a, 2008b).

20. In early 2011, for example, Bank of America, Citigroup, Morgan Stanley, and Goldman Sachs all announced significant increases in base salaries (see Rappaport 2011).

REFERENCES

Adams, Renee B. 2009. "Governance and the Financial Crisis." ECGI—Finance Working Paper 248/2009. Available at http://ssrn.com/abstract=1398583 (accessed June 27, 2012).

Andrews, Edmund L., and Vikas Bajaj. 2009. "Amid Fury, U.S. Is Set to Curb Executives' Pay After Bailouts." *New York Times,* February 4, p. A1, A20.

Angelides, Phil, Brooksley Born, Byron Georgiou, Bob Graham, Heather H. Murren, and John W. Thompson. 2011. *The Financial Crisis Inquiry Report.* Washington: U.S. Government Printing Office (January 27).

Associated Press. 2008. "UBS to Change the Way It Pays Senior Managers." Associated Press Newswires, November 17.

Baker, George P., and Brian Hall. 2004. "CEO Incentives and Firm Size." *Journal of Labor Economics* 22: 767–98.

Bebchuk, Lucian A., Alma Cohen, and Holger Spamann. 2010. "The Wages of Failure: Executive Compensation at Bear Stearns and Lehman, 2000–2008." *Yale Journal on Regulation* 27: 257–82.

Bebchuk, Lucian A., and Jesse M. Fried. 2003, "Executive Compensation as an Agency Problem." *Journal of Economic Perspectives* 17: 71+.

———. 2004a. *Pay Without Performance: The Unfulfilled Promise of Executive Compensation.* Cambridge, Mass.: Harvard University Press.

———. 2004b. "Stealth Compensation via Retirement Benefits." *Berkeley Business Law Journal* 1: 291–326.

Bebchuk, Lucian A., Jesse M. Fried, and David I. Walker. 2002. "Managerial Power and Rent Extraction in the Design of Executive Compensation." *University of Chicago Law Review* 69: 751–846. Available at: http://papers.ssrn.com/abstract=316590 (accessed June 27, 2012).

Bebchuk, Lucian A., Yaniv Grinstein, and Urs Peyer. 2010. "Lucky CEOs and Lucky Directors." *Journal of Finance* 65(6): 2363–2401.

Bebchuk, Lucian A., and Holger Spamann. 2010. "Regulating Bankers' Pay." *Georgetown Law Journal* 98: 247–87.

Bechmann, Ken L., and Johannes Raaballe. 2009. "Bad Corporate Governance and Powerful CEOs in Banks: Poor Performance, Excessive Risk-Taking, and a Misuse of Incentive-Based

Compensation." December 12. Available at: http://econ.au.dk/fileadmin/site_files/filer_oekonomi/seminarer/Management/BankPaper.12.12.09.pdf (accessed June 27, 2012).

Bhagat, Sanjai, and Brian Bolton. 2011. "Bank Executive Compensation and Capital Requirements Reform." Available at: http://leeds-faculty.colorado.edu/bhagat/BankComp-Capital-Jan2011.pdf (accessed June 27, 2012).

Black, Fischer, and Myron S. Scholes. 1973. "The Pricing of Options and Corporate Liabilities." *Journal of Political Economy* 81: 637–54.

Cheng, Ing-Haw, Harrison Hong, and José Scheinkman. 2009. "Yesterday's Heroes: Compensation and Creative Risk-Taking." ECGI—Finance Working Paper 285/2010. Available at: http://ssrn.com/abstract=1502762 (accessed June 27, 2012).

Cimilluca, Dana, Deborah Ball, and Carrick Mollenkamp. 2011. "UBS Raises Tally on Losses—Details Emerge Behind $2.3 Billion 'Rogue' Trading; Small Problem Got Bigger." *Wall Street Journal,* September 19.

Conyon, Martin J., Nuno Fernandes, Miguel A. Ferreira, Pedro Matos, and Kevin J. Murphy. 2011. "The Executive Compensation Controversy: A Transatlantic Analysis." Milan: Fondazione Rodolfo de Benedetti (February 13). Available at: http://digitalcommons.ilr.cornell.edu/cgi/viewcontent.cgi?article=1004&context=ics (accessed June 27, 2012).

Cuomo, Andrew M. (Attorney General, State of New York). 2009. "No Rhyme or Reason: The 'Heads I Win, Tails You Lose' Bank Bonus Culture." July 30. Available at: http://media.ft.com/cms/097ca69e-7d28-11de-b8ee-00144feabdc0.pdf. Data available at: http://www.ag.ny.gov/sites/default/files/press-releases/archived/Bonus%20Report%20Final%207.30.09.pdf (accessed June 27, 2012).

Dash, Eric, and Jack Healy. 2009. "Citi Averts Clash over Huge Bonus." *New York Times,* October 10.

DavisPolk. 2010. "Summary of the Dodd-Frank Wall Street Reform and Consumer Protection Act, Enacted into Law on July 21, 2010." New York: Davis Polk & Wardwell, LLP (July 21).

DiNapoli, Thomas P. 2011. "Wall Street Bonuses Declined in 2010" (press release). Albany: Office of the New York State Comptroller. Available at: http://osc.state.ny.us/press/releases/feb11/022311a.htm (accessed June 27, 2012).

Fahlenbrach, Rudiger, and René M. Stulz. 2011. "Bank CEO Incentives and the Credit Crisis." *Journal of Financial Economics* 99: 11–26.

Farrell, Greg, and Francesco Guerra. 2008. "Top Executives at Morgan Stanley and Merrill Forgo Their Bonuses." *Financial Times,* December 9.

Farrell, Greg, and Julie MacIntosh. 2009. "Merrill Paid Bonuses as Losses Mounted Ahead of Sale to BofA." *Financial Times,* January 22.

Fitzpatrick, Dan, and Kara Scannell. 2009. "BofA Hit by Fine over Merrill—Bank Pays SEC $33 Million in Bonus Dispute; Sallie Krawcheck Hired in Shake-up." *Wall Street Journal,* August 4.

Fitzpatrick, Dan, Kara Scannell, and Chad Bray. 2010. "Rakoff Backs BofA Accord, Unhappily." *Wall Street Journal,* February 23.

Forbes Magazine. 1970–1992. "CEO Compensation: Forbes 500." New York: Forbes. Recent data available at: http://www.forbes.com/lists/2012/12/ceo-compensation-12_land.html (accessed July 9, 2012).

French, Kenneth R., Martin N. Baily, John Y. Campbell, John H. Cochrane, Douglas W. Diamond, Darrell Duffie, Anil K. Kashyap, Frederic S. Mishkin, Raghuram G. Rajan, David S. Scharfstein, Robert J. Shiller, Hyun Song Shin, Matthe J. Slaughter, Jeremy C. Stein, and René M. Stulz. 2010. *The Squam Lake Report.* Princeton, N.J.: Princeton University Press.

Fried, Jesse M. 1998. "Reducing the Profitability of Corporate Insider Trading Through Pre-trading Disclosure." *Southern California Law Review* 71: 303–92.

———. 2008a. "Hands-Off Options." *Vanderbilt Law Review* 61: 453, 468–70.

———. 2008b. "Option Backdating and Its Implications." *Washington and Lee Law Review* 65: 853–86.

Frydman, Carola, and Dirk Jenter. 2010. "CEO Compensation." *Annual Review of Financial Economics* 2: 75–102.

Gauthier-Villars, David. 2010. "Rogue French Trader Sentenced to Three Years—Kerviel Is Ordered to Repay Société Générale $6.7 Billion." *Wall Street Journal,* October 6.

Gauthier-Villars, David, and Carrick Mollenkamp. 2008. "The Loss Where No One Looked—How Low-Level Trader Cost Société Générale." *Wall Street Journal,* January 28.

Gauthier-Villars, David, Carrick Mollenkamp, and Alistair MacDonald. 2008. "French Bank Rocked by Rogue Trader—Société Générale Blames $7.2 Billion in Losses on a Quiet 31-Year-Old." *Wall Street Journal,* January 25.

Goldfarb, Zachary A. 2010. "Cheers at Goldman as Housing Market Fell; Senate Panel Releases E-mails; Executives Reveled in Bets Made Against Market." *Washington Post,* April 25.

Goodman, Peter S., and Gretchen Morgenson. 2008. "By Saying Yes, WaMu Built Empire on Shaky Loans." *New York Times,* December 27.

Hall, Brian J., and Jeffrey B. Liebman. 1998. "Are CEOs Really Paid Like Bureaucrats?" *Quarterly Journal of Economics* 113: 653–91.

Hall, Brian J., and Kevin J. Murphy. 2002. "Stock Options for Undiversified Executives." *Journal of Accounting and Economics* 33: 3–42. Available at: http://papers.ssrn.com/abstract_id=252805 (accessed June 27, 2012).

Harrington, Ben. 2009. "Credit Suisse to Loan Cash Bonuses." *Sunday Telegraph,* January 18.

Hennessey, Keith, Douglas Holtz-Eakin, and Bill Thomas. 2011. "Financial Crisis Inquiry Commission: Dissenting Statement." January. Available at: http://www.advancingafreesociety.org/2011/01/31/financial-crisis-inquiry-commission-dissent/ (accessed June 27, 2012).

Holzer, Jessica. 2011a. "Corporate News: Court Deals Blow to SEC, Activists." *Wall Street Journal,* July 23.

———. 2011b. "A 'Yes' in Say on Pay." *Wall Street Journal,* July 8.

Hulse, Carl, and David M. Herszenhorn. 2008. "Bailout Plan Is Set; House Braces for Tough Vote." *New York Times,* September 29.

Jensen, Michael C., and William H. Meckling. 1976. "Theory of the Firm: Managerial Behavior, Agency Costs, and Ownership Structure." *Journal of Financial Economics* 3(4): 305–60. Available at: http://papers.ssrn.com/Abstract=94043 (accessed June 27, 2012).

Jensen, Michael C., and Kevin J. Murphy. 1990a. "CEO Incentives: It's Not How Much You Pay, but How." *Harvard Business Review* 68: 138–53. Available at: http://papers.ssrn.com/Abstract=146148 (accessed June 27, 2012).

———. 1990b. "Performance Pay and Top Management Incentives." *Journal of Political Economy* 98: 225–65. Available at: http://papers.ssrn.com/Abstract=94009 (accessed June 27, 2012).

MacDonald, Alistair, and Leila Abboud. 2008. "The Fallout at Société Générale: Banks' High-Tech Security Can't Keep Up with Traders." *Wall Street Journal,* January 30.

Murphy, Kevin J. 1999. "Executive Compensation." In *Handbook of Labor Economics,* edited by Orley Ashenfelter and David Card. Amsterdam: North Holland.

———. 2009. Congressional Testimony on Compensation Structure and Systemic Risk. Committee of Financial Services, June 11, 2009. Available at: http://financialservices.house.gov/media/file/hearings/111/kevin_murphy.pdf (accessed June 27, 2012).

———. 2010. "Executive Pay Restrictions for TARP Recipients: An Assessment" (Congressional Oversight Panel hearing on TARP and executive compensation). Marshall School of Business Working Paper FBE 23-10 (October 27). Available at: http://ssrn.com/abstract=1698973 (accessed June 27, 2012).

———. 2011a. "Executive Compensation: Where We Are, and How We Got There." In *Handbook of the Economics of Finance,* edited by George Constantinides, Milton Harris, and René Stulz. Amsterdam: North Holland.

———. 2011b. "The Politics of Pay." In *The Research Handbook on Executive Pay,* edited by Jennifer Hill and Randall S. Thomas. Cheltenham, U.K.: Edgar Elgar.

———. 2012. "Executive Compensation: Where We Are, and How We Got There." In *Handbook of the Economics of Finance,* vol. 2A, edited by George Constantinides, Milton Harris, and René Stulz. Amsterdam: North Holland.

Murphy, Kevin J., and Michael C. Jensen. 2011. "CEO Bonus Plans and How to Fix Them." Harvard Business School NOM Unit Working Paper 12-022; USC Marshall School Working Paper FBE 02-11. Available at: http://ssrn.com/abstract=1935654 (accessed June 27, 2012).

N.Y. Office of the State Comptroller. 2011. "New York City Securities Industry Bonus Pool." Available at: http://osc.state.ny.us/press/releases/feb11/bonus_chart_2010.pdf (accessed June 27, 2012).

Piskorski, Tomasz, Amit Seru, and Vikrant Vig. 2010. "Securitization and Distressed Loan Renegotiation: Evidence from the Subprime Mortgage Crisis." Research Paper 09-02. Chicago: Chicago Booth School of Business (April 15). Available at: http://ssrn.com/abstract=1321646 (accessed June 27, 2012).

Rappaport, Liz. 2011. "Goldman Boosts Partners' Base Pay." *Wall Street Journal,* January 29.

Scannell, Kara, Liz Rappaport, and Jess Bravin. 2009. "Judge Tosses Out Bonus Deal—SEC Pact with BofA over Merrill Is Slammed; New York Weighs Charges Against Lewis." *Wall Street Journal,* September 15.

Solomon, Deborah, and Damian Paletta. 2008. "U.S. Bailout Plan Calms Markets, but Struggle Looms over Details." *Wall Street Journal,* September 20.

Standard & Poor's. 1992–2010. ExecuComp Database. New York: Standard & Poor's. Proprietary data.

Story, Louise. 2009. "Pay Czar Doubts Cuts Will Make Bankers Leave." *New York Times,* October 23.

U.S. Department of the Treasury. 2009. "Special Master Determination Letters, Fact Sheets, and Reports." Available at: http://www.treasury.gov/initiatives/financial-stability/exec_comp/special_reports/Pages/default.aspx (accessed June 27, 2012).

Wallison, Peter J. 2011. "Financial Crisis Inquiry Commission: Dissenting Statement." January. Available at: http://www.aei.org/files/2011/01/26/Wallisondissent.pdf.

White, Ben. 2009. "What Red Ink? Wall Street Paid Hefty Bonuses." *New York Times,* January 29.

Yermack, David. 1995. "Do Corporations Award CEO Stock Options Effectively?" *Journal of Financial Economics* 39: 237–69.

Index

Boldface numbers refer to figures and tables.